"Father Lasa
selecting the mate
just what the faithful want, so that there is scarcely a page
which is not treasured." —The Rosary Magazine, October, 1903

About Father Lasance:

Reverend Francis Xavier Lasance was born in Cincinnati, Ohio in 1860. He studied at St. Xavier College (Now known as Xavier University), then went on to St. Meinrad Seminary in Indiana. He was ordained a priest May 24, 1883, and for seven years he served as assistant and rector in several parishes of the Archdiocese of Cincinnati. Due to a physical breakdown he was forced to give up active parish work in 1890, and after a visit to Europe, he was appointed chaplain to the Sisters of Notre Dame in his native city. During this period, he wrote over three dozen devotional books, for which he received a special blessing from Pope Pius XI in 1927. He died in 1946 at the age of 86.

About *The Young Man's Guide:*

" 'Take care of the boys and the girls will take care of themselves,' has passed into an adage. Here is a practical attempt to aid our young men to tide over the difficult era of dawning consciousness of passionate inclination. Persuade a boy that the true ideal of life is found in the life and passion of our Redeemer, as presented to him by Holy Church, and you do a work entirely necessary for the right formation of his character...A good book, serious enough to be a solid nourishment to the soul, and attractive enough to entertain religiously, is surely one of the best means of saving boyhood and early manhood from shipwreck. Father Lasance has, we believe, gone far towards achieving success in his worthy endeavor.

The first part of the little work is devoted to a doctrinal summary of the Catholic faith, pleasantly stated and driven home by good illustrations. After that, the whole scope of life is divided into an excellent arrangement of topics, embracing the praise of virtue and the condemnation of vice, including a plain and yet guarded treatment of the preliminaries of marriage.

At the end there is found all the material of a good prayerbook...[This is] a book for hard usage and permanent benefit."
—The Catholic World, July 1910

To find more books like this one, visit our website at
www.staugustineacademypress.com

"Remember thy Creator in the days of thy youth"
(Eccles. xii. 1).

"Be thou an example of the faithful in word, in conversation,
in charity, in faith, in chastity"
(1 Tim. iv. 12).

"Rejoice, therefore, O young man, in thy youth,
and let thy heart be in that which is good"
(Eccles. xi. 9).

"Fear God and keep His commandments: for this is all man"
(Eccles. xii. 13).

"What things man shall sow, those also shall he reap...
In doing good let us not fail; for in due time we shall reap"
(Gal. vi. 8, 9).

"To him that soweth justice, there is a faithful reward"
(Prov. xi. 18).

"Listen attentively, my son, to the voice of thy teacher; incline to him the ear of thy heart; receive gratefully the fatherly admonitions of one who loves thee, and resolutely strive to act in accordance with them." —St. Benedict.

Let your watchword be:

ALL FOR THE GREATER GLORY OF GOD
AND IN HONOR OF THE BLESSED VIRGIN MARY.

Saint **Aloysius**

Patron Saint of Christian Youth

Pray for Us.

Saint **Joseph**

St. Joseph Most Chaste, St. Joseph Most Faithful

Pray for Us.

The
Young Man's Guide

COUNSELS, REFLECTIONS AND PRAYERS

FOR

CATHOLIC YOUNG MEN

ABRIDGED VERSION

❖

BY

REVEREND FRANCIS X. LASANCE

❖

WITH ILLUSTRATIONS BY
JULIE STREETER

2012
ST. AUGUSTINE ACADEMY PRESS
LISLE, ILLINOIS

This book is newly typeset based on the 1910 edition by Benziger Brothers. All editing strictly limited to the correction of errors in the original text, minor clarifications in punctuation or phrasing, and the addition of select footnotes. Any remaining oddities of spelling or phrasing are as found in the original.

This book is considered abridged due to the fact that most of the final section, consisting of prayers and devotions as well as the order of Mass, has been omitted. Those prayers which have been retained have been inserted at the end of each chapter, sometimes in a different translation than was found in the original text. All other text herein is unchanged as noted above.

NIHIL OBSTAT
Remy Lafort
Censor Librorum

IMPRIMATUR
✠ John M. Farley
Archbishop of New York

New York, January 3, 1910.

ISBN: 978-1-936639-16-8
Library of Congress Control Number: 2012940966

Editor's Note

The edition you hold in your hands is a faithful reproduction of the original in all ways but one: after much deliberation, we decided to exclude most of the final section of *The Young Men's Guide*. However, we want to reassure the reader that the valuable content you will find in these pages was not changed in any way, except to correct errors of spelling or punctuation in the original.

The reasons for omitting the final section were many and compelling. First, the original book, like most prayer books of its day, was printed as a small leatherbound volume with the thin pages one would find in a missal, making its nearly 800 pages not only much more portable, but much more durable. To print so many pages in an affordable paperback format for today's Catholic families would have resulted in a much larger, heavier and less durable book.

We carefully examined the content of the final section and chose those prayers which every Catholic ought to be familiar with, and placed a selection of these at the end of each chapter of the first section of the book. We also retained the section on preparation for confession, which contained a very thorough examination of conscience. However, the rest of the final section included such things as the order of Mass as it was said in 1910—that is, the Tridentine Mass (or Extraordinary form, as it is commonly known today). For those unfamiliar with it, this may have been of some interest or curiosity; however, for those who attend the Latin Mass, a true Missal would serve far better, since it would contain (again, in more durable form) not merely the order of Mass but also the readings and other propers.

Likewise, the other prayers and devotions, such as the Stations of the Cross, various Litanies, Morning and Evening Prayers, etc. could easily be found in any number of prayer books which would be much more portable than this one.

Another issue was the great deal of redundancy in this section, where, for example, six versions of the same prayer are given, differing only in verbosity or floridity of language. For this same reason, for the prayers we did retain, we sometimes substituted a more widely-known or well-translated version than the one found in the original book. (Though it should be noted that we preferred versions that used *thees* and *thous* rather than the more informal *you*.)

Above all, however, the knowledge that the unabridged version is available through other sources, for those who wish to have the entire book as it was originally published, reassured us that it made sense to provide this abridged version for families who wished to have the content of this unique book at the most affordable price possible. Therefore, we hope you will agree that the current volume is much easier to use without the additional 300 pages and we hope that you will enjoy *The Young Man's Guide* for many years to come.

In Christ,
Lisa Bergman
St. Augustine Academy Press
May 2012

Contents

PART FIRST : THE PANOPLY OF WAR

The Shield of Faith

The Helmet of Hope

The Arrow of the Love of God

The Lance of the Fear of God

The Sword of Respect for Authority

PART THIRD : ON THE JOURNEY OF LIFE

MANHOOD

PART FOURTH : AT THE PARTING OF THE WAYS

WHITHER GOEST THOU?

THE MARRIED STATE

THE PRIESTHOOD

THE RELIGIOUS STATE

A Few Concluding Words

Appendix

Devotions for Confession

PREFACE

The success of *The Catholic Girl's Guide* augurs well, we trust, for the reception which awaits its present companion. Zealous directors of souls have urged us to undertake this work, and we entertain the hope that pastors will introduce *The Young Man's Guide* to the boys of their respective parishes and especially to the boys of "the plain people," as Abraham Lincoln was wont to designate the great body of working classes.

There is more than a grain of truth in the adage, "Take care of the boys, and the girls will take care of themselves." Do we give as much attention and care to the preservation of our boys as we devote to the safeguarding of our girls? Are not our boys and young men exposed to greater dangers in the battle of life? Are not they more constantly and more fiercely assailed by the enemies of man's salvation, and tempted to the gratification of disorderly passions, to every kind of sinful enjoyment—the end of which is temporal misery and eternal ruin?

Hence, any attempt to draw our Catholic youth away from the evil influences that surround them in the world is worthy of approbation; any book that imparts to young men a word of warning and counsels them in regard to the things that make for their spiritual progress and sanctification, for their temporal welfare as well as for their eternal happiness, certainly deserves the hearty endorsement of a Shepherd of souls.

Such a book is the German work entitled *Hinaus ins Leben* by Father Coelestin Muff, O.S.B., a Benedictine of the famous Abbey of Maria Einsiedeln, Switzerland.

We have based *The Young Man's Guide* on this work—inasmuch as it is an English version of the same—revised, amplified, and adapted by us to suit the conditions, circumstances, and requirements of the young men of our own country.

In his preface to *Hinaus ins Leben,* Father Muff says: "*Out into life!* So it is decreed for the young man, who is advancing to maturity; and with Schiller we must add, 'Out into a *hostile* life!'—out into a *struggle,* not only for his material existence and welfare, but much more in behalf of his spiritual and eternal interests.

"To make his young friends in some measure acquainted with this hostile side of life, to point out to them the ways and means to parry the attacks of the enemies of their salvation—this is for a priest, for a pastor of souls, a welcome task.

"It is the aim of our little 'Guide,' in the first place, to furnish a Catholic young man with a correct view of the social and religious conditions of modern life, and to call his particular attention to the forces and influences that are inimical to the preservation of his faith and innocence; it admonishes the young man, on his entrance into the busy world, to put on the '*armatura Dei*' (Eph. vi. 11), the '*armor of God*'; namely, to acquire, to cultivate, and practise various virtues, such as faith, hope, charity, the fear of God, sobriety, humility, obedience, fidelity, and perseverance; it instructs him, especially, how to fight, how to conquer, in the hardest of battles—that which must be fought in behalf of the virtue of chastity.

"In the second place, our 'Guide' is intended to be a support and encouragement to the young man in all the circumstances of his life, and, in particular, to stand by his side at the parting of the ways, when he has to choose a definite state of life—to give him needful suggestions and counsels at this important period of his career in regard to his vocation. By the grace of God, may this little volume be to our young men truly a lighthouse amid the darkness of unbelief and heresy, a bulwark against the ever increasing flood of immorality, an anchor of salvation when the soul is threatened with shipwreck, and a star of hope in the gloom of life."

To enhance the practical value of this work, we have added to the *Counsels and Reflections* a compilation of *Prayers and Devotions*, which, though short, will be found satisfactory for all the ordinary occasions for which a "Prayerbook" is wanted by young men in the world. We certainly desired and planned to add a larger collection of prayers. But this would have made a volume of great bulk, and our young men do not like to carry a bulky book. [***Editor's note:*** *for this very reason, we have omitted most of the Prayers and Devotions from this edition.*]

To Our Lady of the Blessed Sacrament and the Mother of Good Counsel we humbly and respectfully dedicate our little "Guide." May she bless our youthful friends, and pray for them, that they may love and honor Jesus more and more in the Sacrament of His love, that they may learn to know *Him* better, who is "*the Way, the Truth, and the Life*," and, above all, that they may follow Him and walk in justice, holiness, and truth toward that complete beatitude which is the crown of the saints.

F. X. LASANCE.
Cincinnati, Ohio.
Feast of the Assumption
of the Blessed Virgin Mary, 1909.

SOLDIERS of Christ, arise
And gird your armor on;
Eternal life the prize
To be by victors won.
The Cross shall give you might
To scare the hellish foe;
Equipped thus for the fight
In God's name forward go.

On to the gates of Sion, on!
   Break through the foe with fierce endeavor;
We'll hang our colors up in heaven,
   When peace shall be proclaimed forever.

Faith of our Fathers! we will love
   Both friend and foe in all our strife:
And preach thee too, as love knows how,
   By kindly words and virtuous life.

Faith of our Fathers! Holy Faith!
   We will be true to thee till death.

—Oratory Hymns.

PART FIRST
THE PANOPLY OF WAR

The Shield of Faith

1. Is There a God?

THE young man's lot is to go out into a hostile life. What is necessary for him? Behold the warrior, as he goes forth to the field of battle. Is he not amply provided with all needful weapons? When you, my dear young friend, go forth into the world, you are going to encounter mighty enemies, the enemies of your soul. You must, therefore, put on a strong suit of armor, one which is capable of protecting you. And what is this suit of armor? The apostle St. Paul describes it in the following words: *"Put you on the armor of God, that you may be able to stand against the deceits of the devil."* (Eph. vi. 11)

The first and most powerful weapon in this suit of armor is the shield of faith, as the same apostle says: *"In all things taking the shield of faith, wherewith you may be able to extinguish all the fiery darts of the most wicked one."* (Eph. vi. 16) And, indeed, faith is an impenetrable shield against the fiery darts of the devil. When the latter strives to lead us astray, by inciting us to voluptuousness, faith lays bare to our view the abyss of hell, in order that we may behold the torments which will be the punishment of the unchaste. When he desires to dazzle us with the glitter of the riches, honors, and glories which the world has to offer us, faith throws open the portals of heaven, where the highest rewards are prepared for those who persevere in the love of God and the pursuit of virtue. Wherefore contemplate this shield of faith on every side, in order that you may be convinced of its indispensable necessity, may gladly take it into your hand, and grasp it firmly. Let us turn our attention first to the foundation of all faith, of all religion: namely, to the existence of God. *Is there a God?* That is the first question.

"*Is there a God?*" What an unnecessary question, you are saying to yourself. And you are quite right. In regard to this point David says in one of the Psalms: "*The fool hath said in his heart: There is no God,*" and truly; only a man destitute of reason, a man who is mad, could make such an assertion, could question the existence of God.

Let us suppose that you show your watch to a friend, and say to him: "Must not the individual who made this watch, and arranged the works, have understood his business very well? Must he not be a very clever fellow, and possess a first-rate head-piece?" Now, suppose he were to reply: "Oh, nonsense! The watch made itself!" Should you not gaze fixedly at him, and make some such remark as the following: "My good friend, if you are in earnest, and really mean what you say, there must be a screw loose in your upper story." And you would be quite justified in thus addressing him. Yet wait awhile, and pay attention to the practical application of all this.

Fix your gaze upon the splendors of the universe. Behold the countless multitude of the heavenly bodies, as they revolve in their orbits; behold the wondrous creations which are upon this earth, as comprised in the animal, vegetable, or mineral kingdoms. Does not the most consummate imaginable skill, everywhere meet the eye?

But now listen to what certain unbelieving scientists, naturalists, and astronomers say to all this. The friend to whom reference was made above asserted that the watch had made itself. Our scientists go still farther and obstinately assert that the infinitely more wonderful machine of the entire universe, earth, sun, moon, and stars, likewise came into being of itself, having gradually developed out of a mass of primeval matter, which had always been in existence.

How ridiculous and absurd! But let us for a moment assent to the theory of these over-wise gentlemen, let us submit our understanding to them; they owe us, however, a clear and ample explanation of the most important point of all, and are bound to tell us whence came this primeval matter, and the forces at work within it, by means of which the entire universe came into being.

The good gentlemen will thus find themselves driven into a very tight corner, and in order to get out of the dilemma they will be compelled to retreat to a certain extent from the position in which they have entrenched themselves, and say: "If you persist in having a God, you may give the name of God to this primary matter." But this will not help to settle the question, for to have such a God as this is tantamount to having no God at all.

Look forth on some clear and beautiful night in autumn, and contemplate the star-bespangled sky; see how the innumerable heavenly bodies have all their appointed orbits, so that none of them interferes with the others. Examine, moreover, the animal and vegetable kingdoms, and see how everything suits its purpose! Even the smallest plant is formed in its every detail with the most perfect exactitude. And every little creature, down to the insect which crawls in the dust at our feet, is so made as best to fulfil the object for which it was created. "What a piece of work is a man!" exclaims Hamlet; "how noble in reason! how infinite in faculty! in form and moving how express and admirable! in action how like an angel! in apprehension how like a god!" Thus, wherever we look around us in the immense, the boundless universe, we everywhere perceive object, design, and order.

Can not we then comprehend, by means of our common-sense, that all this is not the work of chance, and was not brought into being by unintelligent, unreasoning forces and laws? Must we not rather exclaim in the inspired language of David: *"The heavens show forth the glory of God"*? Yes, let us say with grateful joyous hearts: There is a God; an omnipotent, an all-wise, an infinitely good and bountiful God!

Thank God, dear reader, for the most precious of all gifts, for the grace which enables you to say from the bottom of your heart, and with the most intense conviction: "I believe in God, the Father Almighty, Creator of heaven and earth." Pray that you may always persevere in this faith.

> The fool alone can not descry
> God's work in earth and sea and sky;
> The more enlightened eye can trace
> His all-wise hand in Nature's face;
> And where sight fails, there faith alone
> The great Creator's skill will own.

2. THE CREATOR AND THE CREATURE

IN THE studio of a sculptor a magnificent statue is standing. The famous artist has chiseled it out of pure white marble; the masterpiece is the object of universal admiration. We regard it as a matter of course that the sculptor has every right to do as he pleases with his work, and will only surrender this right to another for a very large sum of money. Yet it can scarcely be said that he created the statue, since the form of it alone is the work of his hands, and not the marble out of which he fashioned it.

Now, dear reader, look once more at the marvelous work of the universe, and all that it contains; look especially at man and tell me whether He—who not only made all this, but created it out of nothing—whether God Almighty has not an absolute, unlimited, and immutable right of possession over it all? Must not, therefore, the whole of creation, and especially man, who is endowed with reason, serve and obey this God as the supreme Lord and Master of all, and do His will in all things?

And it is this relation of dependence and subservience in which man stands to God, which is termed religion.

Religion (from *religare*, "to bind back, to bind fast") expresses the bond of piety by means of which God has drawn man to Himself, in order that we may serve Him as our master, and obey Him as our father. Man must, indeed, serve God; that is, he must both do and suffer His will. But since man is endowed with free will, can he not do whatever he likes? Most assuredly not! For his free will comes not from himself, but is the gift of God. And it is impossible that God can have endowed man with free will in order that ho should do what he likes, but in order that he should do what he ought, and do it quite willingly of his own free will.

All creation fulfils the purpose of its existence; the sun, the moon, and the stars revolve in their appointed orbits, *not voluntarily*, but in unswerving obedience to the laws of nature, with such mathematical regularity that astronomers can calculate their movements with perfect precision. The animal world likewise, *compelled* by the law of instinct fails not to fulfil the object for which it was created. Man, on the other hand, is so constituted that he ought to serve, honor, and worship God deliberately and *of his own free will*.

This consciousness, this conviction that he is bound to honor and worship God, is deeply and ineradicably implanted in the heart of every human being. Hence we find that in ancient times no nation was without its own religion. It is impossible that this universal conviction of mankind can be a deception or a lie; it is, on the contrary, a plain proof that, to quote the words of a Christian writer of the early Church, "the soul is of its very nature religious."

And indeed the most ancient books of Holy Scripture teach us that not only did Abraham and his descendants worship the true God, but that all nations with whom they came in contact had, and adored, their own deities.

Both Greek and Roman historians tell a similar tale. Plutarch, for instance, expresses himself in the following terms: "If one were to wander over the whole world, one might find cities without walls, without literature, and without written laws,...but a city without temples and divinities no one has discovered as yet."

In our own day research has been carried so far that scarcely any country has remained unexplored, or any nation unknown. And all honest explorers bear unanimous witness that just as it was of old, so also in modern times there is no nation which does not possess its own religion.

To go yet further! Religion is the mainspring of all virtue, the solid foundation of all morality; and he who should attempt to found, extend, and perpetuate the kingdom of virtue apart from the kingdom of religion, would be like a man who should build a house upon the sand. Without religion, man is the sport of his passions. He resembles a ship which, being destitute of cable or anchor, is certain sooner or later to go to pieces on the rocks when overtaken by a storm. In a way, religion is to man what the flower is to the plant; if the flower is cut off, the fruit is destroyed at the same time.

Now, my dear young friend, you know what you ought to think of the frivolous way of talking which those adopt who assert that people can get on very well without religion. Yes, they can get on, but after what fashion! Do you, therefore, repeat with heart and voice the following lines:

> Come, sacred Light, from Heaven above
> With power the heart of man to raise
> And teach to hymn his Maker's praise,
> And with thy brightness let him shine
> In presence of the King divine.

3. THE MUSIC OF THE SOUL

APEASANT betook himself to a priest in Rome, and laid before him the following extraordinary doubt. "Your Reverence," he said, "I can scarcely believe that I have a soul!" It may readily be imagined that this unexpected statement caused the priest no slight astonishment. It cost him an effort to discover how he could, in a brief and clear manner, convince the foolish man that he really had a soul. The Spirit of God taught him what to say.

He questioned the doubter thus: "Now, my good man, why can not you believe that you have a soul?" "Because I can not see it!" "Well, then, think of whatever you like"; and after the lapse of a few minutes he inquired: "Have you really thought of something?" "Yes, I have done as your Reverence bade me." "But," continued the priest, "I can not believe that you have thought of anything." "And why not, may I ask?" "Because I can not see your thought." In this convincing manner was the man freed from his doubt.

For, indeed, it would be unreasonable to doubt that we are able to think, will, and remember. On this account it would be equally unreasonable to refuse to believe in the presence within us of a soul endowed with reason.

Thus the power of thought is a proof of the existence within us of an independent and rational soul. But stop! We have reckoned without our host, that is, without the modern unbelieving scientists! They think scornfully of our old-fashioned ideas, and exclaim: "O you silly people! Thought is nothing more than an act of the brain! In order to do this there is no need of a soul; that is to say, no need of a spiritual and independent being."

But pause awhile, you wiseacres, and allow us to ask you a question. From a neighboring house the sound of a masterly performance on the piano reaches our ears. Do you mean to assert that the music is nothing more than an act of the piano, that the instrument plays of itself? Every child would say of you, "these people are too clever by half." Therefore, good gentlemen, we continue to believe that thought is the music of the soul; and that where thoughts exist, there must be a soul capable of thought, just as, where there is the sound of music from a piano, there must be also a performer.

What now is the case of animals, especially those which are most highly trained, as for instance the dog, the horse, or the monkey? Have not they likewise a soul? Certainly the animal possesses sensible impressions, feelings, impulses, a memory, and as far as this goes, one may speak of a soul. But the soul of the animal is essentially and immeasurably removed from the soul of man, because it is not possessed of reason. Even, to use a common phrase, the most intelligent animal is destitute of self-consciousness and reason or understanding. Every child knows that "two and two make four," but no animal could comprehend the fact, though it were to try to do so for a century or more.

Upon us, however, there shines not merely the light of natural reason, but also the sun of faith. The rays of this sun enable us to see that our soul is like unto God, an image of God. Holy Scripture expressly teaches us this, for in the beginning of it we read that God solemnly pronounced these words of vast import: *"Let us make man to our image and likeness."* Thus if man is like God, who is a pure spirit, this likeness can certainly not consist in anything physical or material, but in the possession of a soul, which is a spirit also, made in God's image, simple as God is, living as God is, immortal as God is. Wherefore, lay well to heart the following verse:

> O man, to God's own image made,
> Destined that God to see in light arrayed,
> Keep thou His law, unto thy ways take heed;
> Let love of Him rule every word and deed.

4. DEATH IS NOT ANNIHILATION

IN THESE modern days, when faith has grown cold or vanished altogether, there are people, and even lads of fifteen or sixteen years of age, who, when they are exhorted to reflect from time to time upon death and eternity, merely reply: "I am no child to be frightened with nursery tales; who knows whether death is not annihilation!"

Words like these, when uttered by youthful lips, fill us truly with horror and pity. But how is it possible to speak in this way? Simply because, in the case of those who thus express themselves, the belief in one of the fundamental truths of all religion, the belief in the immortality of the soul, has been destroyed.

Since you, dear reader, must go forth into life and be exposed to the dangers of unbelief, it is of the utmost importance that the conviction that "death is not annihilation" should be deeply rooted in your heart; wherefore, ponder carefully the principal grounds upon which this conviction is based.

Death is not annihilation, but the soul lives on after the death of the body. It is immortal. The very nature of the soul proves this; it is a simple, indivisible being; it can not be separated into parts, or be destroyed.

Now, however, the unbelievers, the so-called materialists, appear upon the scene, and say: "Man does not possess a soul independent of the body, a soul which has its own separate existence." And as proof (?) of this, they assert that since a violent blow upon the head destroys consciousness, the power of thought is therefore dependent upon the brain; the brain being the cause of thought, no spiritual soul is needed for this purpose.

This conclusion certainly appears plausible, but it contains a grievous fallacy. In a similar manner I could "prove" that there is no sun! Just tell me whether, if you close the shutters of your room, the light does not disappear from it; but in proportion as you re-open them, the light streams in again more or less brightly. Therefore the light in the room depends upon the window, the window is the cause of it; hence no other cause is needed, no sun! Thus, my young friend, if you had not seen the sun for yourself, you might believe that there is not a sun at all. In both instances, the fallacy of the deduction or conclusion is obvious. Just as certainly as there is a sun, so certainly does man possess an immortal soul, with an independent existence of its own.

The conviction of all nations bears witness to the immortality of the human soul; it is inscribed by the hand of nature in the heart of every man in characters which can never be effaced. Nature can never deceive. False representations concerning the future life of the soul by no means prove that it is not immortal.

This belief in the immortality of the soul may indeed be dislodged from the head, but never torn out of the heart. "It is difficult," a simple person once remarked to me, "to believe that those whom we love do not merely die, but are dissolved into nothingness." And, truly, all our feelings rise in revolt and the voice we hear within us protests against the assumption that death is annihilation.

No, no, thus it can not be: there shall be a "*Wiedersehen*"[1] of our kindred; we shall meet again those whom we have loved and lost. If, indeed, there were no such future meeting, we should be justified in raising an accusing voice to Heaven, and exclaiming: "Thou hast deceived us by implanting affections within our breast which are only doomed to be disappointed!" Is, then, everything to be ended at the close of this short life, so replete often with suffering, and is only nothingness to remain! Are love and friendship to

1   A reunion, literally "to see again"

be mere empty words, are virtue and justice to exist only in imagination?

What then! The robber and the robbed, the traitor to his country and he who gives his life for his fatherland, the martyr and his torturer, the unnatural son and the model daughter, are they all to share the same fate in annihilation—in the same nothingness? No, it is impossible even to imagine anything so preposterous.

But all has not been said. We have within us a heart which yearns after endless, everlasting happiness! Happiness! The mere mention of this word makes our heart beat more quickly, and stirs our being to its inmost depths. This craving for happiness, this intense longing, must be destined to be satisfied at some future period. But where? Where is this endless and complete happiness for which we long so ardently—where is it to be found? Everything teaches us, everything proves to us, that it can not be found upon earth. Our heart is, indeed, not very large, but the universe does not suffice to fill it. Cæsar, to whom at one time half the world was subject, said with melancholy discontent: "Is that all?"

Therefore, if the longing for happiness is so firmly rooted in our heart, and yet can never find complete or permanent satisfaction upon earth, it follows that it must be possible for man to attain it after this life is ended—that means that death is not annihilation. This reasoning should suffice.

But we have kept the most conclusive argument to the last. We have the words of Christ Himself as a pledge that there is a future life; and He speaks as follows: *"The just shall go into life everlasting, and the wicked into everlasting punishment."*

> There is no death! What seems so is transition;
> This life of mortal breath
> Is but a suburb of the life elysian
> Whose portal we call death.
>   —Longfellow, "Resignation."

5. HISTORY, NOT LEGEND

Pagans thought out for themselves many things concerning the being of God, and then related their imaginings as if they were facts. Such imaginings may be counted by hundreds. But since the world began, no man has ever imagined, in the remotest manner, that the charity of a God could go so far as to lead Him to appear among men in the form of a man, and for their happiness and salvation to deliver Himself up to death. However, this marvel of divine love which it never entered into the heart of man to conceive, and which is sufficient to astonish heaven and earth, found its accomplishment in the only true religion, which is the Christian. *"God so loved the world, as to send His only begotten Son into the world."* Such is the voice which for more than nineteen hundred years has echoed throughout the universe.

Jesus Christ is the name of the only begotten Son of God, who was sent into the world; He in very deed lived and labored in the world; this is an historical fact, no mere tradition, legend, myth, or fable. Listen to some proofs of this.

History teaches by means of the most reliable facts that from the beginning the greatest and most noble among mankind have readily accepted the Christian faith, the holy Gospel. Amongst these we find a proconsul of Paphos, a captain of the Roman cohorts, Dionysius, the Athenian sage, Flavius the consul, a cousin of Emperor Domitian; the most learned, moreover, among the men who lived in those times; Justin, Athenagoras, Minutius, and many others, men prominent among the scientists of the day, jurists, and governmental officials.

But it can not be supposed that all these men accepted the new doctrines, the new gospel, with careless indifference. On the contrary, they thoroughly examined in the first place the holy Gospel and the writings of the apostles, and more particularly they convinced themselves of the facts relating to the life of Jesus.

Furthermore, the disciples and apostles of Jesus bore witness to the truth of their convictions, to the facts of the life of Jesus Christ, by confessing these truths with their blood. When have there ever been impostors in the world, especially where religion was concerned, who have not striven either covertly or openly after notoriety, pleasure, dignities, and riches? Did the apostles, perchance, look for any of these things, or at least aim at attaining them? No, indeed! On the contrary, they knew perfectly well that they had nothing to expect but mockery, contradiction, shame, persecution and death.

With such a prospect as this could the apostles have lied and deceived, could they have invented the history of the life of Christ? No reasonable man could seriously assert such a thing. No; the apostles were themselves completely persuaded of the truth of everything which they preached to the world, and wrote down in the Sacred Scriptures concerning Jesus Christ. Nor did they hesitate for a moment to lay down their life as a testimony to the truth.

Moreover, even Jewish and pagan historians bear explicit witness to the fact that Christ really lived. For example, a Jewish writer, Josephus Flavius, thus expresses himself in the first century: "At that time lived Jesus, a wise man, if indeed he may be called a man. For he performed many wonderful works... When Pilate, in consequence of an accusation brought against him by the most prominent men of our nation, condemned him to be crucified, his disciples still adhered to him. He rose again, and appeared to them alive on the third day, according to what the holy prophets had foretold of him in this, and a thousand other marvelous respects."

Similar is the testimony borne by heathen writers such as Tacitus, Suetonius, Pliny the younger, in regard to Christ. The first-mentioned says that the founder of the Christian religion was condemned to death by Pilate, the Roman governor, during the reign of the emperor Tiberius. Heathen philosophers, such as Celsus and Porphyrius, who lived in the first and second centuries, did indeed write against Christ and His doctrines, but they never called in question the fact of His existence.

"Rejoice in the Lord," then, my youthful reader! Christ has in very deed lived on earth, and, as the Apostle says: *"Christ is our peace."* Christ alone can unite us to God, to the God who created the heavens and the earth, and in whom, to quote the words of the same apostle, *"we live and move and are."* And this Christ is now present in the Holy Eucharist, our Emmanuel, of whom the Angelic Doctor sings: ***Lauda Sion Salvatorem:***

> Sion, lift thy voice and sing:
> Praise thy Saviour and thy King,
> Praise with hymns thy Shepherd true;
> Strive thy best to praise Him well;
> Yet doth He all praise excel;
>   None can ever reach His due.
>
> Jesus! Shepherd of the sheep!
> Thy true flock in safety keep.
> Living Bread! Thy life supply;
> Strengthen us, or else we die;
>   Fill us with celestial grace.
>
> Thou, who feedest us below!
> Source of all we have or know!
> Grant that with Thy saints above,
> Sitting at the feast of love,
>   We may see Thee face to face.

JESUS IS GOD

> Jesus is God! the glorious bands
>   Of golden angels sing
> Songs of adoring praise to Him,
>   Their maker and their king.
> He was true God in Bethlehem's crib.
>   On Calvary's cross true God,
> He who in heaven eternal reigned.
>   In time on earth abode.

Jesus is God! alas! they say
  On earth the numbers grow
Who His divinity blaspheme
  To their unfailing woe.
And yet what is the single end
  Of this life's mortal span,
Except to glorify the God
  Who for our sakes was man?

Jesus is God! let sorrow come,
  And pain, and every ill;
All are worth while, for all are means
  His glory to fulfil;
Worth while a thousand years of life
  To speak one little word,
If by our Credo we might own
  The Godhead of Our Lord!

Jesus is God! O could I now
  But compass land and sea,
To teach and tell this single truth,
  How happy should I be!
O had I but an angel's voice,
  I would proclaim so loud,—
Jesus, the good, the beautiful,
  Is everlasting God!
           —Oratory Hymns.

6. Produce Your Witnesses

We know that Jesus Christ lived upon this earth, not because we have seen Him with our eyes or heard Him with our ears, but because the holy Gospels relate the story of His life, because those who saw and heard Him tell us about Him.

In the first place, it is of the utmost importance to perceive in a clear and convincing manner that everything we are told concerning the life of Our Lord is the truth, and nothing but the truth. This life of Christ, as contained in the Gospel, forms a portion of Holy Scripture, and is inspired by the Holy Spirit of God; it rests, therefore, upon divine authority, and is worthy of absolute belief. But even apart from its divine character, this history is as worthy of belief as the most trustworthy of the earliest records. And why is this? When do you, dear reader, believe that any history which you read is true? Only when you are quite convinced as to its authorship, and the trustworthiness of the author; in particular, when you are able to persuade yourself that the writer knew the truth, and desired to tell it. Well, then, the four evangelists, who related the life of Christ, can come forward and bear witness to its truth.

In the first place, there is no disputing the fact that the authorship of the Gospels has not only been ascribed to these four men, Matthew, Mark, Luke, and John, but that they, and they alone, did write them in very deed. And to this fact the Fathers of the Church who lived and wrote in the time immediately succeeding the apostolic ages, and numerous Christian theologians who shed their blood for the Faith, bear unhesitating witness; heretics, moreover, do the same, inasmuch as they endeavor to prove their false religious opinions by quotations from the Gospel; the Talmud also, the modern legal code of the Jews, acknowledges the gospel miracles as facts; finally, the heathen sages, Celsus and Porphyrius, and even the apostate emperor, Julian, who poured scorn and contempt upon the religion he had so basely abandoned, did not attempt to deny that the life of Christ was written by the four evangelists.

Furthermore, these writers of the Gospel, these witnesses for the truth of it, are entirely trustworthy; their testimony is absolutely reliable. In the first place, they were in a position to tell the truth, since they were well acquainted with the facts. Who indeed could better know the truth than St. Matthew and St. John, who received their vocation as apostles from the divine Redeemer Himself, and who were privileged to be His constant companions, to hear His words and behold His wonderful works? And the two other evangelists, St. Mark and St. Luke, were fully acquainted with the life of Christ, because they wrote their gospels at the suggestion and under the direction of two apostles, St. Peter and St. Paul.

No reasonable man can doubt that the holy evangelists spoke the truth if he attentively considers the manner in which they wrote. Any one who wishes to deceive the reader, to misrepresent circumstances or facts, would certainly not write in so straightforward, frank, and honest a manner as we find that the sacred historians invariably do. He who desires to distort or conceal the truth would assuredly not relate his own faults and failings and those of his dearest friends as the evangelists do. For this reason Rousseau, one of the bitterest enemies of Christ, is fain to confess: "A history like that of the Gospel is not invented." The Gospel possesses such touching, such utterly inimitable marks of truthfulness, that if the author were an inventor and impostor, he would be more worthy of admiration than the one who is the subject of the gospel-narrative. It would be, indeed, a shameless proceeding to reproach an apostle with deceit, unless some further proof were forthcoming. What reasonable motive could they have had to lie? Persecution, chains, imprisonment, death—no one deceives for such gain as this; no one would get himself hung for a lie!

And yet more! The evangelists wrote amid circumstances and in times which rendered it well-nigh impossible for them to deceive.

In the days when Jesus lived and labored, people had sharp eyes and ears, just as in our day, and the enemies of Christianity were not less cunning and malicious than they are at present. Can you imagine that these people would have been good-natured enough to hold their tongues if the disciples of Jesus had related in the Gospel facts concerning Him which were either falsehoods, or, to say the least, gross misrepresentations?   And when, about thirty years after Christ, St. Matthew wrote his gospel, there were still living a great number of those who had formerly been among the bitter enemies of Christ. How would they have attacked the apostle, had he taken upon himself to invent either facts or miracles concerning the life of Christ!

Thus the evangelists stand before us as absolutely reliable witnesses to the truth.   And herein consists the secret of the beauty, simplicity, sanctity, and indestructible power of the holy Gospel. It is not the soul, the mind, the gifts of the writers that we find in them, but the soul, the thoughts, the maxims of Him who forms the subjects of their writings. Jesus lives in the Gospels; He acts, He speaks, He touches the heart, He enlightens and sanctifies. Venerate, therefore, these wondrous pages! Read them in a spirit of faith and with a heart overflowing with the love of God; for

> In Holy Scripture God His truth displays,
> And yet its pages, read in various ways,
> Bring faith to some; cause doubt in other minds:
> That one sucks honey, this one poison finds.

7. Christ is Truly God

THE heir of a mighty monarch once traveling incognito and unattended, visited a lonely mountain valley which belonged to his father's dominions. In order that he might be suitably received, he told the inhabitants his name and his exalted rank. Since, however, no persons throughout the valley had ever seen the crown prince, or even a likeness of him, they refused to believe in his identity without further proof, but required him to show that he was the true and lawful crown prince. And the good people were certainly not to be blamed for requiring such a proof; since otherwise any one who took it into his head to do so, might claim to be the crown prince.

Nineteen hundred years ago, far away in Palestine, a Man made His appearance; He claimed to be, not merely the heir of this or that mighty monarch, but the Son of the King of heaven and earth. Yes, when this Man stood arraigned as a criminal before the chief council of the Jews, and Caiaphas, the high priest, said to Him: *"I adjure Thee by the living God that Thou tell us if Thou be the Christ, the Son of God,"* this Man replied, earnestly and solemnly, *"Thou hast said it, I am He!"*

Thus publicly, earnestly, and solemnly, did Jesus Christ declare Himself to be the Son of God; thus did He announce Himself as true God. And He formerly required of His hearers, as He now in like manner requires of us, that His doctrines should be accepted, and His claims received. We, therefore, on our part, have a perfect right to demand that He should prove to us that we must believe in Him, that He should show His credentials, and prove Himself to be the Son of God, prove Himself to be true God. And indeed, there is not any lack of such proofs, of such credentials. Let us examine this matter somewhat more closely.

He who asserts that He is the Son of God, that He is truly God, must in the first place lead a life absolutely free from sin. When Christ stood before His mortal foes and asked, *"Which of you shall convince Me of sin?"* they were silent. Thus we see that Christ fulfilled the primary condition, that He should be without sin. In order to furnish a proof of His divinity it was necessary that He should do works which only God could accomplish. He must be Lord of the winds and waves, of the devil, of the powers of nature, of the living and the dead. Did Christ perform such essentially divine works, which could not possibly be the result, either of natural causes or of the agency of the devil?

Unbelievers have objected that in order to judge whether we have before us a work which is a miracle, and essentially divine, we need to be thoroughly acquainted with the powers of nature, and also of the devil. To this we make reply that it is only necessary to know what the forces of nature are not able to accomplish. For example, if you, dear reader, are in a room, it is plain that you can not leave that room if every opening to it is closed. Equally true it is, that ordinary mud, if rubbed upon the eye, will not cure blindness; that the devil influences no soul for good, and so on. Therefore whatever exceeds the power either of nature or of the devil, is an essentially divine action.

If, without invoking the aid of God, without first praying for help, Christ performed such actions, He performed them in virtue of His own divine omnipotence. Christ wrought miracles by His own power; the apostles and the saints performed wonders in the name of Jesus and through prayer. If Christ really did this, by so doing He showed Himself to be truly God.

That Christ performed a great number of miracles, the evangelists, the Fathers of the Church, and heathen writers alike testify. I will only mention the occasion on which He raised the dead. At Naim He recalled a dead youth to life by merely uttering this word of command: *"Young man, I say to thee: Arise."*

Christ knew that Lazarus was dead, without any announcement of the fact having reached Him, and He imparted the news to the apostles, and restored Lazarus to life, although he had been four days in the grave. Numerous persons witnessed this marvelous miracle, which caused the enemies of Our Lord to determine upon His death, because they grudged Him His popularity, and feared its consequences. But the Pharisees had no doubt as to the reality of His miracles.

Thus we see that the Saviour was a divine person. He Himself on several occasions asserted it openly, and this assertion was confirmed when He was baptized in the Jordan, by a voice from heaven which declared: *"This is My beloved Son, in whom I am well pleased."*

The adversaries of Christ affirm miracles to be impossible; therefore, say they, there were no miracles at all. Hence I might simply say to any one who had fallen from a ladder: "It is not possible to fall, therefore you have not fallen!" Thus it is utterly foolish to deny the possibility of any fact, the existence of which is self-evident. Therefore even Rousseau, who did not believe in Christ, declared that he who denies the possibility of miracles ought to be placed in a lunatic asylum.

Thus do we perceive that our faith rests upon the most solid basis; Christ is truly God, He has indisputably attested Himself to be such by means of His sinless life and His glorious miracles. Wherefore gaze upon your Saviour with the eye of faith, and say:

> My Lord and God I Thee confess to be,
> Though foes deride, and will know naught of Thee.
> Thy wondrous works reveal to human sight
> Thy love divine, Thy glory, and Thy might.

8. CHRIST CONQUERS

IN FRONT of St. Peter's in Rome there stands a lofty obelisk which the ancient Romans brought over from Egypt. For centuries it remained buried deep under heaps of rubbish; Pope Sixtus V caused it to be set up once more, and this inscription to be engraved upon it: *"Christus vincit, Christus regnat, Christus imperat; Christus nos ab omni malo liberat."* "Christ conquers, Christ reigns, Christ governs; Christ delivers us from every evil."

Christ conquers: He does this by means of His glorious resurrection from actual death, for this is the most striking, the most incontrovertible proof of His divinity. The resurrection of Christ stands forth as a prominent fact in the world's history, and the enemies of Christianity are not less compelled to own its truth than were His adherents and believing disciples. All the attempts of unbelief to argue it away have until now been utterly put to shame, and will be confounded forever. The facts of the Gospel stand as firm as mountains; all storms pass over them without leaving any trace.

Christ conquers; He had Himself foretold His resurrection, and regarded it as a miracle that should prove Him to be the Son of God in the eyes of the whole world. When with a scourge He drove the buyers and sellers out of the Temple, and the Jews asked Him in virtue of what right He acted thus, He replied: *"Destroy this temple, and in three days I will raise it up."* *"But,"* adds the evangelist, *"He spoke of the temple of His body."* In these words Our Lord referred to His future resurrection on the third day. Did this really take place? Yes, in the pages of the Gospel we find it proved to demonstration.

In the first place, the Gospel proves with absolute certainty that the Saviour really expired upon the cross. In order to make certain of His death, a soldier pierced His side with a lance; blood and water flowed from the wound, this being the surest sign that the heart had been pierced and death had actually occurred. Indeed, the wound was so deep, that, at a subsequent period, the apostle Thomas was able to place his hand in it; thus it was a mortal wound. All those who witnessed the crucifixion were convinced of Our Lord's death; the four evangelists are unanimous upon this point. And even the chief priests and scribes, the bitter enemies of Jesus, bore witness to His death, since they asked permission to place a guard at His grave. Moreover, His closest adherents doubted not the fact; they wrapped His body in linen cloths, laid it in a grave, and closed it with a slab of stone.

We now come to the most important point. In order that no deception might be practised, and the body not be stolen, the sepulcher was sealed and guards were placed before it, in compliance with the request of the Pharisees. But it was these very guards who bore the most incontrovertible witness to the resurrection, since they presented themselves on the third day and affirmed on oath they had seen Christ come forth from the sepulcher.

The obdurate Jews, however, went so far in their blindness that after taking counsel, *"they gave,"* as the evangelist tells us, *"a great sum of money to the soldiers, saying: Say you, His disciples came by night, and stole Him away when we were asleep."* What incredible folly is this! Would any man in his senses accept the testimony of witnesses who were asleep? But God, in His wisdom, permitted things to happen in this manner, in order that our faith in the fundamental truth of Christianity, namely, the Resurrection, and therefore in the divinity of Jesus Christ, should be established in a more firm and convincing manner.

Yet a further proof. The risen Lord appeared to His followers. The women who early on Easter morning repaired to the grave declared that they found it empty, as did also the apostles Peter and John. Soon afterward Jesus showed Himself to St. Peter. On the same day He appeared to the two disciples, as they were proceeding to Emmaus. In the following night He appeared to all the apostles when they were gathered together, with the exception of Thomas, to whom He manifested Himself at a later period, when he was present with the others. Furthermore, the Saviour repeatedly appeared to the disciples in Galilee; He ate with them, and made arrangements concerning the Church of the future. On one occasion He appeared to five hundred disciples at once, and on the fortieth day after His resurrection He ascended into heaven in the sight of the apostles.

These appearances could not have been the result of imagination on the part of the apostles; they could not have fancied that they saw what they so earnestly desired to behold; or from the conversation of the disciples on the road to Emmaus, and the conduct of St. Thomas, it is plain that they despaired of proving the truth of Our Lord's claims.

Thus once again let us repeat: Christ conquers! Rejoice therefore, O Christian, to know that our faith is firm as a rock! Yes, verily, firm as a rock! For no fact in the history of the world has been proved in so undeniable a manner as the resurrection of Jesus Christ. Wherefore bow down in a spirit of humility, confidence, and lively faith before this God and Saviour, exclaiming with St. Peter: *"Thou art Christ, the Son of the living God!"* Conquer, reign, and rule in my heart.

> O death! where's now thy mortal sting?
> Where's now thy victory?
> To-day His glorious praise we sing,
> Who triumphed over thee.
> Not triumphed for Himself alone;
> But, by His mighty power,
> Taught us to triumph in our turn,
> Nor dread thy terrors more.
>
> For lo! the dread of death is sin
> And never-ending woe;
> From thence it is our terrors spring,
> From thence our evils flow.
> But now, from sin and hell set free,
> No longer death we'll fear;
> But longing for eternity
> Rejoice when it draws near.
>
> Ye angels, now, who watch around
> The Conqueror's heavenly throne,
> Aid us to make the skies resound
> The victory for us won.
> Aid us to sing His worthy praise
> With one united heart;
> Aid us to walk in all His ways.
> Till we from life depart.
> —Oratory Hymns.

9. Christ Reigns

No doubt, dear reader, the name of Voltaire, the infidel, the enemy of God, is not unknown to you. He lived in France, toward the close of the eighteenth century, and made it the chief aim of his life to carry into effect his well-known saying: *Ecrasez l'infâme*, "extirpate the infamous thing!" Thus did he designate the holy Church of God. And surprising, indeed, it is to see what efforts this man made, and how persistently he endeavored by speech, writings, and actions, to give effect to his favorite saying, to extirpate this holy Church, to uproot it from the face of the earth.

But what did he gain by his proceedings? The outbreak of the most horrible, the most sanguinary revolution the world has ever seen, the slaughter of hundreds and thousands, the dissolution of all order and propriety,—but never the destruction of Holy Church.

And Voltaire does not stand alone in this respect; in all ages there have been enemies of the Church and of God, who, with similar fury and persistence, and with the like weapons, persecuted the Church of God, but never, never could they succeed in uprooting it. And why not? Because the Church is the work of God, because Christ founded it, because Christ *reigns* in the Church and through the Church.

Christ reigns; for (a) He founded a living, infallible authority (Church), commissioning and empowering her to propagate His religion pure and undefiled throughout the whole world; and (b) the Roman Catholic Church now represents this living authority in a legitimate manner.

Christ founded a living, infallible authority. At the very outset He gathered together twelve disciples, designated apostles. To them He said, shortly before His death: "*As the Father hath sent Me, I also send you.*" Thus we see that Christ entrusted to the apostles His own mission; but Christ was sent by the Father as teacher, priest, and king.

As a teacher He taught everywhere, first of all in the Temple, then in the synagogues, in towns and villages, on mountains, on the Lake of Genesareth, in the desert, and so on. And since Christ knew quite well that the apostles were but human, and as such might err and make mistakes, He expressly added to the words we quoted above: *"I am with you all days, even to the consummation of the world."*

Now everything was provided for. And with the consciousness of a mission that was directly divine, the apostles proceeded for the future. They did not ask permission of the emperor Tiberius, for they were sent by Christ.

Furthermore, Christ was a priest; He officiated as such, He absolved souls and healed them, He offered up Himself on Mount Calvary. In like manner were the apostles also sent as priests. They had partaken of the Sacrifice at the last supper, and by Christ's command they were to offer it up in future: *"Do this in commemoration of Me!"* He gave them power to forgive sins: *"Whose sins you shall forgive, they are forgiven them"*; also to baptize: *"Going, therefore, baptize all nations."*

In a similar way was Christ sent as a shepherd, as a king: *Ego sum rex,* "I am a King." But He is not a king like other monarchs; *"My Kingdom is not of this world."* Earthly kings care for the natural, temporal, civil welfare of their subjects, Christ for the supernatural, spiritual, and eternal.

The apostles were likewise shepherds and kings, and as such possessed a threefold power: to give laws, to pass judgment, and to inflict punishment. Of the possession of these powers the apostles were conscious from the very first, since they thus expressed themselves: *"It hath seemed good to the Holy Ghost and to us,"* to lay such and such commands upon you.

Thus we see that Christ founded in very deed a living, infallible authority, with the commission and command to transmit His religion in its entirety to all future generations; this authority is the college of the apostles. Equally certain is it that the Roman Catholic Church, as it exists in the present day, is the legitimate continuation of the college of the apostles. Such a continuation must indeed exist in all centuries after Christ as an infallible teaching authority; for Christ has said: *"I am with you all days, even to the consummation of the world."* Now among all religious systems there is only one which lays claim to the possession of an infallible body of teachers, and this is the Roman Catholic Church alone. When we assert that the Catholic Church is infallible, we mean that she can not err in matters of faith and morals.

If this claim were unfounded, if it were a mere pretension, it would follow that the Church of Christ would today have vanished from the face of the earth. But this is not possible, for were it otherwise, what would become of the promise of Christ: *"The gates of hell shall not prevail against it"*? What would become of the divinity of Jesus Christ Himself?

Thus we see that in one Church alone, in the Roman Catholic Church, does Christ still reign as teacher, priest, and king. Our joy and pride it is that we are children of this Holy Catholic Church.

> Calm when fiercest storms prevail,
> See the Ship of Peter sail;
> Still unharmed from age to age
> Though wild winds and storms may rage.
> Fashioned by a hand all-wise,
> Hell's worst onslaught she defies.

10. A Rock in Mid-Ocean

How small and insignificant was the Church in its origin! Twelve poor fishermen and a handful of disciples—how should they convert the world? But protected and strengthened by their divine Master, the Christian community continually increased, in spite of the bloody persecutions, in the course of which the all-powerful rulers of the mighty Roman Empire caused hundreds and thousands of the Church's children to be slain. After the lapse of a few brief centuries the Roman Empire was shattered to pieces, but the Church had conquered the world.

Fresh enemies arose; heresiarchs appeared and strove to rob the Church of the true faith, or at least to falsify it. They were often most learned and talented men, protected by princes, kings, and emperors. At first they counted a great number of adherents, they endeavored to found churches of their own; but the protection and blessing of the Saviour was not with them, but with His own Church; hence their work came to nothing.

Thus has it ever been, down to the present day, and thus will it continue to be until time shall be no more; all who repudiate or attack the faith of the Church, cast themselves headlong into the raging billows of a stormy ocean, and cause their own destruction upon the rock of the Church. Yes, verily, the Church is a rock in mid-ocean, and this rock is indestructible, because the Catholic Church is the sole possessor of the true faith, and is infallible in proclaiming it.

For the infallibility of the Church as a teacher the word of Christ Himself is pledged. He has made to her a threefold promise.

In the first place, He promised that He would remain with the Church "*even to the consummation of the world.*" Shortly before His ascension, He said to the apostles: "*Going, therefore, teach all nations...and behold, I am with you all days, even to the consummation of the world.*" These words are not addressed to the apostles as private individuals, for otherwise they would be meaningless, since before the close of the first century all the apostles had died, not excepting John. If, therefore, Christ promised to remain with His apostles even to the consummation of the world, it follows that the college of the apostles—that is, the Church in her office as teacher—must continue to exist through all centuries. And if Christ, who is eternal truth, remains with the Church, her teaching must necessarily be infallible. For He does not remain with her in order to teach her error. Rather does He intend to signify, by making use of the words we have quoted above, that He will protect her from all error.

Christ promised, in the second place, that the Spirit of truth should ever abide with the Church. He said to the apostles and their successors: *"I will ask the Father, and He shall give you another Paraclete, that He may abide with you forever, the Spirit of truth...He will teach you all things."*

In these words Jesus promises that the Holy Ghost should so assist the apostles and their successors in their office as teachers that they should only proclaim the true doctrines of Christ. How can those be right who assert that the Church can err, and has already erred; for in that case the Spirit of truth would not be fulfilled, and His divinity would be at an end! Let him who can overthrow this argument!

In the third place, Jesus promised: *"The gates* [the power] *of hell shall not prevail against it* [the Church]." This power of hell, namely, the devil, would certainly overcome, *i.e.*, prevail against the Church, if she would act in accordance with his will and desire. Before all else, however, he wills and desires that the Church should lose the true doctrines of Christ, whereby men are to be saved, and should teach what is false. As soon as he could succeed in bringing this about, he would prevail against the Church. But he can not conquer her, because of the promise of the Saviour; hence it follows that the Church can never err in matters of faith and morals; she must necessarily be infallible.

But as far as you, my dear young friend, are concerned,

what follows from the fact of the Church's infallibility? This especially: make it your constant endeavor to become better acquainted with the true doctrine of the Catholic Church. How much mischief has resulted in the case of individuals, as well as in that of whole families, communities, and states, from the fact that they were in ignorance, either wilful or otherwise, of the true doctrine of the Church. Seek, therefore, a thorough explanation, a clear understanding of all that is taught by the infallible Church. This is more especially necessary in the days in which our lot is cast.

> Come, Holy Ghost, Creator, come,
>   From Thy bright, heavenly throne;
> Come, take possession of our souls,
>   And make them all Thy own.
> O! guide our minds with Thy blest light,
>   With love our hearts inflame;
> And with Thy strength, which ne'er decays,
>   Confirm our mortal frame.
> Far from us drive our hellish foe,
>   True peace unto us bring;
> And through all perils lead us safe,
>   Beneath Thy sacred wing.

11. One True Church: One True Doctrine

CHRIST founded only one Church, for He declared clearly and decidedly: *"Upon this rock I will build My Church,"* and not "My *churches.*" Hence the teaching of Christ is one, the faith is one, the truth is one. This, however, contrasts in the most striking manner with religious indifferentism. What does this term mean?

My young friend, you have perhaps already heard, or will hear at some future day, the foolish talk which asserts it to be a matter of no possible consequence to what religious body one belongs, for one can save one's soul just as well in other churches as in the Roman Catholic Church, since it is only necessary to believe in God, and live a good life. This unconcern in matters of religion is termed "indifferentism."

It is easy to perceive how false and ruinous is such a view of life, as far as religion is concerned. It is doubtless the will of the Saviour that all nations should accept His saving religion, from the time of the apostles and their immediate successors, until the end of the world; hence it is also His will that all nations should listen to the Roman Catholic Church since she alone bears the marks of the true Church of Christ, and it is, therefore, impossible that it should be a matter of no moment to Him whether her teaching should be adopted or not. To assert the contrary would be equivalent to saying that one has an equal chance of saving one's soul whether one does the will of Christ or does it not.

How false and foolish is the saying: "Live right—then believe what you like!" Tell me, how would you answer any one who declared that it does not matter whether one has feet or not, if only one can walk? You would certainly say to such a person: "A truce to this foolish talk, how could one walk without feet?" But mark this, dear reader, feet are not more necessary for walking than is faith in a life which is to be counted upright in the eyes of God. Faith is the rod of an upright life; it is not a matter of indifference to a tree whether it is without roots or whether these are healthy and sound, or rotten and decayed.

There are other absurdities to be pointed out. If it were possible to be saved without the true doctrine, as taught by Jesus Christ, then might the apostles have stayed at home, and it would have been an act of folly on the part of the holy martyrs to lay down their lives for the Faith. They might have argued thus: faith is of no importance, it is quite enough to lead an upright life. Moreover, it would have been quite unnecessary that the Son of God should have become man, and should have taught us the one divine and saving truth.

One more remark: he who declares it does not matter what one believes, says as much as, "It does not matter whether one says: 'God speaks the truth, or God tells a lie'; it does not matter whether one says: 'Jesus is the Son of God, or (horrible is the mere thought) Jesus is a deceiver.' " Is not such a way of speaking both impious and foolish?

Therefore are the effects of indifferentism so ruinous. Ruinous for individuals, for how can he be saved who is conscious that he does not trouble himself about the teaching of Christ? How has a mere belief in the existence of a God been considered sufficient for salvation? Even the devils believe in God. Turks and heathens, too, believe in God. How ruinous for families! What examples do persons who are indifferent to religion set their neighbors, their children! What do they read? All kinds of literature—but no Catholic newspapers or periodicals are to be found on their table.

How ruinous in respect to the Church and to society! There are thousands of mixed marriages, and the children born of these unions ought of course to be baptized as Catholics; instead of which an immense proportion of them are lost to the Church. The harm is no less great in regard to society at large. Religion is rightly considered to be the surest bulwark of the State. But indifferentism can not be looked upon as a power for good in respect to society, since it is not founded upon the fear of God, attention to the voice of conscience, and so on. There is but *one* true Church of Christ—but one true faith—but one true religion.

To conclude: Do not seek a quarrel with others who are not of your faith. But if they attack your Church or your faith, to remain indifferent would be an act of treason in regard to your most precious treasure. Therefore in such a case do not say: "All right, let us talk about this some other time"; but rather quote the saying in vogue among a heathen tribe, "Slay me, but spare my mother"; take your Church under your protection as the guardian of the one, eternal truth.

> What is the greatest treasure mortals can possess?
> What is it raises man into a higher sphere?
> It is eternal truth, the faith which we profess,
> Which gives us hope in life, and peace when death is near.

12. YOUR MOST PRECIOUS TREASURE

A SHORT time since I read in a Swiss newspaper the following account from the pen of a teacher of theology. A celebrated operatic singer, during a stay which he made on the Rigi, said to the professor in the course of a conversation, that three things contributed to human happiness: love, useful occupation (especially in the realm of art), and *religion—a firmly rooted faith*. He confessed that the two first factors are followed frequently by disenchantment. In like manner, he said, fame and applause never confer true happiness.

He had experienced genuine happiness—true peace and contentment—on the day of his first communion, at the time when he possessed deep religious convictions. He had been brought up in a strictly religious manner; now, he said, though in a vague manner he believed in God, he could scarcely be called a believer.

If even this famous singer, whose artistic skill was the admiration of half Europe, and who was loaded with praise and honors, if he regarded as his brightest and happiest days, not those of his success upon the stage, but those of his youth, when he possessed deep religious convictions, there must be something grand and beautiful in this faith; and then is the poet right when he warns you, dear reader, in the following lines:

> Son, let no man take away
> The faith that is thy soul's chief stay;
> Count it as thy dearest treasure,
> Far beyond earth's wealth or pleasure.

*"The kingdom of heaven is like to a merchant seeking good pearls: who, when he had found **one pearl of great price**, went his way and sold all that he had, and bought it"* (Matt. xiii. 45,46).

The one pearl without price is the true faith and the state of grace. Guard this treasure carefully. Sacrifice everything to preserve your faith and the grace and love of God.

Faith is our beacon-light in the storms of life. Faith is our strength and consolation in adversity. Faith is certainly a supernatural treasure of such value that no earthly good whatever can compensate for its loss. Purity of heart is the fairest ornament of a young man; faith is his most precious treasure. It resembles the bright light of the sun, which cheers and enlivens the face of nature, and without which the earth would be dark and dreary, cold and unfruitful. Infinitely more sad, however, would be our life without the bright rays of the true faith.

Hence it follows that to preserve this light, your most precious treasure, with the utmost care, is the first and most important concern of your life. And this is no easy task in the present day, when unbelief is getting the upper hand to an extent which fills us with dismay. Therefore, mark well what you have to do in order to accomplish the task of your life aright, in order to preserve the Faith, which is your most precious treasure.

The first thing is, attend diligently to religious instruction. Faith is a grace in its first origin, and this grace is conferred at Baptism; faith is then implanted as a germ in the heart of the child. The development of this germ is effected by preaching divine truth, by the proclamation of the word of God. Wherefore St. Paul says: *"Faith cometh by hearing"* (Rom. x. 17). On this account you ought highly to prize the proclamation of divine truth by means of sermons and instructions of a religious nature, nor ought you ever to make use of a frivolous pretext to excuse yourself from attending them. Apply to yourself, and not to others, what you hear, and seek to regulate your life accordingly. Make also a daily spiritual reading at home.

The second means of preserving your most precious treasure is to live up to the Faith which you profess. The more zealously any one follows the precepts of the Gospel, the more steadfastly will he be confirmed in the Faith. The more blows a nail receives from the hammer, the more deeply will it be driven in; in the same way will faith become all the deeper, firmer, and stronger, the more cheerfully and readily its precepts are obeyed. Therefore be not slothful in the performance of your religious duties. As soon as you grow careless in this respect, in the same proportion will your faith become weaker and appear less convincing.

The third means is inseparably connected with the foregoing; it is the avoidance of sin. If faith is to be preserved, it is necessary to avoid sin as far as you can, and to lead a life well pleasing to God. For experience teaches that the decline of faith comes from below, proceeds from sin. This is the lower region of life, that of sensuality and animal impulses. Be on your guard against them, do not become their slave; otherwise your faith would Stand in imminent peril.

But before all other means, prayer is the means you must employ, if you desire to keep your faith strong and lively. Faith is, as has been already said, a fruit of divine grace. This was the experience of a young Frenchman, Isnard by name, who lived in the beginning of the last century. He had been a freethinker, but now desired and made an earnest effort to regain the faith he had lost. On this subject he wrote as follows: "I soon found that in the search after truth, the disposition of the heart was the most important thing. I therefore began with *prayer*, and I speedily improved and regained my faith."

Do you therefore apply yourself to prayer. Pray that you may preserve your most precious treasure amid the numerous dangers to be encountered in the world of our own day. Especially in seasons of temptation, pray to God in the language of the Gospel: *"I do believe; Lord, help my unbelief!"* On no account consider your Catholic faith to be of little value. For, as St. Augustine says: "There is no greater wealth, no more valuable possession than the Catholic faith."

> Faith of our Fathers! living still,
>   In spite of dungeon, fire, and sword;
> O, how our hearts beat high with joy
>   Whene'er we hear that glorious word:
> Faith of our Fathers! Holy Faith!
> We will be true to thee till death!
>   —Oratory Hymns.

13. Be on Your Guard!

In the course of my long experience in the cure of souls, I have met with many instances of the manner in which young men who came from thoroughly Catholic neighborhoods and pious families have later on, under the influence of irreligious and impious associations, been unable to keep straight, but have lost their faith, and with the loss of faith, have shaken off all moral restraints. You, my dear young friend, will have to go out into life; you will find yourself in circumstances which are apt to imperil your faith. How important, therefore, it is, that you should be made aware of your danger betimes and so be on your guard against it.

Against this danger to faith St. Paul warned his disciple Timothy, when he wrote: *"There shall be a time, when they will not endure sound doctrine; but according to their own desires, they will heap to themselves teachers, having itching ears; and will indeed turn away their hearing from the truth, but will be turned to fables. But be thou vigilant"* (2 Tim. iv. 3-5). We are living in an age such as he described. There are in the present day only too many men who resemble those whom the Apostle depicts in the words quoted above; men who can not endure the sound doctrine of Jesus Christ, the Son of God, but disparage, blaspheme, and contemn it. Sometimes they express doubts as to a particular dogma; sometimes they jeer at abuses; sometimes they ridicule the external practices and ceremonies of Holy Church. But above all things, they seek to implant in the mind of inexperienced youth, and above all in the soul of the young man who is just entering upon life, the germ of unbelief.

What a misfortune it would be, if such men should succeed in rendering you unstable in your faith, or in causing you to lose it altogether. Beware, therefore, of ever following the false, deceptive, luring light, which unbelief too often kindles in order to lead men astray; it is a light which dazzles, a false show, an *ignis fatuus,* and if you follow it, it will surely injure you, and lead you at last to the fire of hell. Therefore be on your guard against dangers to faith. And what are they? On the present occasion I will only mention three.

Be on your guard against doubts of the Faith. If such doubts present themselves, do not dwell upon them, but pray in all simplicity, and with humility of heart: "O my God, I believe this...because Thou hast said it, for Thou art the eternal Truth." And should these doubts continue to torment you, mention them in all confidence to your confessor or director, and you will receive good advice and instruction; you will be told how to get out of your difficulty. But if fresh doubts regarding matters of faith are suggested to you by unbelievers, the solution of which you fail to see, answer simply: "I am not able to explain this matter to your satisfaction, but of one thing I am quite certain: God can not err, nor can the Church which He guides. Consult a priest; he will give you the necessary explanation of the point in question."

In the second place, avoid the society of those who speak against the Faith and sneer at religion, the sacraments, and ceremonies. If they are persons in your own class, acquaintances to whom you can speak plainly, break the conversation off abruptly and say: "That will do, leave off talking this rubbish, and speak of something more sensible"; otherwise contrive to turn the conversation to some other topic, after defending your faith in a quiet but resolute manner, as well as you can. He who possesses a ready tongue can, in circumstances such as these, completely baffle the scoffer and make him look utterly foolish. I knew a witty Capuchin Father whose sharp tongue frequently did him good service.

On one occasion a stout, pompous gentleman who was sitting opposite to this good Father in a railway coach tried to annoy him by mocking at religion. Among other things he said to him: "Your Reverence, how is it possible that a hell can exist? Where could the Almighty get wood enough to heat such a place?" With a tongue as ready as ever, the Father retorted: "My dear sir, you need not be anxious about this point as long as God has a store of such blockheads as yourself."

In the third place, beware of infidel or anti-Catholic books and writings. Be careful in the choice of your books and magazines. Do not take it into your head that you must read everything which comes to hand. I shall say more in another chapter about the terrible evils which result from the diffusion of books hostile to the Faith and to the Church.

Do you, however, take care that amid the many dangers and temptations which surround you, the light of faith which is within you become not darkness; may it always shine before you and guide you on your heavenward way.

> Lord of eternal purity!
>   Who dost the world with light adorn,
>   And paint the fields of azure sky
>   With lovely hues of eve and morn:

Scatter our night, eternal God,
    And kindle Thy pure beam within
Free us from guilt's oppressive load,
    And break the deadly bonds of sin.

Quench Thou in us the flames of strife,
    And bid the heat of passion cease;
From perils guard our feeble life,
    And keep our souls in perfect peace.

Father of mercies! hear our cry;
    Hear us, O sole-begotten Son!
Who, with the Holy Ghost most high,
    Reignest while endless ages run.
              —Lyra Catholica.

14. POISON IN TONGUE AND PEN

A CERTAIN father, who was a complete unbeliever, caused his children to be educated in Catholic institutions. A friend spoke to him about this strange method of proceeding. The unbeliever, who was a man of education, replied: "I know only too well what a hell upon earth infidelity is, and I am not so unnatural a parent as to allow my dear children to share my fate."

Thus can unbelief be termed a hell! Listen to this, my youthful reader, and note it well: it is the confession of one who was himself an unbeliever. This unbelief, which is a hell in itself and leads to hell, is the fatal poison in modern society, and this poison is presented under all sorts of different forms, especially in two; namely, in speech and in writing.

Too often are people to be found at the present day who rail against religion and know nothing of Christianity except the fact that they were baptized. It is to be wished that these corrupt persons would keep to themselves the poison of unbelief which they have swallowed. However, they are not content to do this, but rush about like mad dogs, and poison others with their bites; and what is most to be lamented is that even the plain people in our country districts are not spared.

If they can not smuggle their poison, contained as it is in bad newspapers, periodicals, and pamphlets, into every household, because some pious and careful father of a family refuses to admit it beneath his roof, they scatter it on the public highway, in saloons, workshops, and manufactories, by means of their irreligious conversation. Whence proceed such expressions as "priest-ridden," "priestly inventions," "let us cast off the yoke of Rome," and so on? Whence comes mocking at prayer, confession, the Most Blessed Sacrament, the veneration of the saints? Whence so many blasphemous expressions? Some individual, perhaps, who, when a child, received but scant religious instruction, goes far away from home and begins to imbibe the poison of unbelief by reading anti-Christian books and listening to unorthodox teaching; he has especially noticed certain catch-words and forcible phrases, and these he repeats whenever he finds himself in the company of others, in order to lure them to destruction. The well-instructed Christian blushes at the folly of it all, but the ignorant take scandal and allow themselves to be led away, while Holy Church sighs daily over these deceivers and deceived. May you never be counted among their number!

Thus is poison also diffused by means of the pen. It is, indeed, a sad pity that so many young persons are poisoned in mind, lose their virtue and their faith, through the medium of books! It is only necessary to go about in cities, towns, and villages, in order to come on the track of the mysteries of iniquity. There are often whole shops full of books and periodicals, and standing at the windows are young persons of both sexes. What are they doing? Who are they? They are thoughtless persons whose hearts are often already corrupted, and who seek to find amusement between their working hours, and therefore patronize these places where trashy periodicals and cheap books can be obtained. Two classes of books and periodicals are to be found there, to which we call your especial attention.

To the first class belong the various kinds of novels, romances, and salacious love stories which awaken sensuality by means of objectionable narratives, and ruin the hearts in which the light of faith still remains, by mingling with these stories contemptuous expressions and subtle attacks in regard to virtue, faith, the Church, and her servants. To the second class belong those irreligious books, newspapers, and pamphlets which openly and boldly blaspheme the Church and religion. The regrettable consequences speedily make themselves apparent. It is true that all these writings contain mere rubbishy scribble, full of lies, exaggerations, and made-up tales, which have been refuted a hundred times over. They put forward accusations and objections which are foolish and groundless. During nineteen centuries, all the enemies of Holy Church have been able to put forward nothing which has not long since been proved by learned Catholic writers to be either a foolish mistake or a malicious falsehood. But the poisoned arrows of falsehood, calumny, and contempt cease not to effect their ruinous purpose. Voltaire, the most notorious among the enemies of religion, stated this fact in the following plain terms: "Only slander right and left; if all you say is not believed, some of it will stick. It is absolutely necessary to lie, and you must not lie in a timid, half-hearted fashion, but in a bold and devilish manner."

And books written upon these lines fly nowadays from town to town, from village to village. But what is to be the fate of the young people who swallow down such poison is this? May God preserve you from this poison!

On the inestimable value of good literature, Father Morgan M. Sheedy once wrote in *Benziger's Magazine*:

"Apart from the influence of our holy religion there is no

one thing which enters more deeply into the warp and woof of our character than the books we read. One of the greatest blessings that can come to any life is the love of books. The practice of keeping, especially before the young growing mind, beautiful and uplifting images and bright, cheerful, healthy thoughts from books, is of inestimable value. Next to the actual society of a noble, high-minded author is the benefit to be gained by reading his books. The mind is brought into harmony with the hopes, the aspirations, the ideals of the writer, so that it is impossible afterward to be satisfied with low or ignoble things. The horizon of the reader broadens, his point of view changes, its ideals are higher and nobler, his outlook in life is more elevated.

"The importance of having great models, high ideals, held constantly before the mind when it is in a plastic condition can not be overestimated. The books we read in youth make or mar our lives. Many a man has attributed his first start and all his after success in life to the books read in his youth. They opened up to him his possibilities, indicated his taste, and helped him to find his place in life.

> Seekest thou for bliss?
> Lo! here it is—
> In quiet nook,
> With well-beloved book.

"Good books are not only our friends; they are also our best teachers. But bad books are a curse and do a world of harm. Evil men, evil lives, evil examples spread a moral pestilence openly and powerfully; but nothing spreads falsehood and evil more surely and deeply than a book.

"But what of the novel? Fulfilling its proper end and aim at elevating the reader and enlarging his knowledge of man and of nature and its mysteries, captivating the wayward fancy, arraying salutary knowledge with true wisdom in pleasing garb, arousing the soul to strive after ideals worthy of man's mind and heart, the novel would play a most desirable part in the betterment of man. We can not deny its immense power, the greater because it reaches many unwilling to read more serious books. Indeed, many masterpieces of fiction are worthy of all the encomiums which the greatest admirer of the novel could bestow on them.

"But the tendency of today, reflected in the popular novel, is to remove all thought of the claims of almighty God, to substitute humanity and philanthropy for religion and Christian charity, and science for revealed truth.

"The other day I was reading the pastoral letter of one of our bishops on 'Christian Instruction.' This is what he wrote: 'Every doctrine of our holy faith, from the existence of God down to the least Catholic practice of devotion, is denied or assailed. Sometimes it is attacked by open hostility, but more often by a chilling indifference, or by a bitter ridicule of all the claims of religion.'

"Now if this be the actual state of things, let me ask: Are we Catholics fully alive to the very grave dangers that beset us from the literature of all kinds that is being daily and hourly issued in such enormous quantities by the publishing houses of America?

"Too many of us seem to have a positive distaste for the best—what has been written by Catholics. In fact, many of us are utter strangers to our own authors, outside of a few great names. We know little or nothing of our greatest writers. Their writings are a sealed book to many. The very name of a Catholic publishing house on the title-page of a book seems to repel rather than attract the purchaser. That is the present situation; it is one to be deplored and must be entirely changed before we Catholics come into the full possession of the literary treasures that are our rightful inheritance."

Bishop Hedley in his pastoral letter, *On Reading*, says:

"There ought undoubtedly to be a great advance on the part of Catholics in the knowledge of religion by means of print. And, happily, it cannot be pretended that there is nothing to read. If we consider, for example, the list of the publications of the Catholic Truth Society, we find among them instructions of every kind: exposition of doctrine, controversy, history, biography, devotion, moral and social papers, besides tales and verse.

"No one is too poor to be able to afford the half-penny or the penny which is the price of most of these brochures and leaflets; whilst there are books and larger pamphlets for those who look for something more extended, and the bound volumes of the series form a small library of the handiest and the most useful kind. For readers of greater education and leisure there are materials in abundance which it is unnecessary to specify at this moment. A catalogue of any of our Catholic publishers will suggest to every one how many subjects there are on which it would be useful to be well informed, and how much there is to be known in the grand and wide kingdom of the holy Catholic faith. No one can love Our Lord who does not know about Him, and no one can be truly loyal to the Church who does not take the trouble to study her.

"If instruction is so deeply important, devotion and piety are not less so. With most of us prayer is very short and very slight. There is one means which will both make us more regular in our daily prayers and deepen our earnestness in that sacred duty. This is *spiritual reading*.

"No one should be without a book about Our Lord, His sacred Heart, His blessed Mother, or the saints. No one should be without a book on the Mass. Besides one's prayer-book, one should have manuals of meditation and of instruction on Christian virtues. More extended devotional treatises will keep alive the piety of those for whom they are suitable. But all Catholics, whatever their condition, should make use of spiritual reading. It is impossible to exaggerate the effect on the lives and characters of Christians of the words of holy men, of the heroic acts of the martyrs, of the example of the lovers of Jesus in every age, of the contemplation of Our Lady's prerogatives and goodness, and, above all, of the story of Our Lord and Saviour Jesus Christ. The *Following of Christ*, and other books of a like nature, are at once a guide to virtue, an encouragement to prayer, and an influence drawing the heart daily nearer to God. The reading of Holy Scripture, of the sermons and conferences of distinguished preachers, and of the penetrating devotional books in which our language is by no means deficient, is adapted to sanctify the house, and to keep out of it, to a greater or less degree, that flood of objectionable printed matter which overflows the land at the present moment.

"Priests and laity can not do more for souls than to encourage by every means in their power good and cheap Catholic literature—*instruction, devotion, tales,* and *periodicals*—and to bring it within the reach of every class of the faithful. All read; they must read, and they will read. Let us strive to check the evils of bad reading by the dissemination of that which is good."

"Everything we read," says Father Matthew Russell, S.J., in *The Art of Being Happy*, "makes us better or worse, and, by a necessary consequence, increases or lessens our happiness. Be scrupulous in the choice of your books; often ask yourself what influence your reading exercises upon your conduct. If after having read such and such a work that pleases you— philosophy, history, fiction—or else such and such a review, or magazine, or newspaper in which you take delight—if you then find yourself more slothful about discharging your duties, more dry and cross toward your equals, harder toward your inferiors, with more disrelish for your state of life, more greedy for pleasures, enjoyments, honors, riches—do not hesitate about giving up such readings: they would poison your life and endanger your eternal happiness.

"Let us often read the *Lives of the Saints*, especially those inner lives in which the details are given in abundance. There we shall learn how we ought to behave toward God, toward others, and toward ourselves, in order to possess true happiness. Nothing is more instructive or more profitable as regards piety and even our temporal interests, properly understood, than the attentive and meditative reading of the *Lives of the Saints*."

15. THE CLOUDED TELESCOPE

WHEN astronomers desire to contemplate the sidereal heavens, they do not take their telescopes into a room filled with smoke, dust, and vapor, but they go out into the open air, at a time when the atmosphere is perfectly clear.

The reason is apparent. They act thus in order that they may see the stars more clearly and distinctly, and keep the lens of their instrument free from smoke and moisture. The same argument applies to faith; it is a telescope by means of which one can see those heavenly and supernatural things which the unaided eye of reason is not able to perceive. But this supernatural telescope must be pure and bright, and not allowed to become dim. How does it become dim; how does unbelief creep into the head and heart? This is the question. Now listen to the answer.

Who drifts into unbelief? Is it the men who spent their youth in prayer and study, and then as priests of God set an example to the world of a pure and blameless life? Is it the virgins consecrated to God who devote themselves in the solitude of the cloister to the contemplation of eternal truths? Is it the courageous youths who do their utmost to safeguard the virtue of chastity, and are careful to cleanse their consciences by a frequent reception of the sacraments? Certainly not! They can see clearly; the lens of their telescope is not dim.

Who drifts into unbelief? Those whose hearts are full of the smoke of sin, of the mist of evil passions; those who are averse to the holy truths of religion and detest its threats and admonitions on account of the sinful lives they are leading. It would be wonderful indeed, if such persons could see as clearly as those who, free from evil passions, follow after truth.

Yes, it is vice, evil, unruly, unbridled passions, which deprive men of their faith. Who is it, for instance, who mocks at confession and communion, or despises and rails at the commands of the Church? It is the man addicted to vice, who finds it difficult to confess the shameful deeds which he commits over and over again. Who begins to doubt about eternal punishment? The man addicted to vice, who trembles at the thought of hell, and heartily wishes that such a place did not exist. It is vice, the sinful gratification of the passions, which has produced heresies, and it is vice which keeps them alive.

There is one vice in particular which gradually weakens and destroys the mental powers of man. Men endowed with the highest gifts may become weak in intellect and memory, and if this happens in regard to worldly affairs, the vice to which we refer attacks all the more frequently and inevitably the supernatural endowments of the soul. "*The sensual man,*" as St. Paul tells us, "*perceiveth not those things that are of the Spirit of God*" (1 Cor. ii. 14). Hence comes the saying of St. Jerome, the Doctor of the Church: "It is difficult to find a heresiarch who was chaste."

If we open the pages of ecclesiastical history, we find this truth confirmed in the most striking manner. We will illustrate our meaning by an example. St. Francis of Sales, the great Bishop of Geneva, had converted 70,000 Protestants. His zeal for souls led him to address himself to a learned Calvinist, the head of this sect in the town of Geneva. He was at that time seventy years of age; his bald head and snowy beard indicated a period of life which must be nearing the portal of eternity. The holy bishop expounded to him, in the most forcible manner, the truths of the Catholic faith, by which alone can we be saved. Beza—for such was the name of the learned old man—Beza confessed himself vanquished and owned that he had nothing more to allege!

Was Beza therefore converted? No! This old man resembled Mount Etna, which, although covered with snow, vomits forth fire—he was the slave of lust. He sighed over his weakness and misery, and pointing to the object of his illicit love, he said: "See, this is why I remain a Calvinist, and can not accept the true Faith." That was his final answer, and he died a heretic.

Hence we can not wonder that there are in the present day so many Christians whose faith has grown cold, or who have lost it altogether, and among their number are to be found— the sight fills me with grief and pain—many young men who went forth into life unspoiled and full of faith. We see how so many of them pander to their passions, and have become the slaves of vice.

Wherefore, my dear young friend, in drawing to a conclusion these instructions concerning faith, I entreat you by all that you hold dear and sacred, to watch and pray, in order that you may not lose your faith! Be ever on your guard in order that the heavenly telescope may not become clouded through sin and vice! Earnestly reflect that it is well to live a Catholic, it is well to die a Catholic. During the course of 1900 years, no Catholic has ever thought of forsaking his religion upon his death-bed; but many infidels and heretics return to the bosom of the Church when they perceive the approach of death. Well is it for them if they do even this! But do you remain faithful to your Catholic faith in thought, word, and deed, even to your latest breath.

"*My just man liveth by faith,*" says St. Paul (Heb. x. 38). Never yield to human respect; be fearless in the confession of your faith; strive to edify others by living in accordance with your faith. The life of faith gives strength, consolation, and peace to the soul in the midst of the trials of life; it is the best assurance of a happy death and of a blissful eternity.

ACT OF FAITH

O MY GOD! I firmly believe that Thou art one God in three Divine persons, Father, Son, and Holy Ghost; I believe that Thy Divine Son became man, and died for our sins, and that he will come to judge the living and the dead. I believe these and all the truths which the Holy Catholic Church teaches, because Thou hast revealed them, who canst neither deceive nor be deceived.

ACT OF SPIRITUAL COMMUNION
BY ST. ALPHONSUS LIGUORI

MY JESUS, I believe that Thou art present in the Blessed Sacrament. I love Thee above all things and I desire Thee in my soul. Since I cannot now receive Thee sacramentally, come at least spiritually into my heart. As though thou wert already there, I embrace Thee and unite myself wholly to Thee; permit not that I should ever be separated from Thee.

The Helmet of Hope

The Helmet of Hope

16. The Protection of the Christian

There is a pious and pleasing legend which runs thus: When our first parents were expelled from the fair garden of Paradise, they wandered sadly up and down. Before them lay the land of toil, overgrown with thorns and thistles. Sighing, they exclaimed: "Alas! Would that the flaming sword of the angel had put an end to our existence!"

Then there breathed forth all at once a gentle breeze from Paradise; trees and shrubs swayed to and fro, and a little cloud, tinged with the roseate hues of dawn, floated down from the hills. A voice came out of this beauteous cloud and spoke as follows: "Your eyes will not be able to behold me, but although invisible, I will be your guide through life. I will dwell in your hearts, and smooth your path. When thou, O man, shalt till the earth in the sweat of thy brow, I will show thee in the distant horizon fields of golden corn and flowery gardens, so that thou shalt imagine thyself to be once more in Paradise."

"But," sighed our first parents, "wilt thou forsake us when we come to die?" "No," said the voice from the cloud, "but in death's dark night I will be to you a light. When your last hour is approaching, my cheering light shall surround you, and you shall behold Paradise open before you."

Our first parents asked: "Who art thou, celestial messenger, who dost bring us consolation?" "I am Hope," was the reply, "the daughter of Faith and Charity." The beauteous cloud melted away, and encompassed the persons addressed, hiding the celestial child from view. But their souls were refreshed and comforted.

My youthful reader, this heavenly child, the virtue of hope, must accompany you on your way through life. Like a helmet of steel, this virtue must guard your head against the blows of fate, which are often so hard. It must be your protection.

You must keep a firm hold on Christian hope; you must cling to it, and never let it go, for such is the will of God. He commands us to hope in Him, and this command is even implied in these words: *"Thou shalt love the Lord thy God with thy whole heart."* Hope therefore in the Lord! Why should we do this? What is the foundation of our hope?

Hope and confidence in God should be your protection and your support throughout your life, because, in the first place, God is almighty, He is infinitely merciful, faithful, and true; therefore He can and will fulfil the promises He has made to us. It is certain that He is able to fulfil His promises. For how could God be almighty if He were not able to do all things, if He could not pardon us, grant us graces, and receive us into heaven? Certainly God has only to will, and His grace penetrates our hearts, filling them with sincere penitence, washing away our sins, abolishing our debt. God wills indeed our sanctification, our salvation, and our happiness, for He is infinitely good. He truly loves all men, and desires to have them all with Himself in heaven. In the most touching manner has He made this clear and plain, since He delivered up His only begotten Son to suffer a most agonizing death. The words of St. John will be true for evermore: *"God so loved the world as to give His only begotten Son: that whosoever believeth in Him may not perish, but may have life everlasting"* (John iii. 16).

Trust in the Lord, for He sealed His promises with the blood of His own Son. Of ourselves we could indeed not deserve eternal happiness, nor the graces needed for its attainments, nor could we ever merit them. But that we could of ourselves not merit, Jesus Christ has merited for us, by means of His bitter passion and death. On this account we have, as the Apostle says: "*Such confidence through Christ toward God.*"

For the same reason St. Ambrose writes, in order to allay our fears: "Behold, whom hast thou for thy Judge! God has committed all judgment to His Son. Can He therefore condemn thee, who has ransomed thee from death?"

Contemplate therefore the merits of Jesus Christ, and when you meditate upon them never let go your hope. If you have already fallen into mortal sin, or if you should ever be grievously wounded by the shafts of sin, hope on; never despair of the mercy and saving grace of the Lord. For if priests and Levites, namely, your fellow-creatures in general, pass you by and abandon you, never will your Redeemer act in this way, never will He give you up for lost. No; your sad plight, your pitiable weakness, and the wounds of your soul will draw Him from afar to your aid, and will touch His sacred heart with compassion. He will act the part of a good Samaritan toward you. He has only oil and wine to bestow upon you, only mercy and loving kindness, if you go to Him with a contrite and humble heart—and a piece of gold, that is to say, Himself in the Most Blessed Sacrament, in order to pay all your debts. Hope in the Lord; He is your protection, your salvation.

> Himself to man our God doth give,
> Our hope, the Lord most High;
> In this hope must the Christian live,
> In this hope he must die.

Apropos of these considerations, some reflections on the number of the saved and lost are not out of order.

As we read in the Gospel of St. Luke (xiii. 23), a certain man said to our blessed Saviour:

"*Lord, are they few that are saved?*" Jesus simply replied: "*Strive to enter by the narrow gate.*"

"It is a question," says Father Walsh, S.J., in his admirable and consoling study, *The Comparative Number of the Saved and Lost*, "about which there is no authoritative decision of the Church, nor unanimous opinion of her Fathers or theologians.

"Many, notably Suarez, hold—as Father Faber does—that the great majority of adult Catholics will be saved. Some, amongst whom we are glad to count the illustrious Dominican, Father Lacordaire, hold or incline to the opinion that the *majority of mankind*, including heathens and heretics, will be saved.

"Pere Monsabre, O.P., Father Castelein, S.J., and Rev. Joseph Rickaby, S.J., advocate this mildest opinion. Father Rickaby says in his Conference, 'The Extension of Salvation': 'As to what proportion of men die in sanctifying grace, and what proportion in mortal sin, nothing is revealed, nothing is of faith, and nothing is really known to theologians. If ever you find a theologian confidently consigning the mass of human souls to eternal flames, be sure he is venturing beyond the bounds of Christian faith and of theological science. You are quite free to disbelieve his word. I do not believe it myself.

" 'The rigor of the older theologians culminated in Jansenism. To the Jansenist the elect were *the few grapes left upon the vine after a careful vintage* (Is. xxiv. 13). Since the extirpation of Jansenism, the pendulum of theological speculation has swung the other way, and theologians generally hope more of the mercy of God, or, at least, speak with less assurance of the range of His rigorous justice.'

"The reasons," continues Father Walsh, "which have induced me to think the mildest opinion, namely, that the majority—and I scarcely fear to add, the *great majority*—of mankind will be saved, are: First, because the study of God's character urges, if not forces, me to do so. Second, because this opinion appears to make most for His greater honor and glory, and for the *merits of Christ*. Third, because the belief in it is better calculated to make us love God, and to serve Him the more from love.

"Cardinal Bellarmine, in one of his expositions of the Psalms, writes: 'David records God's providence in regard of the beasts and the birds in order to let man see that he will never be forsaken by God in His providence. God, who so bounteously feeds beasts and ravens, will never desert those who are made to His own image and likeness.' Is not such Our Lord's reasoning and conclusions as we have them in His Sermon on the Mount: '*Behold the birds of the air; for they neither sow nor do they reap, nor gather into barns, and your heavenly Father feedeth them. Are you not of much more value than they?*' The most learned theologians lay down and prove the following proposition: That God really and sincerely wishes the salvation of all men, *because He is the Creator of all men*. In the words of St. Ambrose: 'God wishes all whom He creates to be saved; would to God, O men, that you would not fly and hide yourselves from Him; but even if you do He seeks you, and does not wish you to perish.' It is more probable that though many can and will fight God to the end and be lost, they will be fewer far than those whom He will tenderly, and in His own way, bring home to Himself. God is not only the *Creator* but the *Father* of all men without any exception. He has commanded us to address Him by this title: '*Our Father, who art in heaven.*' All Christians do so; and a preacher, in his opening instructions, would teach and exhort the untutored savage to believe in and speak to Him as such.

"God is the Father of all men and eminently a perfect Father. We could not imagine such a father casting out, expelling from his home forever a child, until he had tried the proper means to keep him with himself—until the child deserts him, or, by wilful, obstinate, persistent disobedience to his father's will, necessitates his own expulsion. Such a father will do all he well can for the welfare of his children—do everything short of violence to enable his children to succeed in all that is for their good. The dominant desire—wish—will—of such a father must be to make his children happy; his dominant dread and horror, that one of them should be unhappy.

"Our Lord tells us how easy and swift true repentance can be in the case of the *publican*—the notorious and typical sinner—who by making an act of sorrow for his sins, in seven words, went home to his house justified. God is far more ready and generous in forgiving the worst than men—even good men—are in forgiving each other, and bad would it be for the best of us if He were not.

"By way of showing the effect which can be produced by the very thought of God *Our Father*, and belief in Him as such, I may give a fact told to me by the person concerned—now dead for some years. He fell into a state akin to despair about his salvation. A confessor, to whom he opened his mind, told him to go, take his Bible, and write out all the texts in which God calls Himself his Father. He did so, and was blessed with calm and peace before he had written twenty."

The following extracts from the Sacred Scriptures reveal the goodness and mercy of God. Like the psalms of David, which you ought to read and meditate upon, they confirm us in our hope.

"*Say to them: As I live, saith the Lord God, I desire not the death of the wicked, but that the wicked turn from his way, and live*" (Ezech. xxxiii. 11).

"*The Son of man is come to seek and to save that which was lost*" (Luke xix. 10).

"*Behold what manner of charity the Father hath bestowed upon us, that we should be called, and should be the sons of God*" (1 John iii. 1).

"*But I say to you: Love your enemies, do good to them that hate you, and pray for them that persecute and calumniate you; that you may be the children of your Father who is in heaven, who maketh the sun to rise upon the good and bad, and raineth upon the just and unjust. . . . Be you perfect as also your heavenly Father is perfect.*"—Words of our blessed Saviour (Matt. v. 44, 45, 48).

"*Yea, I have loved thee with an everlasting love; therefore have I drawn thee, taking pity on thee*" (Jer. xxxi. 3).

"*The Lord is gracious and merciful; patient and plenteous in mercy.*"

"*The Lord is sweet to all, and His tender mercies are over all His works.*"

"*Every day will I bless Thee, and I will praise Thy name forever*" (Ps. cxliv. 8, 9, 2).

Let us give the good God, our Father in heaven, a service of *Love*, in the spirit of St. Francis Xavier, who said: "O God! I love Thee, not for the sake of winning heaven, or of escaping hell, not for the hope of gaining aught, but solely because Thou art my God."

> "Not with the hope of gaining aught,
>   Not seeking a reward;
> But as Thyself hast loved me,
>   O ever-loving Lord.

> "E'en so I love Thee, and will love,
>   And in Thy praise will sing;
> Solely because Thou art my God
>   And my eternal King."

17. Providence Watches Over Us

Many years ago my path led me by the side of a river, where laborers were engaged in erecting water-works. It was a sultry summer's day, and I pitied the workmen who were obliged to pursue their daily toil in the fierce rays of the sun. I said to myself: "How these poor creatures have to suffer, exposed as they are the livelong day to this blazing heat; and in spite of all their wearisome toil, they perhaps scarcely earn wherewithal to buy clothing and to appease their hunger and thirst!" My sympathy for these laborers caused me to devote my attention to them for a short space of time and to listen to them at their work.

Two middle-aged workmen, whose countenances showed that the cares of a family were weighing upon them, met as they were engaged in wheeling their barrows. "Give me a pinch of tobacco to fill my pipe!" one man said to his comrade; "it's about the only solace a poor man has in these days of want and scarcity. These are hard times indeed; I can scarcely believe that there is a God in heaven!"

But the other replied: "Hold your tongue! Your complaints will not mend matters! You just look at me! I have a sick wife and seven children, and they have all to be supported by the labor of my hands! The bread doesn't go very far in filling their mouths, and my heart is often heavy when I look round on them all. But do you know what sustains and supports me? I have been married for seventeen years, and God has never forsaken me; His hand will not be shortened in years to come, and He will never cease to help me; for Providence watches over us!"

"O what an excellent lesson is this in simplicity and pious trust in God," I reflected; "how suitable, and practical a subject has been chosen!" Providence watches over us! Frequently have I heard these consoling words, but never did they seem so impressive as upon this occasion, when I heard them uttered by a father who had an invalid wife and seven children, and in these hard times had only his scanty earnings wherewith to furnish them with daily bread, and whose confidence in God never wavered for an instant in spite of everything.

Providence watches over us! How does this thought bring comfort to the heart of him who is overtaken by misfortune. But where is confidence in God to be found in this unbelieving age? I make bold to say that neither the poverty of the lower orders, nor the heartlessness of the wealthy classes, but the want of faith and confidence in God, is the principal cause of the evils of the present day; nay, more, amid the evils which surround us, it is itself the most terrible evil of all.

Yet Providence ceases not to watch over us; a thousand examples both in daily life and in history prove this in an incontrovertible manner. But one of the most beautiful and forcible examples to be found in all time is related in the Book of books, in the pages of Holy Scripture.

Let us call to mind the fate of Joseph, when he was in Egypt. Who could appear more unfortunate than he was, when, though perfectly innocent, he was sold by his own brothers, dragged away from home, falsely accused of a most disgraceful crime, and on this account cast into prison! But Providence watched over him! He left the dungeon in order to ascend a throne, than which only a regal throne could rank higher. Thus his misfortune brought about his fortune, and not his alone, but that of his country, his beloved father, and his brethren. Certainly the providence of God manifested itself in this instance in no ordinary manner, and caused all things to work together for good. In order that he might be governor of Egypt, it was necessary that Joseph should be a slave, be loaded with fetters, and thrown into the prison where criminals condemned to death were confined.

Wherefore St. Jerome says: "What we consider to be misfortune, is in reality a blessing." And St. Chrysostom is right when he thus exhorts us: "When any event transcends our power of understanding, we ought not to conclude that is not well done, but rather, since we recognize on the one hand the action of Divine Providence in governing the universe, so ought we in cases which exceed the limits of our comprehension, to adore His unsearchable wisdom." Wonderful truly are the ways of God; who is able to search them out?

What ought therefore to be your resolution? This above all else; never, in any moment of life to murmur and complain, as if God were unjust, as if His providence had ceased to watch over you. But habituate yourself, however severe may be the afflictions which overtake you, to say with patient Job: "*The Lord gave, the Lord hath taken away. Blessed be the name of the Lord.*"

> God it is who makes the soil
> Grateful to the laborer's toil;
> He whom sun and stars obey
> Holds the whole world in His sway;
> Yet from His bright throne above
> Looks upon mankind with love.
> In that bounteous Lord confide,
> For your wants He will provide.

"Two principles," says Father Ramiere, S.J., "form the unalterable basis of the virtue of *abandonment or absolute surrender to Divine Providence.*

"*First Principle:* Nothing is done, nothing happens, either in the material or in the moral world, which God has not foreseen from all eternity and which He has not willed, or at least permitted.

"*Second Principle:* God can will nothing, He can permit nothing, but in view of the end He proposed to Himself in creating the world; *i.e.*, in view of His glory and the glory of the Man-God, Jesus Christ, His only Son.

"To these two principles we shall add a third, which will complete the elucidation of this whole subject, *viz.*: As long as man lives upon earth, God desires to be glorified through the happiness of this privileged creature; and consequently, in God's designs, the interest of man's sanctification and happiness is inseparable from the interest of the divine glory.

"If we do not lose sight of these principles, which no Christian can question, we shall understand that our confidence in the providence of Our Father in heaven can not be too great, too absolute, too childlike. If nothing but what He permits happens, and if He can permit nothing but what is for our happiness, then we have nothing to fear, except not being sufficiently submissive to God. As long as we keep ourselves united with Him and we walk after His designs, were all creatures to turn against us they could not harm us. He who relies upon God becomes, by this very reliance, as powerful and as invincible as God, and created powers can no more prevail against him than against God Himself. This confidence in the fatherly providence of God can not, evidently, dispense us from doing all that is in our power to accomplish His designs; but, after having done all that depends upon our efforts, we will abandon ourselves completely to God for the rest."

"When we will what God wills," says St. Alphonsus, "it is our own greatest good that we will; for God desires what is for our greatest advantage. Let your constant practice be to offer yourself to God, that He may do with you what He pleases." God can not be deceived and we may rest assured that what He determines will be best for us. Can there be a better prayer than this?

"All that is bitter," says St. Ignatius Loyola, *"as well as all that is sweet in this life, comes from the love of God for us."*

18. RESURRECTION AND RECOGNITION

W HEN a socialistic pamphlet is intended for distribution
among the working classes, the author frequently
depicts their misery in harrowing terms. It is true that the lot
of the laboring man is a hard one, and the modern, impious
socialist tells him this over and over again, but hear what sort
of comfort he offers him.

Your Church points you, as a Catholic, to a better life than
this, to a life where you will find rest after your toil, if you,
while on earth, have served God with a clean heart, and have
applied yourself to your daily tasks with a pure intention.
But the writer of a pamphlet such as I allude to, leaves the
unfortunate laborer, whose lot upon earth is so full of hardship,
in doubt whether there is any resurrection and recognition, any
"*Wiedersehen*" of our loved ones, any better life. Who is right,
you with your blissful hope, or this newspaper writer with his
cold and miserable comfort—despair? The question has been
settled long since; Christ rose again, therefore for us also there
will be a resurrection and recognition!

Will this hope perhaps deceive us? Never! An unhappy
mother knelt by the grave of her darling, a boy about ten years
old. She remained kneeling there for hours; she wept until her
eyes were red; she sighed and prayed until her voice failed her;
yet, as the poet tells us:

> When for the loved one lost our tears o'erflow
> The mourning heart is bowed with bitter woe.
> This thought into the heart with solace steals:
> He is not dead whom now the grave conceals.

Assuredly, "he is not dead whom now the grave conceals"!
An inner voice tells us this, and the same voice is heard by all
those nations who honor the last resting places of the dead.
Everywhere, even among the most uncivilized nations, we
find the hope that the sleep of the grave will not last forever,

but that the day of awakening will dawn.

But we, as Christians, have no mere vague presentiments concerning this resurrection and recognition, but the most complete assurance. For Jesus Christ, who is Himself the Eternal Truth, says in clear and solemn accents: "*I am the resurrection and the life; he that believeth in Me, although he be dead, shall live.*"

And there must of necessity be a resurrection, an eternal recompense; it is imperatively demanded by the justice and holiness of God. His eye sees how frequently upon earth licentiousness, crime, injustice, stalk openly abroad or flourish in secret. Where is the penalty, the punishment? Religion has its champions, virtue its heroes, faith its martyrs. Where is the reward?

Or are virtue and vice, innocence and guilt, of equal value in the eyes of God? In that case there would no longer be virtue or vice, guilt or merit; everything would be equal and there would no longer be a question of a Supreme Being, who is holy and just!

Come, let us draw near to a death-bed. We will suppose that we see stretched upon it a young man who is about to breathe his last. He is at an age when life holds out the brightest promise of enjoyment; he is in the bloom of youth, being scarcely more than twenty years of age. He has grown up good and pious, innocent of evil, a spectacle to men and angels. Now death is approaching; the bystanders are dissolved in tears, the dying man alone is calm; he even smiles, a ray of celestial brightness hovers around his wasted features, he exclaims with his final gasp: "Jesus, I am Thine in life and in death! Jesus, mercy!" Now tell me, can God answer the prayer of this angel in the flesh by dooming him to annihilation?

Let us approach another death-bed. Upon it there lies a young man who is about to draw his last breath, but who has been a grief to his family, a disgrace to his relatives. Ever since his boyhood he has been the slave of vice, and he has now become the deplorable victim of his evil passions. There he lies—there he dies—in despair. Now tell me again, can we inscribe upon the bier of the chaste young man, adorned as he was with virtue, words implying his life to have been a delusion? And can we eulogize the miserable victim of vice by affirming that he did nothing wrong? Could God consign these two beings, so radically different from one another, to an equal annihilation? Could they both become, as they lie in the grave, a mere mass of moldering corruption, dust, and ashes—this, and nothing more forever? Is not the mere idea of anything so monstrous abhorrent to the conscience of every man?

No, this can not be, that in death virtue and vice should become mere meaningless terms; rather must each of these two things meet its proportionate recompense.

Do you therefore, my dear young friend, practise virtue and flee from vice; there is a resurrection and a recompense; there is a *Wiedersehen!* "*Take courage, and let not your hands be weakened; for there shall be a reward for your work*" (2 Paral. xv. 7).

"*I know that my Redeemer liveth, and in the last day I shall rise out of the earth; and I shall be clothed again with my skin, and in my flesh I shall see my God; whom I myself shall see, and my eyes shall behold, and not another. This my hope is laid up in my bosom*" (Job xix. 25-27).

"*The just shall live forevermore; and their reward is with the Lord, and the care of them with the Most High*" (Wis. v. 16), "*Who will render to every man according to his works*" (Rom. ii. 6).

'Tis sweet, as year by year we lose
Friends out of sight, by faith to muse
How grows in Paradise our store.
—Keble.

19. HEAVEN ON EARTH

ONCE upon a time a grand banquet was prepared in the palatial residence of a millionaire. The appetizing odors of the viands pervaded the whole house; strains of musical instruments delighted the ear, the gorgeous furniture was a joy to the eye. In the courtyard of the residence stood a horse, calmly munching its hay; the music did not bewilder it and the footmen who hastened hither and thither, carrying dishes filled with all the delicacies of the season, aroused no longing in the horse, who continued to eat the hay with keen relish. The servants thought they would like a little joke, and placed soup, roast meat, and vegetables before the animal; however, it thrust them all aside, and went on eating the hay.

"No one can possibly wonder," I think I hear you say, "if the horse refuses to eat meat, and cares only for oats and hay, since it is its nature to do this." You are perfectly right, but mark this: there are human beings, and unfortunately they are very numerous, who, like this horse and other animals, maintain their position at the manger, and eat their hay and their oats, instead of cultivating an appetite for better food.

You will understand what I am driving at. There are people both young and old, who have no appetite for anything better than the miserable hay and oats of earthly delights: people to whom pleasure and gold seem to constitute a heaven upon earth. They long for animal enjoyments, not for celestial joys. Such persons would willingly learn how to pray, indeed they would go on praying until their voice failed, if only God would grant them just one request. And what, think you, would be this request? Do you imagine that these votaries of pleasure would pray for spiritual and eternal gifts? They can not bear the thought of death and eternity. I have already told you that their heaven is on earth. Their sole wish is that the Almighty would make a bargain with them, and promise that they should never grow old, and never die. You do not hear them say with St. Paul: *"I desire to be dissolved."* Oh, no! but "I desire to remain here, to live forever on earth."

And what would they promise if God would make this bargain with them? The answer is plain enough; they would say: "Keep Thy heaven for Thyself as far as we are concerned, if only we may remain always young, and live forever upon earth in the gratification of all our senses and natural inclinations." Listen to this bit of wisdom from that smart journalist, to whom I referred in the preceding chapter. He writes: "The earth was assigned to us as our abode in order that we might enjoy it to our heart's content, seek for pleasure, and find our satisfaction in it. Those who in exchange for our tears and lamentations offer us nothing but the sight of a dim and distant heaven, only point to a future life, are either not the true friends of the poor man, and of the human race in general, or they are the victims of a morbid self-delusion."

A self-delusion! Pray, where did this scribbler discover this? Certainly not in the pages of Holy Scripture, but in his own brain, and he himself is undoubtedly the victim of a delusion.

One who is certainly far above this newspaper editor has spoken in a very different strain, in that He said: *"In My Father's house there are many mansions: I go to prepare a place for you"* (John xiv. 2).

And the great Apostle St. Paul tells us: *"We have not here a lasting city, but we seek one that is to come"* (Heb. xiii. 14).

"Therefore, if you be risen with Christ, seek the things that are above, where Christ is sitting at the right hand of God: Mind the things that are above, not the things that are upon the earth. For you are dead and your life is hid with Christ in God" (Col. iii. 1-3).

St. Peter admonishes us: *"Dearly beloved, I beseech you as strangers and pilgrims [on earth] to refrain yourselves from carnal desires, which war against the soul"* (1 Peter ii. 11).

"*Blessed be the God and Father of our Lord Jesus Christ who according to His great mercy hath regenerated us unto a lively hope, by the resurrection of Jesus Christ from the dead—unto an inheritance incorruptible and undefiled, and that can not fade— reserved in heaven for you*" (1 Peter i. 3, 4).

Let us quit the polluted realms of the terrestrial heaven and raise our eyes to the true heaven. And why ought we to do this? Because the world and its pleasures pass away. The happiness which it offers us in its honors and riches and pleasures will never satisfy our hearts, which are made for the enjoyment of higher and better things.

Hear the testimony of a man who had enjoyed a very wide experience and had drained the cup of earthly pleasures to its very dregs—I mean Solomon. As he himself plainly states, he had left nothing untried. What was the result? Was he satisfied? No, the refrain of his song is ever the same: "*Vanity of vanities, and all things are vanity.*"

Away, therefore, with this beggarly rubbish, with the "heaven" which the world promises you! You were born to something better, your inheritance is not here! The heaven which is above should be the object of your soul's desires. Thither ought you to direct your eyes, as the marksman directs his eyes to the target. Say with David: "*How lovely are Thy tabernacles, O Lord of hosts! My soul longeth and fainteth for the courts of the Lord*" (Ps. lxxxiii. 2).

Should your lot be a prosperous one in this world, you ought to long far more for that blessed place where your joy will be complete and everlasting. Should afflictions be your portion, bear them with resignation, if only you can attain eternal happiness. Let earth give you what it will, it can not give you heaven; let earth take from you what it will, it can never deprive you of heaven. Therefore farewell, O vain and fleeting world! Draw near, O blissful heavenly dwelling-place! Would that we were already within thy gates, O Paradise! To such a prayer as this, who would not gladly say: Amen?

> O Paradise! O Paradise!
>   Who doth not crave for rest?
> Who would not seek the happy land
>   Where they that loved are blest?
>
> Where loyal hearts and true
>   Stand ever in the light,
> All rapture through and through
>   In God's most holy sight?
>
> O Paradise! O Paradise!
>   'Tis weary waiting here;
> I long to be where Jesus is,
>   To feel, to see Him near.
>
> O Jesus! Thou the beauty art
>   Of angel worlds above;
> Thy name is music to the heart,
>   Enchanting it with love.
>
> O my sweet Jesus! hear the sighs
>   Which unto Thee I send;
> To Thee my inmost spirit cries,
>   My being's hope and end.
>
> Jesus! our only joy be Thou,
>   As Thou our prize wilt be;
> Jesus! be Thou our glory now,
>   And through eternity.

20. TRUST IN GOD: BE OF GOOD CHEER!

WITH courage like that of the lion, the young man rushes forth into a hostile world. It appears as if nothing could prevent him from attaining his highest aims, from realizing his youthful ideals. But alas! no sooner do the first obstacles present themselves, no sooner does he perceive that he will have to struggle and fight, no sooner do a few words of mockery or contradiction sound in his ears, than his lionlike courage vanishes, and he no longer feels the joy of battle; nerveless and inert, he drops his wings.

And if the force of temptation assails him and, weak and inexperienced as the young man is, he falls into sin, and falls very deeply and grievously, then, instead of rising up with courage and energy, he lies in the abyss of his first sin, and abandons himself to cowardice, or even to despair. Never do this, my friend! However hopeless the case may appear, whatever the circumstances may be take courage, be of good cheer, trust in God!

Never think or say: "God will never forgive my sins; He will not grant me the grace which is necessary, if I am to attain heaven; whatever I do, I shall be damned, there is no help for it!" This would be to despair, and despair is a terrible sin, a blasphemy against God. On this subject St. Thomas tells us that there is scarcely a greater sin than despair, and St. Augustine assures us that Judas sinned yet more grievously through despair, than even by betraying his divine Master.

And how awful are the consequences of this sin! The unhappy man who despairs loses all courage, all joy; he falls from sin to sin, because he thinks that nothing can be of any consequence, since he is already lost. Thus in his despair he lives a wretched life while on earth, till he exchanges his misery here below for the everlasting misery of hell.

For this reason I say to you: Trust in God, have confidence in His goodness and mercy. It is, of course, no bad sign that you should feel alarm and terror on account of your sins, that you should regret your past folly, that you should tremble at the thought of the peril incurred by a sinful life. When, after a long winter, it begins to lighten, thunder and rain, it is a sign that spring is near.

Therefore, when the storm agitates the heart of the sinner—that is, when his conscience torments him and exhorts him to repentance, it is a good sign, if he pays heed to the warning voice, and he is happier in his sadness than he was formerly in his sinful pleasures. This is not despair, but a salutary fear of God.

Despair consists rather in a voluntary and deliberate renunciation of all hope of attaining everlasting happiness, and a refusal to have recourse to the means of salvation. But is it possible, O merciful God, that any one can have so little trust in Thee, so little confidence in Thy fatherly love, as to imagine Thee to be unwilling to pardon?

I only wish I could transport him who thus despairs to the far-off land where Jesus lived and suffered for our sake. Behold, I would say to him, here was your Redeemer born, here He lay in the manger for your sake, and yonder, on a mountain near to Jerusalem, He shed His blood upon the tree of the cross. Now, then, tell me, are you a man? If you are a man, this precious blood was shed for you. Tell me again whether you truly repent of your sins and are determined to forsake them without delay, to forsake them, not at some distant day, but at once? If this be the case, then away with your doubts; go on your way—rejoicing, and trust in God!

Dear reader, in whatever circumstance you may find yourself, trust in God! If you find it difficult to curb your unruly passions, to fly from the dangers by which your soul is menaced, to avoid the occasions of sin, and resolutely to turn a deaf ear to the magical enchantments of the world, then, O young man, take courage, trust in God, pray—pray—pray to God with confidence! And if you have to serve an apprenticeship, and submit to the drudgery of learning your business, and if you are obliged to go far away from home and earn your bread in the sweat of your face, then, when you long to repair to some place of amusement, and there forget your weariness and toil by means of drinking, dancing, and gambling, do not give up, but pray to God and trust in Him! Or, as a Religious once wrote in a young man's album:

> Spread thy wings and boldly fly,
> Courage raises to the sky.

Say with the Royal Psalmist: "*I have put my trust in Thee, O Lord; Thou art my God. My lots are in thy hands.*"—Ps. xxx. 15, 16.

"*It is good to confide in the Lord.*"—Ps. cxvii. 8.

"*He will overshadow thee with His shoulders and under His wings thou shalt trust.*

"*His truth shall compass thee with a shield; thou shalt not be afraid of the terror of the night.*

"*For He hath given His angels charge over thee to keep thee in all thy ways.*"—Ps. xc. 4, 5, 11.

In conclusion I will quote the remarkable words which a German statesman addressed upon one occasion to the students at the University of Innsbruck: "We find in the words of St. John (Apoc. xxi. 8) that (among the reprobates) there come in the first place the fearful, the *timidi*, who lack courage to stand up for the cause of God and the Church; next come thieves and other immoral persons. Think what it would be to find yourself condemned to remain for all eternity in the company of these *timidi*, and with them to partake of the cup which eternal justice has prepared for their punishment in the pool burning with fire and brimstone. Wherefore, my friends, do not flag in the fight."

> When afflictions fierce assail,
> Never let thy courage fail;
> Hottest fire, refiners say,
> Melts the gold and hardens clay.

Father Claude de la Columbière's

Act of Hope and Confidence in God

M<small>Y</small> G<small>OD</small>, I believe most firmly that Thou watchest over all who hope in Thee, and that we can want for nothing when we rely upon Thee in all things; therefore I am resolved for the future to have no anxieties, and to cast all my cares upon Thee. *"In peace in the selfsame I will sleep and I will rest; for Thou, O Lord, singularly hast settled me in hope."*

Men may deprive me of worldly goods and of honors; sickness may take from me my strength and the means of serving Thee; I may even lose Thy grace by sin; but my trust shall never leave me. I will preserve it to the last moment of my life, and the powers of hell shall seek in vain to wrest it from me. *"In peace in the selfsame I will sleep and I will rest."*

Let others seek happiness in their wealth, in their talents: let them trust to the purity of their lives, the severity of their mortifications, to the number of their good works, the fervor of their prayers; as for me, O my God, in my very confidence lies all my hope. *"For Thou, O Lord, singularly hast settled me in hope."* This confidence can never be vain. *"No one has hoped in the Lord and has been confounded."*

I am assured, therefore, of my eternal happiness, for I firmly hope for it, and all my hope is in Thee. *"In Thee, O Lord, have I hoped; let me never be confounded."*

I know, alas! I know but too well that I am frail and changeable; I know the power of temptation against the strongest virtue. I have seen stars fall from heaven, and pillars of the firmament totter; but these things alarm me not. While I hope in Thee I am sheltered from all misfortune, and I am sure that my trust shall endure, for I rely upon Thee to sustain this unfailing hope.

Finally, I know that my confidence can not exceed Thy bounty, and that I shall never receive less than I have hoped for from Thee. Therefore I hope that Thou wilt sustain me against my evil inclinations; that Thou wilt protect me against the most furious assaults of the evil one, and that Thou wilt cause my weakness to triumph over my most powerful enemies. I hope that Thou wilt never cease to love me, and that I shall love Thee unceasingly. *"In Thee, O Lord, have I hoped; let me never be confounded."*

ACT OF HOPE

O MY GOD! relying on Thy infinite goodness and promises, I hope to obtain pardon of my sins, the help of Thy grace, and life everlasting, through the merits of Jesus Christ, my Lord and Redeemer.

MEMORARE

REMEMBER, O most gracious Virgin Mary, that never was it known that anyone who fled to thy protection, implored thy help, or sought thy intercession was left unaided.

Inspired by this confidence, I fly unto thee, O Virgin of virgins, my mother; to thee I come, before thee I stand, sinful and sorrowful. O Mother of the Word Incarnate, despise not my petitions, but in thy mercy hear and answer me. Amen.

Te Deum

Thee, O God, we praise; Thee, O Lord, we proclaim.
Thee, O Eternal Father, all the earth doth worship.
To Thee all the angels, to Thee the Heavens and all the Powers:
To Thee the Cherubim and Seraphim cry out without ceasing:
Holy, Holy, Holy, Lord God of Hosts.
Heaven and Earth are full of the majesty of Thy glory.
Thee the glorious choir of the Apostles,
Thee the admirable company of the Prophets,
Thee the white-robed army of Martyrs doth praise.
Thee the holy Church throughout the world doth confess,
The Father of infinite Majesty;
Thy adorable, true and only Son;
Also the Holy Ghost, the Comforter.
Thou, O Christ, are the King of glory!
Thou art the everlasting Son of the Father.
Thou, having taken it upon Thyself to deliver man,
    didst not disdain the Virgin's womb.
Thou, having overcome the sting of death,
    hast opened to believers the Kingdom of Heaven.
Thou sittest at the right hand of God, in the glory of the Father.
Thou, we believe, art the Judge to come.
    (The following verse is said kneeling:)
Thee we beseech, therefore, to help thy servants,
whom Thou hast redeemed with Thy Precious Blood.
Make them to be numbered with Thy Saints in everlasting glory.
O Lord, save Thy people, and bless Thine inheritance!
And govern them, and exalt them forever.
Day by day we bless Thee
And we praise Thy Name forever: yea, forever and ever.
Vouchsafe, O Lord, this day to keep us without sin.
Have mercy on us, O Lord, have mercy on us.
Let Thy mercy, O Lord, be upon us, for we have trusted in Thee.
In Thee, O Lord, have I placed my hope;
    let me not be confounded forever.

V. Blessed art Thou, O Lord, the God of our fathers.

R. And worthy to be praised and glorified for ever.

V. Let us bless the Father and the Son, with the Holy Ghost.

R. Let us praise and magnify Him for ever.

The Arrow of
the Love
of God

THE ARROW OF THE LOVE OF GOD

21. LIFT UP YOUR HEART

IN THE commencement of the last century, Napoleon the Great found himself a solitary prisoner on the island of St. Helena. In order to dispel the ennui which overtook him, he passed in mental review the great men of bygone ages. When he fixed his gaze on Christ, he is said to have exclaimed: "See how He attracted the whole human race to Himself!"

And so indeed it is. The name of Jesus Christ is heard at the cradle of the infant and the grave of the old man, in the cottage and the palace; it is heard by the weak and by the strong; it sounds in the depths and on the heights, in water and on dry land, by day and by night.

Thus have been fulfilled those words of Our Lord: *"And I, if I be lifted up from the earth, will draw all things to Myself."*

He has drawn all things to Himself by the sweet bond of charity. He has given to us poor mortals the most convincing proofs of His infinite love, His divine charity. Let these proofs encourage us; therefore, lift up your heart. Lift it up to the holy mountain, up to the cross, up to Heaven!

To the holy mountain, to Mount Olivet! There behold amid the shadows of night faintly illuminated by the light of the moon, beneath the boughs of the olive trees, a man kneeling on the ground, bowed down as if by a heavy burden, convulsively wringing His hands, His countenance pale as death, while a sweat of blood forces itself through the pores of His skin and trickles down His forehead. And His dearest friends, whom He loved as no friend ever loved his friend, no mother her child, leave Him alone in His agony; they have no word of comfort for Him, they are sleeping; they could not watch with Him one hour, although a short time before they had protested that they were ready to go with Him into prison and to death!

Yet all is not told. His enemies approach like ravenous wolves, and out of their midst one steps forward, who had been His friend, His disciple, and imprints the terrible kiss of treachery upon His sacred forehead.

And they bind the innocent Lamb, the incarnate Son of God, and lead Him away to Jerusalem; they mock and blaspheme Him, they scourge Him and crown His head with cruel thorns.

Now He climbs the steep ascent of Mount Golgotha. With a heavy cross pressing upon His lacerated shoulders, the Man of Sorrows totters along. Having reached the summit, they tear off His clothes, throw Him down upon the cross, stretch His mangled limbs, drive huge nails through His hands and feet, and then set up the cross. Behold the charity of thy God!

Lift up your heart to the cross! There hangs the Lamb of God, suspended upon the tree of shame between heaven and earth. The blood flows from a hundred wounds and trickles down upon the cross. To all this physical torture add the mental anguish which rends His soul at the sight of His beloved Mother standing at His feet. His heart is ready to break with compassion! Furthermore, there is the mockery and blasphemy of the godless bystanders, whose obstinacy, as He knows only too well, will cause all His sufferings to be of no avail as far as they are concerned. And finally, there is the inexpressibly painful dereliction which wrings from His lips the agonizing cry: *"My God, My God, why hast Thou forsaken*

Me?" Now consider all that we have been passing in review and see *"whether there be any sorrow like to this sorrow"*; see whether there be any charity like to this divine charity!

But lift up your heart still higher, lift it up to heaven. If with mortal eyes you are not able to behold the full glory of this abode of the blessed, and if you can not draw near to Him, the Eternal One, because He dwells "in the light inaccessible," do not be discouraged, lift up your heart! For in the light of the bright ray which God will cause to shine upon you, you will be able to form at least some faint conception of the glories of the celestial city.

There in the brilliance of eternal glory, the Son of God sat at the right hand of His Father, not having as yet assumed the nature of man; in the fulness of time the Father sent Him into the world to become man and to die upon the cross. But why did He send His beloved Son to incur humiliation, suffering, and death?

Listen, wonder, and adore! He, the crucified, Himself gives the answer. He solves the problem worthy of a God, in the words which He formerly addressed to Nicodemus: *"God so loved the world, as to give His only begotten Son, that whosoever believeth in Him may not perish, but may have life everlasting"* (John iii. 16).

Thus, again, it was charity which impelled God to an action neither heaven nor earth could possibly have foreseen, an action which would of itself have sufficed to justify the words of the apostle of love, *"God is love!"*

Wherefore, my friend, strive to free your heart from all mere earthly or sinful affection. Lift up your heart to heaven! There alone is an object truly worthy of your love!

> Love, all other love transcending,
> Love from God's own throne descending.
> Blessings free that love unending
> From the cross is ever sending.

St. Francis Xavier's Hymn of Love

O DEUS, ego amo Te!
  Nec amo Te ut salves me,
Aut quia non amantes Te,
Eterno punis igne:

Tu, Tu, mi Jesu, totum me
Amplexus es in cruce.
Tulisti clavos, lanceam
Multamque ignominiam,

Innumeros dolores,
Sudores et angores,
Ac mortem: et hæc propter me,
Ac pro me peccatore!

Cur igitur non amem Te,
O Jesu amantissime?
Non ut in cœlo salves me,
Aut ne æternum damnes me,

Nec præmii ullius spe;

Sed sicut Tu amasti me,

Sic amo et amabo Te,
Solum quia Rex meus es,
Et solum quia Deus es.

O GOD, I love thee for Thyself
  And not that I may heaven gain,
Nor yet that they who love thee not,
Must suffer hell's eternal pain.

Thou, O my Jesus! Thou didst me
Upon the cross embrace:
For me didst bear the nails and spear
And manifold disgrace:

And griefs and torments numberless,
And sweat of agony;
E'en death itself—and all for one
Who was Thine enemy.

Then why, O blessed Jesus Christ,
Should I not love Thee well:
Not for the sake of winning heaven,
Or of escaping hell;

Not with the hope of gaining aught,
Not seeking a reward:
But as Thyself has loved me, O ever-
loving Lord.

E'en so I love Thee, and will love,
And in Thy praise will sing;
Solely because Thou art my God
And my eternal King.

22. All for the Love of Jesus

L OVE is a necessity to every human heart. Man is swayed by love either for good or for evil. Hence it is of the highest importance for every man, and especially for the young man, that an active, practical, abiding, unswerving love of God should dwell within his heart—of the highest importance for the young man, since it is in youth that the war against the threefold enemy—the devil, the world, and the concupiscence of the flesh—is the fiercest and most decisive.

If you, my dear young man, while you are rejoicing in the golden days of youth, fail to gain a mastery over the devil, the world, and the concupiscence of the flesh, the victory will at a later period become very difficult, perhaps even impossible, and in this case you will never win the heavenly crown which is the reward of him who conquers.

But how, and by what means shall you conquer? Solely and wholly through the power of love. For of love the poet sings:

> Love is like the orb of day,
> Love in every heart holds sway;
> Who no more can tune his lay
> To love, may cast his lyre away.

> "Love is your master; for he masters you."
> —Shakespeare.

> "Love aids the hero, bids ambition rise
> To nobler heights, inspires immortal deeds,
> E'en softens brutes, and adds a grace to virtue."
> —Thomson.

> "Love's reign is eternal,
> The heart is his throne,
> And he has all seasons
> Of life for his own."
> —Morris.

> "There is a comfort in the strength of love,
> 'Twill make a thing endurable, which else
> Would overset the brain, or break the heart."
> —Wordsworth.

"Love is strong as death. Many waters can not quench charity; neither can the floods drown it."　　—Solomon (Cant. viii. 6, 7).

But only true love, love to God, has power to conquer the devil, the world, and the concupiscence of the flesh. Wherefore let a true, practical, abiding love of God and of Christ be your guiding star; let it be the mainspring of your life; let it animate and strengthen you.

You must learn to say from your heart with the apostle St. Paul: *"The charity of Christ presseth us"* (2 Cor. v. 14), for then only will you be able to speak of victory. Without love no victory whatever can be achieved, and on no domain. We learn this from sacred and profane history, from the history of the world, from the history of each individual man. Love, as generally understood, conquers in good as well as in evil.

What, for instance, inspired and animated many a patriot to march fearlessly to battle, and to perform those immortal deeds of heroism which are read of in the pages of history? It was love—love of their native land.

What induced Napoleon the Great to give himself no rest, but to drive his triumphal chariot through all the countries of Europe? It was love—the love of fame.

What induces the miser to resist the most powerful of all instincts, the desire for food and drink, and literally to starve himself to death, with a chest full of gold in his possession? It is love—the love of money.

What leads an invalid to conquer fear and anguish, and to submit to a most painful and dangerous operation? It is love— the love of his own life, which makes him risk everything.

What causes a mother so often to give up her own ease and comfort, and sacrifice money, time, sleep, health, and everything she can call her own, for the sake of a sick child? It is love—her great love for her offspring.

And what enables pious married people to conquer their selfish desires? It is love—the love which ought to exist between husband and wife.

What induced St. Vincent de Paul to achieve so heroic a victory over himself, and allow himself to be shut up in prison with the dregs of mankind, with unhappy convicts condemned to the galleys? It was love—love for their immortal souls.

How would it have been possible that untold numbers of holy martyrs, amongst whom were tender virgins and young children, should renounce not only honor, freedom, fortune, health, the joys of family life, but should give up their lives amid terrible torture? It was only possible through the power of love—love for their Redeemer; they said with the Apostle: "*The love of Christ presseth us.*"

And how was the greatest and most glorious victory recorded in the annals of the human race obtained, the victory over sin, death, and hell, the divine victory of the Saviour, when He expired upon Mount Calvary? This was indeed the supremest victory of love—the victory of divine and infinite charity in regard to the poor sons of Adam.

Such, my youthful reader, is the all-conquering might of love. And if you know that it is imperatively necessary for you to overcome the lust of the eyes, the concupiscence of the flesh, and the pride of life, in order to win and wear the victor's crown in heaven, how consoling is the thought that you will be able to conquer through the might of love, through the love of Christ!

And He, the Saviour of the world, has made it so easy for us to love Him, because He first loved us, and has done so very much for us. Ought it not rather to be difficult not to love this divine Redeemer?

Wherefore let a true and all-absorbing love of God enter into your heart and dwell there. This love streams forth from the tabernacle, from the Sacrament of Love. At this moment the Saviour is knocking at the door of your heart. Open to Him; let Him enter in, that He may inflame you with His love. Pray, pray: Heart of Jesus inflamed with love of me, inflame my heart with love of Thee!

Thus shall you conquer through the power of love; conquer your impure and evil passions; this unholy fire will be subdued by the holy fire of a true love of God.

Darkness shrouds your future; who can lift the veil which conceals it? Perhaps it is thick with storms and strife; but if love of Christ reigns in your heart, you will pass in safety through life's long day and death's dark night. Wherefore pray frequently and fervently to your Redeemer in some such words as these:

> O Christ, whose life on earth was love,
> Our hearts with charity inspire;
> Draw all our thoughts to Heaven above,
> Where love fulfils the soul's desire.

ALL FOR THEE, O HEART OF JESUS

How sweet it is to feel, dear Lord,
  That Thou wilt surely see
Each work, or thought, or act of mine
  That may be done for Thee!

That when I try with pure intent
  To serve, to please, to love Thee,
Thy watchful Heart each effort knows,
  Thy blessing rests above me.

Empty my soul of all desire
  Man's idle praise to seek,
Hide me in Thee, for Thou dost know
  How frail I am—and weak.

Take Thou my *all*, since for so long
  Thy providence has sought me,
Make me Thine own since at such cost
  Thy precious blood has bought me.

Live, Jesus, live, so live in me,
  That all I do be done by Thee,
And grant that all I think and say
  May be Thy thoughts and words today.
                              —Leaflets.

23. THE PEARL OF LIFE

S T. JOHN the Evangelist writes thus: *"Before the festival day of the Pasch, Jesus, knowing that His hour was come that He should pass out of this world unto the Father; having loved His own who were in the world He loved them unto the end"* (John xiii. 1). Thereupon, as the other evangelists tell us, Jesus instituted the Most Holy Sacrament of the Altar. This was therefore the token that Jesus loved His own unto the end. The Most Holy Eucharist is indeed the Sacrament of Love; it is in truth a miracle of love. Simply for love of us poor human beings is Jesus Christ really and truly present in the Most Holy Sacrament of the Altar. From the Tabernacle therefore does He unceasingly call to us: *"Come unto Me, all you that labor and are burdened, and I will refresh you!"*

It is especially necessary that you, my youthful reader, should keep your belief in the real presence of Jesus in the Most Holy Sacrament ever alive within your soul. For this reason call to mind the principal foundations of this belief.

The first foundation rests upon the promise of Him who is the Eternal Truth. When Jesus Christ, the God-Man, promises anything, He fails not to fulfil that promise. He solemnly promised to institute the Most Holy Sacrament. When upon one occasion, after the miraculous multiplication of the loaves, the people came to Him in the hope of obtaining a further supply of bread, He referred them to another kind of bread, which He would bestow upon them. And what kind of bread did He mean? He said: *"The bread that I will give is My flesh, for the life of the world,"* that is to say, the selfsame flesh which He offered up on the cross in order that the world—all mankind—should have eternal life. Thus plainly and definitely did Jesus promise that He would really and truly give His flesh to be our food.

But Holy Scripture proceeds to say: "*The Jews therefore strove among themselves.*" And why did they thus strive? Because they deemed it to be absolutely impossible that Jesus would really give them His flesh to eat.

Now consider for a moment: if Jesus had not intended to give His flesh—His real body, not merely bread as an emblem of His body—what would He undoubtedly have answered the Jews? He would certainly have given them the necessary explanation, and said something as follows: "You must not misunderstand Me, good people; I will only give you an emblem of My flesh, only bread to eat." But did Jesus speak in this manner? No! On the contrary, He repeated His former words, and confirmed them with a sort of oath: "*Amen, Amen, I say unto you! Except you eat the flesh of the Son of man and drink His blood, you shall not have life in you. For My flesh is meat indeed, and My blood is drink indeed.*"

And what Jesus promised in this definite and certain manner, He has not failed to perform. At the last supper He truly changed bread and wine into His most sacred body and blood. He expressly said in reference to the bread which He took into His hands, "*This is My body,*" and not, "This bread signifies My body," or, "It will become My body." And at the same time He commanded His apostles: "*Do this in commemoration of Me!*"

And remark yet a third proof: ever since the apostolic ages the Holy Catholic Church has understood the words of Jesus in the very same sense. For example, one of the earliest Fathers of the Church, St. Justinian, who died in the year 566, expressed in the clearest terms the belief of the Church, which had been handed down to him by the apostles. The following are his words: "*We have been taught that this sacred food is the flesh and blood of the Son of God become man.*"

Therefore, enter every church where a lamp glimmers before the tabernacle both by day and night, with ever-renewed and lively faith. There contemplate the love of Jesus, the pearl of our life here below. Be not cold and unmoved like the stone floor, but adore your God with fervor and pray with the deepest reverence. Pierce with the eye of faith the veils of the Blessed Sacrament, and pray with heart and lips:

> Jesus, dearest Lord, I love Thee,
> Because Thou first hast loved me;
> All other love I will resign,
> Conform me to Thy love divine.

PANGE LINGUA GLORIOSI

SING, my tongue, the Saviour's glory,
　　Of His flesh the mystery sing;
Of the blood, all price exceeding,
　　Shed by our immortal King,
Destined, for the world's redemption,
　　From a noble womb to spring.

Of a pure and spotless virgin
　　Born for us on earth below,
He, as man with man conversing,
　　Stay'd, the seeds of truth to sow;
Then He closed in solemn order
　　Wondrously His life of woe.

On the night of that last supper
　　Seated with His chosen band,
He the paschal victim eating,
　　First fulfils the Law's command;
Then, as food to His apostles
　　Gives Himself with His own hand.

Word made flesh, the bread of nature
　　By His word to flesh He turns;
Wine into His blood He changes—
　　What though sense no change discerns?
Only be the heart in earnest,
　　Faith her lesson quickly learns.

TANTUM ERGO SACRAMENTUM

DOWN in adoration falling,
    Lo! the sacred Host we hail;
Lo! o'er ancient forms departing,
    Newer rites of grace prevail;
Faith, for all defects supplying,
    Where the feeble senses fail.

To the Everlasting Father,
    And the Son who reigns on high,
With the Holy Ghost proceeding
    Forth from each eternally,
Be salvation, honor, blessing,
    Might, and endless majesty.

24. IN THE BRIGHT DAYS OF YOUTH

PERHAPS you know from your own experience what homesickness is, the indescribable longing for home, for your dear ones. The saints also knew what homesickness is, but their longing was not for creatures, for earthly goods and possessions. They longed for the heavenly country, the land of everlasting joy, of peace and blessedness, the home of the saints; they longed for that heavenly fatherland, concerning which the Apostle writes: "*Eye hath not seen nor ear heard, neither hath it entered into the heart of man, what things God hath prepared for them that love Him!*" Their longing for heaven was so ardent, that they awaited with holy impatience the hour of their death.

God does not require of us that we should feel homesickness of such a kind as this, but what He does require of all men, and especially of the young, therefore of you, my youthful reader, is that we should love Him and serve Him faithfully. I say that God expects this from young people more especially, since Holy Scripture thus exhorts them: "*Remember thy Creator in the days of thy youth.*" Wherefore love God and serve Him faithfully in the bright days of youth.

It was a blessed, a golden day when your pious sponsors, full of joyous hopes, brought you back from the baptismal font to your parents' house. From that hour, warmed by the sun of divine grace, you grew like a lily among thorns; indeed you knew nothing of the thorns of evil, in the blissful ignorance of your childish innocence. Your soul was like an untarnished mirror; your heart was the abode of celestial peace; your understanding a clear, bright flame. Your will was open to receive all that is good; the frank expression of your eyes reflected the purity of your soul. Your ear had not as yet been polluted by the voice of the tempter; your lips had not tasted the poisonous cup of sin. Your hands were pure and clean; your feet had not walked in the way of transgressors; innocence was depicted in your countenance.

Therefore it is not wonderful that you, endowed as you were with all the qualities of a good child, with obedience, innocence, love of learning, modesty, and with harmless merriment, should have been the joy and delight of your parents and teachers, a spectacle to God, to angels, and to men! Yes, fair and golden were the days of your first youth, which you spent under the parental roof, beneath an unclouded sky.

And how is it with you at present? I do not know, but I hope for the best, and therefore I entreat you to continue to serve God faithfully in the bright days of youth which yet remain to you!

You will understand some day, what you perhaps fail to perceive now, what an unspeakable advantage it is to consecrate the bright days of youth to God; strive to preserve your innocence unsullied to old age—aye, to the grave. What a happiness, what a joy, to be able to say to God, when this mortal life is ended, in the words of the young man in the Gospel: "*All these* [the commandments] *have I kept from my youth*" (Matt. xix. 20).

Wherefore never agree with the fools who say: "*The time of our life is short...Come, therefore, and let us enjoy the good things that are present, and let us speedily use the creatures as in youth...Let us crown ourselves with roses before they be withered.*" (Wisd. ii. 1, 6, 8)

No, never say: "When I am old I will think of God, work for Him, and serve Him. The time to do this has not yet come!" That would be a very presumptuous, foolhardy way of speaking, and one which might cause you bitter repentance at a later period.

Hear what St. John Chrysostom, an illustrious Doctor of the Church, said upon this subject to his audience in a sermon delivered with wonderful eloquence: "Since no one likes to have a decrepit old servant, how much more does God desire and look for the service of the young, in order that He may receive the first-fruits of life. Is it right that any one should spend his youth in the service of sin, and keep his feeble old age, and the dregs of his life for God? To act thus is to offer the pure gold to Satan, and the dross to God; to give the costly pearls to Satan, and to leave the empty shells for God; to bestow the pure wheaten flour upon Satan, and to give the chaff to God; to offer the earliest roses of spring to Satan, and to make a present of the withered leaves to God, to lay the first, best, and rarest fruits on the altar of Satan, and to offer to God those which have lain long under the tree, have been devoured by insects, and allowed to rot."

What an awful punishment is on this account to be dreaded for the dissolute young man! Do you, therefore, make better resolutions, and say to yourself: "I am still young, and I will adorn the bright days of youth with virtues. I will give my heart to Him, to whom alone it belongs, and who asks so earnestly for it in these words: '*My son, give Me thy heart.*' "

The heart of childhood is all mirth,
　　We frolic to and fro
As free and blithe, as if on earth
　　Were no such thing as woe.

But if too soon with reckless faith
　　We trust the flattering voice
Which whispers: "Take thy fill ere death;
　　Indulge thee and rejoice,"

Too surely each succeeding day
　　Some lost delight we mourn;
The flowers all fade along our way
　　Till we, too, die forlorn.

　　　　　　　　　　　　　—Keble.

ACT OF LOVE

O MY GOD! I love Thee above all things, with my whole heart and soul, because Thou art all-good and worthy of all love. I love my neighbor as myself for the love of Thee. I forgive all who have injured me, and ask pardon of all whom I have injured.

JESUS, MY LORD, MY GOD, MY ALL

JESUS, my Lord, my God, my all,
　How can I love Thee as I ought?
And how revere this wond'rous gift,
So far surpassing hope or thought.
Sweet Sacrament, we Thee adore.
O make us love Thee more and more!

O, see, within a creature's hand,
The vast Creator deigns to be,
Reposing infant-like, as though
On Joseph's arm, on Mary's knee.
Sweet Sacrament, we Thee adore.
O make us love Thee more and more!

Sound, sound His praises higher still,
And come ye Angels to our aid;
'Tis God, 'tis God, the very God,
Whose power both man and angels made.
Sweet Sacrament, we Thee adore.
O make us love Thee more and more!

　　　　　　　　　　—Father Frederick William Faber

The Lance of the Fear of God

25. Not Pleasant but Profitable
"Remember thy last end" (Ecclus. vii. 40)

You know how the pious Tobias strove to infuse the fear of the Lord into the heart of his beloved son while the latter was still very young. He was deeply convinced of the truth of the words of Holy Scripture: *"The fear of the Lord is the beginning of wisdom"* (Ps. cx. 10). Therefore it is unnecessary that I should say to you: "If you wish to save your soul, fear the Lord; if it is your heart's desire to dedicate your youth to God, fear the Lord."

But how will you be most surely confirmed in this holy fear of God? By thinking upon your last end, according to the exhortation of the Holy Spirit: *"In all thy works remember thy last end, and thou shalt never sin"* (Ecclus. vii. 40). Therefore comply with this exhortation, and lay to heart the first and most important of these things, namely, death.

You are absolutely convinced that death will not spare you, because it has never as yet spared any one; and you dread its coming because you know with equal certainty that everything does not end at death, but that after death an awful judgment awaits you, and that after the judgment there will follow an eternal life.

Now, what is so terrible about death is not its certainty, but that which is uncertain in connection with it. For as it is sure and certain that we must die, so it is doubtful and uncertain *when, where,* and *how* we shall die.

When shall you die? In regard to this you can never be secure, even for a single moment. Today you are alive, but it is absolutely uncertain whether you will be still alive tomorrow, the day after, in a week, a month, or a year. While you are reading this you are full of the joy and love of life, but who can give surety that this very evening, or tonight, or even the next minute, you may not drop down dead? I repeat my question: who can give surety that it will not so happen?

Some years ago, in a little village in Bavaria, a few peasants were sitting together in a tavern. Over a glass of beer they discussed one thing and another, until at length the conversation turned upon the uncertainty of the time of death. "Certainly," said a stalwart peasant in the prime of life, "certainly no one can know beforehand the precise moment, but of this I am assured: today, at least, I shall not die."

After a time he got up, and prepared to go home; he wished every one good night, and a pleasant meeting on the morrow. Then he left the room, and a few minutes later his companions lifted him up—a corpse! In the dark he had fallen down the steep steps before the door, and broken his neck.

Again, who deems himself more safe from death than a merry young person at a dance? Yet it has happened more than once, that such a one has suddenly expired, the excitement of dancing having brought on an apoplectic attack.

I remember reading some years ago of a young girl, eighteen years old, who returned home late at night from a dance, went to bed, and was found dead the next morning!

Uncertain as it is *when* we shall die, it is equally uncertain *where* we shall die. Shall you die in a sick-bed, fortified with all the last rites of Holy Church; or will death surprise you while you are asleep, or when you are walking out; in your own room, or in some strange place; while you are at work, or when you are engaged in animated conversation; in a saloon or dancing-hall; on the water or on land; when you are on foot, or in a railway coach, and so on? One might go on forever with a string of such questions as these; but what man or angel could answer them?

It may not be pleasant to consider all these uncertainties; but for this very reason reflect upon them, since it is profitable for salvation.

But the *when* and *where* of your death is comparatively of very slight importance. Your eternity depends solely and wholly upon the question of *how* you will die, whether in the grace of God, or in mortal sin.

Therefore *how* will you die? You do not know, I do not know; indeed there is not any one who knows. Only one thing is certain, that so long as a spark of life and consciousness is left to you, you can correspond to the grace of God, you have a chance to save your soul.

Now, my friend, in speaking so seriously about death, I do not wish to make you unhappy, but only to guide you to a good death, only to help you to meet the last enemy with calmness and even cheerfulness. Yes, with cheerfulness! Some years ago I witnessed a death like this in the case of one of my parishioners, a young woman twenty-one years of age. She had always been pious and good, and at the same time merry and cheerful. When death was approaching, she asked that the wreath which was so soon to be placed on her bier, might be shown to her, and as she lay upon her dying bed she seemed quite pleased to look at it. She was indeed a living proof of the truth of the lines:

> *The fear of God* is honor and renown;
> With it the Christian wins a conqueror's crown,
> His portion in this world is peace and joy.
> In heaven 'tis bliss without alloy.

Ever bear in mind the maxim that has caused the conversion of so many sinners, and made so many saints—the memorable maxim that was enunciated by Jesus Christ Himself: "*What shall it profit a man, if he gain the whole world, and suffer the loss of his soul?*" (Mark viii. 36.)

O my God, in the future I will follow more faithfully the example of the saints. I will take to heart the admonition of the Holy Spirit: "*In all thy works remember thy last end.*" I will often go in thought to my deathbed, to God's judgment-seat, to heaven, and to hell. I will endeavor most earnestly to lead such a life now as I would wish to have lived if I had reached the end of my earthly pilgrimage.

"*What does this count for eternity?*" or "*How does this look in the light of eternity?*" was the question proposed to himself by St. Aloysius at the beginning of any important work. Meditate often on the four last things.

> Leaves have their time to fall,
> And flowers to wither at the north wind's breath,
> And stars to set; but all—
> Thou hast all seasons for thine own, O Death!
> —Mrs. Hemans.

> But yesterday the word of Cæsar might
> Have stood against the world; now lies he there
> And none so poor to do him reverence.
> —Shakespeare.

"*Behold, short years pass away; and I am walking in a path by which I shall not return*" (Job xvi. 23).

26. Behind the Veil

A PRIEST, who was conducting the exercises of a retreat, related the following anecdote to his youthful hearers. "Some years ago," he said, "when I was prefect of studies in an ecclesiastical seminary, owing to press of work I sat up one evening until eleven o'clock. At this unusually late hour there came a knock at my door, and when I opened it there stood before me one of the older students, a good and clever young man. His eyes were full of tears. 'Alas! your Reverence,' he said, 'I can not go to sleep, I have committed a grievous sin, I must go to confession.' And when he had done this, he was greatly relieved; he fell asleep in the peace of God, and he told me afterward that he had never slept better in his life."

You will readily guess what gave this young man courage for this self-conquest. It was the thought of eternity, of what lies behind the veil—the thought of eternal damnation. Let us pause and reflect upon hell, upon that which lies behind the veil.

What is hell? Or perhaps I ought rather to ask another question, and say: is there any hell? Only the fool, the unbeliever, can say in his heart: "There is no hell, no eternity." Look at those who so impudently deny the existence of hell; what sort of persons are they? Godless persons, sunk in sin and vice—persons who have every reason to dread hell, and therefore call in question or boldly deny its existence. But, however impudently they may assert the non-existence of hell, in their secret heart they often think very differently. Ever and anon they hear a thunderous, terrifying voice which amid the tumult of passion and sinful pleasure utters these awful words: "You fool, you miserable wretch, if the lessons you were taught in the bright days of youth should be true, if there were in very deed a God, a hell, an eternity, what then—oh, what then!"

Voltaire, the notorious infidel, once received a letter from a friend, in which the latter asserted that he had succeeded in completely banishing from his mind all thought of hell, and all belief in the existence of such a place. Voltaire warmly congratulated him, but went on to say that he himself had not been equally fortunate. Nor did he ever succeed in banishing the fear of hell. When he lay upon his death-bed the thought of hell seized upon him with terrible force, and drove him to wild despair.

Verily there is a hell; but what is hell? Our poor human understanding can never grasp its full signification, much less can words describe it. The words of St. Paul: "*Eye hath not seen*," can be applied to hell in an inverted sense, and we can say: "Eye hath not seen, nor ear heard, neither hath it entered into the heart of man, what things God hath prepared for those who hate Him, and depart out of this life not in His love and grace, but in the state of mortal sin."

This only can we say, that hell is the place of the greatest and never-ending torture, of the *greatest* torture; all the expressions employed in Holy Scripture in reference to hell bear out this assertion, as for example: Hell is "*a land of misery and darkness, where the shadow of death and no order, but everlasting horror dwelleth*" (Job x. 22); or "*He hath reserved [them] under darkness in everlasting chains*" (Jude i. 6); or "*Which of you can dwell with devouring fire*"; or "*Which of you shall dwell with everlasting burnings*" (Is. xxxiii. 14); or "*The unprofitable servant cast ye out into the exterior darkness: there shall be weeping and gnashing of teeth*" (Matt. xxv. 30).

But the greatest torments of hell affect not so much the bodies as the souls of the damned. Think for a moment what pain homesickness inflicts upon the soul of him who endures it, and then consider the lot of him who is condemned to hell. The reprobate will know and *feel* what he has lost by his sins. The pain of loss is immeasurably great. Never shall he enjoy the beatific vision of God; never shall he enter heaven, the home of the saints, the place of everlasting happiness and joy. What horror, what torment, what despair, will seize upon the souls of the damned!

But what more especially makes hell to be hell is its everlasting duration, the utter despair of the damned, since they know that their torments can have no end. That the punishment of hell does indeed last forever is clearly and irrefragably proved by the words of Holy Writ, particularly by the plain and definite pronouncement of the Saviour Himself: "*The wicked shall go into everlasting punishment.*"

Do Thou, O God, grant us living faith, heartfelt love, courage, and strength, a true penitential spirit, and grace of perseverance, that so the horrors which dwell "behind the veil," may not be our portion!

> As thou livest, thou must die;
> As thou fallest, thou must lie;
> As thou liest, so thou must remain,
> For everlasting loss or everlasting gain.

27. CHRISTIAN COURAGE

THE more deeply your heart, dear reader, is imbued with a true fear of God, so much the more will this fear rule and guide you in every circumstance of life, and so much the less will you know any other fear, and so much the more courageously will you at all times and in all places range yourself on the side of God before the eyes of the world. And in our own day it is more than ever necessary to stand up courageously for the cause of Christ. All Christians, but in the first place all men, both old and young, must show themselves to be the courageous apostles of Christ, must fearlessly espouse His cause before all the world, and in every position of life. That is a high, a glorious vocation calculated to fire every youthful heart with enthusiasm.

Christ has said: "*Every one that shall confess me before men, I will also confess him before My Father who is in heaven*" (Matt. x. 32). This open confession of faith in Jesus Christ and the truths He has revealed, this fearless espousal of His cause, is demanded especially in our times. Modern society is to a great extent anti-Christian or inimical to Christ, pervaded by hatred to Christianity in general, and to the Catholic Church in particular.

This was very plainly shown some years ago, when the question of Christian education was debated in the German parliament. On that occasion Count Caprivi, the imperial chancellor, publicly asserted that the whole question centered on this: *Christ or Anti-Christ*. After this courageous declaration, a tremendous hubbub arose, in which all present joined, with the exception of the Center and some members of other parties. The whole of the press, which is hostile to the Church, took up the question later on, and did its best to fan the flame of irritation.

The anti-Christian spirit is still more rampant and obnoxious at the present time in France. There a godless government is making every effort to destroy the Church—to subvert the Kingdom of Christ. Faith in the divinity of Christ is also assailed in the United States and other countries by tongue and pen, and from many a pulpit and platform.

The contemptuous cry of the Jews on Good Friday: "*We will not have this man to reign over us!*" is today the battle-cry of His enemies. Therefore is Christianity to be expelled from the school; from the family, from the legislature. And for the selfsame reason the daily press becomes ever more and more unchristian; ever more shamelessly and impudently are immoral novels disseminated, a truly scandalous kind of literature.

Therefore it is of the utmost importance that the generation of Catholics who are now growing up—I mean Catholic young men—should fearlessly and courageously come forward and espouse the cause of Christ. Even the dread of death ought to induce no one to hold back, much less the dread of temporal loss. God will know how to protect His own in case of need. Think of what the faithful adherents of our holy religion have endured since the so-called Reformation in England and Ireland. Remember that millions of the early Christians shed their blood for Christ, amid the most cruel tortures. Those who confessed themselves to be adherents of the Christian religion were robbed and deprived by the state of their private property; yet the Christians bore all this for quite three centuries.

Sacrifices like these are not required of us: we are not threatened with similar penalties. We ought, therefore, to find it easier to take the side of Christ, and to fight for His cause more cheerfully. Moreover, when you are of an age to take part in elections and voting, you ought not to be false to your character as a Christian; you ought to have the courage of your convictions and act in accordance with your religious principles even if you thereby antagonize or displease the one who gives you employment.

It becomes ever more important also to support with might and main the Catholic press in the fight for Christ. Young men can do much in this respect. They can unite their efforts in this cause, in behalf of which they ought to consider no expenditure of time or money too great. We must give ourselves no rest until there is in every Catholic household at least one newspaper or periodical which, if need be, will courageously fight for the sake of Christ, and fearlessly defend the interests of the Church.

In this manner must we all, and young men more especially, use every possible exertion in order that, in the days in which we live, Christ may once more reign in the whole of our public life. Let us labor and struggle courageously for the spread of Christ's kingdom on earth. You will hear the enemies of Christ and of the Church assert that this is priestcraft! Bear in mind, however, that the Church only commands in the name of Christ. The commands of the Church simply express the will of God. What the sun, shining in the vault of heaven, is for the life of the body, Christianity is for the life of the soul. Christ is the sun of truth and justice for the whole human race. This sun must influence the whole life of man. Therefore, Christians, to the war! Fight for God and the right! Fight for the interests of Christ and his Church! It is a question of the weal or woe of mankind. Vow fidelity to Christ in the following words:

> My God, though all unfaithful be,
> I never will depart from Thee.
> All, all for Christ shall be my cry
> While life on earth goes swiftly by.

28. HUMAN RESPECT

HUMAN respect is a cancer which eats into modern society and does incalculable harm, especially to young men. Take, for instance, a young man, who at his nightly carousals fears to offend or to make himself disliked by his companions, and who therefore goes on drinking until the small hours of the morning. He does not reflect whether he is ruining his health and wasting his money, whether he is bringing vexation and disgrace upon those who belong to him; to all this he pays no heed; he merely says to himself: "What would the others say, if I were not to do as they do?" Oh, this foolish bugbear of human respect! Such a young man we may behold going forth into a hostile world carrying his head very high, and full of self-reliance, but when he comes into the society of those whose beliefs differ from those which he professes, or who mock at religion, what then becomes of his courage? His heart at once sinks into his boots, so that, out of a wretched feeling of human respect, he eats meat on fast days, in order that he may not be jeered and laughed at. He never dares to make the sign of the cross or say grace before meals in the presence of those whose opinions differ from his own. "One must have respect," he says, "for the opinions of others and cultivate their good-will."

It is human respect which keeps so many young men back from a frequent reception of the sacraments, from a regular attendance at divine service both in the morning and afternoon, on Sundays and holydays. "What will people think of me? I shall be considered quite fanatical if I go so often to church." But tell me: what harm is it if you are thought to be pious? Is it not far better that you should be thought to be pious and well-conducted, than that you should be regarded as a toper and brawler?

Let people think whatever they like. Every one is of just as much value as he is in the sight of God, neither more nor less. Therefore we must fear God, as Our Lord says: *"Fear ye not them that kill the body and are not able to kill the soul; but rather fear Him that can destroy both soul and body in hell"* (Matt. x. 28).

Thus many a young man desires to be a good Catholic, but he has not the courage of his convictions; he possesses faith, and his life is blameless as far as he goes; but if he finds himself in society where his religion and religious observances are derided, his faith and his Catholicism are not manifest. He is silent, or perhaps even joins in the mockery and ridicule out of regard for others; that is, in consequence of miserable human respect.

He allows the priests of his Church and her chief pastors to be mocked at and made the object of foolish witticisms. God Himself and His saints are not spared, yet he meanwhile does not consider it to be incumbent on him to stand up and defend the honor of God. Believe me, the hour will come when such a coward will hear these words: *"I know you not! Depart from Me!"* What will it then avail him to have been silent from fear of offending ungodly and unbelieving men?

A young French soldier who fought in the war with China was cast in a widely different mold. One day he heard an extraordinary uproar in that part of the barracks which was in his immediate vicinity, and he went to find out what was the matter. One of his comrades had discovered a rosary in the pocket of a volunteer, and a perfect tempest of contempt, blasphemy, and vulgar abuse had broken forth over its possessor.

Then the young Frenchman showed himself to be a soldier in the true sense of the word, a man of courage, fearless and undaunted, the defender of his religion. "Give me the rosary," he exclaimed amid the tumult; "how can you have the insolence to treat with irreverence and to speak blasphemously about an object of devotion which is so frequently bedewed with many a mother's tears!"

These words were received with a fresh outburst of mockery and curses; but he remained quite unmoved, and never rested until he had gained possession of the rosary. Then with manly decision he said to the mocking crowd: "Believe me, he is a better soldier who has a rosary in his pocket, than one whose mouth is full of blasphemy!"

Can you, my dear young friend, do otherwise than admire such courage and strength of character? Does it not give you pleasure to hear of the conduct of this young soldier, whose name is unknown to fame? It also rejoiced the heart of God, and He will likewise take delight in you, as often as you show yourself to be possessed of a like courage and decision, of true respect, of a proper regard for God and His honor. Truly the present day, in which the world is so far from God, affords ample opportunities for thus acting; wherefore go forth into life with a courageous heart and act like a man: *"Behold, I command thee, take courage and be strong. Fear not, and be not dismayed, because the Lord thy God is with Thee in all things"* (Jos. i. 9). *"If God be for us, who is against us?"* (Rom. viii. 31).

How beauteous is the courage which we find
With childlike confidence in God combined!
Who fears his God shall know no other fear--
He heeds not pitying smile, nor unkind sneer.

VENI CREATOR SPIRITUS

Come, Holy Spirit, Creator blest,
And in our souls take up Thy rest;
Come with Thy grace and heavenly aid
To fill the hearts which Thou hast made.

O comforter, to Thee we cry,
O heavenly gift of God Most High,
O fount of life and fire of love,
And sweet anointing from above.

Thou in Thy sevenfold gifts are known;
Thou, finger of God's hand we own;
Thou, promise of the Father,
Thou Who dost the tongue
    with pow'r imbue.

Kindle our sense from above,
And make our hearts o'erflow with love;
With patience firm and virtue high
The weakness of our flesh supply.

Far from us drive the foe we dread,
And grant us Thy peace instead;
So shall we not, with Thee for guide,
Turn from the path of life aside.

Oh, may Thy grace on us bestow
The Father and the Son to know;
And Thee, through endless times confessed,
Of both the eternal Spirit blest.

Now to the Father and the Son,
Who rose from death, be glory given,
With Thou, O Holy Comforter,
Henceforth by all in earth and heaven.
Amen.

Prayer Before A Crucifix

BEHOLD, O good and most sweet Jesus, I fall upon my knees before Thee, and with most fervent desire of my soul, beg and beseech Thee that Thou wouldst impress upon my heart lively sentiments of faith, hope and charity, true repentance for my sins, and a firm resolve to make amends, as with deep affection and grief, I reflect upon Thy five wounds, having before my eyes that which Thy prophet David spoke about Thee, O good Jesus: *"They have pierced my hands and feet, they have counted all my bones."* Amen.

Prayer to St. Michael

ST. MICHAEL the Archangel, defend us in battle; be our safeguard against the wickedness and snares of the Devil. May God rebuke him, we humbly pray, and do Thou, O Prince of the Heavenly Host, by the power of God, cast into Hell Satan and all the other evil spirits, who wander throughout the world, seeking the ruin of souls. Amen.

Salve Regina

HAIL holy Queen, mother of mercy, our life, our sweetness, and our hope. To thee do we cry, poor banished children of Eve. To thee do we send up our sighs, mourning and weeping in this valley of tears. Turn then, most gracious Advocate, thine eyes of mercy toward us, and after this our exile show unto us the blessed Fruit of thy womb, Jesus. O clement, O loving, O sweet Virgin Mary.

V. Pray for us, O holy mother of God.

R. That we may be made worthy of the promises of Christ. Amen.

De Profundis (Psalm 129)

OUT of the depths have I cried unto Thee, O Lord: Lord hear my voice.

Let Thine ears be attentive to the voice of my supplication.

If Thou, Lord, shouldst mark iniquities, O Lord, who shall stand?

But there is forgiveness with Thee: because of Thy law I wait for Thee, O Lord.

My soul waiteth on His word: my soul hopeth in the Lord.

From the morning watch even until night let Israel hope in the Lord:

For with the Lord there is mercy, and with Him is plentiful redemption.

And He shall redeem Israel, from all their iniquities.

The Sword of Respect for Authority

The Sword of
Respect for Authority

29. A Glance at Nazareth

DIRECT your glance to Nazareth, my youthful reader, and there contemplate the holy family. See what a splendid example of obedience the divine Redeemer gives to all and to young people more especially. Of Him, the incarnate Son of God, it is said in Holy Scripture: *"Jesus was subject to them."* *"He advanced in wisdom and age and grace, with God and men."* *"He advanced in age,"* in this respect it was with the God-Man the same as it is with us ordinary mortals: He continually grew older.

On the contrary, the expression, *"He advanced in wisdom and grace,"* is not to be understood in a purely human sense. Jesus Christ was, as the God-Man, ever full of wisdom and grace. He could not advance in them; but He showed it more and more plainly; He allowed it to appear more and more openly that He was full of wisdom and grace. At present, however, I desire to impress upon your memory these words: *"He was subject to them."* Thereby Jesus became the model of respect for authority, or of the virtue of obedience.

Jesus Christ, as the eternal Son of God, was Himself authority personified, yet *"He was subject."* And to whom was He subject? To a human authority—to creatures. And ought man, a poor, miserable creature, instigated by pride and a false notion of liberty, refuse to acknowledge the authority set over him by his Creator!

Respect and obey authority as God wills that you should do. Obedience is a virtue, an exceedingly precious virtue, and St. Augustine terms it "The mother and root of all virtues"; or, as St. Bonaventure terms it, "A ship which carries one safe to heaven." Obedience, respect for authority, is for all men a most necessary virtue, and for the very young man more especially; for obedience is order, and order must exist wherever God rules and reigns. Disobedience, the offspring of pride, kindled the flames of hell, and peoples its awful realms. Hence St. Bernard says: "Take away self-will, and hell would cease to exist."

Therefore, continue constantly to practise obedience, in imitation of the glorious example set you by the incarnate Son of God during His sojourn in the holy house of Nazareth. It may sometimes be difficult, when pride, obstinacy, or self-will strives to gain the upper hand. But it is all the more necessary that you should now learn to bow your head, and accustom yourself to obey; for at a later period you will find it still more difficult, perhaps even impossible.

But mark this well: your subjection to authority ought not to be the result of stern compulsion, but a Christian virtue. This obedience springs from humility; faith sanctifies it and love lightens its yoke. Only this Christian obedience, obedience for the love of God, can keep its ground under all circumstances, and throughout your whole life.

In an age when respect for both divine and human authority appears to be fast vanishing from the face of the earth, the example of childlike veneration for parents, which was set by a man at the time when he was in high authority, when he was the President of the French Republic, deserves to be mentioned here. I refer to M. Loubet.[1] It is touching to read of the respect and affection with which he clung to his good, simple, old mother.

It was everywhere noticed with approbation that, on the occasion of a visit to Montélimar, he could not be induced to be present at an official reception, to be succeeded by a grand banquet. He preferred to remain at the home of his mother, surrounded by a few relatives and intimate friends. He loved his good old mother with a most tender devotion, and publicly as well as privately showed her every mark of filial love and reverence. This conduct gained him honor in the eyes of all, and the newspapers spoke of it in terms of the highest praise.

Yet why should we look to men for an example of the manner in which the fourth commandment ought to be kept, when the Son of God Himself, in the holy house at Nazareth, furnished the most splendid example of this to young people in all ages. Look at this example, strive to copy it, when you find it difficult to obey.

By the recognition of authority, and by submission to it, the world would become a paradise. Do all that lies in your power, and remember the great reward which is promised to him who obeys: "*An obedient man shall speak of victory*" (Prov. xxi. 28).

> To Nazareth go, and thou wilt mirrored see
> What thy obedience ought, my son, to be.

30. HONOR THY FATHER AND THY MOTHER

O F WHAT continual sacrifices is parental love capable! What is it which turns the hair of the father of a family prematurely gray, what imprints wrinkles on his brow, what causes the once vigorous and stalwart frame to be bent and broken before its time? It is the wearing care and anxiety for the temporal happiness and well-being of his beloved children.

---

1   Émile François Loubet was the 8th President of France.

Then ask your mother what cruel anguish she endured for your sake, how many hours she watched beside your cradle, how much anxiety she has felt on your account? Truly: "New every morning is the love, a tender mother's heart can prove!"

Maternal love! Eight years ago a cadet, seventeen years of age, from the military school at Vienna, slipped from the Traunstein in so unfortunate a manner that he fell into the lake of Gemunden, which lies directly beneath, and there found a watery grave. Every effort to recover the body proved to be without result. Year by year, on All Souls' Day, a lady bowed down with grief, arrives at Gemunden. She is the mother of the poor drowned lad, and she causes herself to be rowed out into the middle of the lake, to the spot where the waters swallowed up her darling son. There, as a token of her unchanging affection, she drops into the lake a wreath composed of the choicest flowers.

Honor your father and mother; honor them by invariably speaking in a respectful manner to them and of them; by never allowing an insolent or unbecoming expression to pass your lips in regard to them, and by never permitting yourself to make any natural or moral imperfections they may chance to possess, the subject of a jest.

Let your whole external demeanor give evidence of your respect for your father and mother. Even if clouds obscure the sun—I mean if real and manifest faults on the part of your parents lessen the brightness of their dignity—search for, and behold the sun through the clouds; namely, in spite of your parents' failings, remember their position of authority. God did not say in the fourth commandment: "Honor a good father, a good mother," but simply: "*Honor thy father and thy mother.*"

In the preceding chapter I quoted an example of childlike respect for parents which was afforded by an official in a very high position. I will now give you another example.

The Blessed Thomas More, the chancellor of England, and consequently the highest personage in the realm after the king, kept his aged father always with him in his own house, and invariably gave him the place of honor. Nor did he ever go from home in order to attend to the business of the State without first asking on his knees for his father's blessing, and kissing the old man's hand.

Again I say, love your father and mother, honor them both in heart and deed. Prove your dutiful affection by never causing grief to your parents, but by being always to them a source of satisfaction. Imitate in this way the youthful Tobias, who was called by his aged parents, *"The light of our eyes, the staff of our old age, the comfort of our life, the hope of our posterity."*

Show your filial love, especially by supporting your parents with the most tender devotedness and the utmost generosity in sickness and old age.

Give proof of your filial affection also by praying daily and fervently for your parents.

Truly the prayer of a good son for his father and mother is certain to pierce the clouds and gain a hearing, exercising, as it does, a holy compulsion in regard to God.

Once more I admonish you, obey your parents; remember how Jesus Himself was subject to Mary and Joseph until He was thirty years of age. He obeyed them! How shameful it is to hear lads who are fifteen, seventeen, or twenty years of age say: "I am no longer a child, it is time to cast off leading strings!" Alas! alas! "I am no longer a child"—such a one is too entirely right! He is no longer a child of God, a child according to the sacred Heart of Jesus, but a child of pride. My dear young man, even should you have attained the age of twenty or thirty years, preserve and give proof of a real childlike affection for your father and mother.

And if perchance your parents sleep in *"God's Acre,"* the best way to remember and to honor them will be to lead an upright and honorable life. If ever in a distant land, amid suffering and affliction and a hard struggle for existence, you miss the kind parents who have been long sleeping in the grave, remember that even then you are not an orphan. Has not Christ Himself taught us to pray: *Our Father, Who art in heaven?*

> In this world the sons of men
> Are beloved by parents twain;
> God is one alone, yet when
> Parents forsake, He will remain.

31. THE PLEDGE OF BLESSING

As a young man, enjoying life, you behold the future spread out before you clad in roseate hues. What you ardently desire for yourself and what your parents and spiritual directors desire for you from the bottom of their hearts, is that good fortune, happiness, and well-being may perpetually encompass your path. But will these wishes be accomplished, will the sun of prosperity perpetually shine upon you, will the blessing of God accompany you in all your ways? What a joy it would be for you, could all these questions be answered in the affirmative, and a pledge, a surety be given you for all this!

Well, it is possible for you to enjoy this satisfaction! God Himself has given you, in the fourth commandment, a certain pledge of happiness and blessing. *"Honor thy father and mother as the Lord thy God hath commanded thee, that thou mayest live a long time, and it may be well with thee in the land, which the Lord thy God will give thee"* (Deut. v. 16).

God has pledged His word clearly and decidedly that He would bless and prosper those who honor their parents.

And numerous examples from history confirm that God has faithfully kept the promise He so solemnly gave. Think of Sem and Japheth, the dutiful sons of Noe, who received the blessing of God through the mouth of their father. Think of young Tobias, who was a model son, the solace and the joy of his aged parents. How abundantly was he blessed! He attained the age of ninety-nine years, living in the fear of the Lord, and he was privileged to see the descendants of his sons to the fifth generation.

And think of Joseph, who was his father's favorite because he was a model son—good and kind, respectful and obedient.

In how striking and remarkable a manner did the providence of God pour richest blessings upon his head! He had great delight in his children and grandchildren, he lived to the age of one hundred and ten years, and died at length a quiet and peaceful death. It went well with him, and he lived long upon the earth. His trials and troubles, too, were the gift of God: they were blessings in disguise.

And if God grants His protection and blessing to good sons here upon earth, how rich is the reward which awaits them in eternity! When, after a long and peaceful life, these good sons, these dutiful children who have so faithfully kept the fourth commandment lie upon their death-bed, they may, as they pass in review the whole of their long sojourn upon earth, discover many faults and failings or even grievous sins, but amid the darkness one bright star shines forth to cheer and comfort them. It is the thought that they always honored their parents, and were ever to them a cause of joy, and never of sorrow.

Now they are standing before the Eternal Judge. He looks graciously upon them, for His all-seeing eye discerns in them a resemblance to Himself, since they were obedient to their parents as He was during His time upon earth. He needs no further testimony, but He calls their parents as if to receive a triumphal reception, and invites them to witness the reward bestowed upon their good children in the sight of the whole world.

Then He says to these dutiful children: "What you did to your parents, you did to Me. Come, ye blessed of My Father, possess ye the kingdom prepared for you from the foundation of the world." But who can depict the indescribable glory and blessedness of that kingdom! Therefore honor your father and mother, in order that you may be a partaker of the eternal joys of heaven.

Remember the warning words of the Holy Spirit: "*Son, support the old age of thy father, and grieve him not in his life. Forget not the groanings of thy mother*" (Ecclus. iii. 14; vii. 29).

> Honor and love your father and mother,
> Cherish them as you cherish no other,
> So shall God's blessing surely attend
> Your path of life to its very end.

32. THE AMBASSADORS OF CHRIST

EVEN under the old covenant, namely in the Book of Ecclesiasticus, the Holy Ghost thus exhorts us: "*With all thy soul fear the Lord, and reverence His priests*" (Ecclus. vii. 31). It is said expressly: His priests; and if this was said in regard to the priests of the old covenant, how much more does it apply to the priests of the new covenant, to the priests of the Catholic Church!

For indeed, these are the ambassadors of Christ to men, the instruments which He employs, in order to bestow the greatest benefits upon us. On the threshold of our life, at its earliest commencement, He sends the priest, in order that, by means of holy Baptism, heaven may be opened to us, and we may be made sons of God, and fellow-heirs of Jesus Christ. He sends the priest, in order that he may instruct us in the truths of the faith, and in the way of salvation, may guide us in the paths of virtue and piety, and prepare us for the worthy reception of the holy sacraments of Penance and of the Altar. Again, He sends the priest, in order that he may be our faithful counselor and sincere friend. He sends the priest when our hearts are bowed with sorrow and when despair threatens to overwhelm us, in order that he may be to us a loving father, and may pour into our wounds the oil and wine of salutary exhortations and divine consolations, and heal us by means of the sacrament of Penance.

Furthermore, God will send the priest when we are overtaken by sickness, even if our relatives desert us. He will send him, in order to help us to save our souls, even if by so doing he were to risk his own life. He will send the priest in order that he may assist us in our last conflict, and bring us pardon in the sacrament of Penance, and give us the food of our souls in the Holy Viaticum, courage and strength in Extreme Unction.

Even after we have breathed our last, God will send the priest, in order that he may pray for us and offer the Holy Sacrifice in our behalf, and thus cause our soul to be delivered all the sooner from the fire of purgatory.

Wherefore thank God, dear reader, for all these great benefits, and reverence His priests—His ambassadors, by whom He sends His gifts.

But non-Catholics and even unreasonable and evil-minded Catholics are often heard to say: "It would be quite right to reverence priests if all priests were worthy ambassadors and instruments of God." Some malicious persons are guilty of a most abominable injustice, in that they lay the open sins and failings of individual priests as a burden upon the shoulders of the whole class and dare to make the infamous remark: "They are all alike!" "They are all of the same cloth!" It is true that God permits unworthy members to be found in every class, members who disgrace the body to which they belong; and in this respect He makes the priesthood no exception. On this account our most holy Redeemer, the Son of God

Himself, tolerated a Judas among His apostles, although they were but twelve in number. Thus there were at a subsequent period, and there will ever continue to be, traitors among priests. This must be admitted, however, that, despite the many temptations and dangers to which priests are exposed in the world, there are but few—very few—who are not true to their high calling.

"They are all alike!" What a shameful slander! When in a community one or another exceptionally vicious individual is found who makes acquaintance with the house of correction, do we on that account condemn the rest and exclaim: "They are all alike!" Would not this be a gross and cruel piece of injustice?

And tell me, if a rich man were to make you a present of a thousand gold coins, all perfectly genuine, with the exception of a few counterfeit and useless pieces, should you on this account despise, abuse, and reject the whole amount? You are doubtless saying to yourself: "No, I should certainly not be such a fool."

Or suppose you have one autumn an apple tree in your orchard loaded with splendid fruit. Because you espy here and there a few rotten, worm-eaten apples, should you, on this account, consider the tree to be worthless, useless, and only fit to be cut down?

The priesthood is a gift which God Himself has bestowed upon mankind; a gift, the value of which can be compared to nothing upon earth, the usefulness of which is illimitable. Can we—ought we—to lightly esteem, or ever despise the priesthood, because here and there it may be found to contain an unworthy member?

The priesthood is indeed for us a magnificent fruit tree, the blessings of which are simply immeasurable. Can we—ought we—calmly to listen and look on, when this tree is reviled, because here and there a rotten fruit is found upon it? Is it on this account to be regarded as worthless or even injurious?

When, some years ago, cholera broke out in Catania, a beautiful town of Sicily, and every one who could possibly do so fled from the plague-stricken place, the priests, with heroic courage, remained at their post in order to bring aid and consolation to the sick and dying. And as they acted, so have all good and worthy priests of the Catholic Church ever acted, from time immemorial, in similar seasons of suffering, sorrow, and want; thus they proved themselves to be, in very deed, worthy ambassadors of Christ to suffering in humanity.

> Revere the priest whom God doth send
> To be thy wise, thy faithful friend;
> To guide thy footsteps on the way
> Which leads to realms of endless day.

33. The Dutiful Child of the Church

A DISTINGUISHING characteristic of a virtuous young man, and one which makes him universally respected, is the honor, love, and obedience he shows his mother. You, however, have three mothers: your earthly mother; your heavenly mother, the Blessed Virgin Mary; and your spiritual mother, the Holy Catholic Church. And how good, how careful a mother is this last! Reflect upon this thought for a few moments, and lay it well to heart. Thus will you love and honor this mother in an ever-increasing degree, and render her a more exact and willing obedience.

If you owe honor, love, and obedience to your earthly mother, how much more to your spiritual mother, the Holy Catholic Church! Bear constantly in mind the words of Jesus: *"He that heareth you, heareth me."* As a good Catholic, true to your convictions, you will never speak in a disrespectful manner of the Church, her doctrines, her services, her ceremonies, or her priests. You will never listen complacently when such conversation is carried on, but, on the contrary, strive to prevent conversation of this nature as far as you are able. Also you will not take in or read books and newspapers which show themselves to be either unsympathetic toward your mother, or openly hostile in regard to her.

You must also love the Church, and rejoice in her prosperity and promote her interests as far as it lies in your power to do so. You must understand that any one who looks on with toleration or indifference when his mother the Church, the Pope, bishops, and priests are persecuted can have in his heart no childlike love for his mother, and can not possibly be a good Catholic.

As a good Catholic you must, before all things, give proof of the respect and love you feel for the Church by carefully obeying her commands and conforming to her decrees. For how could a son be said to love and honor his mother, were he to show himself indocile in regard to her, and heedless of her commands?

In the same way, judge for yourself whether he can really be a good Catholic who says: "I am a Catholic and will remain one; but it is not necessary to bother about Pope, bishops, or priests." Or is he a good Catholic who, on the slightest pretext, neglects to hear Mass on Sundays and holydays, who scarcely ever goes to hear a sermon, and who, when Easter approaches, has to be driven to the confessional? Do you imagine that such people as these in the depth of their heart regard themselves as good Catholics?

There is another highly important thing which you must and will do, if you are a truly good Catholic: you will and must give honor and pleasure to your mother the Church by your good conduct—by an upright life. On this point the words of Jesus are eminently applicable; "*Not every one that saith to Me, Lord, Lord, shall enter into the kingdom of heaven; but he that doth the will of My Father who is in heaven, he shall enter into the kingdom of heaven"* (Matt. vii. 21). Not every one who speaks eloquently for the Catholic cause and appears zealous on its behalf is on this account a good Catholic; but he only who unites to this zeal a good life, a thoroughly upright life. Mark this well!

Those members of the Catholic Church who live in mortal sin—for instance—in sins of intemperance, enmity, or impurity; Catholics who do not give up improper connections, and do not seek to avoid occasions of sin; who steal and cheat, are dead members of the mystical body of Christ, and do but dishonor Him, and put Him to shame.

If, however, such persons show at least a certain regard for the Church and speak well of her ministers, and never assume a hostile position in regard to her, but on the contrary defend her—in short, although they are grievous sinners, but not as much from malice as from human weakness, they are yet better than those merely nominal Catholics, who unite to a sinful life contempt for the commands of the Church and hatred for her priests. For the former sin grievously in one respect, the latter in a double sense, according to the words of Our Lord Himself: *"If he will not hear the Church, let him be as the heathen and publican"* (Matt. xviii. 17).

Wherefore be and remain a good, pious Catholic, true to your convictions, a Catholic who honors and loves his Church, obeys her, and rejoices her by leading a truly Christian life. For it is, and must remain true, that a Catholic who does not honor and love his Church, but refuses to obey her, is not acknowledged by God to be His child. This opinion was expressed 1600 years ago by the Bishop, Doctor of the Church, and martyr St. Cyprian in the beautiful words:

"He who will not have the Church for his mother, can not have God for his father." Therefore see that you are a faithful, dutiful son of this good, solicitous mother.

> Hail, Church of our God, most holy and pure,
> On the rock of St. Peter thou standest secure;
> Sweet Mother of Saints, soon may it be told
> All nations are gathered into thy fold.

34. DILUTED CATHOLICISM

EVEN in everyday life there is nothing so distasteful to sensible and upright people as the duplicity of a man who says one thing, while he means and does another. Here he speaks in one way, there in exactly the opposite; he desires to offend no party, but holds with both sides, his chief object being to gain money and favor. These are mean fellows without any force of character, who, when no more use can be made of them, are universally despised and cast aside. Therefore, even by the sages of old this saying held good: Be true to yourself in thought, deed, and word! Whatever you claim to be, that you ought to be in all fearlessness! Drop all pretense! Dare to be true to your convictions. What does Polonius say, in "Hamlet":

> "To thine own self be true,
> And it must follow, as the night the day.
> Thou canst not then be false to any man."

This axiom should be laid to heart by many a Christian man, be he young or old, who was baptized a Catholic and holds Catholic opinions, but in his words and actions—in what he does and leaves undone—gives evidence that his is a diluted Catholicism; especially by fawning upon such enemies of the Church who can promote his temporal interest, and by ranging himself on their side where important ecclesiastical questions are concerned.

Certainly in this case the admonition holds good: Be true to yourself in thought, word, and deed. You desire to be a

Catholic Christian; very well, but do not be half a one; do not think in one way, and act in another; do not conduct yourself here after one fashion, and there after another; in church like a good Catholic, and in daily life like an apostate; turning about like a weathercock, speaking and behaving in a manner which will please certain persons. Away with this diluted Catholicism, this half-heartedness and miserable sycophancy! Christ has said: *"No man can serve two masters . . . He that is not with Me is against Me"* (Matt. vi. 24; xii. 30). There is no alternative, no neutrality is possible!

It always seems to me that a Catholic Christian who really knows his holy Church, and is aware what a treasure he possesses in her, ought to find it difficult, nay impossible, to kick against the goad of his own convictions, and to speak and act contrary to his belief: and yet the number of staunch, loyal outspoken Catholics, true to their convictions, is constantly diminishing, and that of effeminate, sycophantic waverers is ever on the increase!

These waverers—these men who lack force of character, whose hearts are charged with diluted Catholicism—know and believe, and by listening to sermons and religious instructions can completely convince themselves that the Catholic Church is divine in her origin, holy in her founder, infallible in her doctrines, apostolic in her organization, glorious and wonderful in her saints. Yes, it is true that they know and believe all this. But at the first opportunity, whatever society they may be in, when enemies of the Church mock it and blaspheme this very same Church, her ministers, her precepts, her ceremonies, and her organization, these half-hearted Catholics are silent, and utter no word of defense for their mother; but on the contrary, they perhaps applaud the billingsgate of her adversaries, and even let their own tongues loose against her in vituperation.

Moreover, there are Catholics who believe and know full well that our Holy Catholic Church is the only true Church of Jesus Christ upon earth; and yet they concern themselves very little or not at all as to whether this Church possesses freedom of action and can spread herself everywhere in order to effect the salvation of mankind, or whether she is persecuted and regarded with hostility, and impeded in her sacred vocation, in consequence of which infidelity creeps in everywhere, gradually gains a firm footing, and carries on its seductive, destructive work.

Truly these oscillatory, these unprincipled and cowardly individuals possess only a diluted Catholicism; they are called Catholics, but the name of Catholic sounds in their case only like a nickname.

To all these undecided, half-hearted Catholics may be fitly applied the words of the prophet Elias: *"How long do you halt between two sides? If the Lord be God, follow Him, but if Baal, then follow him."* O ye Christians, how long do you halt between two sides, between the side of your Church and the side of her enemies? If in your heart; you are really Catholic Christians, speak and act as such on every occasion, and in every society.

We live in an age when decision is necessary, when half-heartedness can no more be tolerated in any struggle, whether in matters of religion, or in any other domain. A very momentous time is before us, a period where the civilized world will divide itself more and more into two opposite camps.

*"**Either for Christ or against Christ!**"* such is the watchword, the rallying cry! It behooves us to take a firm stand under the banner of Christ. The future belongs only to resolute, whole-hearted men! Be a man: a dauntless, whole-hearted Catholic.

O sailor, tempest-tossed on life's rough tide,
Seek Peter's bark and gladly there abide;
Fear not though waves run high and wild wind, rage:
She who has storms outlived from age to age
Will bear thee to the shore
Where tempests are no more.

35. A Few Objections

FALLEN man is ever reluctant to submit to the will of another, to obey authority; to do this is irksome to him. This is why so many young people seek to shake off the yoke of obedience. Especially does obedience to the laws and precepts of the Church often appear to them extremely difficult, and often impossible.

As soon as such a command is to be obeyed or such a precept is to be carried out, self-love hunts out every imaginable pretext which can excuse disobedience; meanwhile the evil world with its fatal axioms fails not to aid and abet the disloyal. Let us now examine some of these objections.

For instance, people say: "But the Catholic Church gives so very many admonitions and precepts that one can not always remember them all, much less carry them out into practice."

Now as far as remembering them is concerned, Almighty God has taken care that as soon as any precept is to be observed, and doctrine carried out, it should at once recur in your mind. He has placed a special sentinel at the door of your heart, the voice of conscience. Only follow cheerfully when it calls, and all will be well. For the important matter is to obey your conscience.

"But," you hear people say, "it is impossible to obey the Church in everything." Yet the Saviour has declared definitely and decidedly: *"He that will not hear the Church, let him be to thee as the heathen and publican."* Thus we must hear the Church and obey her; therefore it must be possible to do so, since God commands nothing which is impossible. He makes that possible which would be impossible to our unaided powers, nay more: He even renders it easy with the help of His grace. St. Paul testifies to this truth when he says: "*I can do all things in Him who strengtheneth me*" (Phil. iv. 13).

Especially are objections raised to the laws of the Church concerning marriage; people say, for instance: "But there are many mixed marriages which are perfectly happy; the Church is therefore much too severe when she warns her children so strongly and persistently against contracting such unions."

To this I answer in the first place: If the so-called happiness to be found in mixed marriages must be purchased at the cost of the Protestant bringing up of the children, it is much too dearly bought; and however great it may appear in the eyes of the world, it is a transient kind of happiness, which sooner or later, perhaps not until this brief span of life on earth is ended, must be changed into unhappiness.

I answer in the second place: How small—how very small— is the number of these really and thoroughly happy mixed marriages. If a census were taken in regard to this point, the result would certainly prove anything but satisfactory.

"But the strict regulations of the Catholic Church exercise a tyranny over man's conscience," this is put forward as a further objection. How perverse and stupid this is. Does the Church compel any one, even in the least degree, to become a Catholic, or to remain one? But if the Church declares to those who are in her fold: If you desire to be and remain a Catholic, I require this and this of you, it can as little be called tyranny, as can the rules and regulations for a rifle corps, which its members have to observe. No! tyranny over men's consciences was and is practised in quite another quarter. For example, freedom was formerly the battlecry of the English, when they threw off the ancient faith of their fathers; but on the Catholics of England and Ireland they laid a heavy yoke, and persecuted them with a tyranny and ingenious cruelty which have seldom been equaled in the annals of history.

Liberty and equality are words which echoed throughout France in 1794; but faithful Catholics alone were excluded from this liberty and equality; they were outlawed—under the dominion of *"liberty and equality,"* they met with the same fate which fell the lot of the early Christians under the tyranny of Nero. Therefore the objection that the Church is a tyrant is completely disposed of. The very opposite is true: If ever tyranny was practised, it was practised by the foes of the Church.

You may at times be tempted, my friend, when it is your duty to make a sacrifice required by obedience to the Church, to cloak your want of courage in regard to making this sacrifice, by putting forward such foolish objections. But I entreat you, for the sake of both your temporal and eternal happiness, to beware of yielding to this temptation!

Be true to your faith; true to your convictions!

> I will never forsake thee; I never will be,
> O Church of the saints, an apostate from thee
> Lead thou me on; "I'll follow thee
> To the last gasp with faith and loyalty."

36. SECULAR AUTHORITY

WHERE true faith reigns, there also exists, like an impregnable wall, the recognition of the authority of the State, the duty of obeying the civil powers. This obedience receives its sanction from the Church, which is the pillar of the State and of its ordinances. He, therefore, who heeds not the Church, shakes also the principal supports of every well-ordered constitution. He who incites the citizen to unbelief, and in this manner to disobey his spiritual mother the Church, inclines him to become a traitor to the law and to his native land.

And this is what we especially experience in the present day. While the Church preaches obedience, the godless world, which is separated from her, proclaims treachery against the ruler, the laws, and one's native land; and wherever the Church is ignored, obedience to law and authority is ignored likewise. The Catholic Church will always oppose anarchy and every kind of socialism which ignores God and which is inimical to the eternal interests of man.

It behooves you, my friend, to be ever on your guard that you may not be entangled in the net of the degenerate spirit of the world.

The Church itself cheerfully serves the lawful secular authority in upholding law and order in the State. The best safeguard of your interests, both temporal and eternal, is obedience to the Church.

Let your obedience to the Church be as a sharp sword that will cut to pieces every net which is attempted to be drawn around you by the false principles and specious sophistry of the spirit of evil as manifested in modernism, rationalism, naturalism, and godless socialism.

Keep perpetually engraven on the tablets of your memory the words of the apostles:

In the Epistle of St. Paul to the Romans (xiii. 1, 2, 4, 5) we read: "*Let every soul be subject to higher powers; for there is no power but from God: and those that are, are ordained of God. Therefore he that resisteth the power, resisteth the ordinance of God. And they that resist, purchase to themselves damnation…For he is God's minister to thee, for good. But if thou do that which is evil, fear; for he beareth not the sword in vain. For he is God's minister: an avenger, to execute wrath upon him that doth evil. Wherefore be subject of necessity, not only for wrath, but also for conscience's sake.*"

And St. Peter in his first letter (ii. 13, 15) writes: "*Be ye subject, therefore, to every human creature for God's sake: whether it be to the King as excelling, or to governors as sent by him for the punishment of evil-doers and for the praise of the good...For so is the will of God, that by doing well you may put to silence the ignorance of foolish men.*"

Our holy religion, therefore, plainly commands that we should regard those possessed of lawful authority as the representatives of God and should honor them as such, obeying them cheerfully, as long as they command nothing which is incompatible with the commandments of God and of His Church. Obey therefore, the civil authorities for the love of God, not merely from compulsion or fear of punishment. The example of Jesus Christ and of His apostles teaches this obedience.

The Founder of our holy Church, our Blessed Saviour, gave an example of submission to the laws of the State; He never violated them, unless indeed they were not in harmony with the laws of His heavenly Father. Regarding the coin of tribute, He said to the Pharisees: "*Render to Caesar the things that are Caesar's, and to God the things that are God's* (Matt. xxii. 21).

In the same manner the apostles submitted to the laws of the State as long as it was possible to do this without breaking the laws of God, and they impressed this duty upon others. St. Paul did the same in these words: "*There is no power but from God. Therefore he that resisteth the power, resisteth the ordinance of God.*"

Accordingly, the Catholic Church has always, and in the most positive manner, inculcated obedience to secular authority as a duty and a matter of conscience, and has opposed and condemned those who taught the contrary. Only if the secular authority commands anything which is actually sinful, we must obey God and the Church rather than men. He who asserts that Catholicism teaches the opposite, is a calumniator.

An old soldier was reproached with not having been sufficiently zealous in defending his native land. His reply was an eloquent silence; he showed the scars of the wounds which he had received while fighting his country's battles.

In like manner, we can point to the faithful services which Catholics have rendered to secular authority, even when the latter persecuted and oppressed them unjustly. Need I remind you with what patience, some thirty years ago, the Catholics of Germany and Switzerland bore the sad consequences of the so-called *Kulturkampf*.[1]

Were such obedience practised everywhere, how soon would our deplorable conditions assume a different form! The spirit of the age is a mischievous one, which pervades the nations like some haunting ghost. Can this spirit which teaches men to deny and withstand lawful authority, can it be overcome by force, by blood and iron? We see how this means is employed, alike in great and in petty States, but how unsatisfactory and short-lived are the results!

No, such means are futile. Faith—religion—constitutes the real power, the main source, whence for the individual and for the nation stability, prosperity, and happiness are derived. Keep this faith firmly rooted, ever alive within your heart.

37. FREEDOM

THIS word *"freedom"* is understood by many young people in a totally false sense, and frequently interpreted to their own destruction; hence it is that good, conscientious parents

---

1   *Kulturkampf* refers to the systematic repression of Catholicism by the Prussian Protestant majority following the unification of Germany in 1870. Despite increasingly draconian measures, the Catholics remained defiant, and by the 1890s the aggression had substantially calmed.

and zealous pastors of souls are in constant dread with regard to the young men of the rising generation.

You desire freedom, and you are not to be blamed for so doing. But do not confuse true freedom with absence of all restraint. For this is for the most part fraught with dangers, and its results not unfrequently prove disastrous in the case of young people. I wish to warn you beforehand against these dangers and disastrous results by pointing out to you how you ought to employ your freedom, if you desire to be truly free.

How ought you to employ it? Listen to yonder young man, as he greets his newly acquired freedom: "What luck! Now there will be no more schoolmasters, no more home tasks, no more strict regulations, no being kept in, no scolding and petty fault-finding. Now I will let myself go, and do whatever I choose—just please myself!" A truly remarkable manner this, of enjoying freedom! Certainly this is not enjoying freedom as a reasonable being or as a Christian, since it opens wide the door to the passions which obscure reason and jeopardize one's eternal interests if allowed to have full sway. It is certainly not enjoying freedom as a well-brought-up young man should do, if good manners, and the regard which is owed to the family, are thus trodden underfoot. To act thus is to enjoy liberty like a savage who knows no law, like a wild beast which is destitute of reason.

My dear friend, to enjoy freedom after this fashion is to render yourself unworthy of it, to dishonor and degrade it. Such freedom as this is rebellion against the lawful authority of God, the freedom of sinners, the freedom of evil, of the flesh, of the passions, unreasonable license—yet more—it is bondage itself, according to the words of Holy Scripture: "*Whosoever committeth sin is the servant of sin*" (John viii. 34).

A madman acts in accordance with the promptings of his own fancy, gratifies his impulses and inclinations, but is he therefore to be called truly free? In the same way may every inordinate passion be more or less designated as a sort of madness, which degrades men and destroys their freedom. They are the slaves of their passions.

He who goes into the water for the first time in order to learn how to swim, is guided and held fast by the swimming master by means of a rope, in order that, should he begin to sink, he might be drawn out and rescued without any difficulty. But as soon as the pupil has become somewhat familiarized with the water, and has had some practise in swimming, so that he knows how to keep himself afloat, then he is left free, the restraining rope is withdrawn.

Consider the training of a child. In the beginning leading strings are necessary; careful nurses must guide the child, but only in order to teach it how to walk alone; they have to support its steps, but only in order to show it how to direct them; they have to point out the goal to be aimed at, but only to incite it to hasten toward that goal.

In matters that pertain to morality, the young man who has been properly trained is free to choose between good and evil; but when he has been accustomed to choose the good, he perseveres in it, even when he is far removed from parents and teachers. He knows that freedom does not do away with duty, that it does not confer the right to do whatever he chooses, that it must have reference to God as our last goal and final end, and that, in the case of the free man, the spirit must rule the flesh, and reason hold sway over passion.

Such is true freedom—the freedom which you are bound to choose; it is the freedom which Jesus Christ purchased for you with His precious blood; the freedom which He bestowed upon you with His truth, *"The truth shall make you free"*—in a word, it is that freedom which love gives to the Christian heart, according to the saying of St. Augustine; "Love, and do what you will!" But St. Paul says: "*Love is the fulfilling of the Law*" (Rom. xiii. 10). I know not what your future will be, but this I do know, that it will exactly correspond to the use you make of your freedom; the abuse of it will lead you to shame, the right use of it to eternal felicity. Take your choice!

> Who freedom seeks, true liberty,
> Finds it, my God, in serving Thee.
> Fetters of steel may him confine
> He yields unto no might but Thine.

38. THE CATHOLIC AND HIS NATIVE LAND

How charming is the expression, "My native land! my Fatherland!" At the sound of it the heart throbs more joyously, the blood courses more swiftly through the veins. Love of country is an innate sentiment, the want of which is something unnatural, and is, fortunately, but rarely to be met with.

> "Breathes there the man with soul so dead
> Who never to himself hath said,
>   This is my own, my native land!"

Moreover, true patriotism and love of religion go hand in hand. Remember the Machabees. Their sole reason for having recourse to arms was that they were determined not to see their altars desecrated by profane hands.

But, it is objected, great courage and energy are necessary in order to serve one's country; religion, however, inculcates meekness and resignation; therefore religion makes men cowardly and weak.

This reproach was put forward even by the pagans in the days of Christ and His apostles, but is it fair? Is it just? Most assuredly not. Do not the countless martyrs of the Catholic religion prove that it does not produce weaklings, but that the holy standard of the Cross imparts greater steadfastness than any other standard can possibly do?

Was it weakness and cowardice which caused St. Ambrose to forbid the Emperor Theodosius to enter the sanctuary of God? Was it cowardice and fear which made St. Leo the Pope advance to meet the savage king of the Huns before the fortified city of Rome and induce him to retreat? Or again, was it not courage of the highest order which induced St. Ulrich of Augsburg to oppose with all his might the Hungarians who swept everything before them like a flood? Truly the Catholic religion does not render men weak, cowardly, and indifferent, but infidelity and materialism are inclined to do this. For he who knows no higher interests than mere worldly ones—how should he be willing to risk life and limb for the sake of his country?

Thus religion—*our* holy faith—enables men, above everything else, to carry out into practice the motto which is inscribed on the banners of so many rifle corps:

> Eye, heart, and hand
> For our Fatherland!

The *eye* for the Fatherland! But in order that it may be really useful, the eye—I mean the eye of the mind—must be able to see and perceive what is best and most profitable for the country. But in the case of many a man the vision is obscured by self-interest, egoism, and party feeling. And this is the cancer which at the present day is eating into the greater number of civilized nations; so very many citizens, and among them those who are at the head of affairs, have an eye obscured by selfishness or party feeling. Hence arises the disregard of sacred rights; namely, the flagrant encroachment of the secular power in ecclesiastical affairs. Therefore a free, wide-open, clear eye for the Fatherland! But it is religion alone which gives this freedom and clearness of vision; for it alone teaches men to respect and heed the rights of others; only by its light is the citizen able to perceive what truly promotes the welfare of his country.

The *heart* for the Fatherland—that means the affection of the heart. But this love must be inseparably bound up with religion. I have already said, and experience constantly confirms my assertion, that the love of one's country will be all the stronger, more lasting, more self-sacrificing, and more effectual, the firmer is religious belief.

For this faith, this religious conviction, makes men zealous and enthusiastic in their country's cause; it makes them willing, if need be, to fight and die for their native land, to aid it with all their might. In our own day a mighty prince and ruler recognized this fact. I allude to the emperor of Germany, William the Second, who expressed himself as follows: "No one can be a good soldier who is not also a good Christian."

Finally, the *hand* for the Fatherland! That must be a strong, a faithful hand, a hand which can and will exert itself with all its might in defense of the Fatherland. A strong, a trusty hand like that which the heroes of Switzerland displayed one hundred years ago in Nidwalden and the canton of Schwyz.[1] And a powerful hand, a wrist of iron, such as that which the Tyrolese caused the enemies of their country to feel in the glorious war of independence in the year 1809; such as that which the patriots of Ireland and Poland displayed in their long struggle and heroic resistance to their anti-Catholic persecutors—suffering fire, sword, famine, poverty, sickness, and every kind of privation for the sake of religious principle and love of country.

What strengthened the hand of all these heroes, what rendered them so courageous? It was our holy religion, our Catholic faith.

---

1   After the French Revolution, the French Republican army "liberated" the Swiss and imposed the Helvetian Republic. The Catholic cantons of Nidwalden, Schwyz and Uri united in rebellion against the French, as the new government forbade them to practice their faith.

Does history furnish a more splendid example of patriotism than that of the heroic Maid of Orleans? In her case love of God and love of country were certainly united most intimately. The Blessed Joan of Arc was convinced that God, Eternal Justice, looked with pity upon her oppressed Fatherland and that she was commissioned from on high to deliver her country; hence her undaunted courage, her valor, her energy, her perseverance, and her triumph.

Do you, therefore, my dear young friend, highly prize your holy Catholic religion, faithfully fulfil all the duties it lays upon you, order your life according to the laws it proclaims; then will you in the right way have *eye, heart,* and *hand* for your Fatherland.

> I love thee, my country, the dearest of all,
> I will faithfully serve thee whatever befall:
> A powerful source of courage to me
> The Faith of my fathers ever shall be.

39. The Catholic and Politics

IN SEEING the title of the present chapter you may perhaps shake your head thoughtfully and say: "What, is the author of a book of this nature going to treat of politics?" Yes, I am certainly about to do so! And why should I not, since very weighty reasons impel me to take this course?

You, my youthful reader, are already, or will be sooner or later, of an age to exercise the suffrage, to vote in municipal, state, and national elections, and will therefore enter the realm of so-called politics. Therefore it is for you, as a Catholic, a matter of conscience to learn what are the real, the true Catholic principles which are to be followed in reference to politics. And it is these principles which I now desire briefly to explain.

The Catholic should, before all things, in his relation to politics, never lose sight of the exhortation addressed by St. Paul to the Romans: "*If it be possible, as much as is in you, have peace with all men*" (Rom. xii. 18). That should be the first principle of a Catholic in his intercourse with his fellow men in general, and more especially in regard to politics. It is certainly his duty to have peace with all men, but not under *all circumstances*, not at any price, but only so far as in us lies, as it depends upon us; that is, as far as loyalty to our Catholic beliefs, principles, and convictions permits.

Let us now see how this general principle may be applied to individual matters.

We may consider politics from a fourfold point of view:

1. as politics in reference to mere worldly affairs,
2. to those which concern religious and ecclesiastical matters alone,
3. to mixed questions, and
4. to conditions and circumstances at elections.

Politics occupy themselves, in by far the greater part, with mere worldly affairs; for example, with military and financial questions, postal arrangements, railways, forestry and agriculture, the tariff, trusts, and industries. But even in these matters, faith and religion have no little influence, and certainly ought to have it, in so far as all these things should be ordered and arranged according to the immutable laws of Christian justice, and that no private or party interest should be considered, but only what will best contribute to the welfare of the community, of the city, state, or country at large.

As to matters which deal with purely religious and ecclesiastical questions, no politics should enter into them; *i.e.*, the State ought not to interfere in them. The Catholic, therefore, as a citizen of the State, ought in questions of a purely ecclesiastical nature, to speak and act in accordance with this conviction. It would be acting in direct opposition to St. Paul's injunction—it would be disturbing the peace of a large proportion of one's fellow-men, of all faithful children of the Catholic Church—were one, for instance, to side with those politicians who would depose bishops and suspend priests, suppress religious houses, confiscate their property, and devote churches to secular purposes.

There are, moreover, questions of a mixed character, which concern ecclesiastical and worldly affairs at the same time, as for instance education and the marriage relation. Both Church and State have an interest in these things; therefore they both ought to arrange them in harmony. Before all things, this saying applies: *"Render therefore to Cæsar the things that are Cæsar's; and to God the things that are God's."* It plainly belongs to the Church, and not to the State, to decide what *"things are God's"* since the Son of God Himself appointed the former to be His representative upon earth. Therefore a loyal Catholic ought never to sanction or lend a hand to the encroachments of the State in matters which the Church has decreed to be *"God's."*

A true Catholic and patriot will be interested in elections, especially when there is question of electing men to important offices in the executive and legislative branches of the government; he will determine his vote by asking himself: First, which of the candidates offers the best security or assurance that he will range himself, not with the enemies of the Church, but on the side of justice with fair and upright men. Second, who possesses in the highest degree the integrity, the courage, intelligence, tact, and ability to safeguard and defend the interests of the country, as well as those of the Church.

These are the fundamental principles which ought to guide a faithful Catholic in regard to politics. Follow them zealously and closely; take an interest in elections; perform your duty as a citizen, and vote according to your conscience and convictions.

SUSCIPE
THE PRAYER OF ST. IGNATIUS OF LOYOLA

TAKE, O Lord, and receive my entire liberty, my memory, my understanding and my whole will. All that I am and all that I possess Thou hast given me: I surrender it all to Thee to be disposed of according to Thy will. Give me only Thy love and Thy grace; with these I will be rich enough, and will desire nothing more.

ANIMA CHRISTI

SOUL of Christ, sanctify me.
Body of Christ, save me.
Blood of Christ, inebriate me.
Water from the side of Christ, wash me.
Passion of Christ, strengthen me.
O good Jesus, hear me.
Within Thy wounds, hide me.
Permit me not to be separated from Thee.
From the malignant enemy, defend me.
At the hour of death, call me.
And bid me come to Thee,
That with thy Saints I may praise Thee
For ever and ever. Amen.

The Breastplate

of Justice

The Breastplate of Justice

40. To God the Things that are God's

IN PARIS, on the evening of February 24 1848, an unlooked-for revolution had suddenly broken out and overturned the throne of Louis Philippe, the citizen-king. A furious mob stormed the Tuileries, and threw costly vases, statuary, and paintings out of the windows. While these things were going on, a number of young men passed through the courtyard of the Tuileries; they had succeeded in rescuing the sacred vessels and a crucifix from the chapel of the royal palace. A band of drunken soldiers stopped them, and endeavored to wrest their precious burden from them. "What," exclaimed a courageous young man, holding his crucifix aloft as he spoke, "What, you are fighting for freedom? Let me tell you that this freedom can only be obtained through the cross of Jesus Christ!"

Let us once more transport ourselves to Paris, two and thirty years later. This time no revolution has broken out, everything is quiet. But a vehicle is being driven through the huge city, a vehicle belonging to the government; it has been sent forth by Jules Ferry, the minister of public education, with instructions to the official in charge of the same to remove from all schoolrooms throughout the city every crucifix, and every presentation of Christ. What a contrast have we here! Yonder is a man who holds the crucifix aloft, here we behold one who breaks the cross into pieces! But that is a picture of men in the present day, as they are to be met with so often, and in so many places. They are divided into two great camps: the men who render to God the things that are God's, and those who take from God the things that rightly belong to Him—that is to say, who do not perform their religious duties. I trust that you belong to the former class, that you render to God the things that are God's, that you perform your religious duties.

Among the first and foremost of these duties, I place attendance at divine services on Sundays and holydays, and the suitable observance of these days in a religious spirit. Therefore assist whenever you possibly can at Holy Mass on all Sundays and holydays. For there is nothing in the world more pleasing to God than the sacrifice of the altar. We do not pray alone in Holy Mass, but Jesus Himself pleads in our behalf and prays with us. He offers to His heavenly Father all that He did and suffered His whole life long in order to honor and glorify Him; His obedience, His charity, His humility, and so on. He offers there His body which was crucified, His blood which was shed for our salvation, in a word, He now offers for us the identical sacrifice which He once offered for us upon the cross.

For nineteen hundred years have men journeyed to the Holy Land, in order to gaze--once at least in a lifetime, upon the hallowed spot where the sacred Victim was slain, in order to behold the Mount of Calvary where the precious blood of the incarnate Word was shed, where our Blessed Redeemer, Jesus-Christ, deigned to die for our sins. Now to assist at Holy Mass means in a way to visit the place where Our Lord was crucified, to ascend Mount Calvary in company with our suffering Redeemer. From thence He calls to us especially if it happens to be Sunday: "The day of redemption is here; see, I go forth to Mount Calvary, to the altar, in order to renew the sacrifice of the Cross for the good of your souls. If you love Me, if you wish to show your gratitude for My love, come with Me and assist at the Holy Sacrifice, the oblation of the New Testament."

But this is not the only thing that God can claim on Sundays and holydays; there is something more you owe to Him. The Saviour Himself said: "*He that is of God heareth the words of God*" (John viii. 47). Especially on Sundays and holy days you ought to hear the word of God, as it is proclaimed in sermons and religious instructions.

For all Christians, and especially for young men of your age, it is necessary that they should be repeatedly reminded of the truths of the Faith, and exhorted to do right. Even though you are familiar with the truths of the faith, they are frequently left out of sight, and not taken to heart. And how easily it happens that the thoughtless young man loses his fervor, becomes negligent in the exercises of piety, grows weary of treading the path of virtue, and careless as to right and wrong. Therefore, how necessary and salutary it is that he very frequently, on all Sundays at least, should be instructed, encouraged, and stimulated to walk in the right way.

To be remiss in attending sermons and religious instructions is always a sign of great tepidity. Our Lord said to the Jews: "*He that is of God heareth the words of God; therefore you hear them not, because you are not of God*" (John viii. 47). The same words apply to the Christian who does not go to hear sermons; if you were of God, a child of God, you would take delight in hearing His word; you would willingly hear sermons, and attend catechetical instructions. Happy are those young men who diligently receive the seed of the word of God: "*who in a good and perfect heart, hearing the word, keep it and bring forth fruit in patience*" (Luke viii. 15). To them the promise of Jesus may be applied: "*Blessed are they who hear the word of God, and keep it*" (Luke xi. 28). Notice that Jesus does not merely say: "*Blessed are they that hear the word of God,"* but expressly adds: *"Blessed are they that* **keep** *it."*

Wherefore resolve to keep the word of God; and by so doing render to God the things that are God's.

> Hail, Sunday, peaceful day of rest,
> The Lord's own day, which He has blest;
> Rejoice to sanctify the day
> And in the church your homage pay.

41. A LADDER TO HEAVEN: PRAYER

ONE death-bed scene which I witnessed in the course of my life as a pastor of souls can never fade from my memory. It was the death of one of my former parishioners, a girl who had just left school. She had only been ill for three days when I found it necessary to administer the last sacraments.

When, three or four hours later, I saw that the relentless hand of death was about to cut at her young life, I knelt in prayer beside the bed with all those who were present, and I asked the dying sufferer: "You will pray for us in heaven, my child, will you not?" "Yes," she exclaimed, clasping my hand with a gesture of entreaty, "but you must first pray for me, that I may get to heaven!" And after she had taken leave of every one she repeated, with her failing breath, "Do pray, go on praying! Pray, pray!"

And it is these very words of the dying girl which I repeat to you over and over again: "My dear young friend, do pray, go on praying! Pray, pray, because it is indispensably necessary to do so." Prayer is assuredly the ladder to heaven, without which it is not possible to be saved.

Scarcely anything else in Holy Scripture is commended to us so frequently and with so much emphasis. Over and over again we meet with exhortations to prayer. *"Ask and it shall be given you: seek and you shall find, knock and it shall be opened to you"* (Matt. vii. 7). *"Watch ye and pray"* (Matt. xxvi. 41).

St. Paul bids us: *"Pray without ceasing"* (Thess. v. 17).

Again we are admonished to pray in these words:

"We ought always to pray and not to give up" (Luke xviii. 1).

"Without Me you can do nothing" (John xv. 5).

"Not that we are sufficient to think anything of ourselves as ourselves, but our sufficiency is from God" (2 Cor. iii. 5).

"Amen, Amen, I say to you, if you ask the Father anything in My name He will give it to you" (John xvi. 23).

The Royal Psalmist tells us: *"The Lord is nigh unto all them that call upon Him; to all that call upon Him in truth. He will do the will of them that fear Him, and He will hear their prayer and save them"* (Ps. cxliv. 18, 19).

And what do the saints say? They call prayer the very breath of the soul, and assert that a man who does not pray is a lamp without oil, a body without food, a plant without water, a soldier without arms. St. Alphonsus writes thus: "It is by means of prayer that all the blessed in heaven have attained to eternal felicity. All the damned have been lost because they did not pray; if they had prayed, they would certainly not have been lost."

The same saint urges us to prayer in these words:

"Prayer is a sure and indispensable means of obtaining salvation and all the graces leading thereto. Convinced as I am of the necessity of prayer, I say that all books treating of spiritual subjects, all preachers in their sermons, all confessors in every confession which they hear, should attach the greatest importance to inculcating the necessity of constant prayer on the minds of their readers and hearers, and they should never tire of pressing it on them and of repeating over and over again: *Pray, pray always;* if you pray, you will certainly save your souls; if you do not pray, you will certainly lose them. It is true that many excellent ways of persevering in the grace of God may be recommended to souls; for instance, avoiding occasions of sin, frequenting the sacraments, resisting temptation, listening to sermons, meditating on the eternal truths, etc., all of which are most salutary practices, as every one must admit, but, I ask, of what good are sermons, mediations, and the other means suggested by the masters of the spiritual life, without prayer? Since Our Lord has declared that He will only grant His grace to those who pray for it: 'Ask and ye shall receive' (John xvi. 24). According to the ordinary course of Providence, all our meditations, resolutions, promises, are useless without prayer; if we do not pray, we shall always be faithless to the lights we have received from God and to the resolutions we have taken. Because, in order to do right, to overcome temptation, to practise virtue, to serve God's law, it is not sufficient to have received divine lights, to have meditated, and to have taken firm resolutions. God's actual help is also necessary. Now, this actual help is only granted by Our Lord to those who pray perseveringly for it. The lights we receive, and the earnest consideration and firm resolutions which we make, have the effect of inciting us to have recourse to prayer in the time of temptation and when in danger of offending God; by prayer we obtain the divine help necessary for keeping us from sin, and if, under these circumstances, we were to neglect praying, we should undoubtedly be lost."

This truth is emphasized by other saints:

"Nothing good can be expected from a man who does not pray."—St. Francis of Assisi.

"God bestows some favors without prayer, such as the beginning of faith; others, such as perseverance, are granted only to those who pray."—St. Augustine.

"To enter heaven, continual prayer is necessary after Baptism; for although all sins are remitted by that sacrament, there still remains concupiscence to assail us from within, and the world and the devil to attack us from without."—St. Thomas.

"By prayer is obtained the possession of every good, and deliverance from every evil."—St. Bonaventure.

It follows from these various sayings that without prayer there can be no true virtue—no strength to resist evil, no good death, no salvation. Woe to the man who ceases to pray—he is lost!

The necessity of prayer for every Christian may be deduced from the very essence of Christianity. Through Christ we become children of God: and on this account the Saviour taught us to pray: *"Our Father, Who art in heaven."* How could we say that we had the spirit of a child of God, if we were not to pray?

Through Christ we are made living temples of God. *"The house of God,"* says the Lord, *"is a house of prayer."* A church which is no longer used for prayer becomes a non-entity; it is no more than a ruin. This is an image of a soul which has ceased to pray; it is a crumbling temple. Unhappy soul, to whom prayer has become strange and difficult!

Through Christ we ought also to become His followers; we ought, as the apostle says, to *"put on Christ."* But if we have *"put on Christ,"* if His Spirit lives and rules in our hearts, we can not but pray. For Christ prayed frequently and for lengthened seasons on the occasion of all weighty affairs, and He prayed whole nights at a time.

It is through Christ that we shall finally attain to the eternal vision of God, to eternal communion with Him. How shall we attain to the Beatific Vision and everlasting contemplation of God, if we have not, while still sojourning on earth, learned how to pray, and made it our constant practice to keep ourselves in the presence of God, and by means of prayer, to hold loving intercourse with Him? He who prays not at all, or who does not pray well, is separated from God whilst here below, and will not be admitted to His presence in heaven.

Cling firmly, my young friend, to the ladder which reaches to heaven; by this means ascend to God. And if at times weariness and aridity creep over you, shake off this drowsiness and say to yourself: "I have not yet reached heaven; one unfortunate moment may prove my eternal perdition, therefore I must pray."

Impressed with this truth, you will be more zealous in saying your morning prayers and throughout the day will more frequently raise your mind to God; you will never neglect to attend public worship; you will never lie down to sleep without having in prayer bewailed the faults of the past day. Before all things you must constantly beseech God to bestow on you the gift of prayer.

> Teach, Lord, Thy servant how to pray,
> To make my needs known unto Thee each day
> Then, when my heart is raised to Thee on high
> Grant me to feel that Thou art truly nigh.

With Keble say:

> "Only, O Lord, in Thy dear love
> Fit us for perfect rest above:
> And help us this and every day
> To live more nearly as we pray."

For what and for whom should we pray?

St. Alphonsus Liguori insists repeatedly that in all our devotions, at Mass, at holy communion, in all our visits to the Blessed Sacrament, we should pray for these four graces for ourselves: (1) the forgiveness of our sins, (2) the love of God, (3) the love of prayer, and (4) final perseverance. When these graces are secured, our salvation is assured.

As loyal Catholics we should also pray according to the intentions of our Holy Father the Pope; for his welfare and for the needs and interests of our Holy Mother the Church; for bishops, priests, and superiors; for our country; for universal peace; for the conversion of sinners, heretics, and pagans; and last but not least, for the holy souls in purgatory.

Father Girardey, C.SS.R., in his beautiful treatise on *Prayer*, writes:

"In praying for temporal favors for ourselves, we can claim unconditionally only the *necessaries* of life; in the Our Father we are taught to pray for 'our daily bread'; this does not include superfluities or luxuries; and the words 'deliver us from evil' do not necessarily include, as we have seen, deliverance from physical evils, for the evil here meant is sin and all that leads to sin. We have no reason to hope that God will hear our prayers for those temporal favors that may prove hurtful to our salvation, or that He will exempt us from certain corporal pains and trials, if such an exemption would lead us to sin or endanger our salvation. The granting of such prayers would be, not a favor, but a terrible punishment. We should, then, ask for temporal favors conditionally—that is, under the condition that they may promote our salvation, or at least not hinder it. We ought never lose sight of this saying of our loving Redeemer: '*What doth it profit a man, if he gain the whole world, and suffer the loss of his own soul?*' (Matt. xvi. 26)

"Let us not be so solicitous for temporal favors, which, after all, may prove hurtful to our soul, but let us rather pray for what is conducive to our eternal welfare. When we pray for temporals, and God, in His mercy refuses them to us, it is because they would prove hurtful to us. 'But,' says St. Gregory of Nazianzen, 'he who asks God for a real favor [that is, for a favor that is necessary or useful for his salvation], obtains it, for God is bountiful and generous, and readily bestows His gifts.' 'When you pray,' says St. Ambrose, 'ask for great things; ask not for what is transitory, but for what is eternal.' 'We should pray,' says St. Augustine, 'in that name and through the merits of Jesus Christ. When, however, we pray for what is injurious to our soul, we do not pray in the name of Our Redeemer. In praying for temporals we should be moderate and timid, asking God to give them to us provided they are really beneficial, and to withhold them if they should prove hurtful. Many, when they pray, invoke God, but not as God, for the object of their prayer is opposed to His glory and favorable to their passions. They seem to consider God as a mere servant of themselves and of their passions, such as pride, covetousness, and lust. Let us pray, not for temporals but for heavenly glory and the means of attaining it. The most precious and excellent of temporal things are but insignificant trifles in comparison to what is eternal.'

"Rohrbacher relates in his *Church History* that, among the pilgrims who flocked to the tomb of St. Thomas of Canterbury to seek favors through the saint's intercession, there was a blind man who prayed so fervently for the recovery of his lost sight that he was perfectly cured. After returning home, however, he began to reflect that the restoration of his sight might, perhaps, prove an obstacle to his salvation. He accordingly returned to the tomb of the saint, and, after fervently praying that were his sight ever to be injurious to his soul he should again lose it, he became totally blind once more. He acted most wisely, for it was much better for him to be blind than run the risk of losing his soul. Unguarded looks are often the cause of grievous sin, as is shown by the example of David and of many others.

"When our prayers for temporal favors, either for ourselves or in behalf of others, are not granted, we should consider God's refusal a real benefit rather than a misfortune. In beseeching God for temporals we should be indifferent as to the result of our prayers, being equally ready to accept a refusal or a favorable hearing from Him. If such should be our dispositions, God, when refusing our request, will not fail to compensate us by bestowing on us more excellent favors which we do not think of asking. 'In vain does a child cry for a sword or a live coal,' remarks St. John Chrysostom; 'his parents justly refuse him what may prove very hurtful to him. In like manner, God justly and kindly refuses us what is injurious to us, but, in His goodness, He will give us something better instead.' Let us in all our prayers aim principally at the salvation of our soul, and we shall obtain also temporal favors from God according to this saying of our loving Redeemer: '*Seek ye therefore first the kingdom of God and His justice, and all these things shall be added unto you*' (Matt. vi. 33).

"For whom should we pray? We should first of all, pray for ourselves, because our salvation is our first and most important duty. Although, by the law of charity, we are bound to pray for all men, there are, nevertheless, some for whom we have a special obligation or special reasons to pray. Children should daily pray for their parents, parents for their children, members of the same family and household or community for one another, inferiors for their superiors, both ecclesiastical and civil, and superiors for their inferiors. It is also incumbent on us to pray for our benefactors, both spiritual and temporal, for our relatives, for those who ask our prayers, and who pray for us, for our friends, and for our enemies also, whosoever they may be or whatever evil they may have done or may wish us. We ought, likewise, to pray for the perseverance of the just and for the conversion of sinners, of heretics, schismatics, Jews, and unbelievers. It is a most praiseworthy custom to pray for the sick, for those who are in their agony, for all who are in danger of death, or in danger of losing their innocence, and for all who are in distress, pain, trouble, or sorrow.

"It behooves us daily to remember in our prayers the souls in purgatory, particularly the souls toward whom we have some special obligation, *e.g.*, the souls of our parents, of our benefactors, of those who are suffering on our account. We should endeavor to gain many indulgences for their benefit. If, during our life, we pray for them, God will, after our death, inspire compassionate souls to pray for us when we are in purgatory, for, says our divine Saviour, *'with what measure you mete, it shall be measured to you again'* (Matt. vii. 2)."

42. Raise Your Heart to God: Meditation

WE ARE traveling to an unknown land, to the land of eternity, let us hope, of endless delight. Our life on earth is a voyage to that country. The mistake into which most young people fall, is that they make the journey to eternity in so thoughtless a fashion. You must beware of this folly. Therefore I exhort you to raise your heart to God daily, by means of serious reflection, by means of meditation or mental prayer.

You must already have remarked the wide difference which frequently exists among Christians who dwell beneath the same roof-tree, and form but one family. Unfortunately, one not seldom finds in the present day Christians who commit sin boldly, and even with a sort of pride: but there are, thank God, other Christians who dread nothing so much as sin.

Whence arises this difference? In the case of the latter, from the practice of mental prayer; in that of the former, from the thoughtless manner in which they live their daily life, and never reflect upon higher and eternal things. Truly it is not to be wondered at, if a man who lives in this manner veers about like a weathercock with every wind that blows. He does not live quite like a Christian nor quite like a heathen; he indeed believes in heaven and hell, but in a cold and careless manner.

How does it happen, on the other hand, that the true, earnest Christian stands as fine amid evil examples as an oak which has braved a hundred winters? Let us discover his secret—a secret more valuable by far than the secret of the alchemist. The true Christian also has his temptations; he has to fight with his own concupiscence, with the world, with the devil. But he is not careless and thoughtless; on the contrary, he is watchful and serious; in prayer he meditates upon religious truths and by the grace of God his *faith* becomes fervent and lively, so that he does not fall into grievous sin, but makes steady progress in the way of perfection. The bad and thoughtless Christian, on the other hand, boasts that he believes like any good Christian, but he does not live up to his profession. For this reason one of the saints used to say: "In my opinion, these bad Christians ought to be confined in an asylum for idiots; for how can a sensible, reasonable man believe in heaven and hell, and yet go on sinning?"

St. Alphonsus Liguori says in his *Devout Reflections*[1]:

"We are not created for this earth. The end for which God has placed us in the world is this, that by our good works we may merit Eternal life. '*The end is life everlasting*' (Rom. i. 22). And therefore St. Eucherius used to say that the only affair that we should attend to in this life is eternity; that is, to gain for ourselves a happy eternity, and escape a miserable one. 'The business for which we work is eternity.' If we make sure of success in this business, we shall be happy forever; if we fail in it, we shall be forever miserable.

"Happy he who lives with eternity always in view, with a lively faith that he must shortly die, and enter into eternity. '*The just man liveth by faith*,' says the Apostle (Gal. iii. 11). It is faith that makes the just live in the grace of God, and that gives life to their souls, by detaching them from earthly affections, and reminding them of the eternal goods which God holds out to those who love Him.

---

1   *Devout Reflections on Various Subjects*, translated from the Italian by R. Edmund Vaughan, C. SS. R.

"St. Teresa used to say that all sins had their origin in a want of faith. Therefore, in order to overcome our passions and temptations, we must frequently revive our faith by saying: 'I believe in the life everlasting. I believe that after this life, which for me will quickly finish, there is an eternal life, either full of delights, or full of torments, which will be my lot, according to my merits or demerits.'

"St. Augustine, also, was wont to say that a man who believes in eternity, and yet is not converted to God, has lost either his reason or his faith. 'O eternity!' (these are his words) 'he that meditates upon thee, and repents not, either has no faith, or, if he has faith, he has no heart.' In reference to this, St. John Chrysostom relates that the Gentiles, when they saw Christians committing sin, called them either liars or fools."

Raise your heart to God by meditation, by mental prayer. Only in this way will your *hope,* as well as your *faith,* be maintained and kept from degenerating into presumption or despair.

The sinner often resembles the ostrich, which lives in the sandy deserts of Africa. When it is pursued it buries its head in the sand, that it may not perceive its pursuer, and imagines itself to be unseen; all too late it discovers its mistake; when the fatal bullet has inflicted a mortal wound. After a similar fashion do sinners act. They reflect not upon the mighty hunter, Death, and refuse to think of him; but this does not prevent him from coming, and his cruel arrow fails not to reach its mark. How terrible a thing it is thus to trifle with death!

Wherefore, raise your heart to God, raise it frequently to him, every morning and evening at least! Raise your heart to God in the morning, by making a firm resolution to avoid this or that besetting sin and to overcome our predominant passion. Raise it to God in the evening, by repenting of your sins, by meditating on death, judgment, heaven and hell, and by resolving to lead a more holy, a more virtuous life. Pray every night for the grace of perseverance.

> Lord, Thou hast made this wondrous soul
> All for Thyself alone;
> Ah, send Thy sweet transforming grace
> To make it more Thine own!

MENTAL PRAYER
"In my meditation a fire shall flame out" (Ps. xxxviii. 4)

MAKE at least a short *meditation* every day. *Mental prayer* is a more appropriate and comprehensive term for that spiritual exercise which is so highly praised and commended by the saints and so conducive to holiness and perfection.

Mental prayer is within the reach of all who earnestly desire their salvation. In order to pray with fruit and without distraction it is most useful and almost necessary to spend some time in *meditation* or pious reflection on some supernatural truth, and from this fact the whole exercise is often called meditation instead of mental prayer.

In mental prayer, meditation (the exercise of the intellect) is only a means to the end, which is the elevation of the soul to God—*conversation with God.* When thinking and reflecting the soul speaks to itself, reasons with itself; in prayer that follows it speaks to God. It is plain that mental prayer or meditation is something more than mere spiritual reading.

But we can easily turn our spiritual reading into a meditation, as, for instance, when we read only a few lines at a time from *The Following of Christ*; then meditate, reflect, consider our own conduct in connection with the subject treated, make devout acts and pious resolutions, and finally pray to God for His grace that we may conquer our wicked inclinations, practise some particular virtue, and lead a holy life. After this we can read a few more lines; then meditate again.

Bishop Challoner in his translation of *The Following of Christ* or *The Imitation of Christ*, as this golden book is sometime called, has added some excellent practical reflections at the end of each chapter.

"Meditation," as Madame Cecilia says in her admirable work, *At the Feet of Jesus,* "consists in occupying ourselves mentally and prayerfully with some mystery of the Faith. We call to mind the chief facts, ponder over them, and then stir up our will to regulate our conduct in consequence. Hence meditation is an exercise of the faculties of our soul—*memory, understanding*, and *will*."

"Meditation, as a part of *mental prayer*," says St. Francis of Sales, "is an attentive thought voluntarily repeated or entertained in the mind *to excite the will to holy and salutary affections and resolutions*." It differs from mere *study* in its object. We study to improve our *minds* and to store up information; we meditate to move the *will* to pray and to embrace what is good. We study that we may know; we meditate that we may pray.

"In mental prayer," says St. Alphonsus, "meditation is the needle, which only passes through that it may draw after it the golden thread, which is composed of affections, resolutions, and petitions."

As soon as you feel an impulse to pray while meditating, give way to it at once in the best way you can, by devout acts and petitions; in other words, begin your conversation with God on the subject about which you have been thinking.

In order to help the mind in this pious exercise we must have some definite subject of thought upon which it is well to read either of text of *Holy Scripture* or a few lines out of some other holy book; for instance, *The Spiritual Exercises of St. Ignatius, The Following of Christ, The Spiritual Combat*; Challoner's *Think Well On't*; St. Alphonsus Liguori's *Devout*

Reflections, The Way of Salvation, The Love of Christ, and *The Blessed Eucharist*; St. Francis of Sales' *Introduction to a Devout Life, Meditations for Retreats,* and other works; Bishop Hedley's *Retreat*; Cochem's *Meditations on the Four Last Things,* Baxter's *Meditations for Every Day in the Year*; or any one of the popular books of meditation used by Religious, such as Hamon's, De Brandt's, Segneri's, Vercruysse's, and Ilg's *Meditations on the Life and Passion of Our Lord.* Father Gallwey's *Watches of the Passion,* and Da Bergamo's *Thoughts and Affections on the Passion* are worthy of the highest commendation.

St. Alphonsus says: "It is good to meditate upon the last things—death, judgment, eternity—but let us above all meditate upon the passion of Christ." This saint, the great *Doctor of Prayer,* has given us a beautiful work on "The Passion."

St. Teresa tells us that in her meditation she helped herself with a book for seventeen years. By reading the points of a meditation from a book, the mind is rendered attentive and is set on a train of thought. Further to help the mind you can ask yourself some such questions as the following: What does this mean? What lesson does it teach me? What has been my conduct regarding this matter? What have I done, what shall I do and how shall I do it? What particular virtue must I practise? But do not forget to pray.

Do not imagine, moreover, that it is necessary to wait for a great fire to flame up in your soul, but cherish the little spark that you have got. Above all, never give way to the mistaken notion that you must restrain yourself from prayer in order to go through *all* the thoughts suggested by your book, or because your prayer does not appear to have a close connection with the subject of your meditation. This would simply be to turn from God to your own thoughts or to those of some other man.

To meditate means in general nothing else than to reflect seriously on some subject. Meditation, as *mental prayer,* is a serious reflection on some religious truth or event, united with reference and application to ourselves, in order thereby to excite in us certain serious sentiments, such as contrition, humility, faith, hope, charity, etc., and to move our will to form good resolutions conformable to these pious sentiments. Such an exercise has naturally a beneficial influence on our soul and greatly conduces to enlighten our mind and to move our will to practise virtue.

Meditation is a great means of salvation. It aids us powerfully in the pursuit of our destiny, to know God, to love Him, to serve Him, that we may be happy with Him forever; it helps us to know ourselves and to discover the means of avoiding and correcting our vices, our faults, and weaknesses; it reveals to us the dangers to which our salvation is exposed and leads us to pray with a contrite and humble heart for the necessary graces to cope with temptations, to control our passions, and to lead a holy life. Mental prayer inflames our hearts with the love of God and strengthens us to do His holy will with zeal and perseverance.

As regards the *place of meditation*, St. Alphonsus says:

"We can meditate in every place, at home or elsewhere, even in walking and at our work. How many are there who, not having any better opportunity, raise their hearts to God and apply their minds to mental prayer, without leaving their occupations, their work, or who meditate even while traveling. He who seeks God will find Him, everywhere and at all times. The most appropriate place for meditation, however, is the church, in the presence of Jesus Christ in the Blessed Sacrament."

"Not a few pious persons," says Father Girardey in his *Popular Instructions on Prayer*, "before setting out for their daily occupations, go to Mass in the early hours of the morning, make their meditation during the Holy Sacrifice, and thus draw on themselves the divine blessing for the whole day.

"As regards the *time of meditation*, it would be well if we were to make a meditation both in the morning and in the evening. If this is not feasible, we should, if convenient, prefer the morning to any other part of the day. The reason is because in the morning we are fresh in mind and have as yet hardly any cause for distractions, while later in the day we are apt to be more or less absorbed by our occupations and other worldly matters. Moreover, by a good meditation in the morning we begin the day well, drawing down God's blessing on us, and deriving grace and strength to avoid sin and fulfil our obligations. When we make our meditation in the morning, we ought to prepare its subject on the previous night before retiring to rest, and make thereon some brief reflections before falling asleep, and also after rising in the morning. We ought, moreover, to recall our meditation to mind from time to time during the day, recommending our resolution to the Blessed Virgin by a *Hail Mary*.

"We should endeavor to spend at least a quarter of an hour daily in mental prayer. The saints used daily to spend many hours therein, and when they had much to do they would subtract some hours from the time allotted to their sleep, in order to devote them to this holy exercise. If we can not spend in it half an hour every day, let us at least devote to it a quarter of an hour. The longer and the more fervent our mental prayer, the more we shall like it, and we shall learn by our own experience the truth of the saying of the Royal Prophet: "*Taste and see that the Lord is sweet*" (Ps. xxxiii. 9).

"Pope Benedict XIV granted to all the faithful making mental prayer devoutly for a whole month for at least a quarter of an hour every day, a plenary indulgence, if truly penitent, after confession and holy communion, they devoutly pray for the intentions of the Church and make a visit. This indulgence is applicable to the souls in purgatory."

As to our *petitions* and *resolutions*, Father Girardey says:

"In mental prayer it is very profitable, and perhaps more useful than any other act, to address repeated petitions to God, asking with great humility and unbounded confidence for His graces—such as His light, resignation in adversity, patience, perseverance, etc., but, above all, for the inestimable gift of His holy love. 'By obtaining divine love,' says St. Francis of Sales, 'we obtain all graces'; 'For,' says St. Alphonsus, 'he who truly loves God with all his heart will, of himself, abstain from causing Him the least displeasure, and will strive to please Him to the best of his ability.' If we feel dry or despondent and unable to meditate or pray well, let us repeat many times as earnestly as possible: '*My Jesus, mercy!*' '*Lord, for Thy mercy's sake, assist me!*' '*My God, I love Thee!*'

"Let us offer all our petitions for grace in the name and through the merits of Jesus Christ, and we shall surely obtain all that we ask. 'Mental prayer,' said a holy soul, 'is the breathing of the soul; as in corporal breathing the air is first inhaled and then exhaled, so in mental prayer the soul first receives light and other graces from God, and then by acts of self-offering and love, it gives itself wholly to Him.'

"Before concluding the meditation, we should make some specified good resolution, appropriate as far as possible to the subject of our meditation. This resolution should be directed to the shunning of some sin, of some occasion of sin, to the correction of some defect, or to the practice of some act of virtue during the day.

"The preparation of our meditation consists of (1) an act of *faith* in the presence of God, and of *adoration*; (2) an act of *humility* and of *contrition*, and (3) an act of *petition for light*. We should then recommend ourselves to the Blessed Virgin Mary by reciting a *Hail Mary*, and also to St. Joseph, to our

Guardian Angel, and to our holy patrons. These acts should be brief but very earnest and fervent.

"The conclusion of our meditation consists of these three acts: (1) thanksgiving to God for the light He imparted to us; (2) purposing to fulfil our good resolutions at once; and (3) beseeching the eternal Father, for the love of Jesus and Mary, to grant us the grace and strength to put them into practice. Before finishing our meditation let us never omit to recommend to God the souls in purgatory and poor sinners. In concluding our mental prayer let us, after the advice of St. Francis of Sales, pick out a thought or an affection from our mental prayer, in order to reflect on it or repeat it from time to time during the day."

PRAYERS FOR MEDITATION
From Madame Cecilia's "Retreat Manual"

PREPARATORY PRAYER

ACT OF THE DIVINE PRESENCE

MY GOD, I firmly believe that Thou art everywhere present and seest all things. Thou seest my nothingness, my inconstancy, my sinfulness. Thou seest me in all my actions: Thou seest me in this my meditation. I bow down before Thee, and worship Thy divine majesty with my whole being. Cleanse my heart from all vain, wicked, and distracting thoughts. Enlighten my understanding, and inflame my will, that I may pray with reverence, attention, and devotion.

PRAYER

O GOD, my Lord and my Creator, look graciously on Thy child, the work of Thy hands, and mercifully grant me the help of Thy grace, that all my intentions and acts during this meditation may be directed purely to the service and praise of Thy divine majesty, through Christ our Lord.

Offering of the Resolutions

My God, I offer Thee these resolutions; unless Thou deignest to bless them, I can not be faithful to them. From Thy goodness, then, I hope to obtain this blessing which I ask of Thee in the name and through the merits of Jesus, my divine Saviour.

Holy Virgin, Mother of my God, who art also my Mother, my good angel, and my holy patron saint, obtain for me the grace to keep these resolutions with perfect fidelity.

Ejaculatory Prayers

It would be well if every breath could be a loving sigh, and every moment be filled with the thought of God. If this can not be, form a habit of recollecting yourself from time to time; the more frequently the better. Let the striking of the hour be a signal for recalling the presence of God. Accustom yourself to the easy and frequent use of ejaculatory prayers. We need but to love in order to pray and to sigh for God. These outpourings of the heart proceed from the Holy Spirit; they are a language of love readily understood by this God of love. We naturally think of what we love; hence we can not say we love God if we rarely or never think of Him.

"Aspire to God," says St. Francis of Sales "with short but frequent outpourings of the heart."

"As those who are influenced by human and natural love have their minds and hearts constantly fixed on the objects of their affections, as they speak often in their praise, and when absent lose no opportunity of expressing by letters this affection for them, and can not even pass a tree without inscribing on the bark the name of their beloved; so those who are possessed of divine love have their minds and hearts constantly turned toward the divine object of their love; they are ever thinking of Him, they long after Him; they aspire to Him, and frequently speak of Him: and were it possible, would engrave in the hearts of all mankind the name of their beloved Jesus."

Make use of *Short Indulgenced Prayers.* Ejaculations approved by the Church are certainly most commendable.

St. Philip Neri says:

> "It is an old custom with the servants of God always to have some little prayers ready and to be darting them up to heaven frequently during the day, lifting their minds to God out of the filth of this world. He who adopts this plan will get great fruit with little pains."

43. A Place of Healing for Souls

THERE is a wondrous fountain of health—a marvelous place of healing for souls, which derives its efficacy from the precious blood of Jesus Christ; it is the sacrament of Penance. May you ever be filled in an increasing degree with veneration, and, I had almost said, with holy enthusiasm, for this place of healing for souls.

Picture to yourself a man who, having committed a grievous sin, knows nothing of the sacrament of Penance. He looks into himself, is conscious of the magnitude of his transgression, and the wretched state into which he has fallen. With sighs and groans he exclaims: "How happy I was, in the paradise of innocence! How pure was my soul, on which the heavenly Father's eye looked with pleasure! With what joy and confidence I prayed to Him! How peacefully my days passed, how I rejoiced in the house of my God, on the heart of my Saviour, under the mantle of my dearest Mother Mary, and how brightly there shone from heaven the crown of everlasting glory!

"But now everything is lost; my soul is as hideous as a moldering corpse! And I behold hell open, threatening each moment to swallow me up! Alas! who can help me, what deliverance is possible?"

If an angel from heaven were to appear to this wretched man and assure him that God was ready to pardon all his transgressions, and preserve him from hell, to receive him as His child and admit him to heaven, under this one condition—that he should truly and sincerely repent of his sins and penitently confess them to God's representative—with what joy, with what gratitude, would such a sinner hail the message, and do everything in his power to render himself a worthy recipient of this pardon! This gives you an idea of the rare and, at times, intense, exuberant delight which sincere penitents experience when they return from the confessional—the place of healing for souls.

On this point hear the testimony, not of a holy or specially favored soul, but of a soldier. Yes, it was a soldier, an officer, who had attended one of the sermons preached at a mission given in Paris by Father Brydaine and then had made his confession to him. Afterward he followed him into the sacristy, and spoke thus before all the bystanders: "The king of France with all his treasures, and riches, and pleasures, can not be as happy and contented as I am now. Never in my whole life have I experienced such peace and contentment, such pure, such unalloyed joy and satisfaction as I feel at this present moment."

My dear young friend, if you never, or but rarely, have felt such sensible consolation after you have been to confession, it is no sign that your confession was not a good one. If you have made it with all due seriousness and contrition, you may rest assured that God has forgiven your sins, and bestowed abundant graces upon you.

Thus the sacrament of Penance is, in very deed, the fountain of life, the medicine of salvation, the death of sin, the place of healing for souls, the beginning of all that is good. O blessed Penance, what marvelous change does it effect! That which was lost is found again, that which was spoiled is made new again, that which was dead is restored to life.

All is won, all is saved, for the truly contrite soul, which through the power of this sacrament has regained the friendship of God, and has become once more a child of God and joint heir with Jesus Christ of the kingdom of heaven.

> Have you sinned as none else in the world have before you?
>   Are you blacker than all other creatures in guilt?
> O fear not! O fear not! the mother that bore you
>   Loves you less than the Saviour whose blood you have spilt!
>
> O come, then, to Jesus, and say how you love Him,
>   And swear at His feet you will keep in His grace:
> For one tear that is shed by a sinner can move Him,
>   And your sins will drop off in His tender embrace.
>
> Then come to His feet, and lay open your story
>   Of suffering and sorrow, of guilt and of shame;
> For the pardon of sin is the crown of His glory,
>   And the joy of Our Lord to be true to His name.
>   —Oratory Hymns.

44. Is Confession Difficult?

YOU, my young friend, may belong to the number of those who reply without a moment's hesitation in the affirmative to the question which stands at the head of this chapter. You perhaps consider confession to be a heavy burden. But listen to the opinion expressed on this subject by a famous French poet. I refer to Francis Coppée, whose varied talent is justly admired. He received a Christian education, and for some time subsequently to his first communion performed his religious duties with fervor. But after a few years the errors of youth, and his aversion to confess certain misdeeds, changed this pious frame of mind. Bad books, bad example, and evil associates did the rest, and caused him to become absolutely indifferent to religion.

But serious illness, which prostrated him for years on a bed of suffering, opened the eye of his soul and brought him to sincere conversion—to a truly Christian disposition. He described this change in one of his own works entitled *La bonne souffrance*, or "Happy Suffering." In it are details concerning confession, prayer, and suffering, which are truly sublime and admirable, evincing a depth of thought which could only be expected from an experienced writer on spiritual subjects. Especially to be admired is the subjoined eulogy of confession.

"Surprising and most wonderful," thus run his words, "is the mysterious power of the sacrament of Penance. In it alone does the tortured heart find the consolation which it has elsewhere sought in vain. The world would unreservedly acknowledge the tremendous significance of confession, did not the grossest ignorance and darkest prejudice prevent a clearer insight into the matter.

"Unhappy man, who at every step you take sink deeper under the heavy burden which weighs upon your conscience, come hither, lay aside your false shame. Your apprehensions are groundless, you need not fear that the stranger whom you have chosen for your confidant will betray your dark secret. Speak, therefore, without reserve; confess your whole guilt to him.

"He will answer you with fatherly love, he will only speak of mercy and pardon. As a matter of course he will require you to make reparation for the wrong you have done. Should this be no longer possible, your compunction of heart and your honest confession will be sufficient for him. For your penance he will tell you to repeat certain short prayers, he will raise his hands and pronounce some brief formulas in Latin. You will then depart, freed from your guilt, and as happy as if you had already joined the angelic host."

Now tell me, do these words sound as if confession were a difficult matter, as if it were an intolerable load? On the contrary, the remarkable man who wrote these admirable lines regards it as a great happiness, a blessed privilege to be eagerly desired, that we are allowed to go to confession.

And so indeed it is. Confession only appears difficult to those who do not understand it at all, or whose knowledge is very limited. Therefore I will now proceed to give a few hints as to the right way to make your confession.

Before all things be careful not to make your confession in a mechanical and perfunctory manner. Do your very utmost to awaken a true and heartfelt contrition. That is the principal thing, even if you have only venial sins to confess. And it is not difficult to awaken this true contrition out of love to your crucified Redeemer, and with the assistance of divine grace, which at such times will never fail to come to your aid.

In regard to self-accusation, if it is a question of venial sins alone, do not make things out to be worse than they are in reality. But bear in mind that the value of any confession depends not so much on the completeness with which all little sins and slight imperfections are enumerated, but on the thoroughness of the contrition which is felt, and the strength of the determination to avoid in future both every mortal sin and also every besetting sin or fault to which you are addicted.

Especially observe the following rules:

(a) Never make your confession in too vague a manner, without a definite statement. Do not confuse temptations and sinful inclinations with definite sins.

(b) Do not accustom yourself to enter into details respecting the smallest imperfections, and at the same time, perhaps to pass over certain bad habits and besetting sins. It is far more necessary to lay greater stress upon those faults to abstain from which the voice of God more especially warns you.

(c) After your confession is finished, do not immediately return to your ordinary occupations, nor engage in distracting conversation. Rather let your mind dwell on your good resolutions, and be intent on thanking God from the bottom of your hear for the benefits He has conferred on you.

Follow these rules and you will make a good confession, and confession will seem less difficult to you. Finally, go to confession *regularly* and *frequently*.

Father Von Doss, in his admirable *Thoughts and Counsels for Young Men*, says truly:

> "To receive the sacraments of Penance and the blessed Eucharist only at Easter-time, is to reduce your Catholicity to a minimum, to hang on to the Church, as it were, by the last thread.
>
> "The oftener we go to confession, the easier it becomes. The longer we stay away, the more difficult it is to discover our faults, the more awkward we become in this important business. God grant that this awkwardness and helplessness on the bed of death may not be followed by the most terrible consequences!
>
> "Make the trial. Go to confession often—at least once a month. You will see that it becomes easier with every repetition.
>
> "O my God! I often grieve and lament in secret over the weakness and inconstancy of my heart! Miserable, almost despairing, I look down into the Abyss, to whose verge my sinful passions have dragged me, and I regard myself as lost. I am so utterly the sport of the surging waves, that I fail to struggle against them.
>
> "Vain lamentations! Cowardice! Folly! I can swim up the stream, and bring the waves to a standstill—not by a mere passive looking on, or wringing of my hands; not by an unmanly surrender of myself—but by a faithful employment of those means which He who has created me has placed before me.
>
> "I can escape the abyss which threatens to engulf me—but it is only by repeatedly casting myself into Thy arms, O my God, and by clinging to Thee."
>
> "*A preservation from stumbling, and a help from falling: he raiseth up the soul, and enlighteneth the eyes, and giveth health, and life, and blessing*" (Ecclus. xxxiv. 20).

45. THE TABLE OF THE LORD

THE watchword of these modern times is progress. For instance, no one works any longer by the light of a candle or of a feeble oil lamp; we employ gas or the electric light; no one journeys to Rome on foot, but travels by railway. Progress ought also to reign in the domain of piety and holiness—progress in the use of the means of grace and sanctification. This applies more especially to young people. For in these modern times occasions of sin are so very numerous, dangers to morality so extremely threatening, the attractions and amusements of the world so bewitching, bad examples so enticing, that a young man can hardly be expected to resist them, if he is unwilling to do more than what is absolutely required of him—if he fails to go to confession and to receive holy communion frequently during the year. Let progress be your motto in this respect—progress in the more frequent reception of the sacraments. Draw near, therefore, to the Table of the Lord, in order that you may obtain light to perceive what you ought to do and strength to do the right; grace to avoid sin, and courage to walk persistently in the way of virtue and perfection!

But how often ought you to approach the Table of the Lord? In 1849 Peter Perboir, a missionary priest, met with a martyr's death in China for the sake of Christ. Since the time when he made his first communion he had remained faithful to his resolution that he would receive this food of the soul, the bread of Angels, every month, and the chief feasts of the Church. His devotion on these occasions was so striking, that he seemed to be an angel when he knelt at the altar rails. And it was from this frequent reception of holy communion that he gained strength to become a missionary, and die a martyr's death.

If you are not called to such things as these you nevertheless need strength from above—whatever state of life you may choose—in order to wage a relentless war against the world, the devil, and the concupiscence of our flesh. Seek it, as that saintly missionary did, in frequent communion—in daily, weekly, fortnightly, or at least *monthly* communion. Make it your fixed resolution to approach the Table of the Lord once at least every month; or if this is not possible, not to postpone this sacred duty for more than six or eight weeks. If your circumstances are such that your confessor urges upon you to go to communion once a week, or once a fort-night, follow his wise direction with alacrity.

But many objections are brought forward against the frequent reception of the Eucharist. In the first place it is said that in earlier times people did not communicate frequently, and yet they saved their souls; why should not this custom still prevail?

I reply that, on the contrary, in the first centuries of Christianity it was the universal custom for every one, including grown-up men, and youths also, to receive communion every day.

In the second place you may perhaps say that you are not pious enough to communicate so frequently. But remember that holy communion was instituted not so much for saints as for sinners, just as the physician is wanted not so much for those who are in health, as for the sick and the ailing.

A third objection which you bring forward is that if you go so frequently to communion, you must pull a long face, and never indulge in merriment. Never be merry any more! My dear young friend, it is just the truly pious people—I mean all who seek to keep themselves constantly in a state of grace—who are the most cheerful persons in the world: God grant that your own experience may convince you that such is the truth. "A clear conscience is a soft pillow."

A fourth objection which you bring forward is that if you go to communion so frequently you will find nothing more to confess! So much the better: it is just that which ought to be the result of frequent communion. On the other hand, this will make you able to perceive even lesser failings, so that you will have more to confess than you formerly had.

A fifth objection you may make is that however often you go to confession and communion, you do not improve in the least! Now tell me, how long have you observed the custom of daily or frequent communion? A whole year? Yes. And, of course, you always approached the Holy Table in the proper disposition—with a right intention. In that case, my friend, it is impossible that you can have remained the same, just as impossible as it would be for you to remain cold when sitting close to a blazing fire. Imperceptibly, perhaps, but nevertheless surely, you will make spiritual progress; you will grow in holiness by receiving daily or frequently in your soul The Most Holy God—just as your body grows, though you do not observe it, when you take your meals daily. The Council of Trent calls the Eucharist "the antidote whereby we are delivered from daily faults and preserved from deadly sins."

A sixth objection is thus expressed by you: "I do not like to go to confession." Well, then, go without liking it. No doubt all who go to confession have the same feeling; no one finds a natural pleasure in the act. But no one, for instance, only works just as much is he likes. And if people give themselves immense trouble and wear themselves out for the sake of earthly gain, ought not one to make the trifling exertion which is necessary in order to go frequently to communion for the sake of one's immortal soul and one's eternal happiness? The best things in life are achieved through sacrifice and self-denial. And indeed we ought to be very grateful to God for the easy means He, in His infinite mercy, has given us through the sacrament of Penance to be reconciled to Him after our grievous and frequent lapses into sin.

Lay aside, therefore, your vain fears and specious pretexts, conquer your love of ease, and hasten—hasten frequently—to the fountain of grace which flows forth in inexhaustible fullness from the sacred Heart of Jesus in the Most Blessed Sacrament.

> Flesh of Christ, hail, sweet oblation,
> Pledge and foretaste of salvation;
> Let me forsake all earthly toys
> And only long for heavenly joys.

Veni, Domine Jesu

O Jesus, hidden God, I cry to Thee;
O Jesus, hidden Light, I turn to Thee;
O Jesus, hidden Love, I run to Thee;
With all the strength I have I worship Thee;
With all the love I have I cling to Thee;
With all my soul I long to be with Thee,
And fear no more to fail, or fall from Thee.

O Jesus, deathless Love, who seekest me,
Thou who didst die for longing love of me,
Thou King, in all Thy beauty, come to me,
White-robed, blood-sprinkled, Jesus, come to me,
And go no more, dear Lord, away from me.

O sweetest Jesus, bring me home to Thee;
Free me, O dearest God, from all but Thee,
And all the chains that keep me back from Thee;
Call me, O thrilling Love, I follow Thee;
Thou art my All, and I love nought but Thee.

O hidden Love, who now art loving me;
O wounded Love, who once wast dead for me:
O patient Love, who weariest not of me—
O bear with me till I am lost in Thee;
O bear with me till I am found in Thee.

—Fr. Rawes.

HOLY COMMUNION[1]

FREQUENT and daily communion, as a thing most earnestly desired by Christ our Lord and by the Catholic Church, should be open to all the faithful, of whatever rank and condition of life; so that no one who is in the state of grace, and who approaches the Holy Table with a right and devout intention, can lawfully be hindered therefrom.

A right intention consists in this: that he who approaches the Holy Table should do so, not out of routine, or vainglory, or human respect, but for the purpose of pleasing God, or being more closely united with Him by charity, and of seeking this divine remedy for his weaknesses and defects.

Although it is more expedient that those who communicate frequently or daily should be free from venial sins, especially from such as are fully deliberate, and from any affection thereto, nevertheless it is sufficient that they be free from mortal sin, with the purpose of never sinning mortally in future; and, if they have this sincere purpose, it is impossible but that daily communicants should gradually emancipate themselves from even venial sins, and from all affection thereto.

But whereas the sacraments of the New Law, though they take effect *ex opere operato,* nevertheless produce a greater effect in proportion as the dispositions of the recipient are better; therefore care is to be taken that holy communion be preceded by serious preparation, and followed by a suitable thanksgiving according to each one's strength, circumstances, and duties.

That the practice of frequent and daily communion may be carried out with greater prudence and more abundant merit, the confessor's advice should be asked. Confessors, however, are to be careful not to dissuade any one (*ne quemquam avertant*) from frequent and daily communion, provided that he is in a state of grace and approaches with a right intention.

---

1   Extract from the *Pontifical Decree on Daily Communion.*—Pius X, 1905.

"If the world asks you why you communicate so often, say you do so in order to learn how to love God; to purify yourself from your imperfections, to deliver yourself from your miseries, to seek for consolations in your trials, and to strengthen yourself in your weakness."   —St. Francis of Sales.

"This sacrament is the gift of gifts and the grace of graces. When the almighty and eternal God comes to us, with all the perfections of His thrice holy humanity and His divinity, He surely does not come empty-handed. Provided that you have proved yourself, as the apostle enjoins, He remits your temporal punishment, strengthens you against temptation, weakens the power of your enemies and increases your merits."
                —St. Angela of Foligno.

"The Eucharist heals the maladies of the soul. It strengthens it against temptation. It deadens the ardor of concupiscence. It incorporates us with Jesus Christ."   —St. Cyril of Alexandria.

"Do you wish to love God sincerely, . . . to maintain in your heart the divine and eternal life of Jesus Christ? Communicate *often* and regularly."   —De Ségur.

"One of the most admirable effects of holy communion is to preserve souls from falling, and to help those who fall from weakness to rise again; therefore it is much more profitable frequently to approach this divine sacrament with love, respect, and confidence than to keep back from an excess of fear and cowardice."   —St. Ignatius.

"To communicate every day, and partake of the sacred body and blood of Christ is a most beautiful and profitable practice, for He has clearly said: '*He who eateth My flesh and drinketh My blood, hath everlasting life.*' "   —St. Basil.

"O sacred banquet, in which Christ is received, the memory of His passion is renewed, the mind is filled with grace, and a pledge of future glory is given to us."   —St. Thomas,
Office of the Blessed Sacrament.

"The fruit we ought to derive from holy communion consists in being transformed into the likeness of Jesus Christ. We must endeavor to render ourselves like Him throughout the whole course of our lives; to be as He was, chaste, meek, humble, patient, obedient."   —Rodriguez.

"The body of the Lord is eaten, and the blood - the Lord is received in memory of Our Lord's obedience unto death, that they who live may live no longer to themselves, but to Him who died and rose again for them."   —St. Basil the Great.

46. TRUTH ABOVE ALL

THIS world is a place where truth and falsehood dwell side by side. In the beginning truth alone existed. But the devil, who in Paradise told the first lie, introduced lying into the world.

Truth is frequently compelled to retire into the secret chamber of an honest man's heart; but falsehood stalks proudly among men, haughtily raises its insolent head, triumphs, and diffuses on all sides its poisonous and diabolical doctrines. How stately is the tree of falsehood, how widespread are its branches, how inviting is their shade, how enticing are its fruits! Thoroughly does falsehood understand how everywhere to flatter, to make itself beloved, to win the favor or men.

You, dear reader, are still young and inexperienced, but has it not often struck you that a man who is proficient in the arts of deception, intrigue, flattery, and lying, and who, as is generally the case, possesses, in addition, a ready tongue, can talk glibly, and make things go on all fours, that such a man gains his ends and gets his own way, while another who keeps to the truth, to the plain and unvarnished truth, very often comes out worst?

But do not allow yourself to be deceived by the success of false and untruthful men; whether it last for a longer or shorter period, let not its dazzling appearance blind you. For, indeed, lying may triumph and carry on its diabolical trade for a very long time, but it will not prosper forever; there will certainly come a time, be it sooner or later, when it will be shamefully exposed, and profoundly humiliated; it will be compelled itself to bear witness to the much hated truth.

Then away with all falsehood out of the heart, all deceitfulness from the tongue! Away with all the tricks, wiles, and artifices of the false world! Away with hypocrisy, flattery, cunning, duplicity, as all these children of hell are called! Take to your heart Truth, the gentle, lovable, but too often misjudged daughter of heaven, with all the charming virtues which follow in her train!

Yes, choose this daughter of heaven for your friend and constant companion throughout your life. Let her modesty, sweetness, and amiability inspire you and fill you with enthusiasm! Let your motto always be *Truth above all!*

An honest, upright, straightforward man is a universal favorite. No one can tolerate a liar and a deceiver; he is despised and avoided. Even when he speaks the truth he is not believed.

How often one hears it said: "Such and such a one is not to be trusted; he is one mass of lies and falsehood." Would you like to have a character such as this? And the words of Holy Scripture are, and will remain true: "*A lie is a foul blot in a man.*" Therefore truth above all! Avoid every kind of lie!

Nor allow yourself to be ever persuaded into any kind of dissimulation. Remember the aged Eleazar, who was urged to deny his faith by eating pork: "*His friends desired that flesh might be brought which it was lawful for him to eat, that he might pretend that he had eaten, as the king had commanded.*" But the old man replied: "*It doth not become our age to dissemble.*" Indeed it does not become the old man to dissemble, nor the young man either, nor even a child.

If a young man behaves in a friendly manner to any one's face, but in his heart hates and despises this person, and ridicules him in secret, he plays the part of a hypocrite. In a similar manner did Judas salute and kiss the divine Redeemer on the Mount of Olives, as if he were His closest friend, while by so doing he was guilty of shameful ingratitude and disgraceful treachery.

Truth above all! On this account never allow yourself to be persuaded to fawn upon and flatter any one. The temptation to flatter comes ready to hand when you have to do with people whose favor may be advantageous to you, and whose dislike on the contrary may prove injurious. Avoid extravagant praise of any one's qualities, and never pay compliments which you do not seriously mean. Adhere to the truth!

You may perhaps object and say: "These are evil times; it is not possible to get on without deceit and dissimulation!" But has God changed and altered His commands to please those who lie and cheat? Has He given permission to lie for the sake of gain? But all act in this manner! But if all really do lie and offend God, ought we for this reason to do the same?

No, hold fast this principle: *Truth above all*—and see that you carry it out. And if sometimes, or even frequently, you suffer defeat with your friend, Truth, and this pains and troubles you very much; yet in spite of all never separate yourself from this friend. Remain true to her both in life and in death, and certainly—as certainly as there is a God in heaven—you will conquer with her, and triumph over your enemies and her own "*Magna est veritas et prævalebit!*" "Truth is mighty and will prevail!"

> Let no thought or word of guile
> My heart and lips defile;
> Upright thus in all my ways
> God's goodness I will praise.

47. BE FAITHFUL TO YOUR FRIENDS

THERE is a love which ought to fill your youthful heart, dear reader—that love which is higher, nobler, more sublime than all which earth can offer; that love which restores to the heart the paradise it has lost, that love which comes from heaven and leads to heaven, a pure, holy, unending love—in a word, that true and supreme love which the chosen soul feels for God, her creator, her Redeemer, the only worthy object of an all-embracing, all-surpassing love.

For this love is the heart of man created, and this love ought to inflame your soul.

But be on your guard! For sooner or later, with more or less force, another love will awaken within your breast—a love which, it is true, is not essentially evil, but which is not so elevating, so noble, so holy—a mere earthly love, the love of creatures. You must be very careful that this love should also come from God, be in accordance with the will of God, and be firmly rooted in God.

This applies to the love of one's friends. Let it be real and elevating, and, above all, faithful. The virtue of justice requires that you should be faithful to your friend.

But is it at all proper and desirable to entertain a friendship of this nature? There are not wanting those who assert that one ought not to cherish any particular friendship, or special affection and liking for any one in particular; that in this way the heart is too much engrossed, and the mind too much distracted. But I say that as long as you remain in the midst of an evil world, surrounded by its dangers, temptations, and attractions, it will be useful and profitable for you to maintain and cherish a true and real friendship.

Young people who are in the wide and dangerous world find themselves in a position similar to that of those who climb the treacherous ice-fields of lofty mountains. What steps do they take for mutual protection and rescue in case their lives should be in danger! They are roped together, in order that if one should make a false step, or if the ice should give way under his feet, the others may hold him up, and thus preserve him from death.

Your case will be the same. It will be easier for you to avoid dangers and save your soul if you are united to others in a pious friendship, which is pleasing to God and which is a source of mutual encouragement and support in the practice of virtue.

Certainly it is right to maintain a true friendship. We learn this from the example of the saints, and from that of the Holiest of the holy, Jesus Christ Himself. How deep and tender was His affection for St. John, His favorite apostle, and how He loved Lazarus and Mary and Martha of Bethania!

Moreover, history tells us that St. Peter loved St. Mark with deep affection, and that not less did St. Paul love St. Timothy. St. Gregory of Nazianzen was united to St. Basil by the closest bonds of friendship, also St. Augustine with St. Ambrose, and so on.

But never, in all the records of friendship, can history point to one which equals in faithfulness and unselfish devotion that of Jonathan, the son of Saul. Jonathan knew that David had been chosen by God to inherit the scepter of Saul, and yet he remained absolutely free from jealousy, and even defended his friend with heroic zeal against the hatred of his own father. Beautiful—truly sublime—are the vows which they exchanged; tender and true—beyond death and the grave—was the love which they showed to one another.

Therefore, do you also seek to find a friend, but seek him among your equals, among young men of your own age, and only one who is likely to encourage, and not to hinder you in the practice of virtue. And if you have found such a friend, give thanks to God, and remain faithful to this friend, alike in prosperity and in adversity.

Remain faithful to him as did a certain young artist who wrote to his friend, a famous painter, as follows: "You, as an angel or strength and consolation, have interposed between my self and my passions; when you are near me I feel better and calmer, and as long as you are with me the influences which drag us all down to earth have no power over me. Your gentle restraint and warm encouragement, which I shall never forget, always exerted a most beneficial effect upon me, shedding a ray of pure light upon my soul and dispelling the heavy clouds which darkened my mind."

How good a thing it is to love, while still on earth, as the blessed do in heaven—while yet in this world to hold one another dear and precious, in the same way as we shall hold each other dear and precious when we get to heaven.

Remember the beautiful words of Holy Scripture: "*Nothing can be compared to a faithful friend, and no weight of gold and silver is able to countervail the goodness of his fidelity. A faithful friend is the medicine of life and immortality, and they that fear the Lord shall find him*" (Ecclus. vi. 15, 16). Do you therefore fear the Lord, so that you may find a faithful friend. And such a friend is portrayed in the following lines:

> A friend who with affection true
> Holds up a mirror to your view,
> Shows your conduct, scruples not
> To point out every flaw and blot;
> Who chides you when you go astray
> Diverging from the narrow way,
> Counsels, exhorts, a friend indeed
> Is he, the very friend you need.

48. To Every One His Own

"CUIQUE SUUM!" "To every one his own!" is an ancient maxim of justice. But in the present day it appears to become more and more antiquated and disregarded, and this is one of the principal causes of the deplorable social conditions of modern times.

Some years ago, a very important lawsuit was instituted in Vienna against one of the most prominent financiers. He was accused of embezzlement on a large scale. Counsel for the defendant brought forward, in order to excuse him, the saying that "a man in business nowadays can not afford to be scrupulous, if he aims to make a large fortune," or one can not build a great system of railways with the moral law. In plain and intelligible language this is the same as saying: "in undertakings where it is a question of making money, one must not be too particular. The Ten Commandments have nothing to do with the matter, nor the eternal and immutable laws of right and wrong; against deception, embezzlement, and robbery, they must all be suspended. Away with the antiquated saying: 'To every one his own.' " This is nowadays the rule of conduct in regard to commercial transactions for very many individuals, both on a small and an extensive scale. But to the number of these persons, you, dear reader, must not in any case belong, but you will at all times uphold the first principle of Christian justice: "*Cuique suum*"—"To every one his own!"

Therefore it is a matter of course that you should, before all things, and under all circumstances, remain absolutely faithful to this principle: never in any position of life to appropriate the smallest sum which does not justly belong to you—not a nickel, not even a cent.

Certainly the most indispensable thing for a young man, if he is to prosper in the world is that it can be said of him with truth: "He is absolutely honest: thoroughly upright and trustworthy." Remember the proverbs:

"Unjust gain will bring you pain!"

"No legacy so rich as honesty!"

"Better disaster than dishonor—'tis shorter lived!"

"We are bound to be honest, but not bound to be rich."

"Let Falsehood laugh! Honesty has a heaven all its own."

"Who is the honest man?
He that doth still and strongly good pursue,
To God, his neighbor, and himself most true;
Whom neither force nor fawning can
Unpin, or wrench from giving all their due."
—Herbert.

Therefore:

Give to every one his due
Unto death be honest and true!

Furthermore, it is your duty as a Christian, according to the measure of your age and position, to oppose the hostile division which at the present time eats ever more and more into the heart of human society. Selfishness and unjust exploiting of the poorer classes by the rich and highly placed on the one side, and discontent, hatred, and envy on the other side, namely that of the poor, have brought about this division of society into two hostile camps.

But nothing is so opposed to the spirit of Christianity as this division. The Redeemer desired to break down that wall of separation, and to unite all nations and all classes, as children of the same Father, in one great family of God. He did not remove the differences of nations, stations, and classes. But the difference was to resemble that which exists between the harmonious members of one and the same body, not a separation of hostile elements.

Then again, you ought to look without envy at the greater prosperity of others. If you are animated by true Christian faith, this will not appear so difficult to you. Behold Christ Himself! He, as Our Lord, might have chosen riches, honor, and pleasures to any extent whatever, and mark it well, he could have done this without casting a shadow of sin upon His earthly career—yet He preferred to choose for Himself poverty, contempt, and suffering.

If Our Lord viewed things in this light, every Christian—and you also, as a Christian—must do the same. If Christ said: "*Woe to you that are rich,*" that is to say, woe to those whose hearts cling to riches, then ought the man who does not belong to the upper ten thousand, but earns his bread by means of his toil, look rather with thankfulness to God than with envy and dislike at the classes which are more liberally endowed with the goods of this world. This signifies nothing else except to practise, even in thought, the principle:

"To every one his own," and the precept of brotherly love.

Truly, my friend, if you are obliged to pass your days in strenuous toil, in straitened circumstances, your rebel nature may incite you to discontent, to envy and covetousness. But beware of yielding to this temptation.

For envy and discontent gradually deprive those who indulge in them of the grace of God, and render them unable to enjoy such harmless pleasures as may come in their way. Discontent and covetousness embitter all enjoyment.

But, as I just said, if you are indeed animated by true Christian faith, this envy will be unable to find place in your heart. It may indeed knock at the door, but it can not enter and gain a firm footing there. The shield of faith, the helmet of hope, the breastplate of justice, will ward off these poisonous darts, so that they may not be able to inflict a mortal wound upon the heart.

Be content to play an insignificant part on this world's stage, and by your uprightness and honesty to secure for yourself one day an imperishable reward in heaven. Do not grudge to others a part which is frequently the occasion of eternal perdition. Let every one have his own, give to every one his due, and God will be your reward.

> Friend, be upright, honest, true;
> Give to every one his due;
> Happiness can not be gained
> By what is wrongfully obtained.

SUB TUUM PRAESIDIUM

WE FLY to thy patronage, O holy Mother of God; despise not our petitions in our necessities, but deliver us always from all dangers, O glorious and blessed Virgin. Amen.

THE ANGELUS

*This prayer is traditionally said at 6AM, Noon, and 6PM with at least one person leading (V) and at least one person responding (R). All should be kneeling and a bell should be rung. During Paschaltide, it is replaced by the **Regina Coeli**.*

V. The Angel of the Lord declared unto Mary.

R. And she conceived of the Holy Ghost.

   Hail Mary...

V. Behold the handmaid of the Lord.

R. Be it done unto me according to thy word.

   Hail Mary...

V. And the Word was made Flesh.

R. And dwelt among us.

   Hail Mary...

V. Pray for us, O Holy Mother of God.

R. That we may be made worthy of the promises of Christ.

LET US PRAY: Pour forth, we beseech Thee, O Lord, Thy grace into our hearts; that, we to whom the Incarnation of Christ, Thy Son, was made known by the message of an Angel, may by His Passion and Cross, be brought to the glory of His Resurrection. Through the same Christ our Lord. Amen.

ADORO TE DEVOTE
(HYMN OF ST. THOMAS AQUINAS)

O GODHEAD hid, devoutly I adore Thee,
Who truly art within the forms before me;
To Thee my heart I bow with bended knee,
As failing quite in contemplating Thee.

Sight, touch, and taste in Thee are each deceived;
The ear alone most safely is believed.
I believe all the Son of God has spoken:
Than Truth's own word there is no truer token.

God only on the Cross lay hid from view,
But here lies hid at once the manhood too:
And I, in both professing my belief,
Make the same prayer as the repentant thief.

Thy wounds, as Thomas saw, I do not see;
Yet Thee confess my Lord and God to be.
Make me believe Thee ever more and more,
In Thee my hope, in Thee my love to store.

O Thou, memorial of our Lord's own dying!
O living bread, to mortals life supplying!
Make Thou my soul henceforth on Thee to live;
Ever a taste of heavenly sweetness give.

O loving Pelican! O Jesu Lord!
Unclean I am, but cleanse me in Thy Blood:
Of which a single drop, for sinners spilt,
Can purge the entire world from all its guilt.

Jesu! whom for the present veiled I see,
What I so thirst for, oh, vouchsafe to me:
That I may see Thy countenance unfolding,
And may be blest Thy glory in beholding. Amen.

The Girdle

of Self Control

The Girdle of Self-Control

49. Deny Thyself

WHAT remarkable words are those which St. Paul addressed to the Corinthians: "*I chastise my body and bring it into subjection, lest perhaps when I have preached to others, I myself should become a castaway.*" Thus we see that it is possible for a man who had converted entire nations to the Christian faith to lose his soul if he did not keep his body in strict subjection. This severity in regard to the body is to no one more necessary than to the young man. How is this?

Behold, two rival hosts are opposed to one another in war. That one which, by superior courage and bravery, destroys the other, or puts it to flight, is the victor. In a similar manner do evil inclinations and sinful desire, which are opposed to the law of God, stir within the heart of the young man. If, during the period of youth, these inclinations and desires are resisted and overcome—that is to say, are not indulged and yielded to—then will the body itself gradually become less unruly and finally quite tame. But he, on the contrary, who permits himself to be carried away by sensual desires while he is young will find it more difficult every year to resist them.

In regard to this self-control and self-denial, lay to heart the words of the Redeemer: "*If any man will come after Me, let him deny himself.*" Do not these words teach us, with no uncertain utterance, that without self-denial it is not possible to follow Christ? Or how can you imitate Jesus Christ, live in accordance with His teaching, and at the same time do that which flatters sensuality, and is pleasing to the corrupt desires of the heart? Never can you do this, for here we may quote what Christ has said in another place: *"No man can serve two masters."* To be zealous and faithful in the service of Jesus Christ and at the same time to indulge the flesh, and follow the pernicious maxims of the world, is sheer impossibility; it is equally impossible to turn to the east, and at the same time to face the west.

Do not therefore take alarm, my dear young friend, if I earnestly exhort you to learn how to practise self-denial and renunciation. Every one of those lawful pleasures, so dear to the young, shall be permitted you, but I only wish to keep far from you those which might do you harm, for I am full of affectionate solicitude for your welfare.

Wherein are you to deny yourself, what are you to renounce? The answer is brief and sums thus: First of all you are to renounce whatever is forbidden; you must refuse it, and hold yourself entirely aloof from it. But among all those things which are forbidden, I will here make a brief mention of only three—things which young people in the present day are most unwilling to renounce and deny themselves, but which forge, for the rising generation, iron fetters of the most degrading slavery, and indeed threaten to precipitate them into the yawning abyss of moral and material ruin. These three things are: inordinate love of pleasure, the lust of the flesh, and covetousness or greed of money; renounce them all.

Renounce the love of pleasure. This is in a very special manner the plague of these times. Eating and drinking, pleasure trips, picnics, balls, concerts, and theaters—after such things does the greater number of young men in the present day yearn and strive. Everywhere we hear the piteous cry that young people no longer care to work, but only to enjoy themselves; and the plague of this inordinate love of pleasure no longer dwells in cities only, but spreads more and more in country districts, and even extends its ravage to remote villages. Do you, my friend, take heed while yet there is time; beware of indulging this love of pleasure.

Renounce, moreover, the lust of the flesh. If love of enjoyment wields the scepter, it is no marvel if other vices become more prevalent, if sins against holy purity are more frequently committed; the former is the cause of the latter. To this end contribute also the universal hankering after luxury, instability of faith, immoral reading, indecent pictures, statues, and engravings, dread of work, idleness, and bad examples.

Renounce in the third place the insatiable greed of money. This is closely connected with the love of pleasure. For he who is determined to enjoy himself, to indulge all his desires, must have money, must find a way of getting it in any manner whatsoever. Hence comes the striving and struggling, the longing and reaching after money and goods, which rules the mind, turning it away from God and divine things, and chaining it to the wretched dust of earth.

Renounce it, conquer yourself! Do this at first in little things. For you know that he who desires to fit himself for military service must first participate in many minor maneuvers. The same principle applies to the spiritual warfare.

Without continual conquest of self, without constant self-denial, no other virtue, no true happiness, can be attained. "The greater violence thou offerest to thyself, the greater progress thou wilt make," says the author of the *Imitation*. You must take upon yourself, day by day, the cross of self-denial, of renunciation, not only in order to live an upright life, but also in order to be happy.

To conquer himself the Christian is bound,
But what a difficult task this is found!
The battle is long, the struggle is sore;
The victor's guerdon is joy evermore.

50. Take Up Thy Cross

T HE gentle author of the *Imitation* says:

To many this seemeth a hard saying—'*Deny thyself, take up thy cross, and follow me.*' But it will be much harder to hear that last word; '*Depart* from Me, ye cursed, into everlasting fire.' For they who now love to hear and follow the word of the cross shall not then fear the sentence of eternal condemnation. This sign of the cross shall be in heaven, then the Lord shall come to judge. Then all the servants of the cross, who in their lifetime have conformed themselves to Him that was crucified, shall come to Christ their Judge with great confidence.

Why, then, art thou afraid to take up the cross, which leadeth to the kingdom? In the cross is salvation; in the cross is strength of mind; in the cross is joy of spirit. There is no health of soul, nor hope of eternal life, but in the cross.

Take up, therefore, thy cross, and follow Jesus, and thou shalt go into life everlasting. He is gone before thee carrying His cross; and He died for thee upon the cross that thou mayst also bear thy cross and love to die on the cross. Because if thou die with Him thou shalt also live with Him, and if thou art His companion in suffering thou shalt also partake in His glory (2 Cor. i. 7).

Behold the cross is all, and in dying to thyself all consists, and there is no other way to life and to true internal peace but the holy way of the cross and of daily mortification. Go where thou wilt, seek what thou wilt and thou shalt not find a higher way above nor a safer way below, than the way of the holy cross.

Dispose and order all things according as thou wilt and as seems best to thee, and thou wilt still find something to suffer, either willingly or unwillingly, and so thou shalt still find the cross. For either thou shalt feel pain in the body or sustain in thy soul tribulation of spirit. Sometimes thou shalt be left by God; other times thou shalt be afflicted by thy neighbor, and what is more, thou shalt often be a trouble to thyself. Neither canst thou be delivered or eased by any remedy or comfort, but as long as it shall please God thou must bear it. For God willeth that thou learn to suffer tribulation without comfort, and wholly submit thyself to Him, and become more humble by tribulation.

Thou canst not escape the cross, whithersoever thou runnest; for wheresoever thou goest, thou carriest thyself with thee, and shalt always find thyself. And everywhere thou must of necessity hold fast patience, if thou desirest inward peace, and wouldst merit an eternal crown.

If thou carry the cross willingly, it will carry thee and bring thee to thy desired end; to wit, to that place where there will be an end of suffering, though here there will be no end. If thou carry it unwillingly, thou makest it a burthen to thee and loadest thyself the more, and nevertheless thou must bear it. If thou fling away one cross, without doubt thou shalt find another and perhaps a heavier.

Dost thou think to escape that which no mortal ever could avoid? What saint was there ever in the world without his cross and affliction? Our Lord Jesus Christ Himself was not for one hour of His life without the anguish of His passion. '*It behooved,*' said He, '*that Christ should suffer, and rise from the dead and so enter into His glory.*' And how dost thou seek another way than this royal way, which is the way of the holy cross?...

...The grace of Christ can and does effect such great things in frail flesh, that what it naturally abhors and flees, even this, through fervor of spirit, it now embraces and loves.

To bear the cross, to love the cross, to chastise the body and bring it under subjection; to flee honors, to be willing to suffer reproaches, to despise oneself and wish to be despised; to bear all adversities and losses and to desire no prosperity in this world, are not according to man's natural inclination. If thou look upon thyself, thou canst do nothing of this of thyself. But if thou confide in the Lord, strength will be given thee from heaven and the world and the flesh shall be made subject to thee. Neither shalt thou fear thine enemy, the devil, if thou be armed with faith and signed with the cross of Christ. Set thyself, then, like a good and faithful servant of Christ, to bear manfully the cross of thy Lord, crucified for the love of thee...Drink of the chalice of thy Lord lovingly, if thou desirest to be His friend and to have part with Him. Leave consolations to God, to do with them as best pleaseth Him.

St. Paul says: '*I reckon that the sufferings of this time are not worthy to be compared with the glory to come, that shall be revealed in us*' (Rom. viii. 18).

And St. Peter exhorts us: '*Dearly beloved, think not strange the burning heat, which is to try you, as if some new thing happened to you; but if you partake of the sufferings of Christ, rejoice that when His glory shall be revealed, you may also be glad with exceeding joy'* (1 Peter iv. 12, 13).

Our Lord Himself cries out to us: *'Take up My yoke upon you, and learn of Me, because I am meek and humble of heart, and you shall find rest to your souls'* (Matt. xi. 29).

Know for certain that thou must lead a dying life, and the more a man dies to himself the more he begins to live to God. No man is fit to comprehend heavenly things who has not resigned himself to suffer adversities for Christ. Nothing is more acceptable to God, nothing more wholesome for thee in this world, than to suffer willingly for Christ. And if thou wert to choose, thou oughtst to wish rather to suffer adversities for Christ than to be delighted with many comforts, because thou wouldst thus be more like unto Christ and more conformable to all the saints. For our merit and the advancement of our state consist, not in having many sweetnesses and consolations, but rather in bearing great afflictions and tribulations.

If, indeed, there had been anything better and more beneficial to man's salvation than suffering, Christ certainly would have showed it by word and example. For He manfully exhorts both His disciples that followed Him and all that desire to follow Him to bear the cross, saying: *'If any one will come after Me, let him deny himself and take up his cross and follow Me'* (Luke ix. 23). So that when we have read and searched all let this be the final conclusion, that *'through many tribulations we must enter into the kingdom of God'* (Acts xiv. 21).

—Thomas à Kempis, bk. ii, c. xii.

Do you especially, my young friend, mark the words of Holy Writ: "*It is good for a man when he hath borne the yoke* [the cross] *from his youth*" (Lam. iii. 27).

Wherefore, take the cross which the Lord has destined for you; desire no other, and learn to bear it in your youth, for then it will gradually appear to you to be light and sweet. But it is absolutely necessary for you to learn to bear two things: humiliations and injuries.

Bear humiliations. It is obvious that in order to do this, you must possess and practise true humility. Without this, no salvation is possible for you.

Without humility you can not be a disciple of Him who said: "*Learn of Me, because I am meek and humble of heart.*" If you are destitute of humility, you can possess no other virtue, for humility is the foundation of all virtues, according to the admonition of St. Augustine: "If thou dost desire to erect a spiritual edifice, resolve above all things to found it in humility."

Without humility you can neither be pleasing to God, nor obtain the pardon of your sins, or the acceptance of your prayers. For we are told in Holy Writ: "*A contrite and humbled heart, O God, Thou wilt not despise,*" and, "*The prayer of him that humbleth himself shall pierce the clouds.*"

Do not say that humility degrades a young man; that he will be despised if he is meek and humble. On the contrary, what really degrades a young man, and causes him to be laughed at, and makes him appear small, mean, ridiculous, and pitiable, is pride and arrogance. Look around you and see how true this is. When a young man is full of himself, shows himself an egotist; when he is conceited and vainglorious; when he is inordinately ambitious, striving constantly after places of honor and petty distinctions; when he looks down upon the poor and lowly and fawns upon the rich and powerful; when he ascribes his talents and good qualities, his success and prosperity, only to himself or plumes himself upon an imaginary greatness; when he acts like a snob, shows contempt of others, and is domineering in his conduct; when he holds his head very high and stalks about in his finery as peacocks do; when he indulges in boastful conversation, usurps the largest share of the talk, is self-opinionated, and raves like a fool as soon as he is opposed or contradicted, is not all this very mean, truly ridiculous, vulgar, and pitiable? It is only true humility which makes men great in the sight of God and of their fellow-men.

Our Lord Himself has assured us that: "*He that exalteth himself shall be humbled; and he that humbleth himself shall be exalted"* (Luke xiv. 11). And we are admonished by the Holy Spirit: *"Do thy works in meekness* [humility] *and thou shalt be beloved above the glory of men"* (Ecclus. iii. 19). Strive therefore, to be truly humble, for then you will be able to bear humiliations.

Learn, moreover, to bear injuries and unpleasantnesses. You must inevitably meet with such, but you will only be able to bear them, and bear them with patience, if the daughter of humility dwells within your heart—I mean meekness or gentleness.

Never allow yourself to be drawn into quarrels and strife! And if you are quarrelsome by nature—if you belong to those unfortunate characters which are very touchy, which are hasty and irascible, which bluster and scold, which chatter noisily and thoughtlessly all the livelong day—do you, for the sake of the meekness and gentleness of Christ, learn to control yourself under circumstances of irritation; hold yourself back, be not abusive, learn at least to be silent; in a word, endure.

The important influence which this power of endurance or self-control will have upon your later life, you can not as yet fully estimate, though you may perhaps have some idea of it. Important, indeed, will its influence prove in the family circle, in your intercourse with your neighbors, in the community, in business, and in public life when you are called upon to take an active share in political affairs. And what will be the reward of this patient endurance when you enter upon eternity!

St. Philip Neri one day asked Brother Bernardin Corna, who belonged to his congregation: "Bernardin, the Pope wants to make me a cardinal; what do you think of that?" The Brother replied in all simplicity: "Father, I think this dignity ought not to be refused, for the sake of our congregation." Bravely, and full of holy enthusiasm, St. Philip rejoined: "But paradise, Bernardin, paradise!" The latter immediately answered:

"Forgive me, Father, I did not think of that!"

Alas, thus it is! "I did not think of that, did not think of heaven!" Such must be the confession of many a Christian, many a young man who will not learn to bear humiliations and injuries. But do you think often of heaven, and learn to bear and forbear, learn to be meek and humble of heart.

> Resist the evil, do no wrong,
> Learn to suffer and be strong;
> Unless the passions be restrained
> Abiding peace can not be gained.

51. An Unpleasant Subject—Intemperance

I. Total Abstinence

XENOPHON, the Greek historian, in one of his writings, relates the following incident. When Cyrus, who at a later period became king of Persia, was only twelve years old, he was sent to reside at the court of his grandfather Astyages, king of Media. After a time the king noticed that his youthful grandson never drank wine, and he spoke to him on the subject. Cyrus answered: "I am afraid there is poison in the wine cup. For on the occasion of thy birthday, not long since, I plainly perceived that poison had been mingled with the goblets of wine." "How came thou to think of such a thing, my child?" queried Astyages. Cyrus replied: "I saw that all who drank out of them became mentally and physically incapacitated. At first you all talked, everyone at the same time, very noisily and incoherently, so that no one could understand what his neighbor said, though we boys have been forbidden to behave in this manner. Then you all tried to sing, and the song seemed to please you, though it was extremely absurd. Every one boasted of his strength, and yet, when you stood up in order to dance, you could not even keep on your feet. Thou didst not behave as becomes a king, nor did the guests behave as becomes subjects."

Thus did the youthful Cyrus depict in forcible language the immediate consequences of excess in the consumption of alcoholic drinks. And in this chapter I desire to warn you against the evil effects of intemperance, to exhort you to moderation, and to point out to you the advantages of total abstinence as regards intoxicating beverages. But I am aware that such warnings and exhortations will not be acceptable to many young men, and this is why the present chapter is titled: "An unpleasant subject"; yet I consider you to be open to conviction and so well disposed in mind and heart that you will not contemptuously pass over this "unpleasant subject"— that you will rather read it carefully, and both lay to heart and carry out into practice the kindly admonitions it contains.

"Christianity," says Father Sloan,[1] "has practically overcome and vanquished one after another a great variety of evils; as, for instance, the vendetta, trial by torture, dueling, polygamy, slavery, and the like. Intemperance in the use of intoxicants has to some extent been checked, but in many places it still is prevalent and even popular. That it works great evil and causes dire misery no one will deny. It ruins the home, making the existence of the wife and the mother wretched and at times unendurable. It debauches the youth, and directly or indirectly destroys his prospects of life and his virtue. It debases our men and allures them down to the level of the brute. It causes many a Catholic to become a traitor to his religion and his God by a scandalous life. One fourth of the insane and three fourths of the crime and pauperism found in our land have been attributed to its influence and effects. Directly or indirectly, it has increased enormously the expense of court and jail. Worst of all, it has seduced, and is seducing, thousands, even millions, into the drunkards' hell. Surely it requires no argument to show that a monstrous vice such as this should receive due attention,

---

1   *Vide Sunday-School Director's Guide to Success.*

and that the young should be thoroughly warned against its baneful power. The chief remedy for drunkenness is not to be found in the civil law, but in Christian morality maintained by divine grace."

In an article entitled "Evidence Against Alcohol," by Professor M. A. Rosanoff, which appeared in *McClure's Magazine* for March, 1909, many experiments concerning the effects of alcohol are enumerated, as result of which it may be considered as firmly established that alcohol has a tendency to impair every human faculty.

The conclusions drawn from the experiments by medical experts are as follows:

First, it can hardly be questioned that alcohol has an injurious effect upon the nervous system. Second, it is a false notion that drinking vinous and spirituous liquors with meals helps a laborer in his work. Third, it is a mistake to think that *moderate* drinking is an aid to an artisan or that it increases his efficiency. Fourth, it is positively *not* corroborated by facts that alcohol "*stimulates*" a student to his mental work. Fifth, reports from a large number of cities in the United States, England, and Austria justify the assertion that alcohol is responsible for the presence of one out of four men in every asylum of the insane.

"Intemperance is a fruitful source of *disease* and of *death,*" writes Father Cologan, in his treatise on *Total Abstinence.*[1] "The chief physicians of the present day, including Sir Thomas Barlow and Sir Victor Horsley, have testified to the baneful effects of drink on health and life. Sir Victor Horsley says, whether employed as a food or as a drug, 'the medical profession knows well that it [alcohol] is a potent cause of disease, crime, poverty, and death.' The late Dr. Norman Kerr stated that 60,000 drunkards die every year in the United

---

1   London Catholic Truth Society Publication.

Kingdom, and that 120,000 of our population annually lose their lives, directly or indirectly, through excessive drinking."

The late Sir William Gull, in his examination before the Select Committee of the House of Lords for Inquiry into the Prevalence of Intemperance (1877), said: "I think there is a great deal of injury being done by the use of alcohol in what is supposed by the consumer to be a most moderate quantity, to people not in the least intemperate, to people supposed to be fairly well. It adds to degeneration of tissues. It spoils the health and it spoils the intellect. Short of drunkenness, that is, in those effects of it which stop short of drunkenness, I should say, from my experience, that alcohol is the most destructive agent we are aware of in this country."

Sir Andrew Clarke says: "I do not desire to make out a strong case; I desire to make out a true case. I am speaking solemnly and carefully in the presence of truth, and I tell you that I am considerably within the mark when I say to you that, going the round of my hospital wards today, *seven out of every ten there owed their ill-health to alcohol.* Now what does that mean? That out of every hundred patients that I have charge of at the London hospital, 70 percent of them owe their ill-health to alcohol."[1]

Sir Henry Thompson says: "I have no hesitation in saying that a very large proportion of some of the most painful and dangerous diseases which come under my notice arise from the common and daily use of fermented alcoholic drinks, taken in the quantity which is ordinarily considered moderate."

Dr. Maudsley says: "If men took careful thought of the best use they could make of their bodies, they would probably never take strong drink, except as they would a dose of medicine, in order to serve some special purpose. It is idle to say that there is any real need for persons who are in good health to

---

1   See *An Enemy of the Race:* Catholic Truth Society, London.

indulge in strong drink. At the best, it is an indulgence that is unnecessary; at the worst, it is a vice that occasions infinite misery, sin, crime, madness, and disease."

Lord Brampton, then Mr. Justice Hawkins, said in 1883, at the Durham Assizes, that he "had had considerable experience in courts of law, and every day he lived the more firmly did he come to the conclusion that the root of all crime was drink, it affected people of all ages and both sexes—the middle-aged, the young, the father, the son, the husband, and the wife. It was drink which was the incentive to crimes of dishonesty; a man stole in order that he might provide himself with the means of getting drink. It was drink which caused homes to be impoverished, and they could trace to its source the cause of misery which was to be found in many a cottage home which had been denuded of all the necessaries of life. He believed that nine tenths of the crimes of this country, and certainly of the county of Durham, were engendered within public-houses." At Liverpool, in 1895, he spoke of "that terrible habit of drunkenness which got every one who had it into trouble."

The Right Rev. Dr. Knight, then Bishop of Shrewsbury, has the following passage in his Lenten Pastoral for 1890:

"Is not this vice of intemperance the source of almost every evil, of crimes of violence, of all uncleanness, of blasphemy and loss of faith, the final ruin of soul and body, the shame and disgrace of a man's life and the dishonor of his Church? For all Christians the law of temperance, which is to restrain ourselves from excess, is an obligation; for many, entire abstinence is a counsel which, if followed, will profit them in health of soul and body; while for those who can not otherwise observe the law of temperance it is not a counsel, but an obligation; the strict obligation of avoiding such voluntary occasion as they know by experience will lead them into grievous sin. We are induced to dwell at length on this evil, because of the terrible facts by which it is brought home to us; among the rest by the experience gathered from the reformatories and industrial schools, where, in nearly every instance, the boys and girls who find their way to these institutions come from homes, if homes they can be called, which have been wrecked and defiled by this curse of drink."

The Third Plenary Council of Baltimore says: "The misuse of intoxicating drink is certainly one of the most deplorable evils of our age and country. Intemperance is a constant source of sin, and a copious fountain of misery. It has brought to utter ruin countless multitudes and entire families, and has precipitated into eternal perdition very many souls. All should, therefore, be exhorted by the love of God and country to bend every energy to the extirpation of this baleful evil. To the clergy to whom God has given the office of breaking unto men the Bread of Life, and training them in Christian morality, we chiefly look for helpers in this great work. Let them never cease to raise their voices against drunkenness and the causes and occasions of it, especially in giving spiritual missions to the people.

"We approve, as highly commendable in our times, the practice of those who abstain entirely from the use of intoxicating liquors. We also recognize, as worthy of great praise, the Catholic Total Abstinence Union and the Confraternity of 'the Sacred Thirst,' laboring as they are, by prayer and good works, for the promotion of temperance and relying as they do more on the grace of God, efficacy of prayer, and the sacraments, than on the strength of the human will alone. We recommend these associations, enjoying as they do the blessing of the Holy Father, to the paternal care of the clergy, so that they may flourish more and more, and always adhere to the truly Catholic methods they now follow."

Bishop Hedley in a pastoral letter on *Our Responsibility for Intemperance* says: "As regards the resolution of total abstinence, it is one which, for some people, is absolutely necessary, because there are some who can not save their souls without it. But it is also in the highest degree meritorious in those who do not require it. It is a most admirable practice of Christian self-denial.

"About nine years ago our Holy Father Pope Leo XIII, in a Brief addressed to Archbishop Ireland, of St. Paul, Minnesota, after reciting some of the evils occasioned by intemperance, said: 'Therefore we commend in the highest degree those pious Societies which so nobly propose to practice Total Abstinence from all intoxicants. It can not be doubted that such a pledge (*firma voluntas*) is an opportune and most efficacious remedy for this most grievous evil; and the greater the authority of those who make it, the greater will be the influence of good example in restraining others from intemperance. Especially powerful in this matter will be the zeal of priests.'

"Like all other extraordinary mortifications, it should not be undertaken without consideration and advice. But when prudently taken up and faithfully practised, with interior acceptance of such inconveniences as it carries with it, and without pride, self-sufficiency, or the habit of reflection upon other people, it can not fail to draw the heart nearer to Christ. Moreover, it is a work of splendid brotherly love. It is an example of the most powerful kind. It is a most precious encouragement to the weak and the tempted. Therefore, may God bless all priests and people who join the League of the Cross, and take part in the battle against drink!"

Father Sloan refers to this subject in his *Sunday-School Director's Guide*. He says: "Temperance work can be made a feature of some, or if found desirable, of all, the church societies and sodalities; or a special temperance society can be organized. This society could be broad enough to include in its membership all desirable persons. Its aim and purpose should be to promote a temperance sentiment, to keep the subject alive before the people, and to influence and strengthen the endeavor of all who are laboring for the extermination of drunkenness. Its main effort should be preventive. Total abstinence should be practised by all members who are less than twenty-one years of age, as also by those who find that the use of intoxicants means for them abuse. As to the others, if for the sake of giving good example and encouragement to those less strong, they voluntarily desire to take the pledge, permission should be given to do so. All members should at least practice due temperance.

"In such a society the chief method in vogue is that of taking the pledge. Hence the society's great work is to sign these pledges and to keep them unbroken."

We read in *The Priests' League* for Lent 1909: "Some may ask: What good would membership in the League do me? It does not promise to do its members any good; it does not suppose that those who become its members need any good done them from a temperance point of view. It looks for its members to do good to others, as it is better to give than to receive. Christ chose apostles to bring forth lasting fruit. The League wants members who shall promote sobriety by example and word, especially among those who are of the household of the Faith."

"If we turn to the New Testament," writes Father Cologan,[1] "we find the principles of total abstinence clearly laid down.

"We tell the drunkard that, no matter how dearly he loves his glass, he should give it up to save his soul, because to him even a very little intoxicating drink is likely to lead to excess.

---

1 *Total Abstinence From A Catholic Point of View*: London Catholic Truth Society.

Our Blessed Lord says: '*If thine eye scandalize thee pluck it out. It is better for thee with one eye to enter into the kingdom of God than having two eyes to be cast into the hell of fire*'; that is to say, if anything be an occasion of sin to us, as drink is to the drunkard and to those in danger of becoming drunkards, it is better for us, and it is even our duty, to give it up rather than risk that it should bring us into hell. As for those to whom intoxicating drink is not an occasion of sin, to them we appeal on the principle of charity and zeal for the good of our neighbor; and we ask that for the sake of our weaker brethren, to give them example and encouragement, they would forego what is perfectly lawful. This is quite according to the teaching of St. Paul: '*If because of thy meat thy brother be grieved, thou walkest not now according to charity. Destroy not him with thy meat for whom Christ died . . . All things indeed are clean; but it is evil for that man who eateth with offense*' (so there is no sin in strong drink itself, the sin is in those who misuse it); '*it is good not to eat flesh and **not to drink wine** nor anything whereby thy brother is offended or scandalized or made weak*' (Rom. xiv. 15, etc.). And again, '*if meat scandalize*' (be an occasion of sin to) '*my brother, I will never eat flesh lest I should scandalize my brother.*' From this it is clear that if wine be a source of danger to our brethren, as indeed it is, we do a good and virtuous act in abstaining from it for their sakes."

Moderate drinking is not unlawful; yet for many persons it is not safe. For many young men it is dangerous: nearly all drunkards began their downward career as moderate drinkers.

"It pays to be a total abstainer," as the *Temperance Catechism* says: "first, because the total abstainer saves the money which so many foolishly waste on intoxicating drink; secondly, because total abstainers are generally in a better state of health and less subject to disease, and when they are ill or hurt, they usually recover and are back at work more quickly than those who are not abstainers and thirdly, because they do not lose their place at work through drink and bad company, which is a very frequent cause of workmen and others losing their places."

"Many persons are total abstainers, not because they are reformed drunkards, but from motives of zeal and piety."

Among these motives are: "first, zeal for this salvation of souls in giving example and support to the intemperate who desire to give up their sins. Secondly, penance and satisfaction for one's own sins. Thirdly, atonement to the Sacred Heart for the sins of intemperance committed by others."[1]

Our divine Master Himself admonishes us: "*Take heed to yourselves, lest perhaps your heart be overcharged with surfeiting and drunkenness*" (Luke xxi. 34).

And we are exhorted in the Book of Proverbs: "*Look not upon the wine when it is yellow, when the color thereof shineth in the glass; it goeth in pleasantly, but in the end it will bite like a snake and will spread abroad poison like a basilisk*" (Prov. xxiii. 31, 32).

Read with attention and devout reflection the following address to young men by Father Schuen on intemperance, found in his work, *Outlines of Sermons for Young Men and Young Women*, edited by the Rev. Edmund J. Wirth, Ph.D.

II. THE EVIL OF DRUNKENNESS[2]
"Take heed to yourselves, lest perhaps your hearts be overcharged with drunkenness" (Luke xxi. 34).

ALMIGHTY GOD has made provision of food and drink sufficient to ensure the preservation of life and health.

---

1   *Total Abstinence From A Catholic Point of View*: London Catholic Truth Society.

2   *Outlines of Sermons for Young Men and Young Women*: Schuen-Wirth. (Benziger Brothers.)

Nevertheless, it often happens that the gifts which God puts at the disposal of man are employed in such a manner as to prove not profitable, but rather harmful, to us; they are misused by being employed to excess. Thus it is especially with spirituous drinks, the excessive use of which proves injurious for time and eternity. As a rule, it is men rather than women who are given to excess in this matter. I consider it my duty to warn you against this evil. There may be some amongst you that need that warning very much whilst it is still time, for when the evil has gone too far advice and warning come too late. I will speak to you today on the evil of intemperance; and therefore will consider:

I. Its beginning;

II. Its progress;

III. Its end.

Part I

Drunkenness begins with an inborn tendency to evil, due to the sin of our first parents. "*The imagination and thought of man's heart are prone to evil from youth*" (Gen. viii. 21). "*I know that there dwelleth not in me, that is, in my flesh, that which is good*" (Rom. vii. 18). This propensity to evil is developed in various ways; it is an accursed root from which many poisonous plants grow. One man develops it in the form of anger, another in that of luxury, another in that of avarice, another in that of envy, and still another in that of love for strong drinks. Often the unfortunate tendency manifests itself at an early age, even in childhood. We meet with children that have not yet left school in whom the desire for drink is already developed. The proneness to evil is not a sin in itself, yet it leads to sin if it is let go unchecked. If not resisted with determination it grows rapidly, as a fire spreads if the spark is not stamped out.

The desire for strong drink is developed by frequent indulgence; drink as a habit is an acquired habit. The desire is often contracted through the fault of parents. Many parents are so unwise as to give strong drink to their children—some are foolish to applaud their children if they can drink off a glass like a grown person. It may also be the fault of strangers. There are people so ignorant or malicious as to ply children with strong drinks; they take delight in getting them intoxicated and amusing themselves with their antics. As for adults, their danger very often lies in the company they keep. How often it happens that a friend, so called, teaches another the love for strong drink! Young men often boast of how much they can stand, and by means of ridicule induce their friends to drink more than is good for them.

It may also be through one's own fault that the habit of taking strong drink is acquired. A man may begin by drinking moderately, but on account of the love he has for the associations he meets with in drinking-places, he frequents them more and more and so gradually acquires a love for liquor. He may indeed resist the passion for drink, but unfortunately the number of those who once acquire the habit and resist with any determination is very small. The craving for drink once acquired will not rest without being satisfied. Once the habit is formed it becomes an iron chain, a strong yoke, the man becomes a slave to it and can not break the fetters that bind him. He says: "*Come, let us take wine and be filled with drunkenness, and it shall be as today, so also tomorrow and much more*" (Is. lvi. 12). He can not get rid of the craving; "*If the Ethiopian can change his skin, or the leopard his spots, you also may do well, when you have learned evil*" (Jer. xiii. 23). An habitual drunkard is incorrigible; nothing avails—neither exhortation nor entreaties. He is not moved by calamity nor sickness nor danger of death. If he were placed before the gates of hell and made to look upon the scorching flames, he would not change his manner of life; he would seek to forget the sight by indulging all the more in his bottle.

This is the way in which drunkenness begins—there is an inclination to evil from nature and the habit is developed by indulgence. A man does not become a drunkard all at once—it is a gradual growth. The descent is made by degrees; from month to month, from year to year, it is fixed more firmly, until the lowest round of the ladder is reached.

Part II

The drunkard's course is a life of sin. Intemperance is one of the capital sins; that is: it is a source from which many sins spring. St. Augustine calls it the "parent of all transgressions and the epitome of guilt," the "starting-point of crime and the source of vices." A man given to drink violates his more sacred obligations. Such a one does not sanctify the Sunday. The saloon is his temple and place of worship, it is his home, where he spends the greater part of the night, if the day is not long enough for him. As for hearing the word of God, such an idea does not enter his head. A man given to drink cuts himself off from his family; if he is unmarried, his father and mother, brothers and sisters, give him little concern. If he is married, his wife and children are less dear to him than the enjoyment of strong drink; he is their torment and disgrace.

A man addicted excessively to drink does not shrink from misdeeds and crimes. "*Wine is a luxurious thing, and drunkenness riotous*" (Prov. xx. 1). "*Wine drunken with excess raiseth quarrels and wrath and many ruins*" (Ecclus. xxxi. 38). All the Doctors of the Church agree in saying that there is a close connection between drink and luxury. A man who is a drunkard can not be a pure man. How many sins of this kind are committed on account of drunkenness! Drink makes man quarrel, blaspheme, and commit deeds of violence. A man given to drink can indeed say: *"My misdeeds are gone over my head, and as a heavy burden are become heavy upon me. My bones are putrified and corrupted because of my foolishness"* (Ps. xxxvii. 5, 6).

Such a man's life is a life of misery. It is true the drunkard seems jolly and happy, ready to make friends with all the world, yet the truth is that he leads a wretched existence, for he loses much that constitutes happiness in this life and in the next. He loses his good name. No one feels any respect for him. He is despised by his neighbors and even by his own relatives: *"He is filled with shame instead of glory"* (Hab. ii. 16). He loses his property: *"A workman that is a drunkard shall not be rich"* (Ecclus. xix. 1). All his possessions go to the saloon and at the end of a short time he is a beggar. He loses his position and the means of earning a living. Thus it often happens that a man who started out in life with the brightest prospects, with a fine home and funds at his disposal, becomes a pauper in his old age and ends his days in the poorhouse, if not in a worse place.

A man given to drink brings on himself much that embitters life. He lays himself open to the most bitter reproaches. His own conscience gives him no rest, but torments him continually. *"Tribulation shall terrify him, and distress shall surround him, as a king that is prepared for the battle. The sound of dread is always in his ears"* (Job xv. 21, 24). There are the reproaches of his relatives who rebuke him daily. How much he has to hear that is calculated to wound his self-love and self-respect! He has bodily ailments to endure. "If thou hast overstepped the limits of moderation in drink," says St. Basil, "the next day thy head will be heavy and dull, thou wilt yawn continually and feel giddy." *"Who hath wounds without cause? Who hath redness of eyes? Surely they that pass their time in wine, and study to drink off their cups"*

(Prov. xxiii. 29, 30). The man who gets drunk repeatedly will have to pay a heavy penalty for his indulgence; he will undermine his health and be subject to much sickness and, not unfrequently, to unforeseen death.

PART III

The end of the drunkard is in many cases an unhappy death. Death often overtakes him suddenly. There is no other vice that so frequently brings on an unexpected death as the evil of drunkenness. Some are frozen to death whilst they are intoxicated, others fall into the water and drown, others are killed in a brawl or by accident. If you examine the statistics of accidental deaths, you will find that a very great number of those that were killed were drunkards. Such a death is a terrible misfortune; it makes one shudder to think of being called away from this life in the state of sin, unprepared, incapable even of making an act of contrition or of raising one's thoughts to God. Such a one dies impenitent. If they do not die whilst intoxicated, their death still has many terrors for them. It may be that when laid upon their dying bed and the devil stares them in the face they make an act of contrition and strike their breast in sorrow; yet their life will haunt them; they see that they have given their years to the service of the devil instead of the service of God, and they are not without fear.

The end of many drunkards is eternal damnation. *"Drunkards . . . shall not possess the kingdom of God"* (1 Cor. vi. 10). There is nothing more to be said. The Apostle declares solemnly that the kingdom of God is not for the slaves of their depraved appetites. Our own reason would teach us the same even if the Apostle had not spoken so clearly. The life of a drunkard is a life of sin; can we, then, suppose that the gates of heaven stand open continually to invite such a one to enter? You can not suppose this for a moment; your own good sense must tell you the contrary. For such a one there can be nothing but eternal ruin.

Take the advice of the Apostle: *"Be not drunk with wine"* (Eph. v. 18). If you are concerned about your temporal and eternal welfare, you will be on your guard against excess in drink and will entirely avoid strong drinks, such as whiskey. There is nothing wrong morally in taking drink in moderation, but if you find in yourselves a craving for strong drink, be on your guard, for you are in great danger and total abstinence may be the only salvation for you. The less frequently you are seen in drinking-places the better it will be for your good name, your health, and your eternal salvation. Do not follow the example of some young men who spend their last penny in drink, sit in the saloon half the night indulging in evil conversation, gambling, and drunkenness. Do not let your companions induce you to drink when you do not care for more; never treat or be treated. This latter rule would save the majority of those that in time become drunkards. If you want a drink, pay for it yourself. Be on your guard against associating with young men that are given to over-indulgence; evil companions corrupt good morals. *"Exceed not, and if thou sittest among many reach not thy hand out first. How sufficient is a little wine for a man well taught"* (Ecclus. xxxi. 20-22). *"Be sober"* (1 Pet. v. 8).

III. TEMPERANCE RESOLUTIONS
Suggested by the Cardinal-Archbishop and Bishops of England

THE widespread habit of intemperance is the prolific cause of a multitude of evils. It degrades and destroys the body and soul of innumerable Christians, and is perpetually offering before the throne of God most heinous offenses against His divine majesty. Wherefore, the Cardinal-Archbishop and

Bishops of England have determined to invite the whole of their flock to unite with them in an earnest and persevering endeavor to stem the tide of these evils, and to offer becoming acts of reparation to the offended majesty of God. All are therefore invited to take one or other of the following resolutions, according to their discretion, namely:

1. To offer up *Mass* and *Benediction* this day for the suppression of drunkenness, the perseverance of those who have taken a pledge, and for the spread of the virtue of temperance.
2. To say the *Rosary* once a week for the above intentions.
3. To practise habitually *some specific act of mortification* in the matter of drink, under the direction or approval of a confessor.
4. Never to taste intoxicating drink in a *public house.*
5. Never to take intoxicating drink *out of meal time.*
6. To abstain from intoxicating drink on *Friday and Saturday*, in honor of the passion of Jesus and the sorrows of Mary.
7. To abstain absolutely from the use of *ardent spirits.*
8. To take the Total Abstinence pledge *for a year.*
9. To take the Total Abstinence pledge *for life.*

I firmly purpose—by God's help—to keep the resolution which I have made—to His honor and glory—in reparation for sins of intemperance—and in promotion of the salvation of souls. Through Jesus Christ our Lord Amen.

N.B.: Another good resolution is this, to take a firm and courageous stand against the custom of treating; to trample upon human respect, and to refuse to *treat* or *be treated* in a public place. It can not be denied that the foolish custom of treating in saloons is the cause of intemperance to a great extent and has made a drunkard of many a promising young man. (N. B. added by F. X. L.)

IV. TOTAL ABSTINENCE
FROM A CATHOLIC POINT OF VIEW[1]

T HE Total Abstinence cause is not a war against *drink*. The
Catholic Total Abstinence does not—may not—say that
strong drink is in itself an evil or the creation of the devil.
Long ago there was a religious sect called Manicheans. These
men held that God made that part of the world which was
good, and the devil made the rest which was bad, and wine
and strong drink they said was bad, and crated by the devil.
All this was condemned by the Church as a heresy; for there is
but one Creator of all things—the one Eternal God; "*and God
saw all the things that He had made and they were very good.*"[2]
"Nor," as Cardinal Manning said in his speech at the Crystal
Palace, 1884, "is there sin in these harmless, innocent things,
for this reason: that there can be sin in nothing or in nobody
who has not a will and a conscience to know right from
wrong. Therefore, if this room were full of barrels of beer,
and barrels of wine, and puncheons of brandy, there would
be no sin in these things of themselves. We could set fire to
them and make an end of them. *They* are not the sinners—it
is we ourselves who are the sinners; the men and women who
abuse these things, violating their conscience by their own
free-will—they are the sinners."[3]

No, there is no moral evil, no sin, in these things—wine,
beer, and spirits. In themselves they are good and given to us
by God for our good—although we may say with truth that
inasmuch as a great part of the strong drink of the present day
is "made up" and adulterated, and this inferior adulteration is
passed off as a better article, in this sense such wines etc., are
bad—they are not what they are said to be; but still there is

---

1   Extracts from a pamphlet on Total Abstinence by the Rev. W. H.
Cologan: London Catholic Truth Society.
2   Gen. i. 31.
3   *League of the Cross Magazine*, Oct, 1884.

no sin in them. Listen to St. John Chrysostom on this point: "I hear men say when these excesses happen, 'Would there were no wine!' O folly! O madness! When men sin in other ways, dost thou then find fault with the gifts of God? But what madness is this? What! did the wine, O man, produce this evil? Not the wine, but the intemperance of such as take an evil delight in it. Say then, 'would there were no drunkenness, no luxury'; but if thou sayest, 'would there were no wine,' thou wilt by degrees on to say, 'would there were no steel, because of the murderers; no night because of the thieves.' . . . In a word, thou wilt destroy all things, since they may all be abused."[1]

Nor can the Catholic Total Abstainer condemn the moderate drinker as guilty of sin. There is no sin in taking a glass of wine or a glass of spirits, or in taking a really moderate quantity of them; and we have no right to condemn as sinful a practice against which there is no law, divine or human. St. Thomas and all Catholic theologians teach that the use of wine or of any intoxicating drink is not in itself unlawful; although it may become so for certain reasons, such as danger to the drinker, scandal, a vow not to take wine, etc.

What, then, *is* Total Abstinence? Total Abstinence is the practice of abstaining from intoxicating drink—from *"whatever may make a man drunk."* A Total Abstinence Society is a society of persons who have pledged themselves—promised—to abstain entirely from all intoxicating drink, and are banded together to suppress the vice of intemperance and promote its opposite virtue.

In everyday affairs we have societies and leagues. If there be an evil in the law, we combine—for union is strength—and agitate, and influence public and private opinion, and we do not rest until we have removed that evil. Why, then, should we not combine and agitate and influence opinion—and work, too, with a will—to remove the evil of drunkenness?

1   Hom. lvii. in Matt.

I can not do better than quote from the letter of Cardinal Manning to Fr. Bridgett.[1] His Eminence says: "To meet the invasion of so widely extended an evil [intemperance], it appears to me that a widely extended organization, specifically created for the purpose of arresting drunkenness, and of giving the mutual support of numbers and of sympathy to those who are in danger, is not only a wise mode of counteraction, but, I am inclined to believe, also a necessary provision. It affords external encouragement and support to multitudes who can not stand alone. . . I feel that Temperance and Total Abstinence ought to be familiar thoughts in the mind even of those who have never in all their life been tempted to excess. If they would consciously unite by example, by word, and by influence, to save those who are perishing in the dangers from which they are happily safe, many a soul and many a home now hopelessly wrecked would, I believe, be saved."

From this letter of His Eminence we see the object of a Total Abstinence Society, *viz.*: to arrest drunkenness; to reclaim those who have fallen into this vice; to rescue those in danger; to place as far as possible out of temptation those even who are not in danger—our children, and so to influence society that people may be awakened to the havoc which intemperance is working, and that this vice may no longer be winked at and even encouraged, but may be branded with the disgrace which it deserves, and that society itself may take measures against it. Now it is evident that to carry out this object some organization is necessary—a union not merely of those to whom intoxicating drink is a source of danger, or of those who can not keep sober without the pledge, for if this were proposed, few, if any, could be induced to join such a society, the members of which would be at once known as "reformed drunkards"; but also of those whose sobriety can not be called in question, who would give

1   *Discipline of Drink*, p. 16.

an air of respectability to the society, and throw the shield of their own character over its fallen but repentant and amending members. This union of the temperate with those who have been victims of intemperance, and the pledge, are the great means by which the Total Abstinence Society aims at its object.

What Is the Pledge?

The pledge is a promise—not a vow, nor an oath, but none the less a real binding promise—to abstain from all intoxicating drinks. In other words, he who takes the pledge promises not to drink wine, beer, spirits, or anything intoxicating during the whole time—whether for life, or for a certain number of weeks, months, or years—for which he pledges himself.

The following is the pledge taken before a priest by those who join the League of the Cross:

"I promise to you, Father, and to the League of the Holy Cross, by the help of God's grace, to abstain from all intoxicating drinks."

The pledge does not prevent the taking of intoxicating drinks by medical advice if this becomes *necessary;* but as soon as the necessity ceases, the Total Abstinence must be resumed by any one who wishes to remain a member of the League.

Is the Pledge a Remedy Against Intemperance?

But is the means employed by Total Abstinence Societies the right means—does the pledge really offer a barrier to the progress of intemperance? Does it really reclaim drunkards? Does it keep the weak out of danger? There are two ways of deciding this question: firstly, by the light of experience—for Total Abstinence has now been tried for some years, sufficiently long for us to know whether it is a success or a failure—and secondly, by the very nature of the pledge.

What light, then, does experience throw upon the subject? Cardinal Manning, in a letter published in the *Weekly Register,*

June 6, 1885, said: "The League of the Cross has brought me many consolations in the happiness and Christian life of my people ... What homes we should have had at this day if the last generation had abstained from all intoxicating drinks!" And again: "If we had begun the League of the Cross twenty-five years ago, we should have a hundred thousand more Catholics in London; if twenty-five years ago men and women had been sober, there would have been that number of Catholics more today than there is."[1]

Cardinal Vaughan stated that "experience abundantly proves that for a Catholic the pledge, without the sacraments, is worthless, but that with the grace of the sacraments, it is of much avail."[2] The late Father Rooke, speaking at the Crystal Palace, on the occasion of the festival of the League of the Cross, 1884,[3] said that in his short experience of the work of the League he could tell of the rescue of individuals and of families who were a short time ago sunken in the degrading vice of intemperance, whose homes had been more like pigsties than Christian dwellings—people with no decent clothes because of the pawnshop; people neglecting their most sacred religious duties. By the blessing of God these people had now cast aside their habits of intemperance, and they were now happy, well fed, and well clothed.

The Total Abstinence Union of America comprises amongst its members a great number of the clergy and several bishops—a proof in itself of their opinion as to the benefits resulting from Total Abstinence.

The Third Plenary Council of Baltimore, 1887, says: "Let the exertions of Catholic Temperance Societies meet with the hearty co-operation of pastor and people, and they will go far

---

1   *League of the Cross Magazine*, February, 1887.
2   *Sanctification of Lent*, p. 28.
3   *League of the Cross Magazine*, October, 1884.

toward strangling the monstrous evil of intemperance." The archbishops and bishops of Australia, in their pastoral letter drawn up at the Plenary Council of 1886, "earnestly recommend the formation in every parish of Temperance Societies under the charge of the local pastor."

All this shows that the pledge has been found to be on the whole a useful remedy against intemperance.

From the very nature of the pledge it follows that, as long as it is kept, it must prevent drunkenness. For the pledge is a promise to abstain from intoxicating drink—but without intoxicating drink one can not get intoxicated; this is self-evident, so as long as the abstainer keeps his promise—his pledge—so long must he, of necessity, be a sober man.

Bishop Hedley, in his pastoral letter on Intemperance, after discussing various means to lessen drunkenness, finally refers to one of vast importance in the cause of temperance. In this regard he writes as follows:

"Here we approach the consideration of the *sovereign remedy of all*—the endeavor to obtain God's help and grace through prayer and the holy sacraments.

"Temperance and soberness are spiritual virtues—and virtues, more than other good gifts, depend upon spiritual help.

"It is vain, therefore, to hope to reclaim the drunkard, or preserve the sobriety of young or old, unless you can bring them to the practice of Christian prayer and religious duty. Even if a man reforms through natural motives and native strength of character, the vices of his sobriety are sometimes more disagreeable than those of his drunkenness. But the Christian is, first, humble—knowing that he can neither rise from evil nor remain constant in good without the help of God. Next he is hopeful and full of faith, for he knows that he has a heavenly Father who has nothing nearer to His desires than to draw him to Himself. And thirdly he is obedient—resolutely adopting the means intended by his heavenly Father to save him, and making use of those divine sacraments which convey the precious blood to his weak and sinful soul."

V. How Devotion to St. Joseph Saved a Young Drunkard[1]

VOLUMES could not contain the wonderful favors which are obtained through St. Joseph. He is always ready to befriend his clients, and God is always ready to hear him.

A young man named Joseph had led a good life until the age of twenty. From his childhood he had been devout to his patron saint. When he left school he fell into the company of persons who led evil lives, and little by little he began to do as they did. Among other things he learned to drink, and soon became so fond of liquor that he seldom missed a day without being intoxicated. At last, all his friends knew him for what he was—*a common drunkard.*

He went to the sacraments no more; to church never. Thus several years passed, and one day, while he stood in front of the cathedral watching a man haul a flag to the top of the spire, a sudden impulse led him to enter. He fell on his knees, the tears came to his eyes, and he began to sob and weep. He rose at length and went home, throwing himself on his bed, as he had felt ill all day. The next morning he could not get up; he refused, however, to take a drop of the wine which his sister offered him to steady his nerves.

From that time he would not taste it. He never left his room again; he had been seized with quick consumption, caused by his bad habits.

He lived three months longer. Between midnight and morning each day he would never take anything to quench his thirst. He would say: "I have sinned through thirst, and thus I shall repent and suffer."

1   From *Patron Saints for Catholic Youth,* by Mary E. Mannix

On the morning of the feast of St. Joseph he said: "I think St. Joseph will come for me some time today."

He died at midnight. Later it was learned that he had told his confessor that he had never failed through the evil years to say morning and evening, "*St. Joseph, help me!*" His holy patron had not deserted him.

52. Enjoy Yourself with Moderation and Propriety

St. Philip Neri was a peculiarly cheerful saint; he was merry in the right sense of the word. He was never gloomy or fretful; he could not bear to see melancholy faces about him. He loved to be surrounded by young people, and delighted to see them indulging in harmless mirth. If, on the contrary, he perceived that any one was in a peevish, gloomy mood, he at once asked what was the matter with him. Occasionally he gave such a one a gentle tap on the cheek, and said: "*Be cheerful!*"

I also say to you, my young friend, be cheerful! Who indeed ought to be merry, if not the young? Who would grudge their enjoyment of life to the lamb which gambols in the green meadow, and the young man who delights in the flowery fields of spring? Be of good cheer, be merry, enjoy yourself, but with moderation and in the right way.

If in preceding chapters I have so earnestly exhorted you to practise self-denial and renunciation, to bear and forbear, I am nevertheless very far from wishing to see you hang your head and look peevish and morose, as if you had something bitter in your mouth. No, nothing less than that! To appear as if you were a lamb being led to the slaughter is not only unnatural, but odious.

I am sure that our Father in heaven prefers cheerful people, if only they are pious and well conducted. Sadness is the result of our fallen nature; therefore in no case does it come from heaven, or from God.

"*Rejoice in the Lord always,*" says the Apostle. The Royal Psalmist also encourages us to gladness. Faith and piety gladden the heart by inspiring trust in the goodness and mercy of God.

"*Thou, O Lord, art my protector and the lifter up of my head*" (Ps. iii. 4).

"*Thou hast given gladness in my heart*" (Ps. iv. 7).

"*Let all them be glad that hope in Thee; they shall rejoice forever, and Thou shalt dwell in them*" (Ps. v. 12).

"*I will be glad and rejoice in Thee; I will sing to Thy name, O Thou Most High*" (Ps. ix. 3).

"*Thou hast made known to me the way of life; Thou shalt fill me with joys with Thy countenance; at Thy right hand are delights even to the end*" (Ps. xv. 11). "*I will love Thee, O Lord, my strength. The Lord is my refuge and my deliverer. My God is my helper and in Him will I put my trust*" (Ps. xvii. 3).

"*Though I should walk in the midst of the shadow of death, I will fear no evils, for Thou art with me. Thy rod and Thy staff they have comforted me*" (Ps. xxii. 4).

"*Rejoice to God our Helper*" (Ps. lxxx. 2). "*He will overshadow Thee with His shoulders, and under His wings thou shalt trust*" (Ps. xc. 4).

But it is only the virtuous man who can be merry in the right way, cheerful in the true sense of the word. Real cheerfulness is the inseparable companion of true virtue. Happiness is found in goodness. No one has a right to be cheerful who knows that he is not in the grace of God. The slave of sin, the enemy of God, can indeed lead a merry life in the sense in which the world understands these words, but he must tremble, lament and shudder, whenever he thinks seriously of hell, which yawns beneath his feet.

If you are truly cheerful at heart, then is your soul at peace. Trials may indeed arise, but the clouds will never be so heavy as to prevent the bright and cheering rays of confidence in God to pierce through them and lessen their gloom.

Interior cheerfulness will show itself in your exterior. Your eye will be bright, your countenance serene, your brow unruffled, your bearing firm, your step light.

Cheerfulness is recommended in many passages of Holy Writ. For instance, the Wise Man speaks thus: "*Rejoice, therefore, O young man, in thy youth, and let thy heart be in that which is good in the days of thy youth; and know that for all these God will bring thee into judgment.*" And if David, the royal psalmist, so frequently reminds us in his sacred poems to praise the Lord with joy, how should not the young man do this in the bloom of his youth? All the faithful should heed the admonition of St. Paul to the Philippians: "*Rejoice in the Lord always; again I say, rejoice.*" This saying applies, however, in a very particular manner, to young people.

Let them strive to keep themselves in the grace and love of God and ever to be of good cheer—"*to rejoice in the Lord.*"

One day St. Aloysius found himself in company with some young friends, and engaged in a game of chess. Some one suddenly asked what each member of the company would do if he knew that he was to die within an hour. One said he should repair to the church and engage in prayer; another remarked that the best thing would be to go to confession. But St. Aloysius, whose conscience was completely at peace, quietly said: "I should continue the game, because I am playing in accordance with the will of God, and the wish of my superiors."

That is what it means to be cheerful and merry in the right way, if one preserves at the same time so tranquil a state of conscience that even the unexpected appearance at death would not be able to cause too great alarm and apprehension.

In this way judge the amusements, games, and merry-makings in which you like to indulge, the jokes, witticisms, conversations in which you take delight, the time and money which you sacrifice on your enjoyments. If your conscience does not reproach you, does not whisper to you that your favorite games and amusements are for you an occasion of sin, and the time and money you spend on them a piece of extravagance—then you are enjoying yourself in a proper manner. Continue to be cheerful and merry.

> If aught on earth shall give you pleasure
> God doth that joy bestow:
> See that thou take it in due measure
> Or it may turn to woe.

The human heart craves and seeks unceasingly for happiness. Many find but a small measure of happiness in this life because they lose sight of their eternal destiny—the object of their creation—which is to know God, to love Him, to serve Him, and to be happy with Him. "*Thou shalt love the Lord thy God with thy whole heart and thou shalt love thy neighbor as thyself*" (Matt. xxii. 37, 39). The whole law depends on these two commandments; so Our Lord Himself assures us. The fullest measure of happiness even here on earth is attained by harmonizing one's conduct with the commandments of God, by doing well one's duties to God and man; for this means the possession of a peaceful conscience, a clean heart, a sinless soul; and this is essential to happiness; hence, St. Ignatius says: "Give me, Lord, only Thy love and thy grace; with these I shall be rich enough; here is nothing more that I desire." To be in the state of grace—to have God's love—that is essentially necessary to true happiness. "*Si Deus pro nobis quis contra nos?*" "*If God be for us, who is against us?*" (Rom. viii. 31). The end of man's creation is to glorify God. But in promoting God's glory we are at the same time promoting our own happiness. Ergo, let our watchword be: *"Omnia ad majorem Dei gloriam!"* "All for the greater glory of God!"

> "Know then this truth—enough for man to know:
> Virtue alone is happiness below."
>
> —Pope.
>
> "Happiness and virtue are the same."
>
> —Francis.
>
> "There can be no harmony in our being except our happiness coincides with our duty."
>
> —Whewell.

I. RECREATION
Card-Playing—Gambling—Hobbies—Idleness

S<small>T. FRANCIS DE SALES</small> says in his *Introduction to a Devout Life:* "It is necessary sometimes to relax our minds as well is our bodies by some kind of recreation. John the Evangelist, as Cassian relates, amusing himself one day with a partridge on his hand, was asked by a huntsman how such a man as he could spend his time in so unprofitable a manner. St. John replied:

" 'Why dost thou not carry thy bow always bent?' 'Because,' answered the huntsman, 'were it always bent I fear it would lose its spring and become useless.' 'Be not surprised, then,' replied the apostle, 'that I should sometimes remit a little of my close application and attention of mind to enjoy some little recreation, that I may afterward employ myself more fervently in divine contemplation.' It is doubtless a defect to be so rigorous and austere as neither to be willing to take any recreation ourselves, nor allow it to others.

"To take the air, to walk, to entertain ourselves with cheerful and friendly conversations, to play on the lute or any other instrument, to sing to music, or to go hunting, are recreations so innocent, that in a proper use of them there needs but that common prudence which gives to everything its due order, time, place, and measure.

"Those games in which the gain serves as a recompense for the dexterity and industry of the body or of the mind, such as tennis, ball, pall-mall, running at the ring, chess, and backgammon, are recreations in themselves good and lawful, provided excess, either in the time employed at them, or in the sum that is played for, be avoided."

On this subject of pastimes for young men, Father Schuen writes:[1] "No one can blame you for amusing yourselves, provided you do it in a legitimate manner. This will be the case if your pleasures are innocent. Those pleasures are innocent which involve no danger of sin or scandal, and which are free from danger to health or waste of money, and do not interfere with your duties in life. There are many pleasures of this description; as, for instance, a walk through the woods or fields, a visit to a good friend, the reading of a good and instructive book, an hour spent in music or singing, a game of ball or tennis, and many other similar pastimes.

"Another condition upon which the innocence of your amusements depends is, that you should enjoy them in moderation. All excess is bad, and displeasing to God. Even the best things become evil when carried to excess—just as a most salutary medicine, if given in too large doses, becomes a poison—hence it follows that any diversion indulged in must be enjoyed in moderation. Be on your guard against acquiring a passion for amusements. St. Francis of Sales says: 'There is nothing sinful in making merry at times in harmless way, but we must beware of loving amusements too much.' Many people begin by indulging freely in diversions; gradually they become enslaved by them, and end by pursuing them with intense passion. This is not the way in which we are to seek amusements—we are told: '*Lust shall be under thee, and thou shalt have dominion over it*' (Gen. iv. 7). Be on your guard,

---

1   *Outlines of Sermons for Young Men:* Schuen-Wirth.

also, against loss of time. We should not turn to amusement until all the duties of our station in life are performed; our amusements should not encroach on our time too much, neither should they be prolonged, until late at night. '*See, therefore, brethren, how you walk circumspectly, redeeming the time*' (Eph. v. 15, 16).

"Your amusements to be lawful must be taken with a good intention. The Christian ought not give himself up to mirth merely for the enjoyment of it; he ought to have a higher purpose. The Apostle bids us, '*Mind the things that are above*' (Col. iii. 2). Again he says, '*Whether you eat or drink, or whatsoever you do, do all to the glory of God*' (1 Cor. x. 31). Therefore, let a good intention inspire even your amusements and pleasures. Enjoy yourselves because it is the will of God that you should take recreation after a hard day's work, and let not the mere love of pleasure be the moving spirit of your recreation.

"Proper recreation and rest renew the body and maintain its power of endurance. Recreation is also good for the soul. As a gentle rain at night revives and refreshes the thirsty earth parched by the heat of the midday sun, even so innocent amusements recruit and refresh the mind fatigued with the duties of one's calling. The soul may benefit by innocent recreation, which when taken in the proper manner becomes meritorious and deserving of eternal reward. St. Paul tells us that even drinking and eating can become supernatural acts. '*Whether you eat or drink, or whatsoever you do, do it all to the glory of God*' (1 Cor. x. 31).

"Let your amusements, then, be always of the right kind; let them be innocent, *i.e.*, free from sin; enjoy them in moderation and with a good intention. Religion does not forbid measures of this kind. Your conscience will have no cause to reproach you for them; they may even become a source of eternal reward. '*Rejoice, O young man, in thy youth, and let thy heart be in that which is good.*'

"Among the amusements that are accompanied with danger we [here] mention *card-playing*. In itself an innocent amusement, it quickly degenerates into gambling and sin. It is an amusement in which moderation is difficult. This is especially true of certain games. These games lend themselves easily to playing for money, interest increases, and the small sums soon become large stakes. Usually the young man who began to play for recreation ends by playing above his means; the passion grows and he becomes a gambler. These games are too often prolonged into the late hours of the night or even the early hours of the morning; no recreation is obtained; but on the contrary, greater fatigue is the result. These games, too, keep young men from attending Mass on Sundays; they keep them from their duties."

Card-playing is usually associated with smoking and drinking, and it is indulged in to excess, so that instead of being what it should be—a recreation, it is rather a dissipation—a strain on the mind, a tension on the nerves, a depressor of vitality. An hour of simple card-playing, when no stakes are involved, amid home surroundings, may be unobjectionable; but, when the players sit for many consecutive hours over a game of cards, smoking and drinking, and inhaling the vitiated atmosphere of a crowded room, how can that be a refreshment to the mind and the body? Do not permit your love for any kind of card-playing to grow on you till it becomes a passion and masters you.

To bridle the passions is the task of a man's life. Control your passions so that they do not run to what is evil or overstep the limit of prudence or good sense, even in lawful things. Many professional men who are compelled to lead a sedentary life find sufficient recreation in a brisk walk of half an hour or three-quarters of an hour in the morning and evening.

Many a young man, on the other hand, spends hours and hours of precious time over the card-table—hours which he might employ in certain useful pursuits which would be at the same time a real recreation—a refreshment to soul and body.

Gambling assumes forms of great variety from the throwing of dice or the tossing of a penny or the playing of cards for a glass of beer, or a drink of whiskey in the corner saloon, in roulette and faro and other gaming devices in splendidly furnished apartments where thousands and tens of thousands of dollars are won and lost in a single night. This very morning the newspaper had an item concerning a retired business man, who declared on filing a voluntary petition in bankruptcy that he had lost $110,000 at faro in a gambling house in the city of New York. Despite the fact that the evil results which follow in the wake of gambling are so apparent—as regards both temporal and eternal interests—young men are constantly falling under the influence of this baneful passion. Shun the vice of gambling, if you have any regard for your family, your friends, and your own happiness. Many a debauched, friendless, and miserable vagabond owes his ruin to gambling, and the beginning of his downward course was playing cards and other games of hazard, in which the object was not simple, wholesome recreation, but the winning of a stake or a prize.

What is gaming? And is gaming *in itself* morally wrong? Father Slater, S. J., in his *Manual of Moral Theology* answers these questions:[1]

"Gaming is playing at any game, sport, or pastime for *money* or anything of value which is staked on the result of the game, so that it is lost or won according to the success or failure of the person who staked it.

---

1   Vol. i. pp. 558, 559.

"Clerics are forbidden to play at games of pure chance with scandal to others and *loss of their own time*. While in the United States gaming is considered unlawful and the contract null, the statutes of the different States vary considerably in matters of detail.

"But here we consider the question not as affected by positive law, *ecclesiastical* or *civil*, but as it is in itself.

"Is gaming in itself morally wrong? *Apart from abuse*, to play games of skill or even of pure chance for a stake is not immoral. I may spend my money in moderation on recreation, or I may make a present of it to others, if I choose. There is nothing immoral in agreeing to hand over a sum of money, if I am beaten in a game either of skill or of chance. This perfectly lawful action will however, become unlawful if one of the parties is compelled to play against his will, or if cheating and fraud are practised in the game, or if there is no chance of success on the part of one of the players (unless he knows this and freely consents to play in spirit of it), or if the parties have not the money which they stake or at any rate not the free disposal of it on account of its being required to pay their debts, or to support themselves and their families.

"Moreover, although gaming *in itself* and under the conditions which have just been laid down is not immoral, *yet it is a dangerous pastime for many and easily leads to abuse, sin, and ruin.*"

Speaking of pastimes reminds us of hobbies. "Every man has his hobby," is a well-known saying. It is worth while to have a hobby—some favorite pursuit which is pure in its motive and good in its object, even if it be only for recreation when the day's work is done—some outdoor exercise— some study or occupation which one follows with zeal and enthusiasm in leisure hours.

One of our archbishops said recently in addressing the graduates of an academy: *"A good hobby is the exercise of charity"*—charity like that which engages the members of the St. Vincent de Paul Society or of the various Ladies' Aid Societies—charity in behalf of churches and schools, home and foreign missions, hospitals, orphanages, homes for the aged poor, the blind, the deaf and dumb. A hobby, to say the least, is apt to keep a man out of mischief and to prevent him from utterly wasting his time.

The harder some men have to work, the righter and happier they seem to be. In an interview one of the most prominent and successful merchants of New York was asked: "What do you do in your spare time?" "Work," was his laconic reply.

Probably no man in history used his time to better advantage than did St. Alphonsus Liguori, the founder of the Redemptorists. He was born of noble parents in a suburb of Naples on September 27, 1696. He died on the 1st of August, 1787; in his *ninety-first* year. He made a vow never to lose time. As Bishop of St. Agatha he was a very busy man; he gave much time to prayer; and yet he composed many books of such importance that he has been declared a Doctor of the Church. Butler says: "The little time which he contrived to steal from his pastoral care or his devotions, he spent not in recreation, but in writing, or dictating letters, or composing works for the good of souls, or reading spiritual or theological books. Even when obliged to go out in his carriage, he contrived not to allow a single moment to pass unoccupied."

We read in Bowden's *Miniature Lives of the Saints*: "St. Alphonsus wrote his first book at the age of forty-nine, and in his eighty-third year had published about sixty volumes when his Director forbade him to write more. Very many of these books were written in the half hours snatched from his labors as missionary, religious superior, and bishop, or in the midst of continual bodily and mental sufferings. Yet he counted no time wasted which was spent in charity. He did not refuse to hold a long correspondence with a simple soldier who asked his advice or to play the harpsichord while he taught his novices to sing spiritual canticles." St. Alphonsus said: "Consider every occasion of self-denial as a gift which God bestows on you, that you may be able to merit greater glory in another life; and remember that what can be done today can not be performed tomorrow, *for time past never returns.*"

"*Idleness hath taught much evil*" (Ecclus. xxxiii. 29).

"Nothing," says Father Von Doss, S.J.,[1] "becomes youth less than idleness—laziness. Young man, can your past show anything that gives you a right or a claim to repose?

"And your present life? It demands of you activity, energy, exertion. Idleness is premature old age. To be idle is to decay, to die, to rot. The future imperatively demands of you activity. Care must be taken to educate mind and heart. If time shall soon be no more (Apoc. x. 6) for you, then something must be done now, in order that you may not appear before God like the unprofitable servant in the Gospel, with empty hands, and a buried talent (Matt. xxv. 25). Idleness is the cesspool of the soul. Foul vapors arise from stagnant waters, and idle, dangerous, bad, abominable thoughts from inactive hearts—thoughts which may become desires, and end in shameful actions.

"Idleness effeminates and enervates; it robs the mind of its penetration and the character of its firmness. Idleness is the confederate of all other vices; it opens the way for them into the sick and timid heart. Idleness often gives way to excess in eating and drinking and seeks gratification and pastime in low pursuits. Idleness is inconstant. '*The sluggard willeth and willeth not*' (Prov. xiii. 4). Idleness is cowardly. '*The slothful*

---

1   *Thoughts and Counsels for Young Men:* Von Doss-Wirth.

man saith: *There is a lion without. I shall be slain in the midst of the streets*' (Prov. xxii. 13). Bear in mind that sentence of the Lord, and fear: '*Every tree that bringeth not forth good fruit, shall be cut down, and cast into the fire*' (Luke iii. 9). Insatiable thirst for enjoyment and greedy lust of pleasure, is one of the most devastating distempers of our time, the ever gnawing worm of our generation."

Father Joseph Rickaby, S.J., says in *Ye are Christ's*: "I must deny myself, because many of the things that I desire can not go together; to have one is to give up another. No great end in life is gained without an active and watchful resistance, now to one distracting impulse, now to another. The name for that repressive vigilance is *self-denial*.

"Self-denial is continually practised in view of *mere worldly* success. A good oarsman is made by self-denial, a good marksman, a good musician, and a good scholar. Self-denial is needful because of the variety of our desires. There is, I notice, one desire in me, not the strongest, by no means the most clamorous, a quiet, respectable sort of desire, but endowed with immense vitality, a desire which gradually subdues the rest and outlives them all: what is that? It is the desire of ease, the sheer, pure, undiluted love of doing nothing and vegetating quietly. *Otium, Grosphe*, and the rest, as Horace sings.[1] There are those in whom this desire does not wait the hour of enfeebled old age to attain in majority: it is supreme lord paramount from boyhood onward. Is that my case? The indulgence of that do-nothing desire will not make my fortune in this life: and, for the world to come, when they pray over my dead body, '*Eternal rest give to him, O Lord*,' may not the angels reply: 'Why, this creature entered into his rest

1   This is a reference to Ode 2.16 by Horace, which eulogizes *Otium* (peace and leisure) in a time when war was all too common. Horace contrasts himself with *Grosphe* (Pompeius Grosphus, a wealthy Sicilian landowner) as a way of showing that even prosperity cannot take the place of true peace.

long ago, and has slept throughout life like a dormouse: what claim has he to rest for eternity, who has not labored in time?' I need self-denial to overcome my laziness."

> "Absence of occupation is not rest;
> A mind quite vacant is a mind distressed."
> > —Cowper.

> "An idle brain is the devil's workshop."
> > —Anon.

> "For Satan finds some mischief still
> For idle hands to do."
> > —Watts.

> "He is idle that might be better employed."
> > —French.

> "Rest! Rest! Shall I not have all eternity to rest in?"
> > —Arnauld.

> "When youth sleeps on beds of roses,
> Age on beds of thorns reposes."
> > —Quarles.

> "Rest is for the dead."
> > —Carlyle.

> "Every great and commanding movement in the annals of the world is the triumph of *enthusiasm*."
> > —Emerson.

> "No matter what the object is, whether business, pleasures, or the fine arts; whoever pursues them to any purpose must do so *con amore*."
> > —Melmoth.

II. Happiness in Goodness

SHALL I be happy, if I am good? I know I shall be happy in heaven, but that seems a long way off. Shall I be happy on earth? I ask the question in some anxiety, because I hear a great deal about carrying the cross; and I can not conceive how any one can carry the cross and be happy. Carrying the cross means, I suppose, making oneself miserable. Now, though I should like to be good, I have no mind to make myself miserable. What am I to do? I am to put out of my head forever the notion that carrying the cross means making oneself miserable. There is one indeed who, if I try to be good, will do everything in his power to make me miserable. That is my enemy, the devil, whom St. Peter bid me to *resist, strong in faith* (1 Pet. v. 9). St. Chrysostom says that as a Christian resists thoughts of impurity, so he should resist thoughts of sadness: indeed, the one often leads to the other. And St. Ignatius: "It is proper to the evil spirit to sting, to sadden, to put obstacles in the way, making the soul restless by false reasonings to prevent its getting on. And it is proper to the Good Spirit to give courage and strength, consolation and rest of soul, making things easy and removing all obstacles, that the soul may go on further in doing good." And St. John Chrysostom again: "It is proper to the devil to create trouble and excitement and to shroud the mind in darkness: whereas it belongs to God to shed light, and with understanding to teach us what we need to know." In short, there are two crosses: Our Lord's cross and the devil's cross. Our Lord's cross consists of the labors of my state, and the pain and sorrow that go with labor, of whatever sort it be, as God said in the beginning to Adam: "*In the sweat of thy brow thou shalt eat thy bread: thorns and briers shall the earth bear to thee*" (Gen. iii. 18, 19). This cross I must submit to be nailed to, and never come down till death releases me, never abdicate, never resign. The devil's cross consists of feelings of wretchedness, black discontent, irritation, complaining, downheartedness, and misery—as it were whiffs from the cloud that envelopes Satan in eternal despair. This cross I must fling far from me.

There is no virtue in long faces, even when pious people pull them. To carry Christ's cross manfully, one should be reluctant to know that one has got any great weight of it on one's shoulder. Let me take an example: the case of a young man at college.

A frequent cross with youth is the cross of examinations. I was going to add "in uncongenial matter"; but somehow nearly everything that one is examined in, and has to plod trough during months of preparation, comes to be felt as uncongenial matter. Here are two wrong things to do, and one right thing. The first wrong thing is to refuse the examination, get oneself let off, or let oneself off by ceasing to study. That is like resigning a burdensome office in later life—usually a mistake. It is flinging Christ's cross away. The second wrong thing is to go on studying making oneself miserable all the while with lamentations about the disagreeableness of the task and the prospects of failure. That is adding to Christ's cross, and may likely enough end in casting off both—*quod erat faciendum*, in Satan's plan. The one right thing is to work hard, serenely and faithfully day by day, doing all one can, and committing results to God. The moral is this: the cross of sadness should always be got rid of by a Christian, so far as ever he is able to shake it off: but the cross of arduous and at times disagreeable employment should be held on to and cheerfully borne.   —Father Joseph Rickaby, S. J., in *Ye are Christ's*.

III. A New Virtue

THERE is a virtue which may be new to the hearing of many of us. It was discovered and named by Aristotle; and he called it by the pretty Greek name of *eutrapelia*. *Eutrapelia* may be defined "playfulness in good taste." Aristotle himself defines it: "*a chastened love of putting out one's strength upon others.*" There is in every ordinary boy a disposition to romp, to play the fool, and to destroy property; a disposition which ought to be sternly repressed, subdued, and kept under by those responsible for the boy's education, beginning with himself. Otherwise the boy can have no place in civilized society; he will turn out a young savage. But though repressed, the disposition should not be killed within him and extirpated altogether. It is a defect of character to have no playfulness, no drollery, no love of witnessing or even creating a ridiculous situation. *Eutrapelia* knows exactly when and how to be funny, and where and when to stop. *All things have their season*, says Ecclesiastes (iii. 1, 4); *a time to weep, and a time to laugh; a time to mourn, and a time to dance.* A proud and quarrelsome man is never a funny man. Many a difficulty, many an incipient quarrel, many a dark temptation, is dissipated the moment one catches sight of some humorous side to the matter. A humble man makes merry over his own misadventures; and when he is inclined to storm and rage, listens to a good angel whispering in his ear: "John, don't make a fool of yourself." A merry boy is seldom a bad boy.

Life is not all play: indeed, it is a very serious thing; but on account of its very seriousness we require some play to set it off. That is why you find excellent men and great doers of good with an extraordinary faculty, which they use at times, of talking nonsense and playing the fool. *Eutrapelia* is a blend of playfulness and earnestness. Without earnestness, playfulness degenerates into frivolity. *"O Lord, give me not over to an irreverent and frivolous mind"* (Ecclus. xxiii. 6). We generally wear our lighter clothing underneath, and our heavier clothing above it; and perhaps that is the best way for a man, to veil his *eutrapelia* under a serious exterior. But for a boy the other way about is the better fashion; he should be playful and mirthful to the eye, but have seriousness and earnestness underneath, known only to those who know him well. In the earliest days of the Society of Jesus, there was a novice much given to laughing. One day he met Father Ignatius, and thought that he was in for a scolding. But St. Ignatius said to him: "Child, I want you to laugh and be joyful in the Lord. A Religious has no cause for sadness, but many reasons for rejoicing; and that you may always be glad and joyful, be humble always and always obedient."

—Father Joseph Rickaby, S. J., in *Ye are Christ's.*

Prayer to St. Joseph as Patron

Blessed Joseph, faithful guardian of my Redeemer Jesus Christ, protector of thy chaste spouse the virgin Mother of God, I choose thee this day to be my especial patron and advocate, and I firmly resolve to honor thee as such from this time forth and always. Therefore I humbly beseech thee to receive me for thy client, to instruct me in every doubt, to comfort me in every affliction, and finally to defend and protect me in the hour of death. Amen.

For His Safe-Conduct Through Life

Blessed Joseph, father and guide of Jesus Christ in His childhood and youth, who didst lead Him safely in His flight through the desert, and in all the ways of His earthly pilgrimage, be also my companion and guide in this pilgrimage of life, and never permit me to turn aside from the way of God's commandments; be my refuge in adversity, my support in temptation, my solace in affliction, until at length I arrive at the land of the living, where with thee, and Mary thy most holy spouse, and all the Saints, I may rejoice forever in Jesus my Lord. Amen.

For Grace to Communicate Devoutly

Blessed Joseph, how sweet and wonderful a privilege was thine, not only to see, but to carry in thy arms, to kiss and to embrace with fatherly affection that only begotten Son of God, whom so many Kings and Prophets desired to see, but were not able! O that, inspired by thy example and aided by thy patronage, I may often, with like feelings of love and reverence, embrace my Lord and Redeemer in the Blessed Sacrament of the altar, so that when my life on earth is ended, I may merit to embrace Him eternally in heaven. Amen.

PRAYER TO ST. ALOYSIUS

O BLESSED Aloysius! adorned with Angelic graces, I, thy most unworthy servant, recommend especially to thee the chastity of my soul and body, praying thee, by thy angelic purity, to plead for me with Jesus Christ the Immaculate Lamb, and His most holy Mother, Virgin of virgins, that they would vouchsafe to keep me from all grievous sin. O never let me be defiled with any stain of impurity; but when thou dost see me in temptation, or in danger of falling, then remove far from my heart all bad thoughts and unclean desires; and awaken in me the memory of eternity and of Jesus crucified. Impress deeply in my heart a sense of the holy fear of God, and thus kindling in me the fire of divine love, enable me so to follow thy footsteps here on earth, that in heaven with thee, I may be made worthy to enjoy the vision of our God forever. Amen.

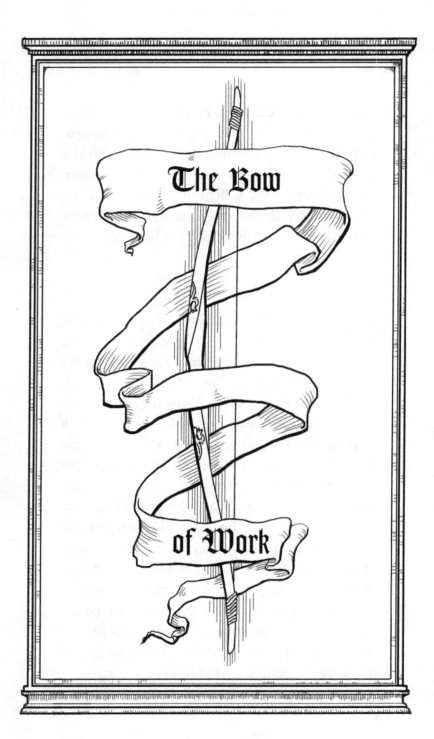

The Bow

of Work

The Bow of Work

53. The Serious Side of Life

THE smiling, careless, innocent days of childhood are but brief; swiftly do they pass away, almost before the young man has begun to learn how great is their value, and to prize them as he ought. Too soon is he compelled to part from the innocent games which gladden a child's heart, and from the merry companions with whom he has spent the greater part of the bright morning of life. Now he is obliged to venture forth, and make acquaintance with the serious side of life.

What is the serious side of life? It is the season of work. Work! Let not the name terrify you on account of the harshness of its sound: the word is not nearly so forbidding and repulsive as it appears at first sight. You must not, as is so often the case, couple with the word "work" an idea of weariness, misery, toil, and humiliation, as connected with a slavish occupation. For work, in the proper sense of the term, includes everything which, unlike the fruit on the tree, does not come to maturity of itself. Work belongs especially to the duties of young men; among his spiritual weapons, I include the bow of work. Therefore do you, my friend, arm yourself with this bow when you sally forth to make acquaintance with the serious side of life.

"In the world's broad field of battle,
    In the bivouac of Life,
Be not like dumb, driven cattle!
    Be a hero in the strife!

"Trust no Future, howe'er pleasant!
    Let the dead Past bury its dead!
Act—act in the living Present!
    Heart within, and God o'erhead.

"Let us, then, be up and doing,
    With a heart for any fate;
Still achieving, still pursuing,
    Learn to labor and to wait."
                                    —Longfellow.

What is the right view of labor? Since man is made in the image of God, he shares in a way in His creative activity. Understand my meaning! Of course, I do not intend to say that he can bring something out of nothing; but he is capable of giving to matter another form, and by the light of his intelligence to rise to the knowledge of higher things.

Now all this is brought about by means of exertion, effort—work. Such work is twofold, being both *mental* and *physical*. Both kinds of work are indispensably necessary for the well-being of human society; they may be termed its body and soul. In this, and in some of the succeeding chapters, we shall direct our attention almost exclusively to the latter kind, to physical labor.

You also, my young friend, will have to experience the grave meaning of the words which God addressed to our first parents in paradise, immediately subsequent to the fall: "*In the sweat of thy face shalt thou eat bread, until thou return to the earth out of which thou wast taken*" (Gen. iii. 19). Work is a law of existence, ordained by God Himself. Every one who refuses to comply with this law incurs the risk of losing, not only his higher vocation here upon earth, but also the crown which is held out to him on a happier shore—the crown of eternal glory in heaven. Therefore you must not hesitate for a single instant to submit willingly to the law of labor, and thus to take the serious side of life in a serious spirit. "*Six days shalt thou labor and shalt do all thy works,*" said God to the people of Israel by the mouth of Moses. On one day of the week man ought to rest from his work, as far as the honor of God or the love of his neighbor does not imperatively demand it. This is required by the third commandment, which God gave of old on Mount Sinai.

St. Paul wrote to the Thessalonians: "*If any man will not work, neither let him eat.*" If you remain idle and slothful, and refuse to work, you rebel against the infinitely wise ordinance of God, and frustrate the end of your creation, as far as in you lies.

Hence it is easy to understand why the saints in all ages have been so very industrious. Never allow a single day to pass without sowing, by means of some useful work, a grain of seed in the furrows of time, which may spring up and bear fruit in eternity.

Listen, also, to what the Holy Ghost says to the idle man in the Book of Proverbs: "*Go to the ant, O sluggard, consider her ways and learn wisdom. Which although she hath no guide, nor master, nor captain, provideth her meat for herself in the summer, and gathereth her food in the harvest. How long wilt thou sleep, O sluggard? When wilt thou arise out of thy sleep? Thou wilt sleep a little, thou wilt slumber a little, thou wilt fold thy hands a little to sleep and want shall come upon thee*" (Prov. vi. 6-11). But not only external and material want shall come upon the sloth-man, but what is infinitely worse, spiritual destitution also—the famine of the soul—for idleness is the parent of all vice. Flee from it therefore, and always bear in mind that:

Swiftly time speeds on its way,
Though we fain would bid it stay;
Employ it well, work while you may,
Night soon succeeds to life's brief day.

54. THE WORTH AND DIGNITY OF LABOR

THE interior of the peaceful house of Nazareth was familiar with strenuous physical labor. Could we have looked in, whom would we have found there engaged at work? Jesus Christ Himself, the God-Man, His foster-father, St. Joseph, and Mary, His virginal mother. From this we may judge the worth and dignity of labor. But men have not always esteemed the value of labor. The ancient heathen considered bodily labor to be altogether contemptible. The man who was free-born felt it to be a disgrace to put his hand to work; even the most enlightened among the Greeks and Romans expressed, in no doubtful terms, their supreme contempt for bodily labor.

And throughout the whole of heathendom we encounter this aversion to labor—this contempt for work. The North American Indian likes to leave work to women, as did the Teutons in days of old.

But since work was necessary, if men were to eat and live, they conceived the idea of slavery. They went so far as to regard common laborers as a separate and degraded class of beings; they considered them as but little superior to brutes. Laborers or slaves were mere animated machines, which might be treated in any manner which seemed good to their owners. They were bought and sold, like any other kind of merchandise; they were cast off, *i.e.*, put to death, as soon as they were no longer of any use. It was seriously doubted whether slaves really possessed a human soul! Such was the view which the heathen took of workmen and work.

Then Jesus Christ appeared, the God-Man and Redeemer. He did not choose for His foster-father an emperor who occupied the throne of the Roman Empire, nor a member of the Roman senate, nor one of the sages of those days.

No; He chose a man who had spent his whole life in hard labor—a carpenter—an artisan, whose workshop was the place he loved best, next to the temple of God.

What a distinction for work does this fact furnish! The greatest honor which God could confer upon any man, He conferred upon an artisan, upon the carpenter, St. Joseph of Nazareth! *"My ways are not your ways,"* is what the voice of the Son of God proclaimed to the whole world even from the manger.

And we may go yet further! He Himself, the incarnate Son of God, willed to labor in the workshop of St. Joseph, until He was thirty years old. And Mary, His most blessed mother, was no fashionable lady, going from place to place in search of amusement and pleasure, delighting in dress, or wasting time in reading silly romances. No, we behold her in the peaceful house at Nazareth, engaged in such domestic occupations as became the wife of an artisan.

Since that day what a different aspect does work assume, viewed in the light of the Catholic faith, and in view of the humble workshop of Nazareth, where Jesus Christ Himself, the God-Man, cheerfully and uncomplainingly helped his foster-father with his work, handling to this end the saw, the hatchet, and the plane.

Heltinger expresses himself ably on this subject in his *Christian Apology*: "Christ, the Son of the carpenter, ennobled work, once and forever, and even the lowest kind of manual labor. The ancient command: *'In the sweat of thy face thou shalt eat thy bread,'* was hallowed by Him, was changed into a blessing, a service rendered to God, and an expression of love to Our Lord.

"And those who were the first to proclaim His doctrines, gained their livelihood by the work of their hands, and by so doing condemned, once and forever, that idleness which devours the fruit of other men's toil. After this, work ceased to be a disgrace, and the Fathers of the Church can scarcely find words enough in which to proclaim the praises of labor. It is indeed a penance for sin, but for the will which is weakened by sin and inclined to evil, it is a shield against temptation; it is a tonic to strengthen man's moral nature, a task performed in the service of Christ, a means of practising every virtue, a school of sanctification, a pledge of rich reward at the hand of God, a well-spring of peace, the honor and the joy of man; for by continuous activity and unceasing effort a man lives a real life, and becomes like to God."

Such, briefly expressed, is the worth and dignity of labor. Learn to honor it and to follow it zealously. Regard your work—be it easy or difficult, lofty or lowly—as a precious memorial, a valuable relic, of the holy house it Nazareth. There, indeed, your work also has been ennobled and sanctified; there it received the patent of nobility, which, in so far as you prize it highly as a valuable jewel, will be for you a source of riches and happiness while you sojourn upon earth, and, what is the most important point, will render you a favorite of Jesus, Mary, and Joseph, and gain for you the right to an eternal reward. Therefore:

> Art thou weary, by thy work opprest,
> Go to Christ and there thou shalt find rest.
> Show Him thy toil-stained hands and see
> His hands that toiled and bled for thee.

55. The Trials of the Workman[1]
"I will hedge up thy way with thorns" (Os. ii. 6)

THE words of the prophet, *"I will hedge up thy way with thorns,"* apply in a greater or less degree to all men; for it

---

1 From *Outlines of Sermons for Young Men and Young Women:* Schuen-Wirth.

was said to the father of the human race and to all his posterity: *"Cursed is the earth in thy work: with labor and toil shalt thou eat thereof all the days of thy life. Thorns and thistles shall it bring forth to thee"* (Gen. iii. 17, 18). Hence it is that thorns spring up everywhere, in the mansions of the rich as well as in the hovels of the poor. Yet there are some states in life where they seem to grow more luxuriantly than in others. Most of you, if not all of you, are in the employ of others, and this is one of the states in life that has its abundance of thorns.

The thorns of the workman may be turned into roses by his being contented with his calling. Contentment with one's calling can be obtained by looking at the world as it is. It is an abode of trials, sufferings, a valley of tears. *"The days of man,"* says Job, *"are like the days of a hireling"* (Job vii. 1). And the author of the *Imitation of Christ* tells us that mortal life is full of miseries, all signed around with crosses (Imit. bk. 2, c. 12). It is not only the state of the workman that has its trials—every state in life has its own difficulties and thorns; there is none where the sky is perpetually serene and where roses bloom forever. In other paths besides the one you pursue, thorns are found to wound the feet of the wayfarer; indeed, they are often of a size of which you have no conception. Many a thorn of which you know nothing is found in the path of the priest, the doctor, the lawyer, the father of a family. Even in the highest ranks of society tears flow in abundance, and *"he that weareth purple and beareth the crown"* (Ecclus. xl. 4) is often crushed to the ground by a heavy burden. Cast your eyes upon the world round about you, compare your work with the work of others more heavily burdened, compare your trials with theirs, and do not complain about your state in life, but be content. Let us also remember that men often conceal their troubles from the world, and that many a man hides a sore heart behind a smiling countenance.

Another source of content is found in looking up to God, whose will we perform. Our holy faith teaches us that there is a divine providence that disposes all things: "*He ordereth all things sweetly*" (Wis. viii. 1). "*The eyes of the Lord are upon the ways of men, and He considereth all their steps*" (Job xxxiv. 21). Holy Scripture teaches us that God disposes all things, especially the ways of man; it must, then, be God's will that we be in the state of life that we find ourselves in. What a consolation for us! As we work, we are doing the will of God. Then again, contemplate the Son of God. He in whom were all things created in heaven and on earth humbled Himself, "*taking the form of a servant*" (Phil. ii. 7). The first thirty years of His life were spent in the workshop of His foster-father, St. Joseph. Ought not this consideration make you contented with your lot?

Another means of turning the thorns of our calling into roses is found in this: that your work may be made meritorious for heaven. Such roses never fade. Nothing is easier than this, for God in His mercy counts to our merit a cup of cold water given in His name. How much more meritorious than a cup of cold water will be your daily labors and trials if offered up to Him! St. Paul exhorts us: "*Whatsoever you do, do it from the heart, as to the Lord and not to men, knowing that you shall receive of the Lord the reward of inheritance*" (Col. iii. 23, 24). If you work for God, not merely for men, all your labors and trials will become valuable for eternity, and will merit for you the "*inheritance incorruptible, and undefiled, and that can not fade, reserved in heaven for you*" (1 Pet. i. 4). The wages you earn upon earth are indeed small, but the reward you may receive for them in heaven is incomprehensibly great. In this manner the thorns in your way may be changed into roses that never fade, and which will be woven into a crown to be placed on your brow for all eternity.

There are many workmen who are honest, conscientious, and careful in the performance of their duties, and who are for this reason trusted and loved by their employers. On the other hand, we must also admit that there are many complaints made today about workmen, and that these complaints are not without some foundation.

Workmen often take no interest in the welfare of their employers; they seem to believe that there must necessarily exist opposition between them instead of a friendly cooperation. Hence they perform their work merely to satisfy their employer sufficiently to retain their situation, and have no intelligent interest in the advancement of his business. That bond which in former times united employers and workmen so that they became almost like members of the same family, the employer looking after the best interests of his workmen, and the workmen looking upon the business of their employer as if it were their own, has for the most part ceased to exist.

Most of the complaints that we hear about workmen would be silenced if they would turn with more earnestness to their holy faith. It is faith that teaches us the nobility of work; by faith we learn that work is commanded us by God. God Himself instituted labor. "*Six days thou shalt work*" (Ex. xx. 9). "*Hate not laborious work, nor husbandry ordained by the Most High*" (Ecclus. vii. 16). "*Endeavor to work with your own hands, as we commanded you*" (1 Thess. iv. 11). That which God has commanded can assuredly be nothing ignoble or vile. Moreover, work has been sanctified by the example of the Redeemer Himself, who came "*not to be ministered unto, but to minister*" (Mark x. 45). For thirty years the Son of God helped Joseph in his work as carpenter. In the light of our holy faith, the calling of a workman is certainly a noble one. By the light of faith, workmen obtain a better understanding of their duties in life, and the first step toward fulfilling them is to know them. Faith leads men to be honest and conscientious in their work.

Conscientiousness is a powerful means of removing the faults commonly complained of in workmen. This springs from faith: worldly motives are generally insufficient to make men truly conscientious. If a workman is conscientious, there is seldom any cause for complaint; he will be diligent in his work, and he will have the interest of his employer at heart; he sees in his work the fulfilment of God's will, and is not disturbed by little difficulties and trials that spring up from time to time; he is willing to make a sacrifice for God's sake.

It is mainly because faith is dying out amongst men that all the countless troubles between laborers and employers arise. Both sides are possessed with a spirit of greed and selfishness; none is willing to consider fairly the just claims of the other, and hence each is continually endeavoring to take unfair advantage of the needs of the other. It is only Christianity that can remedy the evils of the times. What we need is more believing and conscientious workmen and employers. Take in good part the admonitions I have addressed to you; in what I have said I have had nothing but your own welfare at heart. Be upright and honest, so that your employers will have no reason to complain of you, and you will obtain that which is due to you more easily than by opposition and discontent. Every one must admire an honest, diligent workman and will be anxious to recognize his just claims by retaining him. Your calling is not without trials, but you would find just as many, and perhaps greater ones, in every other calling. And do you not know that there is One who counts the drops of sweat upon your brow, and who recompenses every sacrifice? *"I will repay them according to their deeds and according to the works of their hands,"* saith the Lord (Jer. xxv. 14). The workman who is animated with faith and who performs the duties of his calling conscientiously will one day hear the words of Our Lord: "*Well done, good and faithful servant; because thou hast been faithful over a few things, I will place thee over many things; enter thou into the joy of thy Lord*" (Matt. xxv. 23).

> There is One who sees your life,
> Knows your labor, knows your strife;
> One who feels with all your sadness,
> And will turn it into gladness.

56. How Ought You to Work?

IN THE ear of every young man there sounds the call of his heavenly Father, summoning him to go forth and work in the vineyard of this world. The young man ought to learn to labor well and earnestly, and even take delight in his work.

Experience teaches us that industrious young people who love their work, and do it well are almost invariably pious and moral. It is on this account the highest praise for a young man, if it can be said of him with justice that he is industrious, never weary of his work, and always occupied in some useful manner. Employ your time well; be industrious; love your work, it will bring you a blessing both here and hereafter. But mark well *how* you ought to work.

First of all, and before all else, see that you labor for the honor and glory of God; and to this end, every morning at least, before you begin your work, direct your intention. Say with a fervent heart: "*Omnia ad majorem Dei gloriam!*" "All for the greater glory of God!" As often as you begin a piece of work say: "*In the name of Jesus!*"

But a good intention is not enough; you must also perform your work in a state of sanctifying grace; you must take care that your conscience is not burdened by any serious sin. By means of a good intention alone your work does indeed possess something of a supernatural nature, and tends to prepare you for an amendment of life; but while you remain in the state of mortal sin, it can not earn for you a reward in heaven.

If, therefore, an eternal reward is to be paid you for your work from the treasury of God, it must bear, besides the imprint of a good intention, the stamp of sanctifying grace.

And yet one thing more is needful; you must perform your work with patience. He who, while at work, grows impatient, murmurs and complains, is false to the good intention with which he began; his work is no longer done for the honor of God, and therefore loses all claim to an eternal reward.

Wherefore murmur not—do not complain, much less utter words of cursing. Even if you look at the matter from a purely natural point of view, does your work get on any better if you yield to impatience? Can you finish it more quickly if you break out into oaths and imprecations? Most certainly not!

On the contrary, if you are patient about your work, and perform it for the love of God, you will certainly do it with zeal and industry; you will not grow morose and indifferent if you can not complete your task as speedily as you hoped to do. You will not allow yourself to be hindered in your work by useless chatter; no, you will perform it as well as you can—cheerfully and faithfully. You will perform every action as if it were your last, and as if, immediately thereafter, you were to be summoned to appear before God, and give a strict account to Him.

The Blessed Baldomer has taught us by his example how one's daily work may be begun and ended in a manner pleasing to God. He was a locksmith, and employed numerous apprentices. He was much given to prayer, and a lover of work. As a master he held fast to the ancient and admirable custom of beginning everything with God. He arose each morning with his mind on God, and invariably performed his morning devotions with scrupulous care, remembering the old and most true saying, that everything depends on the blessing of God.

He was a daily attendant at Mass, for he bore in mind the divine promise: *"Seek ye therefore first the kingdom of God and his justice, and all these things shall be added unto you."* *"In the name of God,"* he said as he began his work, and then hammered away busily, until evening came, and after the burden and toil of the day, he laid his tools aside with a heartfelt ejaculation of, *"Thanks be to God!"* In this way Baldomer not only gained a fortune, but accumulated a treasure of merit for eternity.

Do you also work in a similar fashion. Employ yourself usefully at every moment of the day, in order that the devil *"who goeth about as a roaring lion, seeking whom he may devour,"* may never find you idle. This is the best way to spoil his little game. Once more let me exhort you: Be very careful to perform your work with a good intention, and in a state of grace. Also strive to be always patient, in order that one day you may purchase, with sterling coins of the realm, an entrance into heaven.

> Cease to lament, O troubled heart,
> What do you gain when you complain?
> For work and prayer we know impart
> The best relief to earthly grief.

57. WORK AND WAGES

SOCIAL questions are very prominently brought forward in the present day. In regard to this subject, the foreground is occupied by complaints concerning the unfortunate relations between capital and labor, between work and wages. Lamentations are rife on the one hand, where it is asserted that the workman may toil and wear himself out, and yet receive a pittance which scarcely suffices to keep the wolf from the door, and which renders it almost impossible to procure the necessaries of life, considering the present high price of provisions.

On the other side the lamentations are just as loud. Workmen can never be satisfied; they demand shorter hours and higher wages, and on account of the excess of production and eager competition it becomes necessary to dispose of goods at a merely nominal price.

And who is in the right? No one can seriously assert that our present social conditions are particularly favorable. But the fundamental cause of all these complaints lies in the fact that human society is, in the present day, no longer permeated by a truly Christian spirit.

If, in our modern times, we had made as much progress in this spirit as we have in discoveries of every kind, there would not be all these complaints. The workman would not have to complain of exploitation and treatment unworthy of a human being on the part of the masters, nor would the latter complain of insolence and excessive claims on the part of the former.

The Christian spirit renders the master just—and more than just—toward the workman; the workman contented, modest, and respectful; the Christian spirit renders the master the father of those whom he employs, and makes them to a certain extent his equals. Yes, if the Christian spirit had governed every strata of society, conditions would have been far more satisfactory; in spite of steam power and machinery we should have more independent workmen. However, if you, young man, belong to the working classes, you must constantly bear in mind the fact that dependence is not degradation. But it forms part of the scheme or economy of divine providence, that many—very many—human beings do, and must live in this or a similar state of dependence.

If this lot has perhaps fallen to your share, see that you do not complain and murmur against the providence of God, and indulge in discontent in regard to your lot; do not consider this dependence to be something degrading, unworthy of a human being, and therefore to be spoken of with contempt. You may, and you should, strive to raise yourself to an independent position, through industry, energy, perseverance, prayer, and the use of lawful means. But to do this by defiance, insubordination, chicanery, unjust demands and actions, would be to rise up against the law and ordinance of God; it would be a sin.

In all your circumstances, in the midst of trials and hardships, fail not to place your trust in God. *"He hath care of you."* In His own good time and way He will reward you if you labor for love of Him, if you do all things, as the Apostle admonishes us, *"in the name of the Lord Jesus Christ."* The demands of workmen in the present day aim only at a just rate of payment. It is otherwise with the reward which God metes out, and which we can merit by our labor, if this is performed in a state of grace, and with a good intention.

God does, indeed, measure out the reward with exactitude, so that no particle of meritorious labor shall remain unrewarded, but He measures it out in rich and overflowing fulness. He rewards everything, not with princely or royal munificence, but with divine bounty, as becomes His divine majesty.

This is told us by St. Paul, in the memorable words with which I conclude this chapter: *"For that which is at present momentary and light of our tribulation, worketh for us above measure exceedingly an eternal weight of glory."*

If thy fortune seem to fail
And thy efforts nought avail,
Chase away all doubt and gloom,
Bravely then thy work resume.
Riches of a higher sphere
Are gained by patient suffering here.

Hard though be thy lot
Christian workman, murmur not;
Soon the light shall dawn
Which ushers in a brighter morn.

58. WORK AND THE SUNDAY REST

UNDER the old dispensation God laid a very special stress on the observance of the Sabbath; while Israel was in the desert, He ordained by the mouth of Moses that anyone who violated this commandment should incur the penalty of death. We, who live under the new dispensation, have to keep the Sunday holy. In the first place we must abstain from servile work on the Lord's Day.

The Sunday rest is, however, no arbitrary requirement for the working man, but a command of nature. A human being is not capable of incessant exertion, like a mere inanimate machine, and even the latter wears out if constantly used. Scientists, and even medical men who are destitute of religious beliefs, and unchristian governments, have publicly proclaimed their conviction that one day of rest in the week is a necessity; they have unanimously asserted how highly important it is that Sunday should be generally observed as a day of rest.

And there is, moreover, something beautiful and elevating in the Sunday rest and Sunday celebration. As soon as he awakes on the Lord's Day, the truly Christian workman feels that he has been transported into a different atmosphere. The cheerful peal of the church bells sounds pleasantly in his ear. He puts on his Sunday coat instead of his dusty blouse, and repairs to church with a joyful heart, in order there to unite with all his fellow-Christians in the worship of God, his supreme Lord and Master. Great and small, high and low, rich and poor, are on the same footing in the house of God, and the meanest workman is conscious that within those walls his dignity as a Christian outweighs marble palaces, high offices of state, kingly titles, and imperial diadems, making them all to appear as mere tinsel.

Yet does many a man imagine in his blindness and thirst for gain that Sunday labor is an advantage to him, and increases his store of money. How short-sighted! If you, my friend, could reckon up the number of those—if indeed any such could be found—who have become rich through working on Sunday, and also those who, in spite of working on Sunday, or, to speak more correctly, because they worked on Sunday, have come to beggary; then would the mere consideration of worldly advantage restrain you from desecrating the day of the Lord. Everything depends on the blessing of God; the curse of God, on the contrary, brings to nought the rarest hopes and wisest calculations. Can not God send down, in the space of one brief hour, lightning and hail, sickness and death? Does His hand not know how to strike the guilty?

A certain judge in his youth had belonged to a society composed of young men who habitually desecrated Sunday, either by work, or excesses of different descriptions. Later in life, however, he had been converted and had amended his ways.

He was, on one occasion, called to pass sentence of death upon a criminal who had been a member of the same society. The judge trembled to think of the danger he had incurred, and asked the unfortunate man before him what had become of his associates of former days. "Your Honor," replied the criminal, "except yourself and me, there is not one left alive; all the others have perished on the gallows, or met some form of violent death."

That is but one instance out of very many which prove that, as He formerly did under the old dispensation, God heavily punishes those who violate the Sabbath. Be very careful, my friend, not to desecrate Sunday either by work, or by indulgence in sinful pleasures. Live in accordance with your faith, be a true and loyal Catholic; then will you live a happy life, and die a peaceful death.

SUNDAY

This day the glorious Trinity
    Creation's work began;
This day the world's Creator rose,
    O'ercoming death for man.

So, while on this His holy day,
    At this most sacred hour,
Our psalms amid the stillness rise,
    May He His blessings shower.

Father of lights! keep us this day
    From sinful passions free;
Grant us, in every word, and deed,
    And thought, to honor Thee.

Assist us, Purity divine,
    Within our hearts to quell
Those evil fires which, cherish'd here,
    Augment the flames of hell.

Saviour, of Thy sweet clemency,
    Wash Thou our sins away;
Grant us Thy peace—grant us with Thee
    Thine own eternal day.
            —*Lyra Catholica.*

59. SUCCESS

"IN *all thy works be excellent*" (Ecclus. xxxiii. 23). If success does not come, it shall not be for want of effort on my part. A good Catholic standing high in his profession or business is a great support to the Church. His example shows that the life of the world to come does not mean the wrecking of the life that now is. But is there not danger of vainglory in the pursuit of success? To this question St. Ignatius makes answer as follows: "When a good soul thinks of doing something that may turn to the glory of God within the area of activity that the Church allows, and thereupon encounters some temptation not to do it, the tempter alleging specious pretexts of vainglory, then the soul could raise its gaze to its Creator and Lord, and if it sees that the thing is not contrary to God's service, it ought to take the very opposite course to the course suggested by the tempter, and say with St. Bernard: *'I did not begin for you, and I will not leave off for you.'* " Besides, success in any profession is not attained except by hard work, and hard work is a wonderful cure for vainglory. Hard work crowds out thoughts of vanity. Work is hard because we are weak. Hard work reveals our weakness and humbles us. Real hard work is not work done with facility and zest, as when a healthy lad runs his mile. Real hard work is gone through in spite of reluctance and pain, and occasional inability to proceed; it is as the limping, hobbling gait of a lame man. The advantages that men are born with, or come in for without labor, or possess henceforth in comfortable security without further need of effort—such are the advantages most likely to turn a man's head with vainglory. Still, labor as we may, some of us will never attain success in this world. God has His own way of treating every soul. Some He leads to heaven by the road of temporal success, but many by the way of failure, poverty, and humiliation, the same by which Himself, as man, mounted to His heavenly throne. Never was there, to human eyes, such an utterly hopeless failure as Christ crucified— accused, found guilty, and condemned, dying the death of a felon and of a slave, deserted by His friends, mocked by His enemies, apparently forsaken by God, and His wonder- working powers taken away from Him—in this plight our blessed Saviour closed His eyes, beholding with His last glance what appeared to be the ruin of His work and the failure of His mission. After such an example, no Christian need be surprised at disaster. There must be other avenues to heaven than the way of the "prosperous gentleman." I will work hard to succeed in my profession and if, with all my hard work, I fail and die a ruined man, still *this hope is stored up in my breast* (Job xix. 27), that my Saviour will love me the better for my failure, and that I shall be the nearer Him on that account in paradise.

—Father Joseph Rickaby, S. J., in *Ye are Christ's.*

'Tis not in mortals to command success,
But we'll do more, Sempronius; we'll deserve it.

—Addison.

"Whatsoever thy hand is able to do, do it earnestly."

(Ecclus. ix. 10)

"Who is the man that desireth life: Who desireth to see good days?
Keep thy tongue from evil, and thy lips from speaking guile.
Turn away from evil and do good: seek after peace and pursue it."

(Ps. xxxiii. 13-15)

"Exhort your hearts, and confirm you in every good work and word."

(2 Thess. ii. 16)

"If thou do well, shalt thou not receive?"

(Gen. iv. 7)

"For He [the Lord] *will render to a man his work, and according*
to the ways of every one, He will reward them."

(Job xxxiv. 11)

"The Lord will reward me according to my justice, and will
repay me according to the cleanness of my hands:
Because I have kept the ways of the Lord; and have not
done wickedly against my God."

(Ps. xvii. 21, 22)

JESUS, MASTER, TEACH ME

TEACH ME, teach me, dearest Jesus,
In Thine own sweet loving way,
All the lessons of perfection
I must practice day by day.

Teach me *Meekness*, dearest Jesus,
Of Thine own the counterpart;
Not in words and actions only,
But the meekness of the heart.

Teach *Humility*, sweet Jesus,
To this poor, proud heart of mine,
Which yet wishes, O my Jesus,
To be modelled after Thine.

Teach me *Fervor*, dearest Jesus,
To comply with every grace,
So as never to look backwards,
Never slacken in the race.

Teach me *Poverty*, sweet Jesus,
That my heart may never cling
To whate'er its love might sever
From my Saviour, Spouse, and King.

Teach me *Chastity*, sweet Jesus,
That my every day may see
Something added to the likeness
That my soul should bear to Thee.

Teach *Obedience*, dearest Jesus,
Such as was Thy daily food
In Thy toilsome earthly journey
From the cradle to the rood.

Teach *Thy Heart* to me, dear Jesus,
Is my fervent, final prayer,
For all beauties and perfections
Are in full perfection there.

—*Leaflets*

"*The life of man upon earth is a warfare*" (Job vii. 1).

"*Fight the good fight of faith; lay hold on eternal life, whereunto thou art called*" (1 Tim. vi. 12).

"*Labor as a good soldier of Christ Jesus, for he also that striveth for the mastery is not crowned, except he strive lawfully*" (2 Tim. ii. 3, 5).

"*Every one that striveth for the masters refraineth himself from all things; and they indeed that they may receive a corruptible crown; but we an incorruptible one*" (1 Col ix. 25).

PART SECOND
CONFLICT AND CONQUEST

The Struggle and the Prize

The Struggle and the Prize

*"The flesh lusteth against the spirit; and the spirit against the flesh;
for these are contrary one to another, so that you do not
the things that you should"* (Gal. v. 17).

60. Your Most Precious Treasure

LET us now direct our attention to the contest in which you
must engage in behalf of holy purity. I desire with all the
fervor of my soul, with all the earnestness at my command,
with the most tender solicitude of a father, to arouse within
your breast an enthusiastic love for this angelic virtue and to
urge you on to struggle with valor and perseverance for its
preservation.

It behooves me also to warn you against the opposite
vice, to point out to you the varied forms which the enemy
you have to encounter is wont to assume, and to describe the
most efficacious means to protect and defend yourself against
all attacks.

In God's name, go forth to do battle manfully on behalf of
the virtue of purity, and to fight with courage and perseverance
against your most terrible enemy, the vice of impurity. It may
help you to fight this battle aright, if you consider with me
and reflect earnestly upon the following points: namely the
prize in the contest, the reward of victory, the enemy, and the
weapons to be employed against him.

The prize that you are to win in the fierce conflict of your youth is something celestially fair and infinitely precious; it is the pearl of virtues, your most costly treasure—purity of heart.

With what a mystic charm, with what grace and beauty, does this virtue of innocence invest the child, the chaste young man. That is what the poet means when he sings of the sweet charm of youth which has never known defilement. And so great is this charm that frequently even the evil man, the libertine, feels its influence, and is filled with veneration. For instance, the poet Heine sings of an innocent child in the following beautiful lines:

> Thou'rt like a tender floweret,
> Innocent and pure and fair:
> I gaze on thee with joy, and yet
> 'Tis not without a shade of care;
> It seems to me I needs must lay
> My hand upon thy head, and pray
> That God would keep thee as thou art,
> So innocent and pure of heart.

How great is the value that most precious treasure possesses in the sight of God! "*And the Word was made flesh, and dwelt among us.*" Yes, in order to atone for our sins, the Son of God submitted to all human infirmities; to hunger and thirst, to heat and cold, to weariness, and the need of sleep, but He did not will to enter the world in the same manner as the rest of mankind, but He chose to set aside the laws of nature, and through a miracle of His omnipotence He was "*conceived by the Holy Ghost, born of the Virgin Mary.*"

And what a love she had for virginal purity! According to the opinion expressed by holy men, she would have been willing to renounce the sublime dignity of becoming the Mother of God rather than to lose the dignity of virginity, by exchanging it for the dignity of motherhood.

And we may go yet farther! The Redeemer permitted the devil to tempt Him in the wilderness, to tempt Him to ambition, even to idolatry, but not to a sin against holy purity. In order to atone for our sins He allowed the Jews to blaspheme and revile Him; but He did not permit them to cast upon Him the merest shadow of an accusation of the sin of impurity.

Fire is opposed to water, and on this account does a flame sputter if a candle is ever so little moistened with water. In the same way does God detest the impure, and love the pure, because He Himself is a pure spirit, and must therefore necessarily abhor the impure, who are like unto the beasts.

With whom is a pure soul to be compared? As Holy Scripture tells us, she can not be compared to anything in this world. "What," says St. Bernard, "is more precious than chastity, which makes an angel out of a man?" The chaste man is especially distinguished for his courage and fortitude in the struggle of life. O my dear young man, if you regard your body as the temple of the Holy Ghost, and desire to preserve it as such, understand, and inscribe it deeply on the tablets of your heart, that in days to come you may be sick, and poor, and wretched, despised by your fellow-men, but if you remain pure of heart, you are and remain a being worthy of veneration, beloved by God as He loves His angels.

If the Redeemer, as He lay in the manger, listened with complacency to the songs of the celestial choirs, He will not fail to receive your prayers as long as you are adorned with the precious jewel of purity, for He then regards you as if you were an angel.

He does not look upon riches, nobility, and honor as the world views these things, else He would not have summoned poor, obscure shepherds to His manger; no, He looks upon a pure heart, upon the heart that is adorned with that most precious treasure—angelic virtue. Therefore Holy Writ says:

"Oh, how beautiful is the chaste generation with glory! For the memory thereof is immortal; because it is known both with God and with men" (Wis. iv. 1).

61. THE VISION OF GOD
*"How blest is he who pure in word and act
Preserves baptismal innocence intact."*

IN THESE words the poet lauds the happiness of a pure and guileless heart. What would Jesus Christ say, were He to come down in person upon earth once more; how would He comfort and encourage the chaste? Not otherwise, assuredly, than He did formerly, in His Sermon on the Mount, when He thus addressed His hearers: *"Blessed are the clean of heart, for they shall see God."* Yes, the vision of God is the reward of the conflict, the bright encouragement for the chaste.

"O how beautiful is the chaste generation with glory; it triumpheth crowned forever winning the reward of undefiled conflicts" (Wis. iv. 2).

"Who shall ascend into the mountain of the Lord? Or who shall stand in His holy place? The innocent in hands and clean of heart" (Ps. xxiii. 4).

During the journey of life every Christian longs to attain the blessed goal, to be admitted into the heavenly paradise. God strews afflictions like thorns along the path of men, in order that their hearts may not cling to earth, nor take delight in the tinsel and false glitter of this world, but seek for true gold, for eternal blessedness, for the vision of God.

If, at any time, the weather becomes dull and rainy while you are traveling through life, and you long more than you ever did before for the everlasting sunshine of heaven, then turn to your diary or journal.

This journal is your conscience. If you find that no sin against purity is inscribed on the pages of your conscience, in that case I congratulate you, and rejoice with your holy angel guardian, for you are "blessed," you are destined to enjoy the vision of God.

According to a remark of St. Gregory the Pope, chastity does not suffice of itself to open to us the gates of heaven. If, for instance, you were merely to keep the sixth and ninth commandments, and in some weighty matter fail to observe some other commandment, you would resemble the foolish virgins, who had no oil in their lamps, and were excluded on this account from the heavenly banquet. For in that case you would be destitute of charity, without which no one can enter heaven.

But note well why *"many are called, but few are chosen."* It is because so few observe the chastity required by their state of life.

On the other hand, a young man who leads a chaste life generally finds no difficulty in keeping the other commandments. If he can fight to a successful conclusion the difficult battle on behalf of chastity—then will he certainly not fail in the easier warfare against the remaining foes of his salvation.

O purity, sweet encouragement for the heart of man! *"The clean of heart shall see God!"*

A legend which was current among the ancient heathen, relates the following circumstance concerning Hermione, the Persian princess. She used to wear a magnificent opal as an ornament for her hair. This precious stone was of infinite value, yet so exceedingly delicate and sensitive that when once but a single drop of water happened to fall upon it, it turned to dust immediately, the wearer sharing the same fate.

Now, dear reader, understand that the celestial blossom of purity is as fair and precious as this opal was said to be, but also just as delicate and sensitive. *"Blessed are the clean of heart, for they shall see God!"*

Aye, they will be blessed, they will see God in a way, even while they continue to sojourn upon earth! The chaste soul resembles heaven; it is a paradise, a garden of delights for the Spirit of God, a throne of the Redeemer, from which grace and blessings flow forth for the entire period during which this soul is united in beauteous harmony with an equally chaste body.

Well, then, does not this pearl of virtues, which leads us to the everlasting vision of God, deserve that we should sacrifice everything, renounce everything, in order to preserve it? Daily—aye, many times a day—and especially in temptation, let us invoke our Queen and our Mother, Mary, the protectress of purity, that she may help us in the conflict for the preservation of chastity; let us say frequently: "*Mary, conceived without sin pray for us who have recourse to thee! Help me to be clean of heart, that thus I may attain to the everlasting vision of God!*"

> "So dear to heaven is saintly chastity
> That when a soul is found sincerely so,
> A thousand liveried angels lackey her,
> Driving far off each thing of sin and guilt,
> And in clear dream and solemn vision
> Tell her of things that no gross ear can hear,
> Till oft converse with heavenly habitants
> Begins to cast a beam on th' outward shape."
> —Milton.

"O holy prerogative of youth," exclaims Father Von Doss,[1] "to be able to practise, in its entire extent, a virtue which is the admiration of heaven and earth! A virtue which is so admirable that, without it, all other virtues lose their brilliancy; so sublime that he who possesses it may be said to equal the angels of heaven; so useful, that the words of Holy Writ are applicable to it: '*All things came to me together with her, and innumerable riches through her hands!*' (Wis. vii. 11).

"Justly, then, is chastity compared to a lily, for this flower not only delights the eye with its brilliant whiteness, but

1   *Thoughts and Counsels for Young Men.*

refreshes the sense of smell by the balsamic odor which it exhales.

"Exceedingly lovely is the lily of chastity, spreading abroad its precious perfume, and refreshing the heavenly Bridegroom, of whom it is said that He feedeth among lilies (Cant. ii. 16). The pure young heart draws him down into its fragrant depths, so that it becomes a veritable garden of the Lord.

"Chastity has the sublime prerogative of not only adorning the soul with its brilliant whiteness, but also of being, at the same time, the best ornament of the body.

"Look into the clear eyes of innocence; what a luster! what quiet majesty! How the purity of God is reflected therein! No springtime sky shines forth as cloudlessly, no dewdrop sparkles as brightly in the rays of the morning sun, no brooklet is as clear. Thus would the angels appear, if they would assume corporal form. O blessed, indeed, are the undefiled in the way (Ps. cxviii. 1), in the dust-covered road of this lower earth!

" '*O how beautiful is the chaste generation with glory! for the memory thereof is immortal: because it is known both with God and with men. When it is present, they imitate it, and they desire it when it hath withdrawn itself: and it triumpheth crowned forever, winning the reward of undefiled conflicts*' (Wis. iv. 1, 2).

"Sublime praise, bestowed upon the virtue of chastity, by the Holy Ghost himself!

"Heaven rejoices over chaste souls, and looks down with pleasure upon them.

"God is a spirit; and the chaste soul approaches the spiritual nature of God, by the overcoming of the flesh.

"The angels are spirits; how much they must love mortals, who, through a fierce combat, obtain as a virtue that which they have by nature, and without any effort or struggle!

"Chastity appears worthy of veneration in the eyes of men. There are none so abandoned as not to highly value that which their cowardice alone prevents them from imitating.

"O blessed religion, which teaches, nourishes, and perfects so admirable and prolific a virtue! By it thou restorest man to himself, preservest his heavenly origin, and in purified heart enkindlest a divine flame.

"And what is the reward for this holy virtue of chastity?

"From the complacency wherewith an infinitely pure God regards chaste souls, measure the grace and the reward he reserves for chastity.

"From the struggle to which the acquisition of this virtue gives rise, and without which, in the majority of mankind, there is no victory—you may form some idea of its recompense, its crown.

"Truly, *'he that loveth cleanness of heart...shall have the king for his friend'* (Prov. xxii. 11).

"Behold how God communicates himself to chaste souls: *'Blessed are the clean of heart, for they shall see God'* (Matt. v. 8).

"See how he prefers them, drawing them close to himself, and permitting them to lean upon his bosom, like the disciple whom Jesus loved (John xxi. 20).

"Mark how he prepares a heaven especially for them; in robes of gladness, and adorned with signs of victory, they *'follow the Lamb whithersoever He goeth'* (Apoc. xiv. 4).

"Behold how he teaches them to sing a new canticle before his throne, one which none but virgins' lips are able to sing (Apoc. xiv. 3).

"O yes, whoever loves purity of heart, has the King of kings for his friend, for his confidant, for his eternal Bridegroom. One spirit with God is he who is joined with Him by self-denial and flight from all vice (1 Cor. vi. 17).

"O heaven of chaste souls, how lovely thou art! What a chosen spot, a high mountaintop, an exclusive sanctuary. *'Who shall ascend to the mountain of the Lord? Who shall stand*

in his holy place? The innocent of hands, and clean of heart'
(Ps. xxiii. 4)."

"Look here, upon this picture, and on this!" says Hamlet.
You have looked with delight upon the lily of purity. Now
look in the opposite direction and contemplate what a monster
impurity is.

Father Schuen says:[1] The alarming growth of this evil
(impurity) makes it necessary to speak in plain, unequivocal
terms upon this subject, which the priest, were he to consult
his own inclination, would fain pass over in silence.

In the scales of divine justice impurity weighs very heavy.
Consider what the sin of impurity really is. It is a profanation
of the image of God. Man has received from God exceptional
favors and privileges: *"God created man to His own image and
likeness"* (Gen. i. 26). *"The man is the image and glory of God"*
(1 Cor. xi. 7). By impurity the image of God is disfigured, for
the impure man gives himself to the gratification of his animal
desires and thereby desecrates his soul, upon which the image
of God is stamped. Luxury is likewise a desecration of the
body. In this a great deal is implied. The body of man is made
a member of the body of Christ in Baptism: *"Know you not
that your bodies are the members of Christ?"* (1 Cor. vi. 15) The
body of the Christian is the temple of the Holy Ghost: *"Know
you not that your members are the temple of the Holy Ghost,
which is in you, whom you have from God?"* (1 Cor. vi. 19)
The libertine makes the body an instrument of bestial lusts,
and thereby degrades and profanes that which is a member of
the body of Christ and a temple of the Holy Ghost. What a
grievous sin this is! Hence you may understand the horror
which God has for the sin of impurity.

Consider in what terms God speaks of this sin. At all
times He has manifested the greatest abhorrence for the sin

1   From *Outlines of Sermons for Young Men.*

of impurity. Holy Scripture gives abundant proof of this. It is said of Onan that the "*Lord slew him because he did a detestable thing*" (Gen. xxxviii. 10). St. Paul exposes the abominable character of luxury in these words: "*Know you not that your bodies are the members of Christ? Shall I take the members of Christ and make them members of an harlot?*" (I Cor. vi. 15). "*He that committeth fornication sinneth against his own body.*" Such is the magnitude of the abhorrence which God has for this sin that under the Old Law certain sins of this nature were punished by death (Lev. xx. 12-13).

Impurity is a grievous sin even in matters that might seem of little importance.

Even a thought freely consented to is a sin worthy of eternal damnation. A thought arises in a moment in the mind, the intellect sees its sinfulness, and the will adheres to it—*a mortal sin is committed.* Such is the teaching of the theologians. What must be the gravity of the sin of impurity when even the thought of an impure thing freely entertained constitutes so grievous a sin!

Consider the sins of the eyes. A glance as quick as thought is cast upon an impure object, and yet such a glance, quick though it be, may lead to mortal sin. "*I say unto you that whosoever shall look upon a woman to lust after her hath already committed adultery with her in his heart*" (Matt. v. 28). What importance attaches to unchaste looks!

Consider the gravity of impure speech. The lips are opened in a moment; how quickly a word is spoken! Yet every impure word is abhorrent to God, and may become a mortal sin. "The tongue," says St. Bernard "is the most to be feared of all vipers; it imparts its poison in a single breath."

If God is ready to punish with eternal hell-fire a mere thought, a look, a word, what must be the gravity of a sin committed in deed against the virtue of chastity! Do not imagine that you can escape the guilt by saying that it is a mere weakness of nature; do not excuse yourselves by referring to the great number or those round about you that may be guilty or these sins. No excuse will avail; God has set His law against this sin and will pronounce judgment according to His justice. Beware of this poison, watch over your thoughts and desires, guard against evil associations; for these things will lead you into the commission of such sin. Never carry the load of such a sin upon your conscience, if you should have fallen into it; the load will bear you down, even to the depths of hell.

God judges and punishes impurity severely in this life. This we can learn from the chastisements which in the past He has sent upon men guilty of this sin. The deluge was largely owing to this sin: "*God saw that the earth was corrupted, for all flesh had corrupted its way upon earth*" (Gen. vi. 12). Remember also the fate of the cities of the plain: "*The cry of Sodom and Gomorrha is multiplied, and their sin is become exceeding grievous*" (Gen. xviii. 20). At Settim four and twenty thousand were put to death by God's command on account of this sin (Num. xxv. 9). How God must hate the sin of impurity can be learned clearly from these punishments.

Besides these punishments by which God showed His judgment of impurity, He has also connected certain chastisements directly with the indulgence of sensuality. These are terrible as they affect the body. Holy Scripture describes them when it says of the impure: "*Rottenness and worms shall inherit men*" (Ecclus. xix. 3). Debauchery often brings most loathsome diseases in its train. Many a one goes about with pallid countenance, an unsteady gait, a living corpse, on account of his sins. Many a one is a mere wreck of humanity on account of sins of impurity committed in his youth. In the hospitals of the larger towns sights may be seen too revolting to describe here, men of whom the doctors can tell you that the seeds of their present condition were laid in their youth by an impure life. *"The Nazarites were whiter than snow, purer than milk...Their face is now made blacker than coals, their skin hath stuck to their bones, it is withered, and is become like wood"* (Lam. iv. 7, 8). Not unfrequently the libertine is carried to an early grave by reason of his sins.

Still more terrible are the consequences of sensuality as they affect the soul. The curse of heaven is poured out upon the soul of the sinner. Sins of impurity inflict a deep wound upon the soul and awaken the terrors of conscience in the breast of the sinner. If persevered in, impurity blinds the sinner and renders him indifferent to his state, it draws him farther and farther from God and produces obduracy of heart, which resists conversion and penance. Sensuality is the parent of impenitence.

God punishes impurity with the greatest severity in eternity. This we know from Holy Scripture, where God states that the impure will be excluded from the kingdom of heaven: *"Do not err: neither fornicators, nor adulterers, nor the effeminate shall possess the kingdom of God"* (1 Cor. vi. 9, 10). *"Know ye this and understand, that no fornicator or unclean person hath inheritance in the kingdom of Christ and of God"* (Eph. v. 5). By the inheritance of Christ the kingdom of heaven is understood, and of this God said: *"There shall not enter into it anything defiled"* (Apoc. xxi. 27). Terrible indeed are the judgments of God as regards the impure; He shuts them out from His kingdom and will not tolerate them in His presence. Nor is this all; they are cast into hell. *"They shall have their portion in the pool burning with fire and brimstone, which is the second death"* (Apoc. xxi. 8). In the fire of hell they will groan forever in despair. *"The smoke of their torments shall ascend for ever and ever: neither have they rest day nor night"* (Apoc. xiv. 11).

Here we see the chastisements meted out to the impure. God punishes them in this life and in the next. *"He shall rain snares upon sinners: fire and brimstone and storms of wind shall be the portion of their cup"* (Ps. x. 6). Even in this life they shall suffer for their crimes, but far more sharp will be their suffering in eternity, when the gates of eternal life shall be closed against them and the gates of death shall open to receive them. *"They will descend to the place where everlasting horror dwelleth"* (Job x. 22).

Today we have considered the gravity of sins of impurity and the chastisements which are inflicted upon the impure. The words I have spoken are words of truth, and they will remain unshaken even if the whole world conspire to treat the matter lightly and to declaim against them as fables. God grant that they may sink deep into your hearts and leave there an everlasting impression. Let these words be before you through life and be with you in the hour of temptation. Form a solemn resolution to abhor this sin from the bottom of your heart. Never listen to the voice of the tempter; the fruit may be pleasing to the eye, but within it is filled with bitterness beyond expression. Be masters, not slaves, of your desires. The means to overcome temptation are found in prayer, custody of the senses, watchfulness over one's thoughts and speech, avoidance of evil companions, and the reception of the sacraments. By the use of these means the soul will live in peace. Go to the sacraments monthly and you will have no difficulty in overcoming temptation. St. Bernard says: "Let the glowing heat of the fire in hell extinguish in thee the fire of sensual desires, let the greater heat overcome the lesser; the horrible crackling of the flames that are unquenchable will banish from your soul all delight in unchaste pleasures."

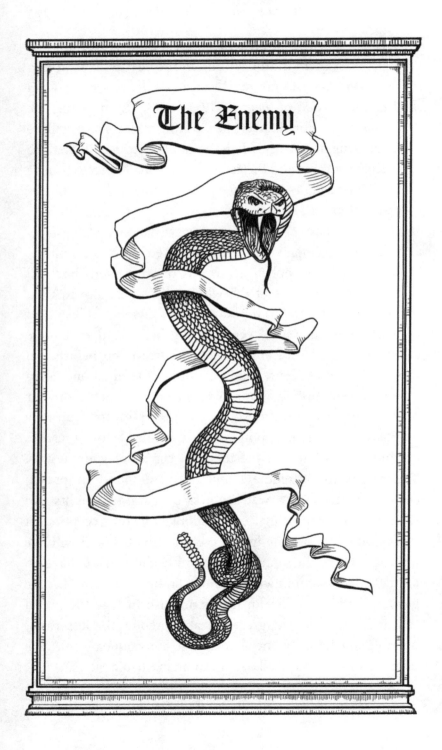

The Enemy

The Enemy

62. The Enemy in Your Own Heart

In every warlike campaign, in every battle, the thing of chief importance is to be acquainted with the enemy, with his power and position, his plans, and the forces he has in reserve. The same thing holds good in regard to the spiritual conflict, especially that which is waged on behalf of the virtue of purity.

It is, first of all, to be observed that the enemy of chastity has planted himself firmly in the heart of every human being; and if I place before your eyes, my dear reader, this position of the enemy with all its dangers, do not allow it to terrify you to such an extent as to cause you to become faint-hearted.

In the world we notice two different things. We observe that even a child is ashamed if he is discovered when doing anything indecorous. We find something similar in the case of the ancient heathen; they sought to hide their sins from the eyes of their fellow-men under cover of the darkness of night. Not only on tables of stone, which God gave to Moses upon Mount Sinai, but also in the book of conscience, it is written: "Thou shalt not offend against chastity." This is our first observation.

Now, who could believe that, in spite of the voice of conscience and the conviction in every nation that this vice is a shameful thing, people are so addicted to it! Whence comes this contradiction—this opposition to reason and conscience? St. Paul answers this question in the name of the whole human race: "*I see another law in my members, fighting against the law of my mind, and captivating me in the law of sin that is in my members. Unhappy man that I am, who shall deliver me from the body of this death? The grace of God, by Jesus Christ our Lord.*"

By these words the Apostle intends us to understand that our reason, our higher self, recognizes sin, especially sins against chastity, as an evil, and regards them with abhorrence; that there is, however, within us a concupiscence, an inclination, a proneness to evil, which allures us, and that this tendency can be resisted and overcome through the grace of Jesus Christ. It is precisely this concupiscence, this proneness to evil, resulting from original sin, which constitutes the first and the most dangerous adversary of holy purity; it is the enemy in our own heart.

An impure thought often steals unperceived into the heart; sinful images are awakened; the imagination clothes them with form and color; sensual desires are stirred up, and the individual finds himself all at once in danger of losing God, of forfeiting heaven and eternal happiness.

Two great mistakes are made concerning this enemy in our own heart and the temptations it excites. Some persons have an exaggerated dread of evil thoughts, but most persons fear them too little. I will say a few words on both points.

If, for instance, when you go to confession you were merely to say that unchaste thoughts enter your mind every day, your confessor would be utterly unable to judge as to the sinfulness of such thoughts. In spite of all these disgraceful suggestions and representations, your soul may be pure and white and stainless as a lily.

A mere thought, on account of which we are not to blame, and in which we take no pleasure, and which we do not desire, is no sin, but only a temptation, only an opportunity for conflict and conquest, a cause and source of eternal merit.

St. Augustine compares evil thoughts to the first sin in paradise, in which these three took part, *viz.*, the serpent, Eve, and Adam. The serpent suggested to the mind of Eve the idea of breaking the command of God; she took pleasure in the thought, and advised Adam to carry it into action; Adam followed her advice and sinned.

The first beginning of an evil thought may be compared to the suggestions of the serpent. Eve represents the lower nature, which takes delight in the contemplation of sin; in the person of Adam we see the human will, which, agreeing to the proposal of Eve, completes the sinful act. If an impure thought enters our mind, it is not a sin, so long as our free will definitely refuses its consent, and we take no pleasure in it.

There are two ways in which our free will may give its consent:

In the first place we may sin through desire if we wish to have the opportunity of doing, seeing, or hearing that which is wrong, or we may sin in reference to the past if we reflect with satisfaction on sins into which we have fallen, and wish to commit them over again. These voluntary wishes and desires are grievous sins, as both faith and reason plainly tell us.

In the second place, the will may give its consent by merely finding pleasure in impure images and thoughts. And this taking delight, willingly and wittingly, this actual pleasure of the will in such images, not the mere impression on the senses, is also a grievous sin. Hence it follows that you must never fail to be on your guard against this enemy in your own heart, and not be careless in regard to impure thoughts.

> How blest is he who ne'er consents
> To any evil deed;
> How pure and beauteous is his life
> Who to God's law pays heed.

63. THE ENEMY IN YOUR EYES

SIGHT is one of the greatest blessings which God has bestowed upon His creatures. The unfortunate man who has lost this precious gift, and is on this account doomed to spend his days in perpetual darkness, can alone appreciate its value aright.

And yet, in the case of how many persons would it not be the greatest benefit, and save them from eternal perdition, if they were to lose their bodily sight! To such individuals one might say what St. Severinus once said to a monk who implored him to ask of God the restoration of his sight. "My son," he said, "do not trouble yourself about the eyes of your body, but rather about those of your soul." To many young persons the saying of the prophet is applicable: "*Death is come in through our windows* [the eyes], *it is entered into our house* [the soul]." The enemy of purity enters into the human heart through the eye.

With what did the first sin begin in paradise? With a longing look Eve gazed at the luscious fruit which hung on the forbidden tree; that look excited a wish to taste the fruit; she yielded to the wish, gathered and ate the forbidden fruit, and gave some of it to her husband; thus was the first sin committed. And if, at a period when as yet no evil concupiscence had stirred within the human breast, the eyes could work irretrievable ruin, how great, how terrible must be the result after the fall, when the enemy in our eyes works in concert with the enemy in our heart! When we see what came of a mere love of eating, we may judge what a much stronger passion will do—unchaste, sensual desire kindled by bold, unguarded glances, and suffered to burst into fierce flames.

Experience teaches that unchaste looks very frequently lead men to a terrible end. We find examples of this in Holy Scripture. The proximate cause of David's sad fall was a bold and sinful look; with this look, the entire edifice of his virtue crumbled away, all his good resolutions were rendered null and void, and he—the man after God's own heart—became a murderer and an adulterer. Putiphar's wife cast unchaste glances upon Joseph, committed adultery in her heart, and would fain have sinned in act as well as in desire.

Yet why should we turn to olden times in order to illustrate our meaning when our own daily observation furnishes only too many melancholy examples of the truth of our assertion?

Pay heed to the warning of Holy Scripture, and say: "I have made a covenant with mine eyes that I should not look upon anything dangerous, lest death should come up through our windows and enter into the soul." Be on your guard against the enemy in your eyes, lest it should gain power over you, and destroy both body and soul. What biting frost is to the flowers in spring, so is an impure glance to the lily of chastity.

The numerous indecent and shameless pictures and engravings to be found in the present day in the pages of certain periodical and illustrated journals are an open grave of innocence. In cities such pictures are too often exhibited in shop windows and on bill boards, or hawked about the streets. It is deeply sad to think how many souls are by this means soiled and ruined. This danger is a very great one for you, my dear young friend. Do not imitate those who say: "We are no longer children! It is quite allowable for us to see certain things, we have reached an age when we ought to be acquainted with such subjects!" Young people who talk in this fashion are, alas! no longer children of God, or at least are not to be counted among His innocent children.

Remark in conclusion that those young men who boldly fix their gaze upon persons of the opposite sex, doing this, not from mere curiosity, but with some measure of sensual desire, are either already unchaste, or will become so before very long. St. Bernard tells us that if persons of different sexes take deliberate satisfaction in gazing at one another and yet no sinful desires arise within them, it is a more wonderful thing than if a dead man were to return to life.

> O Youth, preserve an undimmed eye
> And keep thy heart without a stain:
> The undimmed eye can look on high,
> The unstained heart will peace attain.

64. THE ENEMY IN HUMAN FORM

"COMPANY-KEEPING" is the occasion in which the enemy of chastity appears most frequently in human form. Upon this subject I will speak more at length another time; at present I wish to call your attention to the danger which lurks in the too great familiarity with persons of the other sex under any circumstance.

Such familiarity, though it may begin in a harmless way with a pure feeling of friendly liking, too frequently degenerates into a passion which blinds the understanding and leads to the committal of a thousand sins of impurity, first in thought, then in words, and later also in actions. Alas! how many young persons in this way succumb to the enemy of chastity in human form.

Before all else, avoid clandestine and nocturnal meetings.

Martinian, who is honored as a saintly anchorite, led a pious life upon a mountain for a long series of years. On one occasion there came to him a woman who had lost her way in the wilderness, and implored him, in most effecting language, to give her shelter and protection. What did he do? Remembering his own weakness, he refused to allow her to set foot in his hut. He justly feared that in the form of this woman the enemy of chastity might appear, and bring about his fall. "Fire and straw do not do well together," was his fitting reply.

If, therefore, this holy man, who by years of penance

had practised and confirmed himself in virtue, avoided an apparently necessary meeting with a woman, how much more has a young man, in whom sensuality is strong, and virtue weak, every possible reason to avoid similar occasions!

And in regard to this subject, I must warn you against another great danger! Those unfortunate women, whether married or single, those dregs of their sex who imitate the shameless wife of Putiphar, are still existing in the present day, and are even more numerous than ever.

But if ever, when you come to live in large cities, such a diabolical serpent in human form should present itself to you in a more or less fascinating manner, O then do not delay, do not delay a single instant—I beseech and implore you by all that you hold dear and sacred—but act as Joseph formerly did in Putiphar's house: fly, fly immediately. Your only chance of salvation lies in flight!

The enemy of innocence is especially to be found in the form of immoral companions and associates. To this class chiefly belong those persons who, by their evil and immodest bearing, seek to lead you, and others also, to commit every kind of sinful and vicious action. Such persons are the decoy birds of Satan, by means of which he seeks to entrap others. They are rotten fruit, which spoils that which is sound. They are graves full of corruption, which exhale a pestilential effluvium. Their lascivious and suggestive conversation is an insidious poison, which by imperceptible degrees effects the death of innocence.

These immoral companions do evil themselves, and by their example of immodesty incite others to imitate them.

After this fashion, intercourse with vicious companions corrupted, in days of old, the youthful Augustine. He has left to you, dear reader, in his repentant confessions, the example also of his tears and sorrow; he warns and exhorts you, if the enemy of your innocence presents himself in human form, to fly from him, as you would fly from a roaring lion threatening to devour you.

> O Youth, if this shall be thy aim,
> To lead a life that's free from blame,
> Man's company thou oft must flee
> And learn with God alone to be.

65. The Enemy in Word and Pen

IT IS very sad and deplorable that unbecoming and immodest conversation is so common in our day. Unchaste conversation is carried on in saloons and hotels, in streets and parks, in field and forest, at social gatherings and in workshops, on steamers and in railway coaches, on the way to church, and at the very church door.

Many persons in their perversity seem to find nothing amusing that does not refer to improper and scandalous things. He who can relate the most shameless anecdotes, or make the coarsest witticisms and lewdest play upon words is considered the best entertainer.

In the face of such conduct, your duty is plain. There is in our country a highly dangerous and poisonous snake, which makes a rattling sound with its tail, from which it derives its name of rattlesnake. When the rattling sound is heard, all men become aware that the vile reptile is not far off, and they take care that they are not bitten and poisoned. After a similar fashion do unchaste persons betray themselves by immodest words. If you hear any one talk in this way remember that it is the sound of the rattlesnake; beware, and withdraw yourself in order that this snake, this devil's agent, may not kill your soul with the poison of unchastity. If it is at all feasible, leave such company! If this is not practicable, silence the foul mouth in one way or another—administer to the speaker a sharp, but well-deserved reprimand.

But the enemy of innocence works still greater ruin by means of books and periodicals, than even by words. An immoral book offers to its deluded victim a sweet but deadly draught in a glittering goblet. Other tempters, those with unclean tongues, are obliged when in the company of decent people to respect the laws of morality or conventionality; but improper and salacious literature sneaks in everywhere.

Immoral books are all the more dangerous because they are secret tempters; they ply their nefarious business stealthily and continually. You would be ashamed to remain for any length of time alone with a person of doubtful reputation; you would be careful not to confide in him, because you would fear that injury to your virtue might be the result. On the contrary, one is alone when reading a bad book, alone with the tempter; one can listen to him without being put to shame before others.

The number of these silent but persuasive tempters is legion nowadays. Like a second deluge, the endless number of bad books and periodicals that are prejudicial to innocence and morality pours itself over all strata of society, in cities and villages, extending its ravages even to remote mountain valleys. First in the turbid flood we find bad novels, and indeed the greater number of novels and romances are fraught with danger to morals They almost all relate piquant, sensual love stories, heat the imagination by highly colored descriptions, and these again blind the understanding, enfeeble the will, and ensnare the heart.

The deadly poison is presented and swallowed with the sweet sugar of a showy, attractive style, and a highly interesting tale. But daily experience proves how ruinous are its effects.

Seek the advice of a priest or an educated Catholic layman with regard to the choice of books and periodicals. But do not keep any suspicious book or periodical near you, lest it should fare with you as it did with Eve in regard to the forbidden fruit.

Never allow yourself to be deluded by a striking or high-sounding title; but ask where the book comes from—that is, who is the author and where and by whom it is printed. If this is not stated, the book is presumably trash. Toss it into the fire!

Thank God, there is no longer a dearth of good, first-class novels by Catholic writers of distinction. Good novels certainly serve an excellent purpose. They are capable not only of entertaining, but also of instructing us—and even of encouraging us in the way of holiness and perfection. Young people are inclined, however, to read fiction in excess of what is right and good. Even in regard to reading, there may be a passion that is to be restrained; it is termed a 'rage for reading'. Beware of this. Exercise self-control; do not neglect your duties to gratify your passion for fiction and other light literature.

Pay heed, also, to the admonition of St. Augustine: "Nourish your soul with spiritual reading." Let not a day pass without a short spiritual reading, for instance, from the *Lives of the Saints*, or Thomas a Kempis' *Following of Christ*, or St. Francis de Sales' *Introduction to a Devout Life*.

The pious author of *The Art of Being Happy*, writes: "Everything we read makes us better or worse, and, by a necessary confluence, increases or lessens our happiness. Be scrupulous in the choice of your books; often ask yourself what influence your reading exercises upon your conduct. If after having read such and such a work that pleases you—philosophy, history, fiction—or else such and such a review, or magazine, or newspaper in which you take delight—if you then find yourself more slothful about discharging your duties, more dry and cross toward your equals, harder toward your inferiors, with more disrelish for your state of life, more greedy for pleasures, enjoyments, honors, riches—do not hesitate about giving up such readings: they would poison your life and endanger your eternal happiness."

> "Learning is more profound
> When in few solid authors it may be found;
> A few books, digested well, do feed
> The mind; much cloys, and doth ill humor breed."
> —Robert Heath.

> "A good book is the precious life-blood of a master-spirit, embalmed and treasured up on purpose to a life beyond life."
> —Milton.

66. THE ENEMY IN ALCOHOL

SOME persons assert that the word *alcohol* is derived from the Arabic "*al-ghol,*" *evil spirit.* We will not seek to discover whether this is, or is not, really the case; one thing is true at any rate: namely, that immoderate or very great indulgence in alcohol beverages has such deplorable consequences in regard to morality, that we can say with truth that an impure and evil spirit lurks therein. I mean the enemy of chastity. An eastern legend runs as follows: When Noe began to plant the vine, Satan offered to assist him, on condition that he should receive two thirds of the produce. He then watered the vine with the blood of a parrot, a lion, an ape, and a pig. And since then, so runs the legend, wine (alcohol) possesses this property, namely, that any one who partakes too freely of it, becomes boastful and loquacious like a parrot, furious like a lion, lascivious like an ape, filthy like a pig.

This story is, as I said, only a legend, a parable, but it depicts with admirable precision the ruinous effects of alcohol in regard to morality. We will mention here only one of these effects: alcohol prepares the way for sins against chastity; the enemy of innocence is present in alcohol.

The Wise Man in Holy Writ thus addresses the drunkard: "*Thine eyes shall look after strange women and thy heart speak perverse things.*" And Sirach remarks: "*Wine and women make wise men fall off."* And in Proverbs it is expressly stated: *"Wine is a luxurious thing, and drunkenness riotous."* And St. Paul utters this impressive warning: *"Be not drunk with wine, wherein is luxury"* (Eph. v. 18).

The Fathers of the Church teach the same thing. They term intemperance the grave of chastity, because it is well-nigh impossible to preserve this delicate virtue in the presence of intemperance, which incites to luxury. For instance, St. Augustine writes: "Drunkenness is the mother of all scandalous actions, the sister of impurity, and the shipwreck of chastity." And in another place he exhorts us thus: "Let us flee from drunkenness, in order that we may not fall into unchastity."

As the flames of a fire by means of oil, so are the sensual desires of men aroused and intensified by excess in alcoholic drinks. Therefore St. Jerome says: "Impurity is inseparable from drunkenness." Who indeed does not know the ribaldry, the vulgar jokes and indecent songs, by means of which young men, when excited by drink, irritate and scandalize others.

The unavoidable connection of immorality with drunkenness is constantly confirmed by daily experience. We will give one instance only.

There are in England extensive property owners, whose possessions comprise towns and large villages. Some time ago, a number of them agreed, in order to suppress drunkenness, to close all the drinking saloons existing in their domains. What was the result?

It is related concerning a certain village in Lancashire that for seventeen years drinking saloons were permitted there; for the following fifteen none were allowed. During the former period immorality was rampant everywhere, so that it can be said with truth that in every alternate house an illegitimate child was born. During the subsequent fifteen years matters underwent a complete change, so that at present cases of immorality are of very rare occurrence.

67. THE ENEMY IN THE THEATER

THE theater, the stage, is not merely something indifferent as regards religion and morality, but rather something either highly advantageous or extremely injurious. Undoubtedly the theater wields a powerful influence for good or evil. Good plays of a religious tendency raise the tone of morals. The histrionic art resembles the other arts— poetry, painting, rhetoric, sculpture, and music—in the elevating powers they exercise. For this reason the Catholic Church has taken the fine arts one by one into her service, and thereby aided them to attain their higher perfection. The mystery plays of the Middle Ages were employed by her as a means of religious teaching. For the same reason, Catholic educational institutions in our own day, convent schools, and colleges conducted by Religious, annually have theatrical entertainments. It is the same with Catholic guilds or societies for young men and young women under the superintendence of priests. It is an innocent and harmless pleasure to attend such plays as these.

Dramas, on the contrary, which are performed by professional actors in the theaters of large cities, are frequently fraught with danger for young people. There the spirit of evil, evening after evening, dwells upon its old theme: the concupiscence of the eyes, the concupiscence of the flesh, and the pride of life. Immorality is not seldom, at least indirectly, inculcated. Everything combines to half intoxicate youthful spectators, to lull to sleep their understanding and their will, and, on the other hand, to excite their imagination to its highest pitch, and to arouse sensuality.

The *American Magazine* for May, 1909, published an

article on "The Indecent Stage," in which Samuel Hopkins Adams says:

"At one period of the present theatrical season, one fifth of all the dramatic presentments in New York were of dubious character.

"Half a dozen of them were sheer physical brutishness—the appeal to the Yahoo that lurks within all of us, to the beast that we hold in leash, out of respect to ourselves and our fellows. Sensuality, it is called, in men." He goes on to say that it would be a positive affront "to embalm, in cold print, the rancid innuendoes or the intimate indecencies" of a certain play—one of the most popular of the modern dramas of license.

A certain French writer of plays has himself given an indubitable proof of the immoral tendency of many plays. Why did he forbid his children to witness the performances of the dramas which he had written? For no other reason, than because he believed that their attendance at the theater on those occasions would be injurious to their morals. What a testimony does this afford to the deleterious character of too many plays!

Never go to a play that is performed at a theater of doubtful reputation.

Be on your guard lest your love for the theater develop into a passion. Seek rather to take delight in simple pleasures, which are within the reach of every one. Take delight in beholding the beauteous sights which God offers to our view in the works of creation. Strive by the practice of virtue to be yourself a spectacle to angels and to men. Thus will you, when the toil and suffering of life shall have come to an end, attain to that infinitely glorious sight—the vision of God.

Why should we fear youth's draught of joy,
If pure, would sparkle less?
Why should the cup the sooner cloy,
Which Christ hath deigned to bless?

—Keble.

Lift, O Christian, lift thine eyes
To thy home beyond the skies;
Eternal bliss awaits thee there
With which earth's joys can not compare.

68. THE ENEMY IN PLACES OF AMUSEMENT

"Gather the roses while you may,
Too soon, alas! they fade away."

THUS sings the poet, addressing the young. Gladly and heartily do I concur in the sentiment thus prettily expressed, as long at least, as the tender flower of innocence—the lily of purity—remains intact.

It is, and always has been, a pleasure to me to give pleasure to young people—to be instrumental in procuring for them innocent amusements. My heart rejoices when I see young folks merry and engaged in harmless play.

Bear this in mind, I pray you, when I utter a word of warning with regard to the danger of certain worldly amusements.

Very frequently does the enemy of innocence make his appearance in that favorite resort of young people—the ballroom or dance-hall.

That dancing is, as a rule, fraught with grave perils in regard to chastity, no sensible man will think of denying. I do not mean to say that dancing is in itself, and under all circumstances, a dangerous thing. On the contrary, in and by itself it is a perfectly harmless amusement; that is to say, moving about in time to the music is no more to be objected to than any other kind of gymnastic exercise. Indeed, in many excellent Catholic schools the pupils are occasionally allowed to amuse themselves by dancing. In this case no danger to innocence can possibly exist, any more than when brothers and sisters, or other near relatives, dance together. For these family gatherings the only evil is that they tend to awaken and foster a taste for what so often proves to be a dangerous amusement.

Thus we see that dancing is not, in itself, a danger to chastity; it is rendered perilous only by the circumstances attending it. A great deal depends on the person with whom one dances. If the dancers are of opposite sexes, and not very closely related to one another; if they are quite young, and therefore more likely to have their passions kindled in the intoxication of the dance—then the amusement may assume a dangerous character. An illustration will explain my meaning.

To carry a lighted candle about without any guard against the flame is assuredly not dangerous, but useful and necessary. But if you were to light a fire close to a heap of dry hay, or to take a lighted candle into a room where there had been an escape of gas, what a catastrophe might be the result!

With regard to public dances you will do well if you refrain attending any save those which are conducted under the auspices of Catholic organizations or Church societies and with the sanction of your pastors.

Father Slater, S. J., in his *Manual of Moral Theology* makes the following observations on the subject under consideration.

"Dancing may be a perfectly innocent amusement and it may be a dangerous occasion of sin. No general rule, therefore, can be given as to when dancing must be avoided. Much depends upon the company who join in the dance, upon the *way of dancing*, and upon the subjective disposition of the dancers. If there be nothing objectionable in any of these respects, there is no reason why a young man or a young woman should not be allowed to dance with due caution. If there be ground for objection, and especially if sin has already been frequently committed in similar circumstances, there is an obligation to abstain, unless the occasion of sin is necessary and can be made remote by taking proper precautions. If sin only follows occasionally, there will be no strict obligation to abstain from dancing, provided due precautions be taken in future."[1]

The fact is, the enemy of innocence generally meets and allures the young man amid scenes of noisy worldly festivity— at amusement resorts, concert halls, parks, gardens, summer camps, moonlight parties, pleasure excursions, and picnics. The amusements to which people give themselves up on such occasions, and which fascinate them—these games, carousals, and masqueradings, these sentimental plays and sensuous musical performances, these flirtations and drinking bouts—all have for their object, not moderate and wholesome recreation, but sensual enjoyment, such as unduly excites the imagination, arouses the passions, results in physical and mental depression, enervates the will, makes one indifferent to duty, and opens the door to violent temptations.

The circumstances that attend such festivities certainly constitute rocks on which innocence may easily be wrecked.

Another reprehensible practice which is prevalent in some places, even among country lads, consists in roaming about at night, perhaps past midnight, drinking at intervals, behaving in a vulgar and boisterous manner, annoying and insulting women, disturbing people in the midst of their slumbers by shouting and singing, and indulging in scandalous pranks.

This is certainly very objectionable conduct, a very equivocal pastime; and yet to many young people it appears to cause enjoyment. A decent, self-respecting young man will not engage in such sport, which is fraught with danger to innocence. From such "pleasures" as these he will turn with horror.

---

1   Vol. i. p. 206.

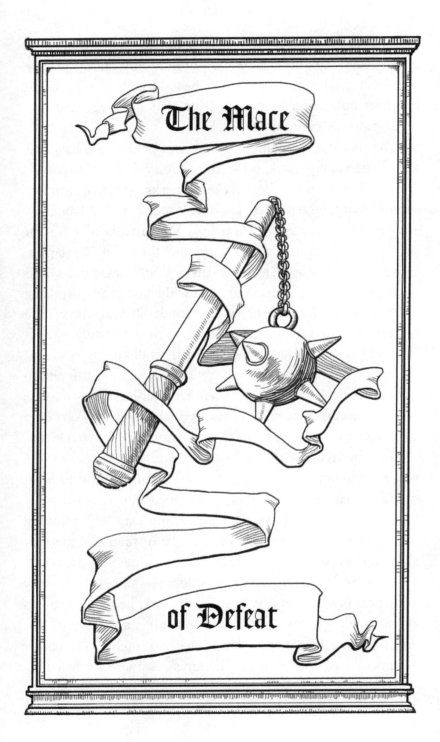

Defeat

69. What a Misfortune!

IF, MY dear young friend, you desire to incite and encourage yourself to persevere in the war you are waging on behalf of the pearl of virtues, you should reflect what a terrible misfortune it is to be defeated in this conflict, and what lamentable consequences such a defeat entails.

Rarely has a mother loved her child so tenderly as Blanche, the holy Queen of France, loved her son Louis, who subsequently occupied the throne of France, and became known to posterity as the saint of that name. One day when this good mother had been giving to her pious son, who was still a boy, many wise counsels, she said in conclusion, with a heart brimming over with maternal solicitude: "O my darling child, you are the most precious thing I have upon earth, more precious than all the gold and jewels which surround us in our palace. Yet I would a thousand times rather see you lying dead at my feet, than know you to have committed one single mortal sin."

Thus also may parents, and those who have the care of souls—thus may I more especially—say to you: You are dear and precious to us, but we would far rather that you should die this very instant in the grace of God, than that you should be conquered by the enemy of innocence, and fall into mortal sin.

I would fain imbue you with a wholesome horror of the vice which is opposed to chastity; therefore I will now depict the consequences of it.

To be vanquished by the enemy of innocence, and given up to the sin of impurity—what consequences does such a state of things entail! It is sad, my friend, but only too true, that when a young man has yielded to temptation, and become acquainted with vice—when after his grievous fall he does not at once arise and break with an iron will the fetters which habit is beginning to forge—the unhappy victim will fall again and again, sinking ever deeper and deeper, until ere long he will despair of being able to extricate himself from the slavery of impurity. Only too many examples of this kind are to be seen. Many a young man, who as a boy was innocent and good, blossoming like a lily in the garden of the Lord, the joy and hope of his parents and confessor, has got into bad ways, because he has become careless about transgressing the sixth commandment.

The first consequence of repeated sins of unchastity is the weakening of the will. "Vice has a will of iron," St. Augustine tells us. This means that passion—the propensity to sin—paralyzes the human will, binds it in fetters of iron. Shall I mention one or two instances?

One young man always had attacks of epilepsy whenever he sinned against purity; of this he was fully aware. Did he seek to amend? No! One day he was found, stretched on the carpet beside his bed—a corpse!

Another young man, a medical student, led an impure life; he knew only too well how unchastity was undermining his constitution and destroying his health. Did he seek to amend? No, he died, and died in despair!

There are certain terrible diseases, which are always, or almost always brought about only by this accursed sin of impurity. In the hospitals of our cities there are entire wards filled with such sufferers. They are mostly young people. Formerly they were strong and healthy, blooming as the sweet-scented roses in June. There they now lie, offensive to all who approach them, their countenances disfigured, their whole body racked by burning pain. There they lie, shunned as if they were suffering from smallpox, their mind tormented by the thought that they might have been quite strong, healthy, and happy. Alas! how pure and innocent I was, how pious and joyful on the day of my first communion! Now my heavenly crown is tarnished, my soul loaded with guilt, my health ruined! My parents and brothers and sisters are overwhelmed with shame and grief through me, perhaps my waywardness brought them to an untimely grave, and then—what an awful account I shall have to render to the strict judge, who has power to condemn me to eternal torments.

The fire of hell—everlasting condemnation—such is the last awful consequence of the vice of unchastity! And who says that this is so? Holy Scripture, the word of God Himself, which teaches that all the unchaste who die in their sins will have to enter a wretched, horrible place, and there be tortured throughout eternity by fierce and devouring flames.

How will the unfortunate creatures curse their sins, how will they wish they had followed the counsels of their confessor, for then they will say to themselves, I might have been happy forever in heaven! But now, condemned and accursed, I am doomed to endure the most horrible torments to all eternity!

But enough has been said! It is well that you should be filled with holy horror by such serious reflections. But if you have already fallen grievously, and are still assailed by fierce temptations, O then never, never lose courage! But under all circumstances say to yourself: *"I can do all things in Him who strengtheneth me."* And bear constantly in mind these lines:

How shortlived the pleasure, how lasting the pain,
Which sinful enjoyments will bring in their train?
Oh, turn a deaf ear to the treacherous voice
Which bids thee in what is illicit rejoice.

PETITIONS OF ST. AUGUSTINE

OH LORD JESUS, let me know myself,
let me know Thee,
And desire nothing else but Thee.
Let me hate myself and love Thee,
And do all things for the sake of Thee.
Let me humble myself, and exalt Thee,
And think of nothing but only of Thee.
Let me die to myself, and live in Thee,
And take whatever happens as coming from Thee.
Let me forsake myself and walk after Thee,
And ever desire to follow Thee.
Let me flee from myself, and turn to Thee,
That so I may merit to be defended by Thee.
Let me fear for myself, let me fear Thee,
And be amongst those who are chosen by Thee.
Let me distrust myself, and trust in Thee,
And ever obey for the love of Thee.
Let me cleave to nothing but only to Thee,
And ever be poor for the sake of Thee.
Look upon me, that I may love Thee;
Call me, that I may see Thee,
And forever possess Thee. Amen.

A Morning Offering

I OFFER to Thee, O my God, the life and death of Thy only Son; and with them these my affections and resolutions, my thoughts, words, deeds, and sufferings of this day, and of all my life, in honor of Thy adorable Majesty, in thanksgiving for all Thy benefits, in satisfaction for my sins, and to obtain the assistance of Thy grace; that, persevering to the end in doing Thy Holy Will, I may love and enjoy Thee for ever in Thy glory.

—*The Garden of the Soul*

Night Prayer

A LMIGHTY and eternal God, I adore Thee, and I *thank* Thee for all the benefits I have received this day through Thy infinite goodness and mercy. Give me light to know my faults and grant me grace to be truly sorry for my sins.

Here examine your Conscience ; then say:

Confiteor

I CONFESS to almighty God, to blessed Mary ever Virgin, to blessed Michael the Archangel, to blessed John the Baptist, to the holy apostles Peter and Paul, and to all the saints that I have sinned exceedingly in thought, word, and deed, (*strike your breast three times:*) through my fault, through my fault, through my most grievous fault. Therefore, I beseech blessed Mary ever Virgin, blessed Michael the Archangel, blessed John the Baptist, the holy apostles Peter and Paul, and all the saints, to pray for me to the Lord our God.

V. May Almighty God have mercy on us, forgive us our sins, and bring us to everlasting life.

R. Amen.

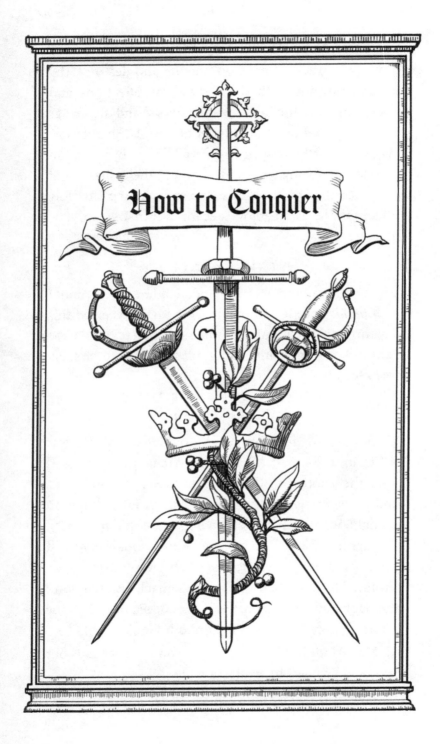

How to Conquer

HOW TO CONQUER
70. TRUSTY SENTINELS

THE worst enemy of man is evil concupiscence, that lust of the flesh which seeks to wither the heavenly flower, the lily of purity and to deprive him of it altogether. At no period is this enemy more daring and persistent than at your present time of life. Sensual desire is kindled like some uncanny fire, and frequently impels to sin with such force that the unhappy young man is obliged to put forth all the spiritual and moral strength of which he is possessed, in order not to succumb in this arduous encounter.

It is of the utmost importance that you should know exactly what are the means to defend and to preserve your chastity. It is of these means that I am now about to speak.

In the first place, let me point out to you the trusty sentinels who will help you to conquer in the fight. The first is the holy fear of God and humility of heart. Happy are you, if you are constantly filled with this holy fear, and never forget that you bear about you the treasure of chastity in very frail vessels.

Take care that you do not talk like so many young men, who indeed are not evil minded, but thoughtless and inexperienced. Such a one witnesses the sad fall of one of his friends. What does he say? "Oh! this will not happen to me," he remarks, "I am not so stupid as he is." Or he exclaims in his conceit: "How can a reasonable being so far forget himself! I should not have believed so and so to be capable of it! No, indeed, I am cast in a very different mold!"

Thus it never occurs to the foolish and conceited young man that a similar misfortune may overtake him. He does not believe that he stands in need of warnings and exhortations; he throws them to the wind. Behold these are the lying utterances of Satan: "*You shall not die.*"

But do you, my friend, be firmly convinced that every one who trusts in himself believes that his footing is firm, and therefore does not fly from the tempter, is certain to be lost. Let him remember those words of Holy Writ: "*He that thinketh himself to stand, let him take heed lest he fall*": let him place humility and holy fear as the first sentinels in the conflict with the enemy of chastity.

A second sentinel is the determination to resist evil thoughts and impulses without a moment's delay. The great and important principle in regard to attacks of disease is to employ, from the outset, suitable methods to resist them. The same principle holds good in regard to disease of the soul.

As soon as you become conscious of impure thoughts, images, and impulses, strive at once to concentrate your thoughts upon something else, upon the work in which you are engaged, or anything else which is harmless and calculated to engross your attention. And in case you are alone, seek, if you possibly can, some companionship which is not dangerous. In every case utter, with all the fervor of which you are capable, some ejaculatory prayer, such as: "*My Jesus, mercy!*" "*Sweet Heart of Jesus, be my love!*" "*Sweet heart of Mary, be my salvation!*" Such ejaculations as these, when uttered with true devotion and childlike confidence, have a marvelous power.

You must avoid all *voluntary and proximate occasions* which are likely to lead to the sin of unchastity. In such a voluntary and proximate occasion does a young man find himself, who without necessity seeks out some place, or lingers in it, or holds converse with persons where it is highly probable, or almost certain, that he will fall into some grievous sin of unchastity.

For example, a young man cultivates a familiar intercourse with a girl—they meet every week, or perhaps several times a week—he is alone with her—very often, possibly every time, they both sin grievously, at least by voluntary indulgence in impure thoughts and imaginations. That is a *proximate voluntary occasion.*

Such proximate voluntary occasions must be avoided at any cost, else nothing is of any avail; follow in time the divine warning: *"Watch and pray!"*

> Be watchful; taken by surprise
> How many fall, no more to rise!
> The storm that wakes the passion's glow
> Shall lay the tender lily low.

71. A Strong Bulwark

I T IS your duty to protect and defend the virtue of chastity, as if your heart were some beleaguered fortress. Nothing contributes to the successful defense of any fortress so much as strong bulwarks. The same argument holds good in a spiritual sense; you must surround your virtue—the favorite virtue of the Saviour and of His Blessed Mother—with mighty ramparts.

One of the most important of these ramparts for the preservation of your purity—an absolutely necessary bulwark for the salvation of your soul—is prayer. Love prayer, and practise it earnestly; then you can not fail to win the victor's crown in your conflict with the enemies of your soul.

In the happy days of childhood, long since past, scarcely had you given the first signs of awakening reason than you were taught to fold your hands in prayer. From the pulpit and in the confessional, at home and in the church, you are exhorted to pray; the sound of the church bell, the sight of the crucifix, admonish you to raise your heart to God in prayer. It is not without the most weighty reasons that I myself have frequently and urgently encouraged you to pray. It behooves young men especially to follow the injunction of St. Paul: *"Pray without ceasing"*; for they are so frequently exposed to the fiercest onslaughts of passion. How otherwise could they in their weakness obtain the strength and grace which are needed in order permanently to resist the blandishments of the world and their own evil concupiscence?

Certainly young people must pray, and pray in the right manner, in order to protect and preserve the pearl of virtues; just as the wise Solomon did in his youth, according to his own words: *"Because I knew that I could not otherwise be continent except God gave it, I went to the Lord, and besought Him"* (Wis. viii. 21).

St. Paul points out to us a special method of prayer for the preservation of chastity in the following words: *"In all things taking the shield of faith, wherewith you may be able to extinguish all the fiery darts of the most wicked one."* By this shield of faith is meant that the truths of our holy religion, more especially serious meditations upon the four last things, will enable us to conquer the fiercest temptations. If such temptations assail you, and dangers threaten you, have recourse to mental prayer. Place before you, as vividly as you can, death, judgment, heaven, and hell. Thus will you be prevented from falling into sin, or at least from remaining in sin, and you will bridle and overcome your passion. Holy Scripture reminds us of this in the following words: *"In all thy works remember thy last end, and thou shalt never sin."*

St. Paul exhorts us to vocal prayer when he says: *"In everything by prayer and supplication with thanksgiving let your petitions be made known to God."* Obey this injunction; pray without ceasing, that you may be kept from temptation, or at least from falling when you are tempted. Our Lord teaches us to pray thus: "*Lead us not into temptation, but deliver us from evil.*" In another place He says: "*Ask, and it shall be given you.*" Ask, and you shall receive strength in temptation, courage in the fight, and deliverance from the bondage of sin, if you have been so unfortunate as to fall into it. As long as a young man continues to pray all is not lost; there is certainly hope for his salvation. But if he grows careless in regard to prayer, or ceases altogether to pray, there is everything to fear, as I know by experience. To take one instance of the many which have come under my observation: A young girl who had formerly been pious and good lost her innocence, to the grief of all who knew her. Her confessor spoke to her upon the subject, and asked how her sad fall had come about. "Alas! reverend Father," she exclaimed, bursting into sobs, "this is what one comes to if one neglects prayer and at last gives it up altogether!" Fain would I say to every young man on the face of the earth: Grow not weary of praying if you would not be lost!

The most precious fruit of prayer is that it unites us to God and renders us heavenly-minded. True prayer is an elevation of the heart to God, in which you hold intercourse with Him. He, the loving Father, during every moment of this sweet communion, infuses more light, fresh love and strength into the heart of the child who kneels before Him. In this way the heart is more and more raised up to God and is excited to pious affections.

When Moses had communed with God for forty days, his face shone with such dazzling brightness that he was obliged to cover it when he came near to the people. We read something of a similar nature in the lives of many of the saints, who, whilst engaged in prayer and contemplation, or after they had concluded these exercises, shone with heavenly radiance.

We poor sinful mortals can not expect to receive from God favors such as these. One thing is certain, however: he who loves prayer, and prays frequently and devoutly, will find his soul to be illumined from on high; he will grow in the love of God, he will strive more and more to please Him, he will more and more despise all that is base, unholy, and impure. He, on the contrary, who does not pray at regular times, who does not raise his heart to God and to heaven, becomes of necessity more and more worldly-minded, loses all relish for higher things, and seeks only the gratification of his lower nature.

Like a pillar of fire, prayer will lead you unharmed through the perils of this world. Prayer will open for you the gates of everlasting blessedness. Never murmur, never despair, whatever may be the dangers and temptations that surround you! You can always pray—if not with your lips, with your heart at least, which is far better. With St. Peter cry out in these words to the sacred Heart of Jesus: *"Lord, save us, we perish!"* But do not pray in a pusillanimous spirit; pray with firm confidence.

> Jesus! eternal Truth sublime!
>   Through endless years the same!
> Thou crown of those who through all time
>   Confess Thy holy name:
>
> Encircled by Thy virgin band,
>   Amid the lilies Thou art found;
> For thy pure brides with lavish hand
>   Scattering immortal graces round.
>
> Keep us, O Purity divine,
>   From every least corruption free;
> Our every sense from sin refine,
>   And purify our souls for Thee.
>
> —*Lyra Catholica.*

Hail thou Star of Ocean!
　Portal of the sky!
Ever Virgin Mother
　Of the Lord most High.

Show thyself a Mother;
　Offer Him our sighs,
Who for us Incarnate
　Did not thee despise.

Virgin of all virgins!
　To thy shelter take us;
Gentlest of the gentle!
　Chaste and gentle make us.

Still as on we journey,
　Help our weak endeavor;
Till with thee and Jesus
　We rejoice forever.
　　　　　—Lyra Catholica.

72. IMPASSABLE BARRICADES

FROM time immemorial barricades have played an important part whenever street fighting has been carried on in large cities. They consist of impediments, artificially constructed, and made of various materials, such as, for instance, beams joined together, or heaps of earth and stones, which render it very difficult for an enemy to pass along the streets.

In the spiritual conflict—in the war against the enemy of chastity—various kinds of mortification and the good employment of one's time may be compared to these barricades. They prevent the entrance of the sin of impurity into the citadel of our heart, or at least render it more difficult. Let us see how this comes to pass.

Why are many young people so weak in regard to the preservation of their chastity? There is no doubt that this is principally caused by want of mortification, by effeminate bringing up. Such a system of bringing up awakens and fosters animal propensities in the human being at an early age, and lays him open to the most terrible temptations later in life. He falls an easy prey to these temptations, because he has but little strength; he is wanting in moral stamina. In this way habits of impurity originate.

He who wishes to prevent sins of impurity from entering his heart must surround it with a thorny hedge of mortification; I mean that he must by severe self-discipline bring his body into subjection to the spirit.

In order to overcome their bodies, the saints ate sparingly, slept but little, wore rough penitential garments, dwelt in caves, sometimes even beneath the vault of heaven, and practised various corporal austerities. In order to vanquish his rebellious flesh, St. Aloysius scourged himself unto blood, St. Francis of Assisi rolled in thorns, St. Bernard immersed himself in a half-frozen pond, even the Apostle chastised his body.

Extraordinary severities are not required of you—not even advisable for you; but without some practice of self-denial and mortification of the senses you will fall into effeminacy and vicious habits.

"There is no alternative," writes St. Alphonsus Liguori; "we must either fight or perish. If the soul does not subdue the body, the flesh will conquer the spirit."

In reference to sensualists who deride the mortification of the flesh, St. Bernard says "If we are cruel in crucifying the flesh, they, by sparing it, are far more cruel; for by the inordinate love of the flesh and the pleasures of the body in this life, they shall merit for soul and body inexpressible torments in the next." St. Philip says: "The perfection of a Christian consists in mortifying himself for the love of Christ. Where there is no great mortification, there is no great sanctity." And St. Francis de Sales admonishes us: "Prayer without mortification is like a soul without a body. Be assured that the mortification of the senses in seeing, hearing, and speaking, is far more profitable than wearing even sharp chains or hair-shirts. It ought to be our principal object to conquer ourselves, and from day to day to go on increasing in spiritual strength and perfection."

Another barricade, a powerful obstacle against the entrance of the spirit of impurity is industry—useful employment. Over and over again does daily experience teach the truth of the proverb: "Idleness is the beginning of every vice"; and it is very especially the beginning of the vice of impurity.

Therefore St. Jerome warns us: "Never let the devil find thee idle." The saint had experienced in his own person how great is the power of industry in repelling temptations. Buried in the desert, terribly emaciated by fasting and chastisement of his body, he felt none the less the sting of the flesh in the most humiliating manner.

Then he applied himself to an occupation so repulsive and tiresome, that only a will of iron, such as he possessed, could expect to carry it through. At last he was able to exclaim: "How grateful I feel to God that my labor and toil have finally helped me to attain the peace and consolation for which I longed!"

Therefore it is a fortunate thing for you, my friend, if you always have plenty of occupation, and have no time left to stand about idle, or to wander aimlessly hither and thither. Indeed, if this is your case, you must give thanks to God that it is so. Think of a spring; it is always clear, because the water is ever in motion. How thick and foul, on the contrary, is a stagnant pool or pond, whose waters are still and motionless. Therefore bar the way to your heart by constant and useful occupation. Let it be your ambition, by indefatigable industry, unremitting activity and endurance, to become a useful member of society, and thus be a credit to your faith, a source of joy to your parents, and a benefactor to your fellow-men.

That man should work is God's good will
And man's own welfare too;
For Satan finds some mischief still
For idle hands to do.

73. A WELL-FURNISHED STOREHOUSE

O F WHAT avail would the most impregnable fortifications and the most powerful weapons be to a general besieged by enemies, and shut up in a fortress, if provisions—the means of life—were wanting to him? He could maintain no permanent resistance, he could not possibly conquer, and there would remain for him no alternative except either to see the garrison perish from hunger, or to surrender at discretion to the enemy.

Such a disaster can never fall to your lot in the war which you wage against the enemy of chastity; for never can spiritual means of support be wanting to you, since well-furnished storehouses stand open to you at all times, from which you may always draw fresh spiritual strength, invincible power, and inexhaustible grace. I understand by these storehouses, the sacraments of Penance and of the Altar.

In confession and communion our merciful Redeemer has bequeathed to the young inexhaustible treasures of grace, which may always enable them to come off victorious in the war against the enemy of their salvation.

It matters not how grievous may be the sins into which a young man has fallen, or how violent and persistent may be the temptations by which he is assailed. If only he goes to confession regularly—with a humble and contrite heart— hell will not secure its coveted prey. Frequent confession and communion are the best means to preserve chastity.

Many holy confessors, like St. Philip Neri and St. Alphonsus Liguori, often enjoined upon such deeply fallen or cruelly tempted young men nothing more for a penance than that they should after their first sin of relapse, again present themselves in the confessional.

If young people really did this with seriousness and perseverance their condition would speedily show a marked improvement.

The richest and most inexhaustible storehouse of divine grace is the most holy Sacrament of the Altar. That necessarily follows from the essence of this sacrament. For who is present there, who gives Himself to you in holy communion? It is He, who once reposed as a little child in the manger of Bethlehem, who passed through all the stages of adolescence—who, when He had attained to man's estate, showed a very special love for the young, who called children to His side, embraced, and blessed them; who so mercifully healed the epileptic young man, the servant of the centurion at Capharnaum, the daughter of the Samaritan woman; who raised to life the widow's son at Naim, and the twelve-year-old daughter of Jairus.

Certainly you know Him, who now as the same merciful Saviour, both God and man, the same loving friend of youth, is still present among us under the eucharistic veil, and so often deigns to descend into our sinful heart in all the plenitude of His grace and love.

Think you that He does not know your struggles and temptations, the manifold dangers which beset the soul He purchased with His own most precious blood? Or do you think He has not the same power which He possessed when, as the Incarnate Son of God, He walked among men and came so frequently and so mercifully to men's rescue and relief; or that He does not feel the same fatherly love, that He is no longer desirous to aid and deliver you? Why these foolish doubts? Go direct to Him, confidently invoke His help; say to Him: *"Jesus, Son of David, have mercy on me!"*

Pray with lively faith, with childlike confidence: *"O sacred Heart of Jesus, I put my trust in Thee!"*

Then will you assuredly feel that strength and consolation are poured into your heart; then will you appreciate the truth of St. Paul's words: *"God is faithful, who will not suffer you to be tempted above that which you are able, but will make also with temptation issue that you may be able to bear it."* You will find that God is true to the promise He made to each one of us by the mouth of His prophet: *"Can a woman forget her infant, so as not to have pity on the son of her womb? and if she should forget, yet will I not forget thee."* How touching, how consoling is this assurance! Surely it must inspire the coldest, the most despairing heart with confidence and hope! The God of love and goodness, of mercy and long-suffering will not forget you when you are tormented by temptation, and exposed to the risk of losing your innocence.

But you must endeavor to receive Him frequently in holy communion.

For the celestial dew contained in this wondrous sacrament imparts divine strength. How could it be otherwise? Holy communion is a union between Jesus and ourselves, a union so intimate that even His almighty love could have devised none closer. He Himself has said: *"He that eateth my flesh and drinketh my blood, abideth in me, and I in Him."* This most intimate union effects a transformation by the fire of divine charity. The partaking of His most sacred body and blood weakens concupiscence and gives the feeble will strength for conflict. By partaking of this sacrament the soul is filled with a joy compared with which the pleasures of sin appear contemptible, and bitter as gall. If Jesus, who as Purity itself, unites Himself so closely to your soul, how can the unclean spirit dare to approach you? If you frequently receive Him in this sacred banquet, if He nourishes, fortifies, ennobles, and sanctifies your soul with His omnipotent grace, must not your lily of innocence ever become stronger, fairer, and more fragrant?

Amid dangers and temptations let this be your prayer:

> In life's hard conflict be Thou near,
> My God, for then no foe I fear;
> Left to myself I needs must fall;
> Strengthened by Thee, I conquer all.

74. HOLY COMMUNION: OUR LIFE AND OUR STRENGTH

PONTIFICAL DECREE CONCERNING DAILY COMMUNION

THE Council of Trent, having in view the unspeakable treasures of grace which are offered to the faithful who receive the Most Holy Eucharist, makes the following declaration: "The holy synod would desire that at every Mass the faithful who are present should communicate not only spiritually, by way of internal affection, but sacramentally by the actual reception of the Eucharist" (Sess. xxii, cap. 6). Which words declare plainly enough the wish of the Church that all Christians should be daily nourished by this heavenly banquet, and should derive therefrom abundant fruit for their sanctification.

And this wish of the Council is in entire agreement with that desire wherewith Christ our Lord was inflamed when He instituted this divine sacrament. For He Himself, more than once, and in no ambiguous terms, pointed out the necessity of eating His flesh and drinking His blood, especially in these words: *"This is the bread that came down from heaven; not as your fathers did eat manna and are dead: he that eateth this bread shall live forever"* (John vi. 59). Now, from this comparison of the food of angels with bread and with the manna, it was easily to be understood by His disciples that, as the body is daily nourished with bread, and as the Hebrews were daily nourished with manna in the desert, so the Christian soul might daily partake of this heavenly bread and be refreshed thereby. Moreover, whereas, in the "Lord's Prayer" we are bidden to ask for *"our daily bread,"* the holy Fathers of the Church all but

Conflict and Conquest

unanimously teach that by these words must be understood, not so much that material bread which is the support of the body, as the eucharistic bread which ought to be our daily food.

Moreover, the desire of Jesus Christ and of the Church that all the faithful should daily approach the sacred banquet is directed chiefly to this end, that the faithful, being united to God by means of the sacrament, may thence derive strength to resist their sensual passions, to cleanse themselves from the stains of daily faults, and to avoid these graver sins to which human frailty is liable; so that its primary purpose is not that the honor and reverence due to Our Lord may be safeguarded, nor that the sacrament may serve as a reward of virtue bestowed on the recipients (St. Augustine, Serm. 57 in Matt. de Orat. Dom., n. 7). Hence the holy Council of Trent calls the Eucharist "the antidote whereby we are delivered from daily faults and preserved from deadly sins" (Sess. xiii, cap. 2).

This desire on the part of God was so well understood by the first Christians, that they daily flocked to the Holy Table as to a source of life and strength. "*They were persevering in the doctrine of the apostles, and in the communication of the breaking of bread*" (Acts ii. 42). And that this practice was to continue into later ages, not without great fruit of holiness and perfection, the holy Fathers and ecclesiastical writers bear witness.

But when, in later times, piety grew cold, and more especially under the influence of the plague of Jansenism, disputes began to arise concerning the dispositions with which it was proper to receive communion frequently or daily, and writers vied with one another in imposing more and more stringent conditions as necessary to be fulfilled. The result of such disputes was that very few were considered worthy to communicate daily, and to derive from this most healing sacrament its more abundant fruits; the rest being content to partake of it once a year, or once a month, or at the utmost weekly. Nay, to such a pitch was rigorism carried, that whole classes of persons were excluded from a frequent approach to the Holy Table; for instance, those engaged in trade, or even *those living in the state of matrimony.*

Others, however, went to the opposite extreme. Under the persuasion that daily communion was a divine precept, and in order that no day might pass without the reception of the sacrament, besides other practices contrary to the approved usage of the Church, they held that the Holy Eucharist ought to be received, and in fact administered it, even on Good Friday.

Under these circumstances the Holy See did not fail in its duty of vigilance. For, by a decree of this Sacred Congregation, which begins with the words *Cum ad aures*, issued on February 12, 1679, with the approbation of Innocent XI, it condemned these errors, and put a stop to such abuses; at the same time declaring that all the faithful of whatsoever class—merchants or tradesmen or married persons not excepted—might be admitted to frequent communion, according to the devotion of each one and the judgment of his confessor. And on December 7, 1690, by the decree of Pope Alexander VIII, *Sanctissimus Dominus*, the proposition of Baius, postulating a perfectly pure love of God, without any admixture of defect, as requisite on the part of those who wished to approach the Holy Table, was condemned.

Yet the poison of Jansenism, which, under the pretext of showing due honor and reverence to the Holy Eucharist, had infected the minds even of good men, did not entirely disappear. The controversy as to the dispositions requisite for the lawful and laudable frequentation of the sacrament survived the declarations of the Holy See—so much so, indeed, that certain theologians of good repute judged that daily communion should be allowed to the faithful only in rare cases, and under many conditions.

On the other hand, there were not wanting men of learning and piety who more readily granted permission for this practice, so salutary and so pleasing to God. In accordance with the teaching of the Fathers, they maintained that there was no precept of the Church which prescribed more perfect dispositions in the case of daily than of weekly or monthly communion; while the good effects of daily communion would, they alleged, be far more abundant than those of communion received weekly or monthly.

In our own day the controversy has been carried on with increased warmth, and not without bitterness, so that the minds of confessors and the consciences of the faithful have been disturbed, to the no small detriment of Christian piety and devotion. Accordingly, certain distinguished men, themselves pastors of souls, have urgently besought His Holiness Pope Pius X to deign to settle, by his supreme authority, the question concerning the dispositions requisite for daily communion; so that this usage, so salutary and so pleasing to God, might not only suffer no decrease among the faithful, but might rather be promoted and everywhere propagated; a thing most desirable in these days, when religion and the Catholic faith are attacked on all sides, and the true love of God and genuine piety are so lacking in many quarters. And His Holiness, being most earnestly desirous, out of his abundant solicitude and zeal, that the faithful should be invited to partake of the sacred banquet as often as possible, and even daily, and should profit to the utmost by its fruits, committed the aforesaid question to this Sacred Congregation, to be looked into and decided once for all (*definiendum*).

Accordingly, the Sacred Congregation of the Council, in a plenary session held on December 16, 1905, submitted the whole matter to a very careful scrutiny; and, after sedulously examining the reasons adduced on either side, determined and declared as follows:

1. Frequent and daily communion, as a thing most earnestly desired by Christ our Lord and by the Catholic Church, should be open to all the faithful, of whatever rank and condition of life; so that no one who is in the state of grace, and who approaches the Holy Table with a right and devout intention, can lawfully be hindered therefrom.

2. A right intention consists in this: that he who approaches the Holy Table should do so, not out of routine, or vainglory, or human respect, but for the purpose of pleasing God, or being more closely united with Him by charity, and of seeking this divine remedy for his weaknesses and defects.

3. Although it is more expedient that those who communicate frequently or daily should be free from venial sins, especially from such as are fully deliberate, and from any affection thereto, nevertheless it is sufficient that they be free from mortal sin, with the purpose of never sinning mortally in future; and, if they have this sincere purpose, it is impossible but that daily communicants

should gradually emancipate themselves from even venial sins, and from all affection thereto.

4. But whereas the sacraments of the New Law, though they take effect *ex opere operato*, nevertheless produce a greater effect in proportion as the dispositions of the recipient are better; therefore, care is to be taken that holy communion be preceded by serious preparation, and followed by a suitable thanksgiving according to each one's strength, circumstances, and duties.

5. That the practice of frequent and daily communion may be carried out with greater prudence and more abundant merit, the confessor's advice should be asked. Confessors, however, are to be careful not to dissuade any one (*ne quemquam avertant*) from frequent and daily communion, provided that he is in a state of grace and approaches with a right intention.

6. But since it is plain that, by the frequent or daily reception of the Holy Eucharist, union with Christ is fostered, the spiritual life more abundantly sustained, the soul more richly endowed with virtues, and an even surer pledge of everlasting happiness bestowed on the recipient, therefore parish priests, confessors, and preachers—in accordance with the approved teaching of the Roman Catechism (Part ii. cap. iv, q. 58)—are frequently, and with great zeal, to exhort the faithful to this devout and salutary practice.

7. Frequent and daily communion is to be promoted especially in Religious Orders and Congregations of all kinds; with regard to which, however, the decree *Quemadmodum* issued on December 17, 1890, by the Sacred Congregation of Bishops and Regulars is to remain in force. It is also to be promoted especially in ecclesiastical seminaries, where students are preparing for the service of the altar; as also in all Christian establishments of whatever kind, for the training of youth.

8. In the case of religious institutes, whether of solemn or simple religious vows, in whose Rules, or Constitutions, or calendars, communion is assigned to certain fixed days, such regulations are to be regarded as *directive* and not *preceptive*. In such cases the appointed number of communions should be regarded as a minimum, and not as setting a limit to the devotion

of the Religious. Therefore, freedom of access to the eucharistic table, whether more frequently or daily, must always be allowed them, according to the principles above laid down in this decree. And in order that all Religious of both sexes may clearly understand the provisions of this decree the Superior of each house is to see that it is read in community, in the vernacular, every year within the octave of the feast of Corpus Christi.

9. Finally, after the publication of this decree, all ecclesiastical writers are to cease from contentious controversies concerning the dispositions requisite for frequent and daily communion.

All this having been reported to His Holiness Pope Pius X by the undersigned Secretary of the Congregation, in an audience held on December 17, 1905, His Holiness ratified and confirmed the present decree, and ordered it to be published, anything to the contrary notwithstanding. He further ordered that it should be sent to all local ordinaries and regular prelates, to be communicated by them to their respective seminaries, parishes, religious institutes, and priests; and that in their reports concerning the state of their respective dioceses or institutes they should inform the Holy See concerning the execution of the matters therein determined.

Given at Rome, the 20th day of December, 1905.

✠Vincent,
Card. Bishop of Palestrina, Prefect.
Cajetan De Lai, *Sec.*

75. Mary, Help of Christians

A T THE close of my instructions in regard to the conflict for the preservation of chastity comes perhaps the most pleasing and consoling of all, the one best calculated to inspire you with a glad hope of victory. Whither does a dutiful son betake himself when any burden weighs heavily upon him? To his beloved mother.

She, the good mother, always has a word of advice, of comfort, and of encouragement. And even the youthful soldier amid the rush and roar of battle thinks, in the moment of greatest peril, of his dear mother far away.

Upon you, my friend, a heavy burden is pressing; the preservation of your chastity; you also are standing in the thick of the battle, surrounded on every side by the enemies of innocence. Do you, therefore, think of your mother, do you also have recourse to your mother; for truly you have a mother in Mary, the ever blessed virgin. She is called by the Church in the Litany of Loretto: "*Help of Christians.*"

Beseech Mary, that her maternal eye may watch over and protect you. St. Bernard, who was so enthusiastically devoted to Mary, addresses you in the following touching words:

"O man, whoever thou art, if thou wouldst not be engulfed in the abyss, turn not thine eye away from the shining star, turn it not away from Mary! If thou wouldst not be tossed hither and thither by the waves of pride and ambition, look up to this star, call upon Mary! If the billows of concupiscence and sensual desires break over thy little bark of life, look up to this star, call upon Mary!

"Keep her in thy heart; let her name be ever on thy lips. If she hold thee up, thou wilt not fall; if she guide thee, thou wilt not go astray; if she protect thee, thou hast no need to fear; if she look favorably upon thee, thou wilt escape the snares of hell, and reach the gate of eternal felicity."

Therefore in the battle with the impure spirit, in which your will is apt to become paralyzed, cling fast to the maternal hand of Mary. This hand is strong enough to help, to protect, and to save you.

Innumerable are the instances in which young persons have been delivered from the most furious assaults of the flesh, and have found grace and strength to overcome them, because they have invoked the Mother of God with the fullest confidence.

The celebrated Father Succhi of Rome was wont to recommend to young men who were inclined to sins of impurity, the following prayer to our Lady: "*My Queen! My Mother!*

remember *I am thine own: keep me, guard me, as thy property and possession.*" The Sovereign Pontiff, Pius IX, granted to all the faithful an indulgence of forty days every time that, when assailed by temptation, they shall say this ejaculation.

St. Anselm thus addresses the blessed Mother of God:

"O Lady, thou art the Mother of Him who pardons and of those who are pardoned; of Him who justifies and of those who are justified; of Him who saves and of those who are saved. O blessed hope! O safe refuge! The Mother of God is our Mother; the Mother of Him in whom alone we hope, and whom alone we fear, is our Mother; the Mother of Him who alone can save or destroy is our Mother."

Father Dignam, S.J. , says: "Go to our Lady, whose love is as the sea; pray her to help you to overcome your faults, to obtain for you never to commit a deliberate fault, never to offend God. She will not only make you very good but very happy.

"Bear this in mind: it was *because of his mother, 'being moved with mercy toward her'* (Luke vii. 13), that Jesus raised the dead man at the gate of Naim. Be careful, when you desire any great favor, to implore the intercession of *your Mother*, of Mary. Ask for great favors and for all graces in the name of Christ's Mother; remind Our Lord of her agony, when, her soul pierced with a sword of sorrow, she stood at the foot of the cross. Have the most unbounded confidence in Mary's intercession."

Our Lord once revealed to St. Catherine of Siena that He had charged Mary to take men, and especially sinners, prisoners, and lead them to Him; and Mary herself told St. Bridget that there was no sinner, no matter how abandoned, who, if he called on her, would not return to God and, by her mediation, obtain forgiveness. Just as the magnet attracts iron, so does she draw the hardest hearts to herself and to God. "Who," exclaims Innocent III, "has ever had recourse to Mary, and was not heard?"

"Mary, the Mother of God, is my Mother," St. Aloysius was wont to exclaim in an ecstasy of delight and gratitude, and like a true servant of Mary he was ever anxious to avoid the least thing that could displease her or her divine Son, and always eager to honor and please her by acts of mortification and by the imitation of her virtues. Let us do likewise—let us carefully avoid whatever is displeasing to Almighty God. "Detach thy will from sin," wrote St. Gregory VII to the Countess Matilda, "and you will find in Mary a mother more willing to protect and assist you than any earthly mother." If you love Mary truly, you will please her by a constant struggle against your passions, by striving to become ever more like to her in virtue, by mortifying yourself in little things, and by performing some devotion in her honor every day. Your constant endeavor should be to please your sweet Mother, and this you will do above all by doing the will of her divine Son, by your fidelity in the service of God, in laboring for your own sanctification, and the salvation of souls.

"True devotion," as we read in *The Little Book of Our Lady*, "comes from God and leads to God. The fundamental rule in regard to the homage which we offer to the Blessed Virgin Mary and the saints is, that it must ultimately be referred to God and our eternal salvation. Our devotion to the Blessed Virgin would be of no avail if it did not tend toward our union with God, toward possessing Him eternally.

"True devotion extends itself to the saints without being separated from the eternal *Source* of all sanctity. *'For other foundation no man can lay, but that which is laid; which is Christ Jesus'* (1 Cor. iii. 11). Let Him be the foundation of our devotion to His holy Mother.

"We are not able to honor our blessed Lady adequately, since, through her, Jesus has come to us. Oh, how great, how sublime was Mary's vocation! God predestined her before all ages to be the Mother of the Saviour of the world. And having called her to fill this most glorious office He would not have her be a mere channel of grace, but an instrument co-operating, both by her excellent qualities and by her own free will, in the great work of our Redemption.

"For thousands of years the world had been expecting the promised *Messias.* The fulness of time has now come. The eternal Father sends a heavenly messenger to Mary, to treat with her of the mystery of the Incarnation. She pronounces the word '*Fiat!*' 'Be it done!' And the heavens open; the earth possesses a Saviour; *Mary has become the Mother of God.*

"Years pass by. The time has arrived when the great sacrifice is to be consummated. We find Mary at the foot of the cross. With the dying breath of Jesus she receives the Church as an inheritance. *Mary becomes our Mother.*

"These are the two great titles which give Mary a claim on our veneration and affection. She is like a fountain from which the waters of grace have spread themselves abundantly over the whole human race. As we have once received through her Jesus, the source of all blessing and grace, so we also obtain through her powerful intercession the various effects and applications of this grace in all the circumstances of life. Her maternal charity, which shines forth in the mystery of the Incarnation, also causes her to take a share in the consequences of this universal principle of benediction. Thus Mary is, by her intercession, the Mother of all Christians, the Mother of all men. Her overflowing charity is an appropriate instrument for the operations of grace.

"Who is better able than Mary to plead in our behalf? She can confidently speak to the heart of her divine Son, where her wishes, her sentiments, find an echo. She fears no refusal. The love of the Son makes Him lend a favorable ear to the request of His Mother.

"Our blessed Lady is able and willing to help us, but in order to secure her powerful and kind assistance we must have a sincere devotion to her. This devotion must be practical: it ought not to consist in words only, but in actions. A person truly devout to Mary will enroll himself in her confraternities, especially in the Confraternity of the Holy Rosary; he will celebrate her feasts, venerate her images, visit her temples, and endeavor to imitate her virtues. Certainly, he cannot be said to have a true devotion toward the Mother of God who does not honor and invoke her by frequent and fervent prayers. Among the various exercises in her honor comes in the first place the Mass of our blessed Lady. Pious historians record many favors obtained by those who celebrated or heard Mass in her honor. The Church also grants special privileges to the Mary-Mass on Saturdays. The Office of the Blessed Virgin, her Litanies, and the holy Rosary are singularly pleasing to her. Let us not imagine, however, that to secure the special protection of the Mother of God our prayers must needs be very long; much will depend upon circumstances; but let us not forget the advice which Blessed John Berchmans gave to his companions at his death: 'The least homage is sufficient, provided it be constant.' Hence, what we have once resolved to do in honor of our blessed Lady must never be put aside or neglected, but must be faithfully persevered in, daily, until death."

Father Basso urges the devout clients of Mary to observe some very commendable practices, as follows:

On rising in the morning and on retiring at night say three *Aves* in honor of the purity of Mary with the aspiration: "By thy holy virginity and immaculate conception, O most pure Virgin, purify my body and sanctify my soul!" Take refuge under her protecting mantle, that she may keep you from sin day and by night. When the clock strikes, salute Mary with an *Ave*. Do the same on leaving or returning to your room, also when passing her pictures and shrines. At the beginning and end of every work or action, say an *Ave*, for blessed is that work which is placed between two *Aves*. Whenever we salute our dearest Queen with the "Angelic Salutation, " so pleasing to her ears, she answers us with a grace from heaven.

An Act of Consecration, the *Salve Regina*, the *Sub tuum præsidium*, the *Memorare*, or some other favorite prayer is said daily by devout souls in honor of our blessed Mother, to obtain from her the grace of a holy life and a happy death. Make with great fervor the novenas preparatory for the feasts of the Blessed Virgin Mary.

Let us conclude this chapter with some special reflections on the Rosary. In the Litany of Loretto the Church calls Mary, "Queen of the most holy Rosary." In his beautiful and instructive sermon on the solemnity of the most holy Rosary, the Very Rev. D. T. McDermott says: "Why is the devotion called *the most holy Rosary?* The Church carefully weighs her words. She selects terms to convey her meaning as precisely as it is possible for language to express it. However language, in its poverty, may fail to express fully the meaning, the Church never indulges in exaggeration. Yet she calls the devotion of the Rosary—*most holy*. And most holy it shall be found to be in its origin, in its prayers, in its object, and in its effects."

The word *Rosary*, as applied to this devotion, means *Garden of Roses*. It is, of course, figurative, and is intended to impress upon all that they will be able to gather flowers of piety and the fruits of every virtue from this devotion.

In Sacred Scripture, our prayers and good works, because of an analogy they bear to them, are likened to material things. For example, our pious deeds are compared to light, in the following text: "*Let your light so shine before men, that they may see your good works, and glorify your Father who is in heaven.*" Good example is likened to the perfume of precious ointments: "*Let us run in the odor of Thy ointments.*" Incense, in the words of holy David, has become a symbol of prayer: "*Let my prayer ascend like incense in Thy sight.*" Men regard those who live soberly, justly, and piously as diffusing around them, by holiness of life, a sweet odor, just as fragrant flowers fill the surrounding atmosphere with perfume. Hence, St. Paul says of those who lead holy lives: "*They are the good odor of Christ unto God.*" And men say of them at death: "*They died in the odor of sanctity.*"

Christians were accustomed to decorate the altars of the Blessed Virgin, and to crown her statues with flowers, because these were emblematic of Mary's virtues. Hence, they hoped their prayers and devotions would be as acceptable to the holy Virgin as the sweet-smelling flowers they offered her were agreeable to men, and that their contemplation of these flowers would lead to the cultivation in their own hearts of those virtues which found in flowers such beautiful emblems. The Rosary is then fittingly called Mary's chaplet or wreath.

The Rosary is a string of one hundred and fifty small beads, divided by fifteen larger ones into tens or decades, as they are commonly called. **The string of beads ordinarily used has but five decades, and is but a third part of the Rosary.**

The arrangement of beads in this manner for the purpose of telling prayers shows that they come to us, not only from the earliest Christian times, but that they were in use among the Jews. And it is not at all unlikely that the Blessed Virgin used something very similar to a string of beads in counting her prayers. So completely identified did beads become (in the course of time) with the counting of prayers, that the word "bead" signified *prayer*. The advantage of a string of beads for those who had a certain number of prayers to say was that it allowed the mind and heart to be concentrated entirely on

God, while the hand mechanically told the number by passing a bead between the finger.

The one hundred and fifty beads represent the psalms of David. The devotion of such of the Jews and of the early Christians as could read and procure books was the reading of the psalms. In order to furnish a substitute to those who could not read or procure books, vocal prayers were assigned to the number of one hundred and fifty—to be told by transferring a pebble (for every prayer) from one pocket to another, or by passing a bead through the fingers.

The Rosary was recited in this form until the thirteenth century. While, since that era it has developed, and been made eminently practical, yet there is nothing in it today that did not spring from the germs it held then.

It was then aptly called the people's psalter. The psalms of David are very suggestive of the Rosary as developed by St. Dominic. Some of the psalms are prophetic, descriptive of Our Saviour's coming, His office, and His reign. These correspond to the Joyful Mysteries. Other psalms are lamentations for sin and prayers for deliverance from sufferings and enemies. These correspond to the Sorrowful Mysteries. Then again there are those which are hymns of thanksgiving and praise, psalms of victory. These correspond to the Glorious Mysteries. The fifteen larger beads denote the mysteries of the Rosary. The arrangement of the Rosary in this form, with its meditation on the mysteries, is generally credited to St. Dominic. It matters not whether the Rosary of today was given to the saint by the Blessed Virgin herself, who is said to have appeared to him, or whether it was the result of an inspiration of grace. It has proved its title to heavenly origin by its fruits. *"A good tree can not bring forth evil fruit; neither can an evil tree bring forth good fruit; wherefore, by their fruits you shall know them."*

The one great object of this devotion is to impress upon

men the truths connected with the Redemption. When the number, the piety, the heroic virtues of those joined together in the devotion of the Rosary are considered, it must appear manifest that this form of prayer is simply irresistible with God.

Just think of the number of holy souls joined in the confraternities of the Rosary, some still in the world, others in religious communities! Many of these, like Aloysius, are angels in human flesh, who add bodily mortifications to innocence of life. Others are holy penitents, like Magdalen, Augustine, and Mary of Egypt, who honor God more by their penance than ninety-nine just who need not penance. Think, then, of this countless number of devout men and women, who every day recite the Rosary piously for themselves and their brethren! Think of the dying who, in momentary expectation of seeing God, devoutly offer the prayers of the Rosary as their last petitions to heaven in behalf of their brethren and themselves! Think of those who were once members of these confraternities, who are now among the elect of God, and who constantly watch over the welfare of these fellow-members on earth. Think of the prayers, almsdeeds, mortifications of all those united in the Rosary, as presented to Jesus Christ through the hands of His Mother, and may it not be said they do a holy violence to heaven? *"The kingdom of heaven suffereth violence, and the violent bear it away."* How truly may it be said of those who through this devotion, learn the virtues of Mary, and exhibit them in their daily lives: *"They that explain me shall have everlasting life."*

The Rev. Mother Francis Raphael, O. S. D. (Augusta Theodosia Drane), writes, in *The Spirit of the Dominican Order*: "If we examine the special devotion of our saints, we shall find that the mysteries of the Rosary were like an unseen thread running through them all. Take the story of Magdalen Angelica, whose life was divided according to the three parts of the Rosary. At the commencement of her religious conversion she kept entirely to meditation on the Joyful Mysteries, in order to obtain a childlike gaiety and innocence of heart. Then when she had received the habit of religion, she took the Sorrowful Mysteries to meditate upon, and with them entered upon a long course of austerities and disciplines. And at last she passed on to the Glorious Mysteries; and heaven rained down a very deluge of light and consolation into her soul, so long left disconsolate on the cross of her agonizing Spouse. This light was so divine and wonderful that it often became visible, encircling even her body in a bright luminous cloud. 'She acquired all her perfection,' says her biographer, 'through the meditations of the Rosary'; and when one Rosary Sunday, toward the close of her life, she knelt before our Lady's altar, and prayed for innocence of heart, the divine Mother spoke to her and said: 'Be of good heart, my daughter; for that which thou prayest for, thou already hast.'"

In *The Rosary Magazine* we read the following interesting communication: "The Holy Father Pope Pius X has offered a signal mark of his love for the Rosary in granting, July 31, 1906, to all those who piously carry the beads about with them, an indulgence of one hundred days and as many quarantines. This indulgence may be gained daily, provided, of course, that one be in a state of grace. Rosarians will recall that this privilege was long enjoyed by members of the Rosary Confraternity, Pope Innocent VIII, in a bull dated Feb. 26, 1491, having conferred it in the blessed hope that such a plenitude of favor might spread devotion to the Rosary over land and sea. In 1899 Pope Leo XIII published a catalogue of indulgences in which the above did not appear. As Rosarians rejoice that this favor is again ours, and we fervently pray that a still wider propagation of the Rosary devotion may result, and that the desire of the Venerable Pontiff to bring all things to Christ may be speedily realized.

"An indulgence of five years and five quarantines can be gained by Rosarians each time the holy name of Jesus is reverently pronounced in the recitation of the Dominican Rosary."

We read in *The Sentinel of the Blessed Sacrament*: "It was our Lady herself who, at Lourdes, excited us to the devotion of the Rosary. She passed through her fingers a long Rosary of glittering beads, smiling the while upon Bernadette, who was reciting her chaplet.

"If we desire to gather the fruit, we must bend the branch. If we long to possess Jesus, we must draw Mary to us. The Rosary is the sweet and powerful means of finding Jesus through His Mother. What, in truth, does Jesus eucharistic long for? What does He desire in abiding with us, except to live always in our thoughts, in our love? '*Do this in commemoration of Me*,' did He say when giving us the Eucharist. Now, the Rosary responds to the same desire. As the Blessed Sacrament contains Jesus, with all the graces and virtues of His past states, so the Rosary calls up before the mind's eye all His mysteries. Therefore it is that, after the Eucharist and the liturgical offices, which successively recall to us all the feasts of Our Lord, the Rosary is the very best way of continually contemplating the life of Jesus Christ and of uniting ourselves to Him.

"If we afford so much pleasure to father, to mother, to friends, by a hearty greeting, how much more must our fervent 'Angelic Salutation' please Jesus and Mary! Oh, then, let us repeat, without tiring, this filial salutation, and Jesus and Mary will help us *now and at the hour of our death!*"

76. St. Joseph, the Universal Helper

LIKE stars in the sky, through the long light of Time, shine out the saints, gracious, serene, and holy, and, like the celestial orbs, exercising a beneficent influence upon successive generations of men. Amongst them all, as some planet of surpassing radiance, is Joseph, the descendant of kings, the carpenter of Nazareth, as though in that one person were united the extremes of earthly rank. Down through the centuries his influence has been felt, comparatively still and small at first, but gradually expanding into its full importance, until in these past three centuries he has become the Father of Christians, the Patron of the Universal Church. "The saint of Scripture," says Cardinal Newman, "the foster-father of Our Lord, he was an object of the universal and absolute faith of the Christian world from the first: yet devotion to him is comparatively recent. When once it began, men seemed surprised that they had not thought of it before; and now they hold St. Joseph next to the Blessed Virgin in their religious affection and veneration."

Religious literature resounds with the praises of him who was emphatically called in Holy Writ "*the just*." In prose and in verse, his noble, majestic figure has formed the theme of many a beautiful or striking passage. In art, Joseph appears almost from the first and in a variety of ways. Now he is seen in some gorgeous canvas of Raphael or Perugino, or the more homely but forcible and lifelike presentations of the Dutch artists. Now he is feeble and old, the austere guardian of the Lily of Nazareth; again he is in a vigorous middle age, the defender and supporter of the royal Son and Mother; with a gravely intellectual head, portraying the wise and prudent guardian of his Immaculate Spouse; or in comparative youth, the strong protector of the flight into Egypt.

The saints in all ages have chosen St. Joseph as their special advocate at the throne of grace, holding—with that most modern of the beatified, whose cause has been introduced at Rome, Father Eymard, Apostle of the Blessed Eucharist—that St. Joseph is the helper of all Christians. "Happy the soul," says he, "who is devout to St. Joseph. It is a certain pledge of a good death, of salvation, and of eternal happiness. St. Joseph is also the patron of afflicted souls; for he had many trials and troubles. In your griefs, therefore, always have recourse to St. Joseph."

But no tribute was ever stronger to the power of the Patriarch of Bethlehem than that of the Virgin of Avila. Says St. Teresa:

"To render the Lord propitious to my prayers, I took glorious St. Joseph for my advocate and protector, and recommended myself most earnestly to him. His help was shown forth in the most striking manner. That tender father of my soul, that beloved protector, hastened to draw me from the condition in which my body languished, as he had snatched me from the greater perils of another kind which threatened my eternal salvation. . . . I do not remember ever to have asked anything of him which he did not grant me. What a picture I should place before your eyes, were it given me to trace out the signal favors which God has bestowed upon me, and the dangers both of soul and body from which I have been delivered, through the mediation of that blessed saint! The Most High gives grace to the other saints to help us in such or such a want, but glorious St. Joseph, as I know from experience, extends his power to all. Our Divine Lord wishes in this way to make us understand that, as He Himself was subject to St. Joseph in the land of exile, recognizing in him the authority of a foster-father and guardian, so He is still pleased to do His will in heaven by hearing and granting his requests. . . .

"Therefore the number of souls who honor him begins to be great, and the happy effects of his mediation every day confirm the truth of my words. Knowing now by my own experience the amazing influence of St. Joseph with God, I would wish to induce every one to honor him by a particular cultus. Hitherto I have always seen that persons who had a real devotion to him, sustained by works, made progress in virtue; for that heavenly protector favors in a special manner the spiritual advancement of souls who recommend themselves to him. I will content myself then, with conjuring, for the love of God, those who do not believe me to make the experiment. They shall discover for themselves how advantageous it is to honor that glorious Patriarch with a special devotion."

And this testimony of the great Carmelite is, in fact, the testimony of the ages: that St. Joseph never refuses to aid those who confide themselves and their affairs to his patronage. As expressed on one occasion by a contemporary preacher, this saint has been set over the human race in the character of father and head of the family; so that temporalities may be recommended to him with all confidence, in the certain hope that, if the thing asked for be not prejudicial to the petitioner, it will be granted; or, failing that, something of greater value shall be given in its stead. Were it possible to set down here the numberless favors granted through the mediation of that saint, even in temporal concerns, by religious who best know how to ask, or by devout souls in the world, it would be simply incredible to the unbelieving many. The venerable Patriarch of Bethlehem proves himself a veritable haven of refuge amid the trials and the needs of this transitory life; and above all in the last and greatest trial which, for each in turn, closes life's drama.

—*The Ave Maria*, March, 1909.

Prayer To St. Joseph
For the Preservation of Chastity

GUARDIAN of virgins and father, holy Joseph, to whose faithful care Christ Jesus, innocence herself, and Mary, the Virgin of virgins, were committed: I pray and beg of thee, by these dear pledges, Jesus and Mary, free me from all uncleanness, and make me with spotless mind, pure heart and chaste body, ever most chastely to serve Jesus and Mary all the days of my life. Amen.

> The Sovereign Pontiff, Pius IX, by a rescript of the Sacred Congregation of Indulgences, Feb. 4, 1877, recalling all indulgences hitherto given, granted to all the faithful who, with at least contrite heart and devotion, shall say this prayer, *an indulgence of one hundred days*, once a day.

Ejaculation

St. Joseph, model and patron of those who love the sacred Heart of Jesus, pray for us.

> One hundred days; indulgence, once a day.
> —Leo XIII, Dec. 19, 1891.

"Take thou courage and show thyself a man" (3 Kings ii. 2)

"Watch ye, stand fast in the Faith, do manfully" (I Cor. xvi. 13)

"A man he seems of cheerful yesterdays
And confident tomorrows."　　　—Wordsworth.

Of manners gentle, of affection mild;
In wit a man, simplicity a child.　　　—Pope.

"Virtue itself offends, when coupled with forbidding manners."
—Middleton.

"Roughness is a needless cause of discontent.　Severity breedeth fear, but roughness breedeth hate; even reproofs from authority ought to be grave, and not taunting."—Lord Bacon.

In simple manners all the secret lies:
Be kind and virtuous, you'll be blest and wise.
—Young.

"The greatest man is he who chooses right with the most invincible resolution; who resists the severest temptation from within and without; who bears the heaviest burdens cheerfully; who is calmest in storms, and most fearless under menaces and frowns; whose reliance on truth, on virtue, and on God is most unfaltering."　　　—Seneca.

PART THIRD

ON THE JOURNEY OF LIFE

On the
Journey
of Life

MANHOOD

77. MANLINESS

MANLINESS implies self-control, conscientiousness, moral courage, fearless discharge of duty in the face of obloquy and prejudice, firm determination to do what is right because it is right and pleasing to God, without regard to human respect, expediency, or popularity, a steadfast adherence to one's religious principles and convictions—in a word, an upright Christian character.

> "Self-reverence, self-knowledge, self-control,
> These three alone lead life to sovereign power:
> Yet not for power—power by herself
> Would come uncalled for—but to live by law,
> Acting the law we live by without fear;
> And because right is right, to follow right
> Were wisdom in the scorn of consequence."
> —Tennyson.

"*Act like a man; take courage and do; and be not dismayed*" (1 Paral. xxviii. 20).

"*Do ye manfully, and let your heart be strengthened—all ye that hope in the Lord*" (Ps. xxx. 25).

"*Behold, I command thee, take courage and be strong. Fear not, and be not dismayed; because the lord thy God is with thee in all things*" (Jos. i. 9).

"*If God be for us, who is against us?*" (Rom. viii. 31).

"*He that feareth man shall quickly fall, he that trusteth in the Lord, shall be set on high*" (Prov. xxix. 25).

> *"I myself will comfort you; who art thou, that thou shouldst*
> *be afraid of a mortal man, who shall wither away like grass?"*
> (Is. li. 12).

> *"Who is he that can hurt you, if you be zealous of good?"*
> (1 Peter iii. 13).

Strive to be a manly man! A manly man is a man of character; one who is controlled by conscience; one who does his duty under all circumstances; one who is swayed by reason, by faith, by moral principles—not by every passing impulse, not by transient emotions, not by fancy or caprice, not by human respect. A manly man is one who is endowed with the courage of his convictions; one who is conscientious, sincere, truthful, honest, upright, just and charitable, unselfish and magnanimous, kind and gentle; one who practises what he preaches, whose life is consistent with his faith; one who heeds the admonition of his Creator: *"Walk before Me and be perfect"* (Gen. xvii. 1); *"Thou shalt be perfect and without spot before the Lord thy God"* (Deut. xviii. 13); one, in fine, who may be called truly a Christian gentleman—who seeks to please God first and always, and then observes the Golden Rule: *"As you would that men should do to you, do you also to them in like manner"* (Luke vi. 31).

Vacillation of mind, feebleness of will, unsteadiness of purpose, want of courage, energy, and perseverance—these militate against success in the battle of life, and impede a man's progress in the way of virtue and perfection.

A firm will underlies every good and strong character, and to the lack of it must be attributed much unhappiness and misery in the world.

Strength of character includes both firmness of will and the power of self-restraint. A man, for instance, who yields to anger, and whose bursts of fury make his subjects tremble, may appear to be strong, as he ruthlessly bears all before him, but he is really weak—pitiably weak. He has not conquered himself; he is mastered by his passions. He lacks self-control, and therefore he is not strong. That man is great, that man is strong, who subdues his feelings, suppresses his evil inclinations, and bridles his passions.

> "*The patient man is better than the valiant, and he that ruleth his spirit than he that taketh cities*" (Prov. xvi. 32).

> "He is most powerful who has himself in his power." —Seneca.

> "He who reigns within himself and rules passions, desires, and fears, is more than a king." —Milton.

> "There never did and never will exist anything permanently noble and excellent in a character which was a stranger to the exercise of resolute self-denial." —Sir Walter Scott.

Father Von Doss, S.J.,[1] says: "There are characters so wavering that one is scarcely able to describe or portray them. Now joyous, now sad; sometimes disposed to good; again inclined to evil; at one time impetuous, at another hesitating, in constant agitation, in eternal waves of commotion—their hearts remain even to themselves inexplicable riddles. Such men are tossed on the ocean of life, like ships without rudder or helm.

"Do you not know that it is said of the fool that he is changed as the moon (Ecclus. xxvii. 12), and of the just man that he is an everlasting foundation? (Prov. x. 25)

"Alas! for those soft, unstable characters which are capable of being molded at will!

"Who shall discover in such a youth the man of the future? He is full of inconsistencies. In his changeable nature timidity sometimes yields to a spirit of enterprise; coldness, to that of enthusiasm. He is given to violent and easily formed attachments! Although susceptible to virtue, yet evil impressions leave behind in his heart far deeper traces.

1 *Thoughts and Counsels for Catholic Young Men:* Von Doss-Wirth.

"This inconstancy takes such a hold on some, that even their exterior—their looks, carriage, gait, speech, and gestures—bear testimony to it.

"God grant that a young man of that sort may never be approached by a seducer! What an easy prey he would find!

"There are characters so flighty that even God's grace seems inefficacious in their regard. Interior admonitions, salutary inspirations, good example—all these, and even more, produce no effect; for the volatile soul pays no attention to them, refuses to cooperate with them.

"Pitiable characters, who can be transformed into reliable men only with great difficulty and the most indefatigable perseverance!

"Yet such natures are by no means incorrigible.

"No, young man! despond not! Earnest efforts must be successful.

"First of all, be humble, and acknowledge your inconstancy. Then, endeavor to cope with it in detail.

"Have the courage necessary to keep a strict watch over yourself for a time; and by continually renewing your good resolutions fight against the failings you discover within you.

"Accustom yourself to quiet and reflection. Do not act precipitately nor impetuously. Render an account to yourself of all that you do.

"Do not permit your feelings to get the upper hand; rather strive to become the master of your own heart.

"Nothing is more disgusting than a sentimental piety.

"Nothing is further from perfection than that external piety which derives its sweetness from the feelings alone.

"Nothing is more inefficacious than a piety which lives only on impressions.

"Of course, there is a sensible devotion, and it is of value: for it is a gift of the Holy Ghost, and may be made an excellent means of virtue. But there is, also, a disposition of the heart—we may call it a sort of dainty piety—which is a great drawback to virtue. It inflates the spirit, and leaves the heart empty. It seizes upon the spiritual tid-bits, while good, substantial food is wanting to the soul.

"Do you know in what manly piety consists? In this—that man's will (which constitutes his manliness) be employed in its full strength for God's honor and glory, in His holy service.

"If a commandment of God is to be kept, it is ready to keep it.

"If a good fight is to be fought for principle and virtue, it is ready for action.

"If a difficulty is to be overcome, it is ready for the task.

"Manly piety does not, by any means, despise or disregard external practices of piety, but it regulates them and brings them in harmony with the duties of one's station in life: it keeps away everything extraordinary, and despising the mere appearance, and insisting more upon the interior spirit, it reaches to the heart. Proceeding to sacrifice, it labors and toils, struggles and conquers.

"Does it appear to you, that too much is required of you when you are asked to cultivate such manliness?

"Make, at least, the attempt, and begin. *'Lift up the hands which hang down, and the feeble knees'* (Heb. xii. 12).

"There are children enough, and plenty of weaklings. Be manly; and, although young in years, put to shame those who call themselves mature, although not such either in thought or deed.

"The world needs men—not grand geniuses or plausible talkers. It is not sentimentality and dreams that will save it, but acts and deeds. It was not merely by revelations and visions that the saints became such, but by spiritual combat, by self-denial, and overcoming the enemies of their souls.

"'*Expect the Lord, do manfully, and let thy heart take courage, and wait thou for the Lord*' (Ps. xxvi. 14).

"There is only one thing of which a man ought to be ashamed—of evil—to do evil, or to have done it.

"But, miserably enough, he is often ashamed of the very opposite, of avoiding evil and doing good.

"The thought of being ridiculed, blamed, or despised by others, disquiets him; he becomes confused and alarmed; he acts contrary to his better convictions. The inspiration to good is slighted, the favorable opportunity passes—he is overcome— conscience, virtue, God, are surrendered!

"Young people yield easier than others to this false shame, this foolish fear—because their imaginations are so lively, their minds so susceptible to all impressions.

"How many conversions from evil to good and from good to better, does not this human respect prevent! How much evil does it cause, how much good does it not frustrate!

"What will they think of me? What will they say to it? They will laugh at me, ridicule me. How can I separate myself from this, or from that? How can I give up this one or that one? They will think hard of me; it will look odd and singular!

"The whole world is full of such cowards; and often those who boast most of their independence are the most pitiful slaves of this mean passion.

"Honor—much-abused word! Does honor consist in cowardly compliance, in a more than untimely readiness to please? in sacrificing conscience? in surrendering our highest and best convictions?

"Has he honor who lies down in cringing servitude—the bond-slave of a word, a jest, a look, a reproach?

"Coward!—for such you are, and as such you are regarded even by those to whom you yield—*coward!* Why do you suffer yourself to be thus enslaved?

"Are those whom you so much fear your legitimate lords and masters?

"God alone is, by right, your Lord and Master. From Him you have your being; He can take it away from you at His pleasure, whenever He wills—and not they. He shall one day judge you. His good pleasure must be of more value to you than all the displeasure of men. God's displeasure can not be outweighed by all the good pleasure of men.

"'*Be not afraid of them that kill the body, and after that have no more that they can do. But I will show you whom you shall fear: fear ye Him who, after He hath killed, hath power to cast into hell. I say to you, fear Him*' (Luke xii. 4, 5).

"Alas! what an insult do you offer to God by preferring man before him! Are you, then, ashamed of God?

"What is more honorable than to serve God? to do His holy will? Is He not the King of heaven and earth? Is He not the best, the highest, the loveliest, and the most beautiful?

"How, if God should, one day, be ashamed of you? If, on the terrible judgment day He let you perish in your nothingness? If, then, He should deny you, as you deny Him now, if He should refuse to know you? What then?

"'*Whosoever shall be ashamed of Me, and of My words, of him shall the Son of man be ashamed, when He shall come in His majesty*' (Luke ix. 26), says the Lord—and He will keep His word.

"Tell me, at least, before whom are you ashamed?

"Before the good and virtuous? Before those who will, one day, come with the saints of heaven to sit in judgment over the world?

"Is it not rather before sinners, evil-doers, perverts, and fools? Yes, indeed—fools. The Sacred Scripture says: '*Fools hate them that flee from evil things*' (Prov. xiii. 19). Yes, indeed—sinners. '*The worship of God is an abomination to a sinner'* (Ecclus. i. 32). And again: *'He that walketh in the right, and feareth God, is despised by him that goeth by an infamous way'* (Prov. xix. 2).

"Are you so sensitive as to the recognition or respect of men? Why, then, do you not labor for the esteem and praise of the just and good?

"Why all these cowardly fears? Is virtue, then, something disgraceful? What has any worth, if not it, and it alone?

"Riches vanish, honors evaporate, pleasures slip away— virtue, valuable in itself, recognized by God, fostered by the noblest and best of men—an object of envy, even to the wicked—virtue remains, reaches even beyond the grave— crowns, and is crowned—reigns in, and for, all eternity! *'They that instruct many to justice shall shine as stars for all eternity'* (Dan. xii. 2).

"Can it be possible that you are ashamed of your nature, of your existence, of your destiny? Unheard-of folly! Is the bird ashamed of flying, the fish of swimming? And is not the service of God your nature, your element, your end and aim? *'Fear God, and keep His commandments: for this is all man'* (Eccles. xii. 13).

"You are afraid of being thought singular, odd, queer, peculiar?

"But, are you not aware that, as a virtuous man, you will always be singular, odd, queer, peculiar, in a world of sinners?

"Not to be singular in the sense of the wicked, is to renounce all virtue.

"If you do not walk in the broad way of destruction, you are singular; if you walk in the straight path, and seek the narrow gate, you separate yourself from the vast multitude that rush through the wide portals into everlasting ruin.

"Remain singular! The singular ones go into heaven, whilst the children of the world remain outside.

"Say, young man, what will become of you, if you accommodate yourself to the sentiments and conduct of certain youthful companions? If you praise what they praise, blame what they blame, do as they do? Do they not travel in crowds upon the broad road of sin and sensuality?

"No, you have a conscience; you have your principles, drawn from the Gospel; act according to these, and ask for nothing else.

"It is time for you to become a man; to be, in the fullest sense of the word, manly. You talk and dream so much of self-dependence, where is it?

"Is there question of principles? The loosest are those of the majority; they are favored. Honor, revenge, dueling, suicide, are permissible, or at least excusable, acts. As to morality, if one only avoid the most flagrant crimes, if he but escape talk and publicity—for the rest, human weakness deserves some indulgence; we are not angels.

"Here, a double-meaning word is spoken—you remain silent; there, a smutty one—you show no sign of disapproval; again, a vulgar one—you laugh at it. And, in order to avoid all suspicion of narrow-mindedness, one at last joins in, applauds, contributes his share, outdoes—yea, vies with the rudest in nastiness, and thereby purchases for himself among young libertines and low companions the unenviable reputation of being a good fellow—of a young man that knows how to live— who lives and lets live—a liberal, broad-minded young man full of 'go.'

"In the dictionary of worldlings and sinners, intemperance is excusable weakness; idleness—necessary relaxation; endless, and too often passionate play—pastime; reading of sensual books— culture, knowledge of the world; extravagance—generosity; vanity and affectation—civility; flattery—courtesy; untruth—

necessary reticence; ambiguity—prudence; dishonesty—clever calculation.

"'*Woe to you that call evil good, and good evil; that put darkness for light, and light for darkness; that put bitter for sweet, and sweet for bitter*' (Is. v. 20), for men's sake!

"The slave of human respect is like a puppet, involuntarily performing all the motions which Satan and the world compel it to.

"Pitiful role!—especially for a young man who should carry his free, noble brow high in air, and not suffer it to bear the brand of a miserable bondage to creatures!

"Evil companions may sneer at you because you discharge the duties of your station; because you study, labor, and make good use of your time. Answer: *I know what I am about!*

"They may entice you to carousals, to dangerous amusements. Say: *I will not go with you!*

"They may press you to learn the cause of your change of life. Tell them: *That concerns me alone!*

"They may mock at your altered demeanor. Let them go on; blunt arrows do no harm.

"They may laugh at your conscientiousness. Pity their want of conscience.

"Contradict when and where necessary; have courage; defend yourself. Here defiance is necessary and right.

"The worst thing that could happen to you in this case would be the best—that such people would let you alone.

"Oh, happiness, to be rid of such perverse and false friends, and to be able, at last, to breathe freely once more!

"'*Thou hast broken my bonds: I will sacrifice to Thee, the sacrifice of praise*' (Ps. cxv. 16, 17), to serve Thee as I must; to love Thee as I can; to be guided only by holy fear, as I should!

"'*Whosoever shall be ashamed of Me and of My words, of him shall the Son of man be ashamed*' (Luke ix. 26).

"*Thou shalt not follow the multitude to do evil; neither shalt thou yield in judgment, to the opinion of the most part, to stray from the truth*" (Ex. xxiii. 2).

"*But if you also suffer anything for justice's sake, blessed are ye. And be not afraid of their fear, and be not troubled*" (1 Peter iii. 14).

"*For God hath scattered the bones of them that please men; they have been confounded, because God hath despised them*" (Ps. lii. 6).

"*With him that feareth the Lord, it shall go well in the latter end, and in the day of his death he shall be blessed*" (Ecclus. i. 13).

St. Aloysius is the perfect model for all young men in regard to purity and manliness. Pope Benedict XIII named him patron of youth.

Father Rickaby, S. J., commenting on this in *Ye are Christ's*, says: "Our Lord, we may say, has ratified and carried into effect the nomination of his Vicar. St. Aloysius has taken a strong hold on our boys. This seems to be some part of the reward given him of God even on earth, where he renounced so much. Then again every Catholic boy appreciates that virtue which is the chief ornament of his age—the virtue of which Aloysius is so brilliant an example, and whence he derives his name of Angelic. Many also are held to the saint by ties of gratitude; for his intercession on behalf of the young is singularly powerful with God. There are those who ascribe to some devotion done in his honor the settlement of their vocation. On the other hand, here is an authentic story of a boy delivered through St. Aloysius from the calamity of being pushed forward to the priesthood against his will. In a clerical seminary in Italy, about the year 1850, on St. Aloysius' day, the boys used to write letters to the saint, which lay before his statue all day, and then were burned or given back unread. The bishop of the diocese insisted on taking up one of these letters and reading it, to see, as he said, that the boys did not write nonsense. No representations of the Jesuit rector, from whom this story comes direct, could stop him. The letter he happened to get hold of ran to this effect: 'Dear Aloysius, my parents will have me here, because they want me to be a priest: I have no vocation: can you get me out of it?' The thing was settled that day. Furthermore, it is plain to any one who will study his life, that Luigi Gonzaga was a high-spirited, energetic, and courageous boy, with the makings of a soldier or a statesman in him, one quite capable of filling the high position he was born to. The efforts of the Marquis, his father, to retain him, though he had two younger brothers, Rudolf and Francis, are a testimony to his fitness for being the head of a noble house. People useless in the world are seldom much good in the Church. Heroic sanctity requires high courage. One reason why sanctity is so rare is because high courage is rare. A 'muff' will never make a canonizable saint. A boy's instinct soon discovers that there was nothing of the 'muff' in Luigi Gonzaga."

78. POLITENESS[1]
"The attire of the body, and the laughter of the teeth,
and the gait of the man, show what he is" (Ecclus. xix. 27).

THERE is a certain sort of harsh, repellent virtue, and it may be that some souls are called to it.

There is also a pleasant sort of virtue to whose influence it must be credited, if the kingdom of good is extended here below.

How beautifully politeness becomes a well-educated young man! How it increases his amiability, and elevates his morally good qualities, making them worthy of imitation!

If virtue is the precious pearl, politeness or manners is the artistic setting which delights the eye and enhances the value of the jewel.

1   *Thoughts and Counsels for Young Men*: Von Doss, S.J., adapted by Rev. A. Wirth, O.S.B.

Politeness and virtue are most intimately connected. Both spring from a common root: self-denial—both have a common enemy: selfishness.

The worldling, in order to please the world, does many things that are not easy, nor to his taste. He molds himself into certain forms, abandons views and inclinations that are near and dear to him, puts restraints upon himself, bears insults, overlooks slights, keeps back what he would like to say, and speaks when he would rather remain silent. He is determined to please every one, no matter at what cost; he must maintain his position, he must rise. Hence, for a miserable pittance or reward he becomes the inglorious victim of vanity, selfishness, and human respect.

Not so with the virtuous man. He, too, makes sacrifices, even a sacrifice of himself, but for the love of God—for a divine reward. Without sacrificing his conscience (which belongs to a higher Lord), he endeavors in all other things to become all to all.

He restricts himself for the sake of others, accommodates himself to their tastes, is indulgent where he can be; he praises what is praiseworthy, and knows how to soften a necessary rebuke by sympathy and friendly interest. Cheerful without excess, he is obliging, affable and polite, without cringing; modest with superiors, benign with his equals, and condescending to inferiors.

O the power of love! O holy violence of self-denial!

Shall not such politeness, arising from such motives, and purchased at the price of such sacrifices, bear on its brows the stamp of genuine virtue?

Is it not as far removed as heaven is from earth, from that artificial whitewash, from that smooth veneering that chills us with its deadly coldness, because it originates from loveless, selfish hearts, and is destitute of all heavenly warmth and unction?

Politeness and urbanity, culture and courtesy, have value only as far as they proceed from, and aim at, charity. If their source is true self-denial, if they rest upon the esteem of the neighbor, as faith teaches us, they are laudable, meritorious, and pleasing to God.

The eulogy or example of a polite companion, or of an educated man of the world, is neither a sufficient nor worthy motive for cultivating that which, only through faith, is raised from a mere social to a Christian virtue.

Just because genuine politeness originates from charity, and promotes charity, it should be no stranger to you, young man, no matter what vocation or state of life you may embrace. Learn it for God's sake by self-observation, and the observation of educated and refined persons.

You will avoid many faults against charity if you remove what is contrary to good manners. Yes, good manners will even be to your own gain, because through their influence you will learn to treat yourself with a kind of veneration.

Consider it not below your dignity to pay attention to courtesy even in minor things. Dress, carriage, looks, gestures, gait, speech—nothing is to be overlooked.

Even Holy Writ—that most solemn and sacred of all monitors—disdains not to lay down rules of conduct, which are always rules of wisdom, as well as rules of charity. Though these, in general, refer to the whole outward man, they, in particular, regard the most abused of all our instruments of sense, the tongue.

A man is known by his look, and a wise man, when you meet him, is known by his countenance. For *"the attire of the body, and the laughter of the teeth, and the gait of the man, show what he is"* (Ecclus. xix. 27).

"*The heart of fools is in their mouth, and the mouth of wise men is in their heart*" (Ecclus. xxi. 29).

"*A wise man will hold his peace till he see opportunity, but a babbler and a fool will regard no time*" (Ecclus. xx. 7).

"*He that answereth before he heareth, showeth himself to be a fool, and worthy of confusion*" (Prov. xviii. 13).

"*He that uses many words, shall hurt his own soul*" (Ecclus. xx. 8).

"*It is the folly of a man to hearken at the door, and a wise man will be grieved with the disgrace*" (Ecclus. xxi. 27).

"*A fool will peep through the window into the house, but he that is well taught will stand without*" (Ecclus. xxi. 6).

"*If thou sittest amongst many, reach not thy hand out first of all: and be not the first to ask for a drink*" (Ecclus. xxxi. 21).

"*Be not hasty in a feast. Use as a frugal man the things that are set before thee*" (Ecclus. xxxi. 17-19).

"*Leave off first, for manners' sake, and exceed not, lest thou offend*" (Ecclus. xxxi. 20).

Do you, perhaps, believe that good manners or courtesy were a matter of indifference to the Saviour of the world?

Behold the picture which the ancient prophets presented of the *Messias!*

"*He shall not cry; neither shall his voice be heard abroad. The bruised reed he shall not break, and the smoking flax he shall not quench: he shall bring forth judgment unto truth. He shall not be sad nor troublesome*" (Is. xlii. 2-4).

"*If any man will take away thy coat, let him have thy cloak also. And whosoever shall force thee to go one mile, go with him other two. Give to him that asketh of thee, and from him that would borrow of thee turn not away*" (Matt. v. 41-42).

"*When thou art invited to a wedding, sit not down in the highest place*" (Luke xiv. 8) "*because every one that exalteth himself shall be humbled*" (Luke xiv. 11).

"*Have no strife amongst you as to which shall be first; for the great ones of earth do this. He who is the greatest among you, let him be as the least: and he that is leader, as he that serveth*" (Luke xxii. 26).

"*Be natural as children*" (Matt. xviii. 31). "*Be wise as serpents, and simple as doves*" (Matt. x. 16).

And did not the apostles teach the same?

"*Render to all their dues: fear, to whom fear, honor, to whom honor*" (Rom. xiii. 7).

"*Communicating to the necessities of the saints, pursuing hospitality*" (Rom. xii. 13).

"*Rejoice with them that rejoice; weep with them that weep*" (Rom. xii. 15).

"*If it be possible, as much as you can, have peace with all men*" (Rom. xii. 18).

"*Let your modesty be known to all men*" (Phil. iv. 5), that all may be edified by your good conduct.

"*We are a spectacle to the world, to angels, and to men*" (1 Cor. iv. 9).

How easily may courteous manners, ennobled by a modest reserve, dispel the popular prejudice against virtue, and awaken in the rudest and most vicious mind a strong desire to imitate him who is none the less a Christian because he is a polished gentleman!

79. CHEERFULNESS

ST. PAUL admonishes us: "*Rejoice in the Lord always: again, I say, rejoice!*" (Phil. iv. 4). And the prophet Habacuc sings: "*I will rejoice in the Lord, and I will joy in God my Jesus. The Lord God is my strength and He will make my feet like the feet of harts; and He, the conqueror, will lead me upon my high places singing psalms*" (Hab. iii. 18, 19). There is an apostolate of *cheerfulness* as well as of prayer and of preaching by word and example. Like a sweet, fragrant flower by the roadside, whose bright loveliness is a joy to every one who passes by, our cheerfulness is a blessing to all with whom we come in contact. A young man, merely by being cheerful, exerts a quiet yet potent influence for good. Let us bear this in mind: that we can be helpful to souls, that we can encourage them and strengthen them in good by our cheerfulness and amiability. The author of *The Art of Being Happy* tells us: "It is well to do our duty, but sometimes this is not enough for the happiness of others and our own. We must do our duty with joy, with eagerness, with love. We must not keep count of what we do, nor stop strictly and sternly at the exact limit of duty. Let us learn to devote ourselves generously, above all when there is question of fulfilling certain obligations of our state, position, etc., by which we do good to our brethren. Let us learn to show always a smiling face, although our work is distasteful to us or overwhelms us. And after having worked hard let us take care not to recall in conversation the pains we have taken, the fatigue that we have imposed upon ourselves. Then our duty accomplished will please every one: God first, then men, and last of all our own poor heart."

Our Lord Himself has said: "*Be of good cheer!*" And He said this substantially many times. Jesus was indeed a man of sorrows, but He was not a sad man. His face must always have reflected the serenity of His soul. He was meek and humble, gentle and amiable. "*He went about doing good to all.*"

From the Gospel narrative we can glean that Jesus possessed a cheerful temper, serenity mingled with tender seriousness, a most engaging presence, and a winning personality. Children came to Him willingly and loved to linger near Him, and how can any one imagine Him embracing and caressing little children without a smile of loving-kindness? Men followed Him in crowds, fascinated by His charm of manner and of speech. And into woman's heart came the thought: What happiness to be the mother of such a son!

Among the saints—the close followers of Christ—St. Francis de Sales pre-eminently commands our admiration and our love for his Christlike characteristics of cheerful serenity, meekness, humility, patience, charity, kindness, sweetness of temper, and suavity of deportment. Like Our Saviour, the gentle Bishop of Geneva loved to make use of comparisons drawn from nature to illustrate his sermons, which are so replete with good cheer and helpfulness.

As we read in the introduction to *The Mystical Flora of St. Francis de Sales*: "In this he holds a place peculiarly his own. His images do not recall scenes of Cappadocian gloom, like those of St. Basil, nor, like St. Jerome's, the harshness of the desert. But rather, as the clear blue waters of the lakes of his own Savoy soften without distorting the rugged outlines of the overhanging hills, which they reflect bright with sunshine, gay with flowers, and crowned with teeming vines, so does his gentle spirit present to our minds the loftiest doctrines in all the grandeur of truth, and yet clothed in images of beauty that charm the fancy while they flash new light upon the understanding. But most of all is this true of him as he comes in from the garden with comparisons gathered from the flowers that bloom therein." The spiritual comparisons of St. Francis drawn from plants and flowers make clear to us "how one may draw good thoughts and holy aspirations from everything that presents itself in all the variety of this mortal life."[1]

Ornsby, in his life of the saint, says: "There appears in the mind of St. Francis de Sales that union of sweetness and strength, of manly power and feminine delicacy, of profound knowledge and practical dexterity which constitutes a character formed at once to win and subdue minds of almost every type and age.

1　Devout Life, pt. ii. c. xiii.

As the rose among flowers, so is he among saints. From the thorny, wood-fiber of the brier comes forth that blossom which unites all that can make a flower lovely and attractive; and from the hot and vehement nature of the young Savoyard came a spiritual bloom, whose beauty and fragrance were perfect in an extraordinary degree. All things that command respect and attract love were found in St. Francis."

And this explains his power as a spiritual guide, his mighty influence over sinners, his success as a peacemaker, and his helpfulness to all with whom he came in contact.

As followers of Christ, and in imitation of the saints, let us cultivate the habit of cheerfulness and pray for the spirit of gladness, which is rooted in charity, in the peace of a good conscience, in gratitude to God for His blessings, in Christian hope and confidence, in perfect submission to the divine will; and let us do this not only for our own good, but also for the happiness and betterment of others.

> Every life is meant
> To help all lives; each man should live
> For all men's betterment.[1]

"*Servus servorum Dei*," "Servant of the servants of God," is one of the titles of the Pope. The Prince of Wales has borne for his motto "*I serve*," since the fourteenth century. In a way we are all one another's servants. St. Thomas Aquinas says: "That therein one man excels another man is given him of God that therewith he may serve other men." Our blessed Saviour tells us of Himself: "*The Son of man came not to be ministered unto, but to minister*" (Matt. xx. 28). At the Last Supper He washed His apostles' feet, saying to them: "*I have given you an example.*" His example and His teaching are that the highest must not disdain the lowest, and that all are to serve all. Now we can all serve or help others by our cheerfulness

1   Alice Cary.

and amiability. A cheerful person creates a wholesome moral atmosphere around him, and exerts an invigorating influence upon his environment.

There is great merit also in cheerfulness, when it is cultivated from a supernatural motive, when it is the fruit of divine and fraternal charity. It requires self-control and self-denial to maintain cheerfulness under all circumstances—in sickness, in pain, in sorrow, in poverty, in misunderstanding, and in unpleasant surroundings. Christian cheerfulness implies something more than natural temperament; it means self-denial—self-control. Natural disposition should not be offered as an excuse for being morose and rude. By the grace of God and with an earnest effort we can overcome our evil nature. You find yourself refreshed by the presence of cheerful persons; why not make earnest efforts to be helpful to others by your own cheerfulness and amiability? Strew the road with flowers for others, and in turn your own pathway will be scattered with roses.

Montaigne says: "The most manifest sign of wisdom is contented cheerfulness, and it is undoubtedly true that a cheerful man has a creative power which a pessimist never possesses."

> A merry heart goes all the day;
> A sad tires in a mile.

Lew Wallace tells us, "A man's task is always light if his heart is light," and there is wisdom in the Spanish proverb: "Who sings in grief procures relief."

The presence of a good and cheerful man acts like an invigorating tonic upon all around him. Nothing disturbs his equanimity, which springs from the peace of God in his heart. The author of *The Imitation* says: "The joy of the just is from God and in God, and their rejoicing is in the truth. If there be joy in the world, truly the man of pure heart possesses it.

Rejoice when thou hast done well."

Father Dignam, S.J., says in his *Retreats*: "All discouragement comes from pride. Failure has nothing to do with pleasing God. A soul who fails and makes an act of contrition twenty times in the day will probably have given God more glory, and done more for Him, than one who has gone quietly on all day without failure; God created some people (it may be said) to serve Him by failure; for they give Him glory by their acts of contrition and humiliation, while if they had succeeded, their pride would have made them displeasing to Him."

The thought of heaven and of that blessed time when we shall see God in the fulness of His beauty ought to keep our hearts overflowing with peace and joy. We can be always bright and cheerful if we keep our eyes directed toward the eternal shores, to the blessed land of the saints, where the sky is ever cloudless, where the sun of happiness never sets, where a perfect torrent of delight inundates the soul, where, as the beloved disciple tells us, "*God shall wipe away all tears, and death shall be no more, nor mourning, nor crying, nor sorrow shall be any more; for the former things are passed away.*"

Apropos of this subject, Father Henry Calmer, S.J., of blessed memory, who for many years filled the pulpit of St. Xavier's, Cincinnati, and held vast audiences spellbound by his eloquence, wrote the following lines while visiting a Trappist monastery:

ETERNITY

The silent monks prayed in their oaken stalls;
In the tangled grass by the abbey walls
Bloomed the roses red with their drooping leaves,
And roses pink as the dreams youth weaves,
And roses white as when love deceives;
How they bloomed and swayed in the garden there,
While the bell tolled out in the warm still air:
"Eternity!"

"Eternity!" the great bell rang.
"Leave life and love and youth," it sang;
And the red rose scattered its petals wide,
And the pink rose dreamed in the sun, and sighed,
And the white rose pined on its stem and died.
O Life, Love, Youth! Ye are sweet, ye are strong,
But barren lives shall bloom in a long
                    Eternity!

Where peace and interior joy abound, there also cheerfulness of mien and manner ought to be found. Happiness presupposes peace—a threefold peace: Peace with God, peace with ourselves, and peace with our neighbor. That man is happy who lives in peace.

In the holy night when our Saviour was born, the angels sang: "*On earth, peace.*" On the eve of His Passion, Our Lord said to His disciples in His touching farewell address: "*Peace I leave with you, My peace I give unto you.*" And after the Resurrection, He greeted His followers repeatedly with the words: "*Peace be to you.*" Peace must be a great blessing, a priceless treasure; it is indeed happiness.

The Church prays for peace daily in the Canon of the Mass. "*Dona nobis pacem!*" is the third petition of the *Agnus Dei*: "Give us peace!" And in the beautiful prayers before communion the Church again asks for peace. "*Pax huic domui!*" "Peace be to this house!" the priest says on entering a sickroom to administer the last sacraments. "*Pax!*" is the simple device of the illustrious Order of St. Benedict, in connection with the watchword: "*Ut in omnibus glorificetur Deus!*" "That in all things God may be glorified!" This is substantially the same as the chant of the angels: "*Gloria in excelsis Deo et in terra pax hominibus!*" "Glory to God in the highest and peace on earth to men of good will!" To seek God's glory means peace and happiness to man. His glory and our happiness are inseparably united. This is man's destiny, as the little catechism teaches: "To know God, to love Him, to serve Him and to be happy with Him forever." This is true philosophy: Man tends naturally to happiness as to his last end, "a state of freedom from all evil and enjoyment of every good that can be desired, joined with the certainty of its everlasting duration."

In this world, real happiness consists in the peace and joy of a good conscience and in the hope of an eternal reward which springs from a well-spent life. "In the next world," as Archbishop Meurin says in his *Ethics*, "happiness consists in the fullest knowledge of the infinite truth, which is God Himself, in the most ardent love of the supreme goodness and beauty, which again is nothing else but God, and in the perpetual possession of supreme bliss, which consists in everlasting friendship and union with God."

The will of God, then, is this: that in the present life, in whatever circumstances divine Providence may place us, we live virtuously, avoiding evil, and doing good.

Peace with God implies the state of grace, a good conscience, submission to and fulfilment of the divine will. Peace with self implies the mastery over one's passions, the consciousness of duty well done, the approval of one's conscience. Peace with one's neighbor implies the commandment of love, the observance of the golden rule: "*As you would that men should do to you, do you also to them in like manner*" (Luke vi. 31). This threefold peace is the basis of happiness. A cheerful Christian gentleman is a rebuke to the world, whose votaries make it a matter of reproach against religion that it sends men to learn the solemn lessons of the grave and casts a blight upon life, that meditation on the eternal truths tends to stifle endeavor, to paralyze our energies, and to sadden our days. Religion really tends to gladden our hearts and to make our days calm and tranquil.

"*Rejoice in the Lord always!*" We ought always to be cheerful, and our joy should find expression in deeds of kindness and helpfulness to all with whom we come in contact. We ought to heed the words of Our Lord to His followers: "*Be of good cheer!*" Life today is so strenuous that there is constant need of relief from its strain, and a sunny, cheerful, gracious soul is like a sea breeze in sultry August or like a "draught of cool refreshment drained by fevered lips."

The author of *The Floral Apostles*, referring to the crocus and the primrose as the emblems of cheerfulness, says: "Cheerfulness furnishes the best soil for the growth of goodness and virtue. It is also the best of moral and mental tonics. '*A glad heart maketh a cheerful countenance, but by grief of mind the spirit is cast down*' (Prov. xv. 13). '*A joyful mind maketh age flourishing; a sorrowful spirit drieth up the bones*' (Prov. xvii. 22)."

We can all acquire greater cheerfulness by assuming the right mental attitude toward our environment and circumstances, by looking habitually at the bright side of things, by training ourselves persistently to see the good and pleasant things in our common, daily life.

Some persons seem to have eyes only for the disagreeable things that happen to come into their life; they forget or overlook their blessings, and brood over their trials and misfortunes.

The soothing line in *The Rainy Day* "Behind the clouds is the sun still shining," does not comfort them. Stevenson says:

> "Two men looked out through their prison bars.
> The one saw mud and the other stars."

Let us learn to look at life not to find misery and discomfort in it, but to find goodness, gladness, and beauty. The author of *The Art of Being Happy* relates the following anecdote: "A poet was gazing one day at a beautiful rose-tree. 'What a pity,' said he, 'that these roses have thorns!' A man who was passing by remarked: 'Let us rather thank our good God for having allowed these thorns to have roses.' Ah! how we also ought to thank God for the many joys and blessing that He grants us in spite of our sins, instead of complaining about the slight troubles that He sends us."

"A doctor who has made a specialty of nervous diseases," so we read, "has found a new remedy for the blues. His prescription amounts to this: 'Keep the corners of your mouth turned up; then you can't feel blue.' The simple direction is: 'Smile; keep on smiling; don't stop smiling.' It sounds ridiculous, doesn't it? Well, just try turning up the corners of your mouth, regardless of your mood and see how it makes you feel; then draw the corners of your mouth down, and note the effect, and you will be willing to declare 'there's something in it!'" A good suggestion in regard to any past trouble or humiliation is this: "Let it go!" "Forget it!" An optimist writes: "If you had an unfortunate experience this last year, forget it. If you have made a failure in your speech, your song, your book, or your article, if you have been placed in an embarrassing position, if you have been deceived and hurt by one whom you looked upon as a friend, if you have been slandered and abused, do not dwell upon it, do not brood over it; forget it! There is not a single redeeming feature in these memories. Do not make yourself unhappy by keeping on the walls of your heart the pictures of vanished joys and faded hopes. Forget them. Count your blessings. Be of good cheer."

As regards those faults of our neighbors that irritate us, it will help us to be more cheerful and amiable if we remember our own shortcomings, which they have to endure. St. Paul admonishes us: "*Bear ye one another's burdens and so you shall fulfil the law of Christ*" (Gal. vi. 2). Do not look for mistakes or faults to censure in others; let us rather look for an excuse for our brethren; let us admire their virtues and imitate them.

The author of *The Art of Being Happy* says: "There is a word which can not be said too often to every Christian whom God has destined to live, converse, and labor in the society of his fellow-creatures: *Be indulgent.* Yes, be indulgent; it is necessary for others and it is necessary for your own sake. Forget the little troubles that others may cause you; keep up no resentment for the inconsiderate or unfavorable words that may have been said about you; excuse the mistakes and awkward blunders of which you are the victim; always make out good intentions for those who have done you any wrong by imprudent acts or speeches; in a word, smile at everything, show a pleasant face on all occasions; maintain an inexhaustible fund of goodness, patience, and gentleness. Thus you will be at peace with all your brethren; your love for them will suffer no alteration, and their love for you will increase day by day. But, above all, you will practise in an excellent manner Christian charity, which is impossible without this toleration and indulgence at every instant."

In conclusion, then, let us resolve to be cheerful and amiable at all times and under all circumstances. By keeping this resolution we shall glorify God, gain much merit ourselves, and be a blessing to others.

80. KINDNESS

"LET us be kind if we would promote the interests of the Sacred Heart, of which kindness was the special characteristic. Let it not be in isolated acts—'few and far between'—no, it must be like prayer—an *habitual disposition* of heart, which is ready to manifest itself without any effort, at all seasons and in all circumstances, and thus it will be with hearts which are united to that Heart of love. Kindness will flow from them, as it were, naturally, just as the flowers give forth their perfume, the birds their song, and as the sun shines down alike on good and bad as it goes in its daily circuit—because all this is of their very nature. In the most trivial things of daily life the spirit of kindness should render itself evident. . . .

"Kindness is as the bloom upon the fruits—it renders charity and religion attractive and beautiful. Without it, even charitable works lose their power of winning souls; for, without kindness, the idea of love, the idea of anything supernatural— in a word, of Jesus, is not conveyed to the mind by the works performed, even though they be done from a right motive. There is such a thing as doing certain exterior actions, which are intended to be charitable, ungraciously. Now, actions thus performed do not manifest the kindness of the Heart of Jesus, nor will they be efficacious in extending the empire of His love, or in winning souls to His kingdom. The fruit may be sound, but the bloom is not on it; hence it is uninviting. . . .

"How many a noble work has been nipped in the bud by the blast of an unkind judgment; how many a generous heart has been crushed in its brightest hopes by a jealous criticism; how many a holy aspiration, destined to bear abundant fruit for God and souls, has been forced back into the poor heart from whence it had ascended, there to be stifled utterly and forever, leaving that heart, as the poet so graphically represents it 'like a deserted bird's nest filled with snow,' because unkindness had robbed it of that for which, perhaps, alone it cared to live. How much, then, we may believe has been lost to the world of all that is good and great and beautiful through the instrumentality of unkindness—and if it be thus, what developments, on the other hand, may we not expect, in the order of grace as well as of nature, in the hearts and minds of men beneath the genial sun of kindness.

"Even in the common things of life, and in the natural order, how striking are the results of the passage of this Heaven-sent missioner, this angel of light and consolation.

"If we reflect upon it, kindness is but the outcome and

exemplar of the divine precept: *Thou shalt love thy neighbor as thyself.* There is nothing we personally so much appreciate as kindness. We like others to think of us kindly, to speak to us kindly, and to render us kindly actions and in a kindly manner. Now, we should know how to put ourselves in the place of others, and thus we should testify to them that kindliness that we value so much ourselves.

"When our divine Lord came down upon earth, He came not only to save us by shedding His blood for us, but to teach us by His example how to co-operate with Him in extending the Kingdom of His Father. And one of the most powerful means which He employed for this purpose was kindness, gentleness, and forbearance. '*The goodness and kindness of God our Saviour appeared*' (Titus iii. 4), by which words we learn that kindness is not altogether synonymous with goodness, but, as it were, a luster, a bloom, an attraction superadded to it.

"We might regard this sweet reflection from the Heart of Jesus from many points of view, but it is especially under one aspect that we have been considering it; namely, as a powerful weapon in our hands for the efficacious exercise of our apostolate. Kindly thoughts of others will be productive of prayer in their regard, at once fervent and affectionate—prayer such as the loving Heart of Jesus willingly listens to; kindly words and deeds will draw souls to the love of Him whose spirit they behold so attractively reproduced in His members. As the wood-violets give forth their perfume from beneath the brushwood that conceals them from view, telling us of their unseen nearness, so kindness reveals to us the nearness of Jesus, the sweetness of whose Spirit is thus breathed forth.

"Such is the kindness which is that great missioner sent by the Heart of Jesus to exercise an apostolate of love upon earth, and so to promote the glory of God and the salvation of souls." —*The Voice of the Sacred Heart.*

Thoughts from Father Faber on Kindness

THE worst kinds of unhappiness, as well as the greatest amount of it, come from our conduct to each other. If our conduct, therefore, were under the control of kindness, it would be nearly the opposite of what it is, and so the state of the world would be almost reversed.

*

Kindness is the overflowing of self upon others. We put others in the place of self. We treat them as we would wish to be treated ourselves. We change places with them.

*

Kindness adds sweetness to everything.

*

Of great consequence is the immense power of kindness in bringing out the good points of the characters of others.

*

A kind act has picked up many a fallen man who has afterward slain his tens of thousands for his Lord, and has entered the Heavenly City at last as a conqueror amidst the acclamations of the saints, and with the welcome of its Sovereign.

*

Kindness has converted more sinners than either zeal, eloquence, or learning, and these three last have never converted any one unless they were kind also. In short, kindness makes us as Gods to each other. Yet while it lifts us so high, it sweetly keeps us low. For the continual sense which a kind heart has of its own need of kindness keeps it humble.

*

Kindness is infectious. One kind action leads to another. Our example is followed. This is the greatest work which kindness does to others—that it makes them kind themselves.

*

A proud man is seldom a kind man. Humility makes us kind, and kindness makes us humble.

*

A kind man is man who is never self-occupied. He is genial, he is sympathetic, he is brave.

*

If a man *habitually* has *kind thoughts* of others, and that on supernatural motives, he is not far from being a saint.

*

There is one class of kind thoughts which must be dwelt upon apart. I allude to *kind interpretations*. The habit of not judging others is one which it is very difficult to acquire, and which is generally not acquired till later on in the spiritual life.

*

Now, the standard of the Last Judgment is absolute. It is this—the measure which we have meted to others. Our present humor in judging others reveals to us what our sentence would be if we died now. Are we content to abide that issue? We ought to cultivate most sedulously the habit of kind interpretations.

Men's actions are very difficult to judge. Their real character depends in a great measure on the motives which prompt them, and those motives are invisible to us. Appearances are often against what we afterward discover to have been deeds of virtue.

*

What mistakes have we not made in judging others! Have we not always found in our past experience that, on the whole, our kind interpretations were truer than our harsh ones?

How many times in life have we been wrong when we put a kind construction or the conduct of others? We shall not need our fingers to count those mistaken upon.

*

Kind words are the music of the world.

*

We must say something about *kind suffering.* Kind suffering is, in fact, a form of kind action. With the Christian, kind suffering must be almost wholly supernatural. There is a harmonious fusion of suffering and gentleness effected by grace, which is one of the most attractive features of holiness. What is more beautiful than considerateness for others when we ourselves are unhappy?

*

To be subject to low spirits is a sad liability. Yet, to a vigorous, manly heart, it may be a very complete sanctification. What can be more unkind than to communicate our low spirits to others, to go about the world like demons, poisoning the fountains of joy? Have I more light because I have managed to involve those I love in the same doom as myself? Is it not pleasant to see the sun shining on the mountains, even though we have none of it down in our valley? Oh, the littleness and the meanness of that sickly appetite for sympathy which will not let us keep our tiny Lilliputian sorrows to ourselves! Why must we go sneaking about, like some dishonorable insect, and feed our darkness on other people's light? We hardly know in all this whether to be more disgusted with the meanness, or more indignant at the selfishness, or more sorrowful at the sin. The thoughts of the dying mother are all concentrated on her new-born child. It is a beautiful emblem of unselfish holiness. So also let us hide our pains and sorrows. But while we hide them, let them also be spurs within us to urge us on to all manner of overflowing kindness and sunny humor to those around is. When the very darkness within us creates a sunshine around us, then has the spirit of Jesus taken possession of our souls.

*

Rightly considered, kindness is the grand cause of God in the world. Where it is natural, it must forthwith be supernaturalized. Where it is not natural, it must be supernaturally planted. What is our life? It is a mission to go into every corner it can reach, and reconquer for God's beatitude His unhappy world back to Him. It is a devotion of ourselves to the bliss of the Divine Life by the beautiful apostolate of kindness.

*

Let us conclude. We have been speaking of kindness. Perhaps we might better have called it the spirit of Jesus. What an amulet we should find it in our passage through life if we would say to ourselves two or three times a day these soft words of Scripture: "*My spirit is sweet above honey, and my inheritance above honey and the honeycomb*" (Ecclus. xxiv. 27).

81. THE CORRECT THING[1]
FOR MEMBERS OF CHURCH ASSOCIATIONS

IT IS THE CORRECT THING: For members of church associations to comply with the rules and regulations.

To be present if possible when meetings are called.

To have a certain amount of humility in regard to one's own ability.

To always withdraw at once from any organization which is not working in harmony with the pastor of the parish.

To refuse to accept an office if one is not willing and able to discharge its duties.

To remember that everybody can not be first.

To approach holy communion on the regular communion days in a body.

1   From *The Correct Thing for Catholics*, by Leila Hardin Bugg. Benziger Brothers.

It is *Not* the Correct Thing: To belong to any society or organization which is not approved by the pastor.

To refuse a contribution (to the Church or for a Church festival) in a discourteous manner.

To give a donation as if conferring a personal favor on the one who solicits it.

To preface one's donation by the remarks that Father Blank is always begging; that Father Blank-Blank, the former pastor, thought of something besides money; that one would be glad to get into a parish where there were no debts, and where priests preached on the gospel instead of money—money all the time.

To head a subscription list with a large contribution to some charity enterprise when one's pew rent and church dues are unpaid.

The Correct Thing in Business

It is the Correct Thing: To act as a gentleman in a business transaction, no matter how far his associate may forget himself.

To be scrupulously honest because it is right to be so, and not because "honesty is the best policy."

To remember that all rich men are not knaves nor all poor ones angels.

To make the best of one's opportunities.

To remember that a life need not necessarily be a failure because it is not crowned with wealth.

To be punctual to the second in keeping a business appointment.

To remember that a five minutes' delay has sometimes turned the tide of a young man's destiny.

To devote one's business hours strictly to business and one's time of recreation to something else.

To pay a good man what his services are worth, and not merely the minimum at which they can be obtained.

To avoid all misrepresentation in a business transaction.

To receive every one courteously, whether rich or poor.

To give a reproof, where necessary, in private.

To remember that a frowning demeanor does not always imply a dignified one by any means.

To hold one's word as sacred as one's bond.

To avoid all transactions that are classed in lump as shady.

To remember that adulation to power and arrogance to poverty mark a plebeian in mind as well as in origin.

To be manly at all times.

To remember that ill-gotten gains will turn the downiest couch into a bed of thorns at the hour of death.

To remember that everybody admires a manly man.

The Correct Thing for a Citizen

It is the Correct Thing: For a citizen to remember that he owes a duty to the community in which he lives.

To know the difference between statesmanship and political wire-pulling.

To remember that a trickster holding office is a standing reproach to the community which permitted his election.

To let love of country be second only to love of God.

To know that the very least a loyal son of his country can do is to cast his vote for good men.

To contribute cheerfully to all public enterprises.

To remember that a bad Christian never made a good citizen.

To answer in the negative Scott's immortal question:

> Breathes there a man with soul so dead
> Who never to himself has said
> This is my own, my native land?

It is *Not* the Correct Thing: For a man to think that he can rightfully live only for himself.

To claim the benefits of citizenship, and to shirk its burdens.

To think that rights have not their corresponding obligations.

To imagine that it is unworthy of a gentleman to take an interest in politics.

To think that a man entitled to the ballot, who holds aloof from the polls and then talks about political corruption, is not partly to blame for such a state of affairs.

THE CORRECT THING IN CHURCH

It is the Correct Thing: To always be in time for Mass and other services in the church.

To remember that the church bells are rung for a purpose and not merely to keep the sexton busy, and that it would be well therefore to obey their call.

For every member of a parish to rent a pew or at least a seat in the parish church.

To take holy water upon entering the church.

To make the sign of the cross on the person and not in the air.

To genuflect on the right knee and to have it touch the floor.

To remember that the King of kings is present on the altar, and to order one's conduct accordingly.

To avoid whispering, laughing, and looking about in church.

To walk gently up the aisle if one is unavoidably detained until after the services have begun.

To make a short act of adoration on bended knees after entering the pew.

To be devout and recollected at the different parts of the Mass.

To remember that mere bodily presence in the church with the mind wandering to temporal concerns, does not fulfil the precept of hearing Mass.

To pay attention to the sermon, and make it the subject of one's thoughts during the day, as also during the week.

To remember when special collections are to be taken up, and to have a contribution ready in your hand.

To make a practice of putting something in the contribution-box every Sunday. To train children to this practice.

To listen to the music as a means of elevating the heart to God.

For a gentleman occupying a pew to move in or rise and let ladies pass in before him.

For pew-holders to offer seats in their pews to strangers.

To be punctilious in following the ceremonials of the Church—standing, kneeling, etc., at the proper times.

For Catholics to keep away from Protestant services.

To take an earnest Protestant to hear a good sermon.

To remain kneeling until the last prayers have been said and the priest has retired to the sacristy.

It is *Not* the Correct Thing: To be late for Mass or any church service.

To stalk hurriedly and noisily up the aisle.

To ignore the holy water font at the entrance.

To make the sign of the cross as if fanning off flies.

To give a little bobbing curtsy, instead of the proper genuflection, before entering one's pew.

To whisper, laugh, or cause any distraction to those around.

To deliberately turn around, stare up at the choir, or at those entering the church.

To go to sleep, or read during the sermon

To be in an ecstatic condition of devotion when the contribution-box approaches.

To forget all about the special collections for the orphans, the church debt, the Pope, etc.

For a person occupying the end seat to scowl forbiddingly at all those who seek to enter the pew.

To kneel on only one knee, or to emulate the position of the bear when saying one's prayers.

For members of the congregation to find fault with the sermon, criticise the clergyman, and retail gossip on their way home from church, as is done in China and other places in the Orient.

It is the Correct Thing: To be willing and ready at all times and under all circumstances to give the reason for one's religious belief when asked to do so by a sincere seeker after truth.

To avoid argument merely for the sake of argument.

To say nothing needlessly to wound the feelings and religious opinions of those out of the Church.

To refute calumnies against the Church when they come under one's notice.

To be firm always in one's adherence to the teachings of the Church, even at the risk of giving offense to others outside her pale.

To remember that "a liberal Catholic," in the sense in which the term is usually understood, is often no Catholic at all.

To remember that example is more powerful than precept.

To understand that, whilst it would be wrong for a Catholic to go to a Protestant church, it is not wrong for a Protestant to go to a Catholic church, simply because it is one of the fundamental doctrines of all Protestant denominations that religion and religious opinions are very much a matter of private interpretation of the Bible; that two persons may belong to one church and yet not both believe exactly the same thing, and that all churches are alike pleasing to God in proportion to the sincerity of their members. In brief, that the Catholic Church forbids her children to participate in religious services outside of her pale, and the Protestant churches leave their members to do as they please in the matter.

It is *Not* the Correct Thing: To be careless about what one says, and the use of expressions calculated to give offense.

To weakly agree to slanders on the reputation and integrity of the Church or her ministers.

To manifest surprise and impatience at the failure of any one to grasp a truth that seems so plain to oneself.

To imagine that because one can not see a truth it is therefore not so.

For a Catholic to say that one Church is as good as another; for every intelligent Protestant knows that a consistent Catholic can not think so, and that a Catholic who says he does is telling a deliberate falsehood.

To act in any way that would bring reproach on the Church or give scandal to those either in or out of the fold.

In life's bright morn I see thee depart,
I see thee go with a trembling heart;
Farewell, dear Youth, so joyous and free,
God's blessing ever abide with thee.

When thou dost stand where the ways divide
May thy Angel-guardian be at thy side;
God grant thou may'st choose the narrow way.
And from it may thy footsteps never stray.

> *"Wenn Du am Scheidewege stehst,*
> *Und Pflicht and Wunsch den Kopf verwirren,*
> *Du wirst im Pfad nur selten irren,*
> *Wenn Du den Unbequemsten gehst."*
> —F. W. Weber, *Gedichte.*

PART FOURTH

AT THE PARTING
OF THE WAYS

At the Parting

of the Ways

WHITHER GOEST THOU?

82. THE DECISION

LET us suppose that you are on a walking tour in a neighborhood as yet unknown to you. You come to a spot where one road leads straight before you, another to the right, and a third to the left. Is it not very important for you to know which of these three roads you ought to take in order to reach the desired goal?

You have really set out on a pilgrimage like this; for your whole life is nothing but a journey to heaven. You may possibly have already reached the crossroad, or will reach it before long; you must come to a decision, and enter upon one of these paths in life.

But which are you to choose? Life in the world, especially the *marriage state*, the *priesthood*, or the *religious life?* All these roads have one and the same goal—they all lead to heaven. But each has its own special and peculiar difficulties, so that not all who walk along these paths reach the goal with equal facility and with the same happiness.

Those who are really qualified to tread the path they have chosen, will reach their goal easily and happily with the help of God. When you arrive at the parting of the ways it is of the highest importance that you should choose the right way— that is—the state of life destined for you by God. Lay well to heart the momentous character of this decision.

The three states mentioned above, life in the world, or matrimony, the priesthood, or the religious life, are the only *vocations*, properly so called; certain doctors, lawyers, tutors, tradesmen, artisans, farmers, and so on, apparently represent so many different vocations, to make use of an expression commonly in vogue.

But these are really no *vocations* in the proper sense, for they impose upon those who embrace them no essentially different obligations, as in the states of matrimony, the priesthood, and the religious life; they are simply trades, occupations, professions, distinct positions in life. Now as regards the three states or vocations, properly so called, God, whose wise providence guides and orders all things, bestows upon each individual human being, an immortal soul with all the special aptitudes and capabilities which are required to lead him to the goal which he is destined to reach. When, therefore, a young man has arrived at the parting of the ways, there sounds in his ear more or less plainly, sometimes within his own heart, sometimes from an exterior voice, the call of God: "I have destined you to be the father of a family; I have thought to lay upon you the dignity and burden of a priest; I desire to see you lead a pious life within the walls of a convent."

Thus does the call of God sound in the ear; of all men in innumerably different ways. One hears the call in his own heart from his childhood days; another hears it for the first time when the moment of decision arrives. God calls one suddenly by some extraordinary event, others again, and the greater number, by the force of circumstances and environment.

How immensely important therefore it is to recognize and follow this call of God. God made man to know Him, love Him, and serve Him in this world, and to be happy with Him forever in heaven; this is the final goal and highest end of all men!

The commandments also are the same everywhere and for all men; but it is not everywhere and for all men equally difficult to keep these commandments. Therefore every state is not for every one, and every one can not reach heaven with the same facility in every state.

If you are not destined for life in the world, for matrimony, you will scarcely be able to save your soul in the married state, or will only succeed in doing so with great difficulty. On the other hand, if you are called to the matrimonial state, to remain unmarried would place a great obstacle in your heavenward way.

And if it be the will of God that you should enter a Religious Order, it would be difficult for you to work out your salvation in the world.

Therefore St. Gregory of Nazianzen says: "He who makes a mistake as to his vocation will fall from one error to another all his life long, and at the end of it may possibly even find himself deceived as to his hope of heaven."

It is easy to see the reason which lies at the root of this. If a young man refuses to follow the clear call of God, because to do so would involve a sacrifice, he forfeits many graces.

You have, as yet, perhaps not reached the parting of the ways, and years may elapse before the moment for a decision arrives. You may already be filled with anxious dread lest you should make a wrong choice, and wreck your prospects of happiness. But fear not, be of good courage! There is a sure and simple means of choosing aright. In the meantime be truly chaste and pious, and your choice can not fail to be a happy one.

> Many are the ways that here
> Lead unto a higher sphere:
> One thy God has traced for thee,
> Best and safest that will be.

83. GOOD ADVICE

WHEN a parish priest, a director of souls, surveys the young people belonging to his flock, he asks himself with a heavy heart the important question: "What will become of all these who are dear to me?" A similar inquiry forces itself upon me in regard to the youthful readers of these pages. And in regard to you, who are perusing this chapter, I ask myself whether you, well-meaning as you are at present, will always remain virtuous, be happy, and get to heaven at last.

I can not tell; I can only wish it with all my heart. But one thing I do know: that it will go well with you, and that you will in all probability save your soul, if you embrace the state of life for which you are destined by God.

Therefore it is incumbent on me to do everything in my power in order to help you to make a wise choice. Therefore lay well to heart the good advice which I am now about to offer you, in view of such a choice.

My first piece of advice is: take counsel of yourself. But you must do this calmly, without prejudice. Your heart should resemble a delicately balanced pair of scales; you must weigh all things fairly. You must not try to discover where and how you can most speedily grow rich and enjoy the vanities and amusements of the world. A young man who should take counsel of himself in such a fashion as this, and look at things from a purely material point of view, without reference to God and to his eternal salvation, would be greatly in danger of making a bad choice. Therefore I beseech you not to expose yourself to any such risk.

Take counsel with yourself in such a manner as will enable you to say to God in a spirit of resignation: "Speak, Lord, for Thy servant heareth. I desire nothing but what is Thy will. If only I can do Thy will it is a matter of indifference to me whether I am rich or poor, whether happiness or sorrow is my portion, whether my life is full of work, or spent in ease and without exertion. All this of no consequence, if only I can please Thee, O my God, and save my soul in the end."

In this resigned frame of mind examine yourself; review your characteristics, peculiarities, and inclinations, good and bad; think over your past; notice what are your passions and temptations; consider the strength or weakness of your will. Then compare with all this the duties, difficulties, and dangers of the state of life upon which you purpose to enter. If you feel compelled to say to yourself: "When I remember the weakness of my will and the force of the temptations which assail me, I do not think that I am capable of fulfilling the duties of that state, or of overcoming the difficulties which it presents," it becomes plain that this road to heaven is too steep for you.

Consider your case as you would that of a friend who had similar faults and the same inclinations. One is usually more unprejudiced in regard to others than one can hope to be if the matter under consideration is a personal nature. Why should you not feel the same affection for yourself as you do for a friend? Why should you not take counsel with yourself in the same manner in which you would seek to advise him? Ask yourself the question which St. Aloysius was wont to put to himself whenever he was obliged to come to an important determination: "How does this look in the light of eternity?" or "What does this count for eternity?"

Act in respect to yourself as you will wish you had done when you come to lie upon your death-bed. There can be no safer rule than this. For in the presence of death, matters are viewed in their true light, and no longer seen through colored glasses. How extremely foolish it would be to embrace a state of life which would furnish cause for bitter repentance in your last hours!

My second piece of advice is: Take counsel with others.
But who is to counsel you, and to whom ought you to listen?
Here great caution is necessary; there are counselors who
present themselves unasked, and to whom it would be wrong
to listen. On no account lend your ear to bad Catholics, to
persons who have no faith or who have not a good reputation.
In regard to the supernatural their understanding is either
darkened or extinguished altogether; the eyes of their mind
are blind as far as the eternal truths are concerned—how, then,
could they advise others, how point out to them the right road
to heaven? There are yet other counselors to whom it would
be most inadvisable to listen. I mean worldly persons, who are
entirely absorbed in material things. For higher interests they
have no perception; their thoughts are set upon nothing else
but money, honors, and pleasures. Persons of this class usually
deplore the entrance of a young man into a Religious Order.

Nor ought you to listen to the advice of those who have
anything to gain or lose from your choice as regards the goods
of this world. Finally, do not be advised by persons who know
nothing about the state of life that you may be thinking of
adopting, as, for instance, the religious state. Their ignorance
imbues them with the most absurd ideas and vehement
prejudices, in regard to such a state of life. How could they
form a correct judgment?

From whom, then, are you to seek counsel? Holy Scripture
exhorts you: "*Keep continually to a wise man, who fears
the Lord.*" It is very important to remember this when the
choice of a state of life is under consideration. And why is it
so? Because he who desires to give good advice must often
offend this or that individual with regard to whose temporal
interests the results of his advice may prove to be prejudicial. If
counsel is sought from persons who fear man rather than God,
what misery may not be the consequence of following their

advice, since in giving it they view things from a purely human standpoint. As a rule, your natural advisers, given you by God, are your parents. But there are exceptional cases in which they rank among the evil counselors I have enumerated above; and in these instances their advice can not be relied upon.

Under all circumstances your best adviser is plainly your confessor. You ought not only ask his advice, but faithfully to follow it. He knows you as no one can know you, except God alone; he knows your good and bad qualities and inclinations. Therefore do not, in your youthful folly, be influenced by the fear that his advice will not coincide with your own wishes. Rather give thanks to God that you have at least one friend whose intentions are pure, whose motives are disinterested, and who will be able to prevent you from taking a false step. Consult your confessor and follow his advice; it will be for your good. The Holy Ghost refers to the priest, the confessor, when He exhorts you in the words I have quoted above: "*Keep continually to a wise man, who possesseth the fear of the Lord.*"

84. EFFECTUAL MEANS

THE right choice of a state of life is certainly a great desideratum, since it is a matter of so much consequence in relation to your success and happiness. In order to make a happy choice, follow the good advice offered you in the preceding chapter, and make use of the *effectual means*, which I am about to point out to you.

In the first place, keep your heart constantly directed toward heaven. Have but one desire—namely, to know and to do the will of God. God will then bestow his grace upon you, and you will be certain to make a wise choice. No one ought to wait for an extraordinary call, such as the apostles and many great saints received. However, if you keep your heart constantly directed toward God, He will enlighten you with

His grace. He will give you prudent counselors, and so ordain external circumstances that you may be led as if by the hand of your guardian angel to the state of life God intends for you.

Truly the ways of God are wonderful and manifold. Sometimes He impresses on the heart of a young child a desire for a particular state. Consequently, later on in life there can arise no question as to making a choice, the question having already been decided. To others He signifies His will only when a choice has to be made; and these often enter with joy of spirit into a state for which they had long experienced a rooted aversion.

In the second place, keep your soul pure. Very much— everything, indeed—depends upon this. The brighter and more transparent is the glass of a window, the more readily do the rays of the sun penetrate into the room, but the dimmer the glass, the darker will the apartment be. The soul may be compared to glass, to a mirror, into which the beams of divine grace shine, and in which they are reflected. If you desire to be enlightened from on high in your choice of a state of life, keep your heart clean; preserve therein the bright light of innocence. If this light is obscured or extinguished by sin, delay not to rekindle it by means of contrition and confession.

In the third place, be diligent in prayer. From what has already been said you must plainly perceive that prayer is of the utmost importance in choosing a state of life. For, in the one hand, you seek to choose the state of life which will best promote your eternal salvation; on the other, the world, the flesh, and the devil strive to decoy you into taking the wrong road.

There are two epochs in the life of every individual when the devil lays snares for him with particular cunning. The first is when he ceases to be a child; then comes the crisis, the critical period when the result of previous training will show in the innocence and purity of the youth or maiden, or the reverse be unhappily the case. I believe this critical period has already passed with you; I confidently hope you have successfully stood the test and preserved your innocence.

But with yet greater cunning and force will the devil attack you either now or a few years hence when you come to choose a state of life. Should he succeed in inducing you to take the wrong road, he will expect to emerge victorious from your final, death-bed struggle. Therefore, my dear young friend, pray, pray! Pray for light, that the mists may disperse and the road of life stretch clearly before you; pray for strength to resist your passions whatever sacrifices it may cost you; pray simply that you may know and do the will of God.

In the fourth place, receive frequently and worthily the sacraments of Penance and of the Altar. These sacraments will maintain the purity of your soul, and the Giver of grace will descend into your heart with His light and strength. After each communion entreat Our Lord, with earnestness and confidence, to teach you what are the designs of His sacred Heart in regard to you, and to strengthen you to make any sacrifice that may be necessary. And on your communion days give some time to serious reflection. Imagine that you are stretched upon your death-bed. Ask yourself, if you were in that awful hour, what state of life you would wish you had chosen. Would it not be a cause of bitter regret if you had acted in accordance with your own self-will, instead of following the advice of your confessor?

I can not refrain from mentioning one more means for arriving at a right decision—namely, a true, filial, confiding love and devotion to Mary. On the present occasion I will only make two brief remarks in regard to the devotion. If you desire wisdom and enlightenment concerning the choice of a state of life, the surest way to obtain it is through Mary for she is

"*Sedes sapientiæ*," the "Seat of wisdom." And if you wish to attain eternal salvation in the state which you may choose, the surest way to realize this is through Mary, for, as a great saint tells us, "a true servant of Mary can never be lost."

Do not imagine that thoughts like these are suited only for a young man who is about to enter the cloister. These reflections are not intended for this one or that one, but for all who desire to choose aright so as to ensure their eternal salvation.

As you ought to beware of rashness in choosing a state of life, so ought you to guard against over-anxiety. Do not lose heart in presence of the momentous decision. Make use of the means I have pointed out to you; look constantly toward Heaven. Keep your soul pure; be diligent in prayer; frequently approach the sacraments; practise devotion to Mary; regard her as your Mother; and look with cheerful confidence into the future. Eternal peace and joy follow the earthly struggle. The way of the cross leads to the crown of immortal glory.

> Gentle Star of Ocean!
>   Portal of the sky!
> Ever virgin mother
>   Of the Lord most high!
>
> Break the captive's fetters;
>   Light on blindness pour;
> All our ills expelling,
>   Every bliss implore.
>
> Show thyself a mother;
>   Offer Him our sighs,
> Who, for us incarnate,
>   Did not thee despise.
>
> Virgin of all virgins!
>   To thy shelter take us!
> Gentlest of the gentle!
>   Chaste and gentle make us.
>
> Still, as on we journey,
>   Help our weak endeavor;
> Till with thee and Jesus
>   We rejoice forever.

THE MARRIED STATE

85. OUGHT YOU TO MARRY?

ALL three states of life, namely, the Priesthood, the Religious state, and the Married state, are, as I have frequently remarked, ordained by God; but every state is not for every one, and it is not a matter of indifference in the sight of God which state is chosen.

The reason why I speak here of the married state in the first place, is simply because a very large majority of young men are called to this state, and also because it is usually the first which is considered. We now proceed to ask the first decisive question: are you called to the married state? Ought you to marry?

The answer to the question, "Ought you to marry?" depends upon another question: "Do you think yourself capable of fulfilling the duties of the married state?" In order to answer this question, you must learn what these duties really are, and I will now proceed briefly to set them before you.

One of the chief among these duties requires that husband and wife should live together in concord, love, and conjugal fidelity until death. They must remain together, since marriage is indissoluble. Only when it pleases Almighty God to sever the bond by taking husband or wife out of the world may the survivor marry again.

How should married people live together? First of all, in peace and harmony. They should aim at the same goal, and strive after one and the same thing. For this end they must be united, avoiding anger, quarreling, and dissension.

The following apposite anecdote may be related here. Two married persons who lived unhappily together, carried their dispute one day so far as to come to blows. A neighbor who heard what was going on suddenly shouted: "Fire! Fire!" The quarrel was forgotten; husband and wife eagerly inquired where the fire was burning. "In hell," was the unexpected reply, "and thither married people must go who persist in living in enmity, anger, and dissension." The lesson to be drawn from this is that married people should live together in love and harmony, not in strife and discord. They should seek to please one another, they should pray for one another, and bear with one another. And they should live in conjugal fidelity, that is, they should keep the solemn promises made to one another at the altar.

Another important duty is that of mutual edification. They should edify one another by a Christian life; they should set one another a good example, they should seek to sanctify one another, so as finally to reach heaven. This is the most lofty aim, the highest goal of a union which a sacrament has rendered holy.

Just as Christ loved His own, not merely until His own end, but in such a way as to enable them to attain their final goal, which is eternal felicity, so must the husband love his wife in such a manner that they may both attain their final end, eternal blessedness. Therefore they should pray together, together attend divine service, and receive the sacraments.

Married people have another important duty: they must bring up their children in the fear of God.

At the day of the last judgment we who have the care of souls do not fare like private individuals; we have not merely to answer for what we have personally done or left undone, but when we have given an account of this we shall be asked about the condition of those who have been entrusted to our care.

In the same manner shall fathers and mothers be judged, not only in regard to what their own lives have been, but also as to the manner in which they have brought up their children. This duty in regard to the proper training of children ought of itself to suffice to cause you, if you are a young man thinking of matrimony, to reflect very seriously and not to answer the question: "Ought I to marry?" with thoughtless haste in the affirmative.

But when, and under what conditions, may the reply be an affirmative one? In order briefly to sum up everything, I say to you: If you have reached a suitable time of life, if you are at least twenty-four or twenty-five years of age, if you are sound both in body and mind, if you are not afflicted with any hereditary disease; if you have a fair prospect of being able, in the pursuit of your calling, to maintain a family; if you possess the requisite endowment and capacity to fulfil the difficult duties which devolve upon parents, and to be the head of a well-ordered household, and if you think that you can preserve your chastity and promote your sanctification better as a married man than as a bachelor, then you ought to marry. But on the other hand, it would not be right to refuse to found a family, merely from love of a free and comfortable existence. May God enlighten and direct you; may God bless you.

> The selfsame faith and mutual love,
> The selfsame hope for joys above,
> Such bonds alone in wedded life
> Will joy secure, and banish strife.

86. THE COMPANION OF YOUR LIFE!

I F YOU have reached a suitable age, and feel yourself called to the married state, then are you confronted with the most important affair—namely, that of seeking and selecting the partner of your life.

Then the momentous inquiry presents itself: Whom ought I to marry, with whom ought I to commence a courtship, and to what ought I principally look? I will now endeavor to reply to these questions, and to furnish you with a few practical hints.

In the first place, look for genuine piety, modesty, intelligence, and common-sense. A woman must necessarily possess true piety; without this she is unfit to make a man happy, or to bring up children properly. It is quite certain, however, that a young woman is destitute of real piety, no matter how frequently she may go to church, if she is guilty of disobedience, impertinence, untruthfulness, and duplicity in regard to her father and mother, or if she has a loose and biting tongue, from which no one is safe.

Beware of marrying such a one; most probably she would be the same in regard to you as she is in regard to her parents and other persons. Furthermore, if a girl is conspicuously vain, indulges her pride, dresses in an immodest and unseemly manner, is excessively fond of frequenting picnics and dancing places, and is not ashamed to parade her real or imaginary charms even in the house of God and during divine service, or if she seems in a tremendous hurry to get married—such a one could never satisfy you: she would never make you happy.

Do not allow your choice to depend altogether upon minor considerations, such as physical beauty, finished manners, a charming deportment, wealth, and worldly possessions.

Physical beauty ought not to decide. When I say this I am far from meaning that you ought to marry a deformed or ugly person or one in regard to whom you feel from the outset a repulsion or aversion. No, certainly not; but undue importance must not be attached to beauty, because it offers no security for a happy marriage.

"A beautiful body," says St. Chrysostom, "which is not the dwelling of a virtuous soul can hold a husband captive but for a very short time." And the same holy Doctor of the Church writes in another place: "How many husbands have come to a deplorable end, although their wives were possessed of remarkable beauty; others, on the contrary, have led a very happy life, and attained to a ripe old age, at the side of a wife possessed of but little physical attractiveness."

Worldly possessions, property, and money ought also to be a minor consideration in regard to the choice of a wife. Money need not be left altogether out of the question; but it is plain that he who looks only to the dowry, marries not the individual, but the money. To such a one may fitly be applied the saying of the holy Doctor whom we have just quoted: "It seems as if the wife were to be bought. Such conduct dishonors the gift of God, and treats a holy sacrament as if it were an ordinary transaction."

I chanced to read of an instance of this style of transaction in a newspaper the other day. A very wealthy man wanted to get a son-in-law still richer than himself. He met with a young man to suit his ideas, and proposed to give him, in the event of his marrying his daughter, a very handsome sum as her dowry. The gentleman, however, who probably loved money more than he loved the girl, demanded a still larger sum. The squabble which ensued was a long one; at length the bargain was satisfactorily concluded, and the marriage took place. The young lady does not appear to have been more sensible or noble-minded than her parent, or else she would have said to him, "Father, you can do with your money what you please, but this sordid fellow shall not have me! I want a husband who wishes to marry *me*, not my *money!*"

If money ought not to play a principal part it is, as a rule, desirable that your betrothed should stand on nearly a similar footing with yourself in regard to property; in any case she ought not, by means of an enormous dowry, to make a rich husband out of a poverty-stricken creature. For believe me, there would then be the greatest danger of her making of you a henpecked husband, and that in accordance with the saying, "Money rules the world"; she would try to rule you; there would be breakers ahead in the sea of life.

Whom, therefore, ought you to marry? A person endowed with those qualities which will enable you to attain, in common with her, the end for which God has intended you in your particular state of life. Therefore seek a bride who, as has already been explained, is truly pious, modest, intelligent, and sensible; who, moreover, thoroughly understands housekeeping, and takes pleasure in it; one who is thrifty, economical, neat, and careful; one who sees that everything is properly done and who does not shirk taking part in household duties herself.

Finally, see that your betrothed is about on the same level with yourself in regard to age and education. Remember the well-known lines of Schiller:

> Heart with heart together meeting,
> See they are in concord beating;
> Life is long, and passion fleeting.

87. The Time of Courtship — "Company-Keeping"

You are aware that it behooves you at all times to watch and pray, and keep strict guard over your innocence, but never is this so necessary as during the time of courtship.

That is the most dangerous time for young people. If they forget God, the period of their engagement often witnesses the ruin of their innocence, their peace of mind, and the happiness of their life.

This topic is consequently among the most important for those whose office it is to instruct young men and give them practical advice for their guidance in moral and spiritual matters. Let me tell you plainly what a Christian young man ought to think about courtship, and how he ought to conduct himself during that period.

A Christian young man ought to seek to know betimes what is allowed and what is forbidden in regard to courtship. He ought not to wait to know this until he has fallen deeply in love, and perhaps even made improper proposals. In this case the eye of his conscience would be dimmed; it would be impossible for him to judge aright.

For those who have already sinned together, warnings usually come too late; persuasions, entreaties and exhortations are equally thrown away; if such persons were to see the abyss of hell yawning before them, or if some one were to rise from the dead in order to warn them, they would continue to pursue their evil way, saying it was impossible for them to desist from it.

Therefore, I say to you, before entering upon any courtship learn what is the right view to be taken in regard to company-keeping. But what is this right view? Careless persons who enter upon a courtship are ready to assert that company-keeping is nothing bad, but rather something beneficial and useful, since it is the necessary preliminary for marriage.

To this it may be replied, that under certain conditions, courtship is nothing evil, but profitable and permissible; but how few courtships there are which fulfil these conditions and which do not appear to be dangerous and even sinful!

Father Schuen says in regard to this subject:[1]

Young people of opposite sexes fall in love with each other, get engaged to be married and not unfrequently remain in that state for a very long time, sometimes for years. Over this state of things heaven has reason to mourn and hell to rejoice. How so, you may ask—is there anything wrong in keeping company with a person that you intend to marry? I answer that, in itself, there is nothing wrong in keeping company, but that the time and other attendant circumstances very frequently convert it into a proximate occasion of sin, and that it can become very wrong. Love-affairs are frequently very lightly entered into; but they are often attended by great dangers and sad consequences.

That two persons who intend to get married should previously become better acquainted with each other is reasonable and right; in fact, ordinary prudence and the future happiness of the two demand as much. If they meet at times, provided they do not remain alone too much and especially at night, and then enter the married state in a proper and legitimate manner, such acquaintance can not be found fault with. But in many cases there is no prospect, or only a very remote one, that marriage will follow; at times there is not the slightest intention of marriage between the two that keep company. Or, when there is an engagement of marriage, they are constantly together; they are averse to the presence of other persons; they prefer to sit for hours in the dark; they wander about in secluded and out-of-the-way places; they are at every dance that is held for miles around. The Christian code of morals can never sanction such company-keeping. Such a method of courtship is fraught with the greatest dangers and generally constitutes a proximate occasion of sin.

Holy Scripture condemns this. *"Can a man hide fire in his bosom, and his garments not burn? Or can he walk upon hot*

1   *Outlines of Sermons for Young Men:* Schuen-Wirth.

coals, and his feet not be burned?" (Prov. vi. 27, 28.) "Are you," asks St. Augustine, "more masters of yourselves than David, or wiser than Solomon? Now, if too familiar intercourse with women, and the seduction of their caresses were the ruin of these great men, how will it fare with those who purposely seek such familiarity with the opposite sex, who perhaps live in the same house with them and frequent every amusement in their company?"

St. Jerome calls illicit acquaintances the "death-agony of a moribund chastity."

Even that mildest of moralists, St. Francis de Sales, points out the great danger of undue familiarity: "These erotic friendships evoke so many temptations, dissipations, and jealous feelings, not to speak of other things inimical to the peace of the soul, that the better feelings of the heart are completely crushed and destroyed by them." St. Alphonsus, the prince of moral theologians, says: "I maintain as a general principle, that it is a matter of great difficulty for any one who keeps up an intimacy of this kind to preserve himself from proximate occasion of sin."

The same conclusion becomes evident if we consider the frailty of human nature. We know that the heart of man is prone to sin. Through the fall of our first parents a great misfortune came upon them and their posterity. Man has become exceedingly weak; the door of the heart is always open to evil. St. Paul testifies to this: *"I know that there dwelleth not in me, that is, in my flesh, that which is good. I see another law in my members, fighting against the law of my mind, and captivating me in the law of sin, that is in my members"* (Rom. vii. 18, 23). The human heart is especially prone to the sin of impurity. A single look, a single grasp of the hand, is sufficient to awaken the fire of passion. Witness the case of David (2 Kings xi. 2 seq.).

Ask yourselves now whether there is anything wrong in these familiar associations with persons of the opposite sex. They are dangerous in the highest degree. Two young persons, by nature most frail, meet frequently in the twilight or the dark, in solitary places—the passions are enkindled, flames are unchecked—and you ask is there any danger! If the hermits of the desert, with all their prayers and austerities, with their diet of roots and vegetables, could subdue nature only by hard struggles, what is not to be feared when it is a question of two lovers, who perhaps seldom pray and practise little if any self-denial? They will not stop short of the greatest sins if they continue their illicit company-keeping.

The ordinary consequence of dangerous familiarity is a multitude of sins. The river of iniquity that flows from them is not a single stream, but forms many most destructive currents. In the first place we must mention impurity. Indulgence in love-affairs, carried on without safeguards, results almost inevitably in violations of chastity. He who put his hand into the fire is burned; he who scrambles over a thorny hedge tears his clothes; he who casts himself into the mire will be soiled; and he who keeps up an undue intimacy with a woman will fall into grievous sins. Experience proves only too well the truth of this statement. If such a one does not go astray at first, he will fall into sin all the surer as time goes on. At the outset they will indulge in silly conversations, then love becomes a passion and the understanding is darkened—and when passion obtains a firm foothold, the will forms a thousand evil desires; sinful words and unchaste deeds not unfrequently follow.

Another evil is the grief which is caused to parents. How much grief, how much sorrow, parents endure on account of the misdeeds of their children! Their sons and daughters do not obey them, they scorn their advice and admonitions. The parents foresee only too clearly the end of the dangerous entanglements which their children have gotten into, and they mourn over them in bitterness of soul. Often these associations lead to theft. The young man goes into excessive expenses to make presents to his "company," he wants to dress above his means, to take his "company" to dances and amusements; his income is not sufficient and the deficiency must be supplied from his father's coffers. These intimacies lead to scandal. The young couple live on a footing of intimacy, they are seen together almost daily, and yet months and years go by without marriage. People suspect easily that things are not right, and in many cases there is good reason for the suspicion.

Another evil that follows is frequently a desecration of the sacraments. Full and open confessions of guilt are frequently not made; a feeling of shame keeps the couple from declaring their sins as they should. Such confessions are sacrilegious and so also is the communion which follows. Or, if they confess their sins, they are not willing to remove the proximate occasion of sin; they go from one confessor to another; they leave his admonition unheeded, give a half-hearted promise to avoid the occasion, without a firm will to do so. The absolution is nothing but empty words that can never remit sin. Thus the sacraments are profaned for years, and the mysteries of the Faith are abused in the most shameful manner.

Intimacies of this kind cause many tears. Sins are always a source of sorrow, but this is especially true of sins of impurity. They bring with them evils not only in the matter of eternal salvation, but even in a temporal way. Disgrace often falls upon those persons guilty of such sins. As the man grows older, he looks back with deep regret at the years spent in contempt of the law of God. On his deathbed they become a source of anguish and fear.

Not unfrequently such young men die suddenly, and have no time for repentance; they have filled the measure of iniquity, and are called to give an account of their doings. Others become hardened in vice and never repent. They are plunged into the abyss, and mourn their sins for all eternity.

These dangerous intimacies bring on consequences bitter as the sting of a serpent; they are attended by great dangers and sad consequences. I have not overdrawn the picture; I have spoken nothing but the truth. Make no excuses to palliate the danger of which I have spoken today. Experience shows that the reality is, if anything, worse than I have pictured it. I made the proper allowance. There is no fault to be found with company-keeping within certain limits. Where there is an earnest intention of marriage, and the engagement is not of too long duration, and the visits are made to the family, and proper hours are kept, there can be no objection. What I condemn, and what every Christian must condemn, are the courtships without reference to marriage, the intimacies protracted for years, the visits where the young people are together for hours and alone. These are nothing but proximate occasion for sin and often a living in habitual sin. For persons living so, there can be no hope of absolution in the confessional which is valid before God unless they abandon the occasion. If you are carrying on an acquaintance of this kind, I beg of you, if you love God, if you love the salvation of your own soul, break it off at once. Do not answer that you have done nothing wrong as yet; if you continue, you can not remain free from sin. Cut off the hand that scandalizes you, pluck out the eye that is a source of sin and cast it from thee. Make a generous resolution now, and God will sustain you with His grace. If you do, you will always bless the day on which you conquered yourself.

> Each state and calling here below
> Has its own joy and its own woe;
> Yet sorrowful beyond the rest
> A marriage that God has not blest.

88. MARRY A CATHOLIC

A s REGARDS the choice of a wife, I have another, and a very important point to mention—namely: *Marry a Catholic!* On no account conclude a mixed marriage—therefore avoid engaging yourself to a non-Catholic.

First of all it must be remarked that no offense to Protestants is intended when Catholics are warned against marrying them. Protestants ought to hold similar opinions, looking at the matter from their own point of view, and, indeed, they frequently do. To prove the truth of what has just been said, I will give two extracts—the first from a Protestant newspaper—they are fraught with useful lessons for Catholics. My first quotation runs thus:

"A mixed marriage is always a sad mistake, and any one who forms such a union must make up his mind to experience a good deal of trouble and unhappiness. If the children are brought up as Catholics, the Protestant husband or wife must look on while they say their beads, must hear them invoking the saints, and must tolerate other practices and devotions which are distasteful and annoying to Protestants. If the children are Protestants, discontent and reproaches are sure to follow on the Catholic side; and if some are brought up as Catholics, others as Protestants, the family is divided."

Parents and children ought to profess the same faith. A Protestant artisan who had married a Catholic, and whose only child died, expressed himself as follows: "Standing beside the death-bed of our child, I felt how great a gulf separated my wife from me. In my opinion, mixed marriages are very deplorable." Truly, no one who cares about his own salvation and that of his children ought to contract a mixed marriage.

My second quotation is taken from a pamphlet entitled *A Word of Warning to Protestants*. It runs thus:

"How unhappy a wife must be, who has been brought up a Catholic, and reflects, every time she attends divine worship, that her children are being educated as Protestants. And the opposite case is just as painful. Nor do I think that the religious discussions which must arise between husband and wife can be very edifying. These discussions can scarcely be avoided if each is in earnest in regard to his or her beliefs. And if religion is to be a forbidden subject, what will become of the children?"

A Catholic priest could not much better or more forcibly express his disapproval of mixed marriages, than do these extracts from Protestant sources. Listen to the decision of the Catholic Church concerning mixed marriages. She has always declared her disapproval of them, and advised—nay commanded—Catholics to avoid contracting them. More than fourteen hundred years ago, several Councils, among them those of Elvira, Laodicea, and Chalcedon, forbade Catholics to marry heretics, unless the latter promised to become Catholics.

Two special reasons induced and compelled the Catholic Church to come to this decision. In the first place, a union between a Catholic and a Protestant can never be a perfect marriage, can never be what marriage ought to be. For marriage is a sacrament, and ought to be regarded and treated as such. How can this be, when the Protestant considers marriage to be a merely civil contract?

Married people should live in the closest union, the most perfect harmony; they ought to have but one heart and one soul. How can this be, when they hold such widely different opinions in regard to the most sacred and important of all subjects—namely religion?

Moreover, married people ought to help one another on the way to heaven. How can they do this when one takes the road to the right, and the other treads the path which turns to the left? Furthermore, married people ought to give their children a religious education, and they should co-operate in carrying on the good work. Again, I ask, how can they do this, when their views in regard to religion differ so widely?

Finally, there is another important reason: Mixed marriages are extremely seldom happy marriages. Upon this subject a learned theologian writes as follows: "There is perhaps not one single instance to be found of a mixed marriage in which (although they may have lived peaceably together) the husband and wife did not, after the lapse of years, express the conviction that it would have been better for them had they never met. There was a flaw in their mutual relations, a sore spot, which could never be healed."

Therefore be warned in time, and resolve never to court a young woman who is not of your faith, that you may thus never contract a mixed marriage.

> Though love may clasp the nuptial band.
> Yet wedded bliss no storm can stand,
> Unless the selfsame faith both share
> And make God's service their first care.

The Priesthood[1]

89. The Call to the Priesthood

"Neither doth any man take the honor to himself but he that is called by God, as Aaron was" (Heb. v. 4).

THE priesthood is so sublime a state, that no one should embrace it without a clearly known vocation to it.

No, no man takes this honor to himself *but he that is called by God, as Aaron was.*

A negative inclination for this holy state would certainly not be sufficient. You feel no disinclination to it; it does not appear impossible to you to fulfil its chief duties—celibacy especially; you imagine yourself free from certain violent temptations; you are not destitute of the necessary talents. Is that all that is required for a vocation to the priesthood?

Much less might that be considered a call to it, which rests purely upon exterior reasons or worldly motives.

It is much to be desired that you become a priest. Pious desire! if the honor of God is its sole object—if it be subordinate to the will of God.

Priests are the representatives of God upon earth. They form a separate state. The Lord is their portion (Ps. xv. 5), and their duty consists in being a chosen generation to the Most High (1 Peter ii. 9), and in helping men to reach their eternal destiny.

---

1 From *Thoughts and Counsels for Young Men*: Van Doss-Wirth.

The vocation of priests is to heal, to pray, and to offer sacrifice.

They cleanse men from the stains of the soul; they educate them for heaven; they fulfil, in regard to the erring, the duties of the Good Shepherd; they pour oil and wine into the wounds of the soul; they give refreshment to weary mortals; they assuage suffering and impart strength.

They praise God in their own name and in that of all the faithful; they make supplications, they give thanks, they petition for new graces and blessings.

They celebrate the most sublime mystery of the New Law, and daily offer up to the Eternal Father the immaculate Lamb of God, who taketh away the sins of the world, in expiation of their own sins, and those of mankind, and for the obtaining of innumerable graces and blessings.

They are God's coadjutors (1 Cor. iii. 9); they are the ambassadors of Christ (2 Cor. v. 20); they are the dispensers of the mysteries of Christ (1 Cor. iv. 1).

They are saviours of souls.

To save souls! O sublime work! O work most acceptable and glorious to God! God's own work!

O heart of the priest, large as the universe, high as the heavens, restless as fire, glowing with love of the apostles, thirsting like the Saviour's heart—who can conceive thy longing desires, hopes, sufferings, joys, struggle and triumphs!

By reason of his vocation, the priest is obliged to a much higher degree of perfection than the rest of the faithful.

As he excels the latter in dignity, so it is becoming that he should by far excel them in nobility of soul and in sanctity of life.

He is the salt of the earth. Woe to the salt, if it lose its savor (Matt. v. 13), for then it is unfit for seasoning.

He is a light. Woe to the light that proves to be an

ignis fatuus! Woe to the light that is extinguished, or hidden under a bushel!

He is the city of God, set upon a mountain (Matt. v. 14). Woe to the mountain that is so surrounded by mists and vapors, that the city on its top is lost to the sight of the expectant pilgrim!

If souls are committed to the priest's charge, and if he is to lead them to heaven, he must surely walk himself in the way of salvation.

If he is to educate mankind in spirituality, he must certainly labor unceasingly at his own spiritual perfection.

How dare the curse of sin adhere to the hands that have been made especially to bless?

Shall the mouth which is to announce the words of life, be the mouth of one spiritually dead?

Shall the priest's actions contradict the word of edification, and pull down instead of building up?

You ask for the marks of a true vocation to the holy priesthood?

First, pay attention to the preliminary conditions:

Do you possess the necessary talents? Erroneously, or rather, almost blasphemously, it is asserted, sometimes, that anything is good enough for God. Hear what He Himself says on this point: *"The lips of the priest shall keep knowledge, and they shall seek the law at his mouth, because he is an angel of the Lord of hosts"* (Malach. ii. 7). And do you suppose that the priestly eloquence, by means of which the Holy Ghost speaks to the faithful, can exist without a solid, scientific foundation?

Is your life spotless? A youth spent in purity is, of course, the best recommendation, yet, on the other hand, penitents are not excluded from the priesthood—penitents, that is, such as have expiated and are still expiating the transgressions whereby they once criminally desecrated their youth; penitents, who, after having long since, and most energetically, renounced their evil habits, prepare themselves by a pure present for a still purer future, and leave no means untried to grow and advance in virtue and holiness.

As regards the marks themselves, there are very many; the greater the number you possess, the more certain your call.

Is your intention a perfectly pure one? Do you seek in the priesthood God, your own, and your neighbor's salvation, and nothing temporal—such as honor, prosperity, ease, comfort? Is it God, above all, that urges you to embrace this state? Have you heard this call repeatedly?

Do you perceive an interior urging to this holy state? Does the thought of your future priesthood calm and refresh you?

Is the honor of God really dear to your heart? Have you a lively desire to save souls?

Do you find pleasure in spiritual things? Do you love prayer, the sacraments, spiritual reading, intercourse with pious and spiritual persons?

If you are truly called to the priestly state—that is, to a life of sacrifice—how is it you are not able to make a sacrifice of evil in yourself, to give up a favorite sin, to overcome a favorite inclination?

Prove yourself—aye, prove yourself very seriously. From almost all other states one may recede; but here, there is no return; once bound, you are bound forever. Thou art a priest forever, according to the order of Melchisedech.

Blessed you, if you are called to re-enforce the sacred phalanx which gives to the Church militant her heroic champions and leaders in the battle!

Once more: the call must come from above. This is the only legitimate gate to the fold of Jesus Christ, of which it is said: *"He that entereth not by the door into the sheepfold, is a thief and a robber"* (John x. 1).

Yes, young man, God must call you. Woe to him who intrudes uncalled into that holiest of states, in which the sacrilegious intruder not only does no good, but effects, alas! an infinite injury to himself and others!

O terrible utterance of the Eternal Truth: "*Every plant which is not planted by God shall be rooted up*" (Matt. xv. 13), since it brings forth no fruit; it is useless in itself and to others; it is fit only to be cast into the fire and to be burned. Pray—pray fervently—that you may know and do the will of God.

> " 'Tis Thy good pleasure, not my own,
> In Thee, my God, I love alone;
> And nothing I desire of Thee
> But what Thy goodness wills for me.
> O will of God, O will divine,
> All, all our love be ever Thine.

> "To Thee I consecrate and give
> My heart and being while I live;
> Thou, O my God, alone shalt be
> My love for all eternity.
> May heaven and earth with love fulfil,
> My God, Thy ever-blessed will."

The Religious State

90. The Happiness of a Religious Vocation

I SHOULD not consider that I had entirely completed the task I set myself in writing these pages, were I not to add a few words concerning the religious state. In many countries, the present time is certainly not favorable to it. Religious are harassed, persecuted and chased out of the quiet retreats they have chosen for themselves. These persecutions are, however, quite unable to stifle the sublime vocation to the life of the cloister. The vital sap which circulates so abundantly within the Church produces continually, in this direction also, fresh buds and blossoms. And it is in the peasant, artisan, and industrial classes that youths are ever and again to be found, whom the voice of God calls, and forcibly impels to enter the hallowed precincts of the cloister. What are we to think concerning this vocation to the religious life? Lay to heart, in the first place, the happiness of such a vocation.

The judgment of the short-sighted world is entirely false when it imagines the life of a Religious to be joyless, melancholy, depressing and more or less unhappy. The monk must indeed renounce much which men regard as pleasure and enjoyment, but only to be compensated a hundred-fold by higher and purer joys. Have you ever seen a vine pruned? The process seems to hurt the vine and bitter drops, like tears, ooze from the stem; yet it proves to be for its good, and increases its value. Thus it is with a Religious. All the sacrifices which he has perchance to make, do but augment his happiness; they increase that peace which, as Christ says, "*the world can not give*." And the same divine Redeemer gives this assurance to those who serve and follow Him: "*My yoke is sweet, and My burden light.*"

Consider attentively another remarkable utterance which the Saviour spoke. When St. Peter asked: "*Behold, we have left all things and have followed Thee. What therefore shall we have?*" Jesus answered and said: "*Amen, I say to you, there is no man that hath left house, or parents, or brethren, or wife, or children, for the kingdom of God's sake, who shall not receive much more in this present time, and in the world to come, life everlasting*" (Luke xviii. 29, 30).

Life everlasting! This promise does not surprise us. But the other is very remarkable. Even *in this life* the disciples who follow Christ wholly and entirely will be bountifully rewarded. They will receive a hundredfold, far more than they have left, even *in this time*; liberty of spirit, peace, interior joy, happiness, confidence in God, brotherly love.

It is, however, true that those who enter the cloister take human nature with them; and there also is much human frailty to be found. But in spite of all this, there is but one spirit which pervades the cloister—the spirit of love—a fraternal co-operation in all undertakings. That is the blessing of Christ: the happiness of a religious vocation.

This happiness is mirrored in the daily life of a true Religious. The whole day is consecrated exclusively to God by means of obedience, cheerful labor, and religious exercises. His first awakening in the early hours of the morning is a pious upward glance to the most holy Trinity, whom he adores, and to whom in his prayers he offers up his life, his will, his heart, and its desires.

In the course of the day, wherever he may be, whatever he may do, he remembers that he is in the house of God, and in the service of God. In this way, a laborious and wearisome life seems a paradise to him, dearer than any transitory enjoyment in the palaces of this world.

And in the evening, before he lies down to rest, he closes his day's work in the presence of the blessed Sacrament of the Altar, and commends his spirit to the sacred Heart of Jesus. And in spirit, at least, he is never separated from the hallowed precincts of the sanctuary; in thought and desire he is always united with Jesus in the Tabernacle, and he can truly say with the prophet: "*My soul hath desired thee even in the night.*"

We can form an idea of the sublimity of the religious state, if we reflect on the example of Jesus, the God-man. He led a life of more than angelic purity, a life of mortification, renunciation, and self-denial, and He willed to be born of a pure virgin, and loved Joseph more than any other man, on account of his virginal purity.

When a young man, imitating this great love of Our Lord for purity, takes refuge in the cloister, treading the pleasures of the world under his feet, in order in virginal purity to follow the chaste Lamb of God and His immaculate Mother, will he not then enjoy that sweet delight of pure souls which is unknown to the children of the world? His happiness is indeed a foretaste of the peace and joy of heaven. Finally, Jesus Christ came, not to do His own will, but He humbled Himself and became obedient unto death, even to the death of the cross. If a Religious imitates this example also, and places himself, for his whole life, under obedience to his spiritual superiors will he not reap the blessing and the fruits of such a sacrifice? Sublime is the religious state and truly great is the happiness of a Religious. But do you, my friend, trust in God; leave it to Him, whether this happiness is, or is not to be your portion. Pray for guidance and be ever ready to do the will of God with a cheerful and generous heart.

> Jesus, day by day
> Lead us on life's way.
> Naught of danger shall we reckon,
> Following where Thou dost beckon.
> Lead us by the hand
> To our Fatherland.

*   *   *

> Lead, kindly Light, amid the encircling gloom;
>   Lead Thou me on!
> The night is dark, and I am far from home.
>   Lead Thou me on!
> Keep Thou my feet; I do not ask to see
> The distant scene—one step enough for me.
>
> I was not ever thus, nor pray'd that Thou
>   Shouldst lead me on.
> I loved to choose and see my path, but now
>   Lead Thou me on!
> I loved the garish day, and, spite of fears,
> Pride ruled my will: remember not past years.
>
> So long Thy power hath blest me, sure it still
>   Will lead me on.
> O'er moor and fen, o'er crag and torrent, till
>   The night is gone;
> And with the morn those angel faces smile
> Which I have loved long since, and lost awhile.
>   —Cardinal Newman.

91. THE SACRIFICES OF A RELIGIOUS VOCATION

HAPPY are those who are called to the religious state! But we must not look exclusively at the happiness and advantages which accompany life in the cloister, but we must also weigh the sacrifices which it entails. A religious house is no place for lotus-eaters. No one ought to enter the cloister with the idea of exchanging a life of effort and struggle in the world for a quiet and comfortable existence. He who seeks nothing but this in an Order, nothing but sweet tranquility and undisturbed comfort, will find himself bitterly deceived. Reflect merely upon the trials of community life. Consider one of the essential conditions of life in the cloister—namely, this one—to live with many others and to be dependent upon others. The rules of every convent, quite apart from the question of contact with many others, with many different characters, make demands which are absolutely incompatible with a desire for self-indulgence and self-satisfying solitude.

The Ego we love so well, and cherish so tenderly, can no longer make its claims felt. It is not necessary to think of a specially strict Order where the regulations are peculiarly stringent, but the obligatory observance of the vows is merely to be reflected upon—to possess nothing of one's own, to live in subjection to a superior; this done, it will at once be clearly perceived that self-will can no longer hold the scepter there.

Thus we see that the life of a true Religious is a life of constant sacrifice. For he relinquishes all those things which are most calculated to bind poor human beings down to earth. The evangelical counsels, which the Saviour Himself has given, and to the observance of which the Religious pledges himself, can not be faithfully carried out without grievous sacrifices on the part of the carnal man. Every one knows what these counsels are: voluntary poverty, virginal purity, and constant obedience to a spiritual superior. And Religious pledge themselves to the conscientious observance of these counsels under pain of grievous sin when they pronounces their vows either for their whole life, or at least for a definite period.

It must certainly involve a sacrifice to pronounce the vow of poverty, for instance, and to keep it faithfully. Or can it be easy for a young man who possesses a fortune of his own, and can dispose of it as he pleases, to renounce now and for all future time all claim to call anything his own, or to appropriate anything for his own use without the permission of a superior? Can it be easy for him during the whole of his life in the convent to ask, like a child, for permission to keep a trifling gift, or to exchange it or give it away?

The vow of chastity also involves a great sacrifice, namely, the complete renunciation of married family life— the observance of virginal purity for the Saviour's sake. This sacrifice is peculiarly pleasing to Our Lord.

The Saviour came into the world in a state of poverty; He renounced everything, and was cradled on the rough straw of the manger. But one thing He never gave up; even in the stable His eye wanted to rest upon virginal souls! Therefore He willed to see Mary and Joseph beside the manger. Poor as He came into the world, He also died; His death-bed was the hard wood of the cross. But there also, amid the gloom and sufferings, two lilies of purity, Mary and John, were at the foot of the cross.

Like these lilies ought all those young men to be, who are planted in the chosen garden of the Lord, in the religious state. This life of virginal purity involves a perpetual conflict, an endeavor to obtain the crown of angels while dwelling in mortal flesh. But this conflict, this struggle, can be termed nothing but sacrifice, renunciation, self-denial.

The third vow is the vow of obedience. How many sacrifices does this single word imply! St. Gregory the Great once said that it is not so difficult to give up one's possessions; but it is difficult indeed to renounce oneself. By obedience one gives up oneself as one gives up one's own will.

This also involves sacrifices. They are often secret sacrifices of which no one knows anything, which the world does not know, which no one extols, but which cut to the quick the inmost soul. But how exalted are these sacrifices, these conquests of self! How richly will the Father, who seeth in secret, reward them one day!

Thus we see that obedience requires continual sacrifices at the hands of a Religious: not one single instant is he—if we may so speak—free from the yoke. Obedience calls him in the morning, and commands him in the evening; obedience orders everything in the house, prescribes the hours of work and the form of that work, the time for prayer and the length of that recreation. Obedience guides and controls his every step and movement.

Little enough is the room left for the exercise of self-will. By the practice of obedience a ceaseless war is waged against self.

Therefore if you, my friend, think that you are called to the religious state, examine yourself carefully to discover whether you have strength and courage to make these sacrifices.

Remember the words of St. Paul: "*I can do all things in Him who strengtheneth me.*"

The help of divine grace will not be wanting to you in the event that you should be called to make the sacrifices involved in the religious life. If you have the necessary talent and dispositions, go forward courageously. Take up the mighty weapon of obedience; with it combat the enemies of your salvation. Through disobedience man separated himself from God, his creator and final end: through obedience he must return to Him. Even should you remain in the world you will still have to walk in the way of obedience. *Perfect* obedience to their Superiors is demanded of Religious; faithful obedience to the commands of God and of holy Church is incumbent on seculars.

ALL FOR THEE, O HEART OF JESUS

HOW sweet it is to feel, dear Lord!
    That Thou wilt surely see
Each work, or thought, or act of mine
    That may be done for Thee!

That when I try with pure intent
    To serve, to please, to love Thee,
Thy watchful Heart each effort knows,
    Thy blessing rests above me.

Nothing unnoticed, *nothing* lost—
    Unlike the world—in all things
Grateful art Thou for all I do,
    For great as well as small things.

Empty my soul of all desire
    Man's idle praise to seek,
Hide me in Thee, for Thou dost know
    How frail I am—and weak.

Take Thou my *all*, since for so long
    Thy providence has sought me,
Make me Thine own, since at such cost
    Thy precious blood has bought me.

A Few Concluding Words

92. Farewell

How touching is the account given us in Scripture of the farewell which the youthful Tobias took of his blind father and his weeping mother in order to go forth into a strange country. How touching is the lamentation *"Woe, woe is me, my son, why did we send thee to go to a strange country, the light of our eyes, the staff of our old age, the comfort of our life, the hope of our posterity?"*

A similar feeling of sadness steals into my heart, now that I have arrived at the conclusion of these instructions. You, my young friend, are about to go forth into life, into all the thousand perils and pitfalls which in the present day, more than ever, threaten to ruin both the faith and the innocence of a young man.

But I comfort myself with the thought that I have every reason to say, with the aged father of Tobias: *"I believe that the good angel of God doth accompany him, and doth order all things well that are done about him."*

This good angel, I know, is your guardian angel, and this little book also, I trust, will serve as your guardian and your guide also. It will accompany you when you go forth into the world, and remain always at your side. It depends only upon you that this companion should remind you what is to be done, and what is to be left undone; you must simply take counsel with it by reading this little volume attentively.

I will now, in taking farewell, briefly recapitulate under five resolutions all that has been said. You must impress these resolutions indelibly on your memory, and adhere to them faithfully.

First Resolution. *I will be careful to say my daily prayers regularly, and never to omit hearing Mass on Sundays and holydays without absolute necessity.*

This resolution may be epitomized in one word: *Prayer.* Prayer is the pivot on which the spiritual life of every Christian, and certainly of every Catholic young man, revolves; prayer is the very breath of the soul, its vital breath. And bear in mind that by prayer is meant both *vocal* and *mental* prayer. Read attentively what is said in this book on mental prayer or meditation. Try to make at least a short meditation every day, or a spiritual reading with pious reflections and devout affections from a book like *The Following of Christ* or *The Lives of the Saints.*

With the Royal Psalmist you should be able to say: "*I had in mind the eternal years*" (Ps. lxxvi. 6).

"*In all thy works, remember thy last end, and thou shalt never sin*" (Ecclus. vii. 40).

"*We have not here a lasting city, but we seek one that is to come*" (Heb. xiii. 14).

"*The number of the days of men at the most are a hundred years: As a drop of water of the sea are they esteemed: And as a pebble of the sands, so are a few years compared to eternity*" (Ecclus. xviii. 8).

Say a little prayer daily for the grace of a happy death, *e.g.*, the *Memorare*, or "*Jesus, Mary, and Joseph, assist me in my last agony!*" "*Jesus, Mary, and Joseph, may I breathe forth my soul in peace with you.*"

Cultivate a tender love and a fervent devotion to Jesus in the Most Blessed Sacrament of the Altar, and to the Mother of Jesus, the ever Blessed Virgin Mary. Cultivate a practical devotion by *imitating* the virtues of Jesus and Mary in your daily life.

Second Resolution. *I will make it my practice to receive the sacraments regularly—at least once a month.*

Here you may impress on your mind the word: *Sacraments.* Confession and communion constitute a never-failing source, a fount of grace, whereby the life of the soul may be evermore renewed, maintained, and strengthened. It is truly an indispensable condition for the preservation of the supernatural life of the soul, that it should draw strengthening waters out of the Saviour's fountains.

Third Resolution. *I will carefully avoid everything likely to endanger my faith, especially bad companions, infidel and immoral publications, and luxurious living.*

See that the light of faith which is in you be not darkened or weakened by listening to conversation opposed to faith and to the Church, or by reading books, pamphlets, and newspapers which have a similar tendency, or by an immoral course of life on *your* part.

Fourth Resolution. *In confession I will always be careful, candid, and sincere in regard to the sixth commandment.*

This commandment reminds you that you ought to make every effort in order to safeguard and preserve that fairest ornament of your youth, innocence—chastity. The most effectual means to this end is childlike candor in confession. This candor will be your salvation. But alas for you if you do not tell the whole truth, or if you gloss over your transgressions, and conceal your temptations or the perils to which you are exposed.

Fifth Resolution. I will join the *Sodality*, or *The Young Men's Society*, and other Catholic and charitable organizations connected with my parish church, according to my means and circumstances, such as *The League of the Sacred Heart, The Society of St. Vincent de Paul* or of *The Holy Name* or of

The Propagation of the Faith.

Do all you can to further the interests of your parish, church, and school. Your heart should be aflame with a zeal for the House of God as was the heart of David, who was able to say truly: "*I have loved, O Lord, the beauty of Thy house and the place where Thy glory dwelleth*" (Ps. xxv. 8).

The resolution in regard to joining the *Sodality, The Young Men's Society,* or *The Catholic Club* of your parish church, is of particular importance. These associations aim at preserving their members from wandering into forbidden paths or to lead them back into the right road, when they have gone astray. Revere and love your pastor; second all his efforts for the welfare of your society; be kind and helpful toward your associates.

In conclusion I will adopt the words which the aged Tobias addressed to his son: "*All the days of thy life have God in thy mind, and take heed thou never consent to sin, nor transgress the commandments of the Lord our God. Take heed to keep thyself, my son, from all fornication; never suffer pride to reign in thy mind or in thy words, for from it all perdition took its beginning. May you have a good journey, and God be with you on your way, and His angel accompany you!*"

"*In doing good, let us not fail; for in due time, we shall reap, not failing*" (Gal. vi. 9).

WISHING

Do you wish the world were better?
Let me tell you what to do.
Set a watch upon your actions,
Keep them always straight and true.
Rid your mind of selfish motives.
Let your thoughts be clean and high.
You can make a little Eden
Of the sphere you occupy.

Do you wish the world were happy?
Then remember day by day
Just to scatter seeds of kindness
As you pass along the way.
For the pleasures of the many
May be ofttimes traced to one,
As the hand that plants the acorn
Shelters armies from the sun.

—Leaflets.

To Jesus, Mary, and Joseph

Jesus, whose almighty bidding
    All created things fulfil,
Lived on earth in meek subjection
    To His earthly parents' will.
    Sweetest Infant, make us patient
        And obedient for Thy sake;
    Teach us to be chaste and gentle,
        All our stormy passions break.

Blessed Mary! thou wert chosen
    As Mother of thy Lord;
Thou didst guide the early footsteps
    Of the great Incarnate Word.
    Dearest Mother! make us humble;
        For thy Son will take His rest
    In the poor and lowly dwelling
        Of a humble sinner's breast.

Joseph! thou wert called the father
    Of thy Maker and thy Lord;
Thine it was to save thy Saviour
    From the cruel Herod's sword.
    Suffer us to call thee father;
        Show to us a father's love;
    Lead us safe through every danger;
        Till we meet in heaven above.

ALL FOR THE GREATER GLORY OF GOD AND
IN HONOR OF THE BLESSED VIRGIN MARY!

Appendix

This section contains selected excerpts from the Prayerbook that formed the second half of The Young Man's Guide. Other excerpts may be found at the end of each chapter.

❀ Quit ❀

- Gossiping.
- Anticipating evils in the future.
- Faultfinding, nagging, and worrying.
- Dwelling on fancied slights and wrongs.
- Scolding and flying into a passion over trifles.
- Thinking that life is a grind and not worth living.
- Talking constantly about yourself and your affairs.
- Saying unkind things about acquaintances and friends.
- Lamenting the past, holding on to disagreeable experiences.
- Pitying yourself and bemoaning your lack of opportunities.
- Writing letters when the blood is hot, which you may regret later.
- Thinking that all the good chances and opportunities are gone by.
- Carping and criticising. See the best rather than the worst in others.
- Dreaming that you would be happier in some other place or circumstances.
- Belittling those whom you envy because you feel that they are superior to yourself.
- Dilating on your pains and aches and misfortunes to every one who will listen to you.
- Speculating as to what you would do in some one else's place, and do your best in your own.
- Gazing idly into the future and dreaming about it, instead of making the most of the present. *—London opinion.*

❈ A Rule of Life ❈

"He that shall persevere to the end, he shall be saved."

1. Daily conduct.—Have a fixed hour for rising in the morning; bless yourself with holy water, and as soon as possible after your toilet recite devoutly your morning prayers. During the day make at least a short meditation or a spiritual reading. It is commendable to read daily from the *Lives of the Saints*. Hear Mass; make a visit to the Most Blessed Sacrament and to Mary, the Mother of Jesus. If you can not go to church, make your visit and adoration at home, turning toward the nearest tabernacle and receiving holy communion spiritually. Recite the *Angelus*; say the beads. In the evening examine your conscience and recite your evening prayers.

2. *Confession and Communion.*—Receive the holy sacraments frequently—once a week or, certainly, once a month. Go as often as you can to holy communion, with the advice of your spiritual director. When you commit any sin, make an act of contrition immediately and resolve to amend; if it is a mortal sin, confess it as soon as possible.

3. *Occasions of Sin.*—Avoid idleness, bad companions, low theaters and public balls, immoral books, sensational newspapers, salacious literature, foolish novels and romances, games of chance, and every occasion of sin. In temptations, bless yourself, invoke the most holy names of Jesus and Mary, and think of death. *"He that loveth danger shall perish in it."*

4. *Sundays.*—*"Remember that thou keep holy the Sabbath-day."* Be not satisfied with hearing a Low Mass on Sundays. Hear sermons as often as possible, and listen attentively to the word of God. No matter how poor an orator a priest may be, no matter how plain his language or how unattractive

his delivery, remember that he is the representative of Christ, and that you can always find in every sermon sufficient matter for reflection and application to your own life and circumstances. Faithfully attend the meetings of the Sodality or Young Men's Society, and never absent yourself unnecessarily from afternoon or evening services and benediction.

5. *Pious Practices.*—Keep yourself in the presence of God. Accustom yourself to saying short ejaculatory and indulgenced prayers. Keep a crucifix, holy pictures, and holy water in your room. Carry your beads with you. Wear a scapular, and a medal of the Immaculate Conception. Support your parish priest and your parish church in all good works. Help the poor and the orphans according to your means. Frequently think of death and eternity.

6. *Blessed Virgin Mary.*—If you love Jesus, you will love and honor His blessed Mother. Be most devout to her and daily perform some acts of piety in her honor. A pious *Servant of Mary* will erect a *home altar* in honor of the heavenly Queen and Mother of God before which he will recite his prayers. On our Lady's feast-days he will place an offering of fresh flowers on this altar. Hear Mass and receive holy communion on the great feasts of the Blessed Virgin. Daily renew your act of consecration and say the *Memorare* for a happy death. Cultivate her virtues, especially purity, modesty, meekness, humility, charity, patience, resignation to the will of God and devotedness to duty.

7. *Retreat.*—Make a spiritual retreat once a year.

8. *Spiritual Communion.*—An act of spiritual communion like the following should be made frequently, and especially at Mass: "My Jesus, I believe that Thou art truly present in the holy Sacrament of the Altar. I adore Thee. I praise Thee and thank Thee for all Thy blessings. I am sorry that

I have offended Thee by my sins. By this act I wish to make reparation to Thee for all the insults and injuries committed against Thee in the sacrament of Thy love. I love Thee with my whole heart. Come to my poor soul; unite Thyself to me . . . ✠ . . . I thank Thee, my good Jesus. Oh! never, never leave me. Let me not be separated from thee by sin."

9. *In the hour of Death.*—When you are dying, make acts of contrition and of love. Pronounce the sweet and holy name of "Jesus."

In life and in death, praise and be submissive to the holy will of God.

Strive to become a saint. For *"this is the will of God, your sanctification."*

> *"The number of the days of men at the most are a hundred years; as a drop of water of the sea are they esteemed: and as a pebble of the sand—so are a few years compared to eternity."*
> —Eccles. xviii. 26.
>
> *"Now to the King of ages, immortal, invisible, the only God, be honor and glory, for ever and ever. Amen."*
> —1 Tim. i. 17.

❋ DEVOTIONS FOR CONFESSION ❋

BEFORE CONFESSION

CALL to mind that this confession may be the last of your life. Therefore, prepare yourself for it as if you were lying sick upon your death-bed, and already at the brink of the grave. Ask God to give you the grace to make a good examination of conscience, the light to see your sins clearly, and the strength to make a sincere confession and to amend your life.

PRAYER

MOST merciful God, Father in heaven, relying on Thy goodness and mercy I come to Thee with filial confidence to confess my sins and to implore Thy forgiveness. Thou wilt not despise a contrite and humble heart. Bless me and receive me again into Thy favor; I acknowledge that I have been most ungrateful to Thee, but I sincerely repent and detest the wrong I have done, and I desire henceforth to walk in the way of perfection in accordance with Thy holy will.

O Jesus, my Saviour, my good Shepherd, I have strayed far from the path that Thou hast marked out for me; I did not follow in Thy footsteps; I wandered into forbidden places. Repentant and sorrowful, I beg to be admitted again into the fold of Thy faithful followers. I want to confess my sins with the same sincerity as I should wish to do at the moment of my death. My Jesus, I look to Thee with confidence for the grace to examine my conscience well.

O holy Spirit, come in Thy mercy; enlighten my mind and strengthen my will that I may know my sins, humbly confess them, and sincerely amend my life.

Mary, my Mother, immaculate spouse of the Holy Ghost, refuge of sinners, assist me by thy intercession.

Holy angels and saints of God, pray for me. Amen.

EXAMINATION OF CONSCIENCE

BEGIN by examining yourself on your last confession: Whether a grievous sin was forgotten through want of proper examination, or concealed or disguised through shame. Whether you confessed without a true sorrow and a firm purpose of amendment. Whether you have repaired evil done to your neighbor. Whether the penance was performed without voluntary distractions. Whether you have neglected your confessor's counsel, and fallen at once into habitual sins.

Then examine yourself on the Ten Commandments; the Commandments of the Church; the Seven Capital Sins; the duties of your state of life; and your ruling passion. Calmly recall the different occasions of sin which have fallen in your way, or to which your state and condition in life expose you; the places you have frequented; the persons with whom you have associated. Do not neglect to consider the circumstances which alter the grievousness of the sin, nor the various ways in which we become accessory to the sins of others.

THE TEN COMMANDMENTS OF GOD

1. **I** AM the Lord thy God, Who brought thee out of the land of Egypt, and out of the house of bondage. Thou shalt not have strange gods before Me. Thou shalt not make to thyself a graven thing, nor the likeness of anything that is in heaven above, or in the earth beneath, nor of those things that are in the waters under the earth. Thou shalt not adore them, nor serve them.

2. Thou shalt not take the name of the Lord thy God in vain; for the Lord will not hold him guiltless that shall take the name of the Lord his God in vain.

3. Remember that thou keep holy the Sabbath day.

4. Honor thy father and thy mother, that thou mayest be long-lived upon the land which the Lord thy God will give thee.

5. Thou shalt not kill.
6. Thou shalt not commit adultery.
7. Thou shalt not steal.
8. Thou shalt not bear false witness against thy neighbor.
9. Thou shalt not covet thy neighbor's wife.
10. Thou shalt not covet thy neighbor's goods.

THE SIX COMMANDMENTS OF THE CHURCH

1. To hear Mass on Sundays and holy days of obligation.
2. To fast and abstain on the days appointed.
3. To confess at least once a year.
4. To receive Holy Eucharist during the Easter-time.
5. To contribute to the support of our pastors.
6. Not to marry persons who are not Catholics, or who are related to us within the fourth degree of kindred, nor privately without witnesses, nor to solemnize marriage at forbidden times.

THE SEVEN DEADLY SINS, AND THE OPPOSITE VIRTUES

1. Pride . . . . Humility.
2. Covetousness . . . . Liberality.
3. Lust . . . . Chastity.
4. Anger . . . . Meekness.
5. Gluttony . . . . Temperance.
6. Envy . . . . Brotherly love.
7. Sloth . . . . Diligence.

THE FOUR SINS WHICH CRY TO HEAVEN FOR VENGEANCE

1. Wilful murder.
2. The sin of Sodom.
3. Oppression of the poor.
4. Defrauding the laborer of his wages.

Nine Ways of Being Accessory to Another's Sin

1. By counsel.
2. By command.
3. By consent.
4. By provocation.
5. By praise or flattery.
6. By concealment.
7. By partaking.
8. By silence.
9. By defense of the ill done.

The Seven Spiritual Works of Mercy

1. To admonish sinners.
2. To instruct the ignorant.
3. To counsel the doubtful.
4. To comfort the sorrowful.
5. To bear wrongs patiently.
6. To forgive all injuries.
7. To pray for the living and the dead.

The Seven Corporal Works of Mercy

1. To feed the hungry.
2. To give drink to the thirsty.
3. To clothe the naked.
4. To visit and ransom the captives.
5. To harbor the harborless.
6. To visit the sick.
7. To bury the dead.

Preliminary Examination

WHEN did you make your last confession? Did you take sufficient pains to awaken contrition?

- Did you omit to confess a mortal sin, either intentionally or through forgetfulness?
- Did you intentionally neglect to say the penance which was imposed on you, or were you so careless as to forget it?
- Have you carried out the resolutions you made at your last confession or have you paid no heed at all to them?

Appendix

Examination on the
Ten Commandments of God

1 Have you doubted in matters of faith? Murmured against God at your adversity or at the prosperity of others? Despaired of His mercy?

- Have you believed in fortune-tellers or consulted them?
- Have you gone to places of worship belonging to other denominations?
- Have you recommended yourself daily to God? Neglected your morning or night prayers? Omitted religious duties or practices through motives of human respect?
- Have you rashly presumed upon God's forbearance in order to commit sin?
- Have you read books, papers, and periodicals of anti-Catholic or atheistic tendency? Made use of superstitious practices? Spoken with levity or irreverence of priests, religious, or sacred objects?

2 Have you taken the name of God in vain? Profaned anything relating to religion?

- Have you sworn falsely, rashly, or in slight and trivial matters? Cursed yourself or others, or any creature? Angered others so as to make them swear, or blaspheme God?

3 Have you kept holy the Lord's Day, and all other days commanded to be kept holy? Bought or sold things, not of necessity, on that day? Done or commanded some servile work not of necessity? Missed Mass or been wilfully distracted during Mass? Talked, gazed, or laughed in the church? Profaned the day by drinking, gambling, or in other ways?

4 Have you honored your parents, superiors, and masters, according to your just duty? Deceived them? Disobeyed them?

- Have you failed in due reverence to aged persons?

5 Have you procured, desired, or hastened the death of any one? Borne hatred? Oppressed any one? Desired revenge? Not forgiven injuries? Refused to speak to others? Used provoking language? Injured others? Caused enmity between others?

6 (and 9) Have you been guilty of any sin against holy purity in *thought, word*, or *deed?*

7 Have you been guilty of stealing, or of deceit in buying, or selling, in regard to wares, prices, weights, or measures? Have you wilfully damaged another man's goods, or negligently spoiled them?

8 Have you borne false witness? Called injurious names? Disclosed another's sins? Flattered others? Judged rashly?

10 Have you coveted unjustly anything that belongs to another?

Examination on the Precepts of the Church

Have you gone to confession at least once a year? Received holy communion during Easter-time?

- Have you violated the fasts of the Church, or eaten flesh-meat on prohibited days?
- Have you sinned against any other commandment of the Church?
- Examine yourself also in regard to the Seven Capital Sins and the nine ways of being accessary to another's sin.

After the Examination

Having discovered the sins of which you have been guilty, together with their number, enormity, or such circumstances as may change their nature, you should endeavor to excite in yourself a *heartfelt sorrow* for having committed them, and a sincere detestation of them. This being the most essential of all the dispositions requisite for a good confession, with what humility, fervor, and perseverance should you not importune Him Who holds the hearts of men in His hands to grant it to you!

CONSIDERATIONS TO EXCITE IN OUR HEART TRUE CONTRITION FOR OUR SINS

CONSIDER Who He is, and how good and gracious He is to you, Whom you have so often and so deeply offended by these sins. God made you—He made you for Himself, to know, love, and serve Him, and to be happy with Him forever. He redeemed you by His blood. He has borne with you and waited for you so long. He it is Who has called you and moved you to repentance. Why have you thus sinned against Him? Why have you been so ungrateful? What more could He do for you? Oh, be ashamed, and mourn, and despise yourself, because you have sinned against your Maker and your Redeemer, Whom you ought to love above all things!

Consider the consequences of even one mortal sin. By it you lose the grace of God. You destroy peace of conscience; you forfeit the felicity of heaven, for which you were created and redeemed; and you prepare for yourself eternal punishment. If we grieve for the loss of temporal and earthly things, how much more should we grieve for having deliberately exposed ourselves to the loss of those which are eternal and heavenly!

Consider how great is the love of God for you, if only from this, that He hath so long waited for you, and spared you, when He might have so justly cast you into hell. Behold Him fastened to the cross for love of you! Behold Him pouring forth His precious blood as a fountain to cleanse you from your sins! Hear Him saying, "*I thirst*,"—"I thirst with an ardent desire for your salvation!" Behold Him stretching out His arms to embrace you, and waiting until you should come to yourself and turn unto Him, and throw yourself before Him, and say, *"Father, I have sinned against heaven and before Thee, and am no more worthy to be called Thy son."* Let these considerations touch your heart with love for Him Who loves you so much, and love will beget true contrition, most acceptable to God.

Say an *Our Father*, a *Hail Mary*, and a *Glory be* to obtain true contrition. Then add the following:

INVOCATIONS

O Mary, conceived without sin, pray for us who have recourse to thee!

Indulgence of 100 days, once a day.—Leo XIII, March 15, 1884.

Holy Virgin, Mary immaculate, Mother of God and our Mother, speak thou for us to the Heart of Jesus, Who is thy Son and our brother!

Indulgence of 100 days, once a day.—Leo XIII, Dec. 20, 1890.

AN ACT OF CONTRITION

ETERNAL FATHER! I am heartily sorry for having offended Thee, and I detest all my sins, because I dread the loss of heaven and the pains of hell, but most of all because they offend Thee, my God, Who art all-good and deserving of all my love. I firmly resolve, with the help of Thy grace, to confess my sins, to do penance, and to amend my life.

APPROACH the confessional with the same recollectedness and reverence as would fill your heart if Christ our Lord were seated there in person ready to hear your confession. The priest is really the representative of Christ.

When you kneel down, say: *Bless me, Father, for I have sinned*, and then begin the *Confiteor*, proceeding as far as *Through my fault*, etc.

The Confiteor[1]

I CONFESS to Almighty God, to Blessed Mary, ever virgin, to blessed Michael the archangel, to blessed John the Baptist, to the holy apostles Peter and Paul, and to all the saints, that I have sinned exceedingly in thought, word, and deed, through my fault, through my fault, through my most grievous fault.

Then tell when you made your last confession and begin the avowal of your sins. Confess all your sins with a contrite and humble heart, and conclude thus:

For these and all the sins of my past life, especially my sins of (*naming certain sins*), **I am heartily sorry, beg pardon of God, and absolution of you, my Father;** *then finish the Confiteor:*

T HEREFORE, I beseech the blessed Mary, ever virgin, blessed Michael the archangel, blessed John the Baptist, the holy apostles Peter and Paul, and all the saints, to pray to the Lord our God for me.

Listen then with humility and docility to the instruction of your confessor, and during this time avoid all recurrence as to the confession itself, remembering that sins forgotten after a serious examination are really comprised in the absolution. Accept with submission the penance imposed, and if any obstacle that you foresee will prevent your accomplishing it, state this respectfully.

While the priest pronounces the words of absolution, endeavor to excite an act of perfect contrition. Should your spiritual Father deem it proper to defer absolution, acknowledge your unworthiness, and do not murmur. Leave the confessional resolved to use every effort, by amendment of life and sincere repentance, to obtain God's pardon, which His minister will ratify.

---

1   Editor's Note: this form was used prior to the Second Vatican Council. The *Confiteor* is now rarely used in the Confessional.

THANKSGIVING AFTER CONFESSION

ETERNAL FATHER! I thank Thee, I bless Thee, for Thy goodness and mercy. Thou hast had compassion on me, although in my folly I had wandered far away from Thee and offended Thee most grievously. With fatherly love Thou hast received me anew after so many relapses into sin and forgiven me my offenses through the holy sacrament of Penance. Blessed forever, O my God, be Thy loving-kindness, Thy infinite mercy! Never again will I grieve Thee by ingratitude, by disobedience to Thy holy will. All that I am, all that I have, all that I do shall be consecrated to Thy service and Thy glory.

Sacred Heart of Jesus, I place my trust in Thee.

Indulgence of 300 days.—Pius X, June 27, 1906.

Jesus, my God, I love Thee above all things.

Indulgence of 50 days, each time.—Pius IX, May 7, 1854

O DIVINE Spirit! penetrate my soul with true horror and loathing of sin. Grant that I may be more exact in the fulfilment of all my duties, and strengthen me by Thy grace, that I may not again yield to temptation.

Sweet heart of Mary, be my salvation.

Indulgence of 300 days, each time.—Pius IX, Sept. 30, 1852.

Mary, our hope, have pity on us!

Indulgence of 300 days, each time.—Pius X, Jan. 8, 1906.

IN CONCLUSION, reflect on the following verses from the Psalms:

"BLESSED *are they whose iniquities are forgiven, and whose sins are covered."*

"Blessed are the undefiled in the way; who walk in the law of the Lord."

"I cried with my whole heart, hear me, O Lord: I will seek Thy justifications."

"*I cried unto Thee, save me: that I may keep Thy commandments.*"

"*I will praise Thee, because Thou hast heard me, and art become my salvation.*"

"*O praise the Lord, for He is good and His mercy endureth forever.*"

"*The Lord is my helper; I will not fear what man can do unto me.*"

"*I will please the Lord in the land of the living.*"

"*The perils of hell have found me. O Lord, deliver my soul.*"

"*I have acknowledged my sin unto Thee, and mine iniquity I have not concealed.*"

"*I said, I will confess against myself mine iniquity with the Lord, and Thou hast forgiven the wickedness of my sin.*"

"*Thou art my refuge from the trouble which hath encompassed me, my joy. Deliver me from them that surround me.*"

PSALM 102

BLESS the Lord, O my soul, and let all that is within me, bless His holy name.

Bless the Lord, O my soul, and never forget all He hath done for thee.

Who forgiveth all thy iniquities; Who healeth all thy diseases.

Who redeemeth thy life from destruction; Who crowneth thee with mercy and compassion.

Who satisfieth thy desire with good things: thy youth shall be renewed like the eagle's.

The Lord doth mercies, and judgment for all that suffer wrong.

He hath made his ways known to Moses: his wills to the children of Israel.

The Lord is compassionate and merciful; long-suffering and plenteous in mercy.

He will not always be angry; nor will He threaten forever.

He hath not dealt with us according to our sins; nor rewarded us according to our iniquities.

For according to the height of the heaven above the earth: he hath strengthened his mercy towards them that fear him.

As far as the east is from the west, so far hath He removed our iniquities from us.

As a father hath compassion on his children, so hath the Lord compassion on them that fear Him.

For He knoweth our frame; He remembereth that we are dust:

Man's days are as grass, as the flower of the field so shall he flourish.

For the spirit shall pass in him, and he shall not be: and he shall know his place no more.

But the mercy of the Lord is from eternity and unto eternity upon them that fear him: And his justice unto children's children,

To such as keep his covenant, And are mindful of his commandments to do them.

The Lord hath prepared his throne in heaven: and his kingdom shall rule over all.

Bless the Lord, all ye his angels: you that are mighty in strength, and execute his word, hearkening to the voice of his orders.

Bless the Lord, all ye his hosts: you ministers of his that do his will.

Bless the Lord, all his works: in every place of his dominion, O my soul, bless thou the Lord.

HELP us, Joseph, in our earthly strife,
E'er to lead a pure and blameless life.

Indulgence of 300 days, once a day.—Leo XIII, March 18, 1882.

EJACULATORY PRAYERS TO OBTAIN A GOOD DEATH

JESUS, Mary, and Joseph, I give you my heart and my soul.

Jesus, Mary, and Joseph, assist me in my last agony.

Jesus, Mary, and Joseph, may I breathe forth my soul in peace with you.

The Sovereign Pontiff, Pius VII, by a decree of the Sacred Congregation of Indulgences, April 28, 1807, granted to all the faithful, every time that, with at least contrite heart and devotion, they shall say these three ejaculations: an *indulgence of three hundred days*; and an *indulgence of one hundred days*, every time that, with the same dispositions, they shall say one of these ejaculations.

Additional titles available from

St. Augustine Academy Press

Books for the Traditional Catholic

Titles by Mother Mary Loyola:

Blessed are they that Mourn
Confession and Communion
Coram Sanctissimo (Before the Most Holy)
First Communion
First Confession
Forgive us our Trespasses
Hail! Full of Grace
Heavenwards
Holy Mass/How to Help the Sick and Dying
Home for Good
Jesus of Nazareth: The Story of His Life Written for Children
The Child of God: What comes of our Baptism
The Children's Charter
The Little Children's Prayer Book
The Soldier of Christ: Talks before Confirmation
Welcome! Holy Communion Before and After

Titles by Father Lasance:

The Catholic Girl's Guide
The Young Man's Guide

Tales of the Saints:

A Child's Book of Saints by William Canton
A Child's Book of Warriors by William Canton
Illustrated Life of the Blessed Virgin by Rev. B. Rohner, O.S.B.
Legends & Stories of Italy by Amy Steedman
Mary, Help of Christians by Rev. Bonaventure Hammer
The Book of Saints and Heroes by Lenora Lang
Saint Patrick: Apostle of Ireland
The Story of St. Elizabeth of Hungary by William Canton

Check our Website for more:

www.staugustineacademypress.com

Printed in the USA
CPSIA information can be obtained
at www.ICGtesting.com
CBHW020137211123
1989CB00001B/1